# The Blessing of Abraham, the Spirit, and Justification in Galatians

# The Blessing of Abraham, the Spirit, and Justification in Galatians

*Their Relationship and Significance for Understanding Paul's Theology*

CHEE-CHIEW LEE

☙PICKWICK *Publications* • Eugene, Oregon

THE BLESSING OF ABRAHAM, THE SPIRIT, AND JUSTIFICATION
IN GALATIANS
Their Relationship and Significance for Understanding Paul's Theology

Copyright © 2013 Chee-Chiew Lee. All rights reserved. Except for brief quotations in critical publications or reviews, no part of this book may be reproduced in any manner without prior written permission from the publisher. Write: Permissions, Wipf and Stock Publishers, 199 W. 8th Ave., Suite 3, Eugene, OR 97401.

Pickwick Publications
An Imprint of Wipf and Stock Publishers
199 W. 8th Ave., Suite 3
Eugene, OR 97401

www.wipfandstock.com

ISBN 13: 978-1-61097-372-4

*Cataloguing-in-Publication data:*

Lee, Chee-Chiew.

The blessing of Abraham, the Spirit, and justification in Galatians : their relationship and significance for understanding Paul's theology / Chee-Chiew Lee.

xvi + 240 pp. ; 23 cm. Includes bibliographical references.

ISBN 13: 978-1-61097-372-4

1. Bible. Galatians—Criticism, interpretation, etc. 2. Bible. Galatians—Theology. 3. Holy Spirit—Biblical teaching. 4. Abraham (Biblical patriarch). 5. Justification (Christian theology)—History of doctrines I. Title.

BS2685.52 L33 2013

Manufactured in the U.S.A.

# Contents

*Foreword* by Douglas Moo   /   vii

*Abbreviations*   /   ix

1   Introduction: The Juxtaposition of the Blessing of Abraham and the Spirit in Galatians 3:14   /   1

2   Justification by Faith: The Context of Galatians 3:14   /   18

3   The Beginning of the Blessing of Abraham: Genesis and the Rest of the Pentateuch   /   61

4   The Spirit's Role in the Blessing of Abraham: Development in Other Old Testament Texts   /   95

5   The Spirit's Temporary Absence in the Blessing of Abraham: Development in the Second Temple Literature   /   136

6   The Spirit's Relationship with the Blessing of Abraham in Galatians: Implications on Justification by Faith   /   182

*Bibliography*   /   213

# Foreword

As a single book with two distinct divisions, the Bible poses a challenge to everyone who seeks to understand its ultimate meaning. How are we to integrate the OT and NT into a single story and single message for the church? This question has challenged Christian interpreters since the beginnings of the church, and it continues to attract considerable attention from the scholarly community. Many interpreters find more contrast than continuity; and Paul is often singled out as a particularly notorious instance of one who forces the OT to say what it did not originally mean in order to commend Christ and his people as the fulfillment of God's first testament promises.

I therefore welcome a book, such as the one I here commend, for its argument for continuity across the testaments. But it is not only its conclusion that I welcome. Facile claims for harmony between the testaments are all too common; too many sweep awkward exegetical details under the rug in order to keep conclusions neat and tidy. Not the least of the virtues of Chee-Chiew Lee's book is her determination to tackle the specifics of the text at the same time as she seeks to move from those specifics to wider biblical-theological conclusions. Her work is marked by careful and even innovative exegetical work in both OT and NT as well as stimulating reflection on larger theological themes.

Dr. Lee begins with a simple yet difficult exegetical question: how are "the blessing of Abraham" and "the promise of the Spirit" to be related in Galatians 3:14? She argues convincingly, I think, that the two are not to be equated—the "blessing" is *not* the Spirit—but that the Spirit functions as both the evidence of the presence of that blessing and the means by which that blessing can be perpetuated. She bases this conclusion on the way in which key OT prophetic texts speak of the eschatological gift of the Spirit in relationship to God's fulfillment of his promises to the patriarchs. Among other important consequences, this argument enables her to shed light on the vexing issue of the unity of the argument of Galatians

## Foreword

and to set the work of God's Spirit in the new covenant in a rich biblical-theological context.

I trust that her book, and its argument, will attract the attention they deserve.

Douglas Moo
Wheaton, IL, 2012

# Abbreviations

| | |
|---|---|
| 1 *En.* | 1 *Enoch (Ethiopic Apocalypse)* |
| 1 Macc | 1 Maccabees |
| 1 Pet | 1 Peter |
| 1 Thess | 1 Thessalonians |
| 1–2 Cor | 1–2 Corinthians |
| 1–2 Kgs | 1–2 Kings |
| 1–2 Sam | 1–2 Samuel |
| 11QPs | Qumran *Psalms Scroll* |
| 11QT[a] | *Temple Scroll*[a] |
| 1QH[a] | *Hodayot*[a] or *Thanksgiving Hymns*[a] |
| 1QpHab | *Pesher Habakkuk* |
| 1QS | *Serek Hayaḥad* or *Rule of the Community* |
| 2Q18 | Qumran Hebrew manuscript of Ben Sira |
| 4Q196 | Qumran manuscript of Tobit |
| 4Q225 | Qumran manuscript of *Jubilees* |
| 4Q252 | *Commentary on Genesis A* |
| 4Q504 | *Divrei Ha-me'orot* or *Words of the Luminaries* |
| 4QDeut[q] | Qumran manuscript of Deuteronomy |
| 4QDibHam | *Divrei Ha-me'orot* or *Words of the Luminaries*; also named as 4Q504 |
| 4QpNah | *Pesher Nahum* |
| 8HevXIIgr | *The Greek Minor Prophets Scroll from Nahal Hever* |
| AB | Anchor Bible |
| *ABD* | *Anchor Bible Dictionary.* Edited by D. N. Freedman. 6 vols. New York, 1992 |
| *ABR* | *Australian Biblical Review* |
| AD | anno Domini |

## Abbreviations

| | | |
|---|---|---|
| AGJU | | Arbeiten zur Geschichte des antiken Judentums und des Urchristentums |
| AnBib | | Analecta Biblica |
| *Ant.* | | *Jewish Antiquities* |
| *AThR* | | *Anglican Theological Review* |
| *b. Yevamot* | | Babylonian Talmud *Yevamot* |
| *BBR* | | *Bulletin for Biblical Research* |
| BC | | before Christ |
| BCE | | before the Common Era |
| BDAG | | Bauer, W., et al. *Greek-English Lexicon of the New Testament and Other Early Christian Literature*. 3rd ed. Chicago, 2000 |
| BDB | | Brown, F., et al. *A Hebrew and English Lexicon of the Old Testament*. Oxford, 1907 |
| BECNT | | Baker Exegetical Commentary on the New Testament |
| BETL | | Bibliotheca Ephemeridum Theologicarum Lovaniensium |
| *BHQ* | | *Biblia Hebraica Quinta*. Edited by A. Schenker, et al. Stuttgart, 2004– |
| *BHS* | | *Biblia Hebraica Stuttgartensia* |
| BibIntS | | Biblical Interpretation Series |
| *BN* | | *Biblische Notizen* |
| BNTC | | Black's New Testament Commentary |
| *BRev* | | *Bible Review* |
| *BSac* | | *Bibliotheca Sacra* |
| *BV* | | *Biblical Viewpoint* |
| *BZ* | | *Biblische Zeitschrift* |
| BZAW | | Beihefte zur Zeitschrift für die alttestamentliche Wissenschaft |
| BZNW | | Beihefte zur Zeitschrift für die neutestamentliche Wissenschaft |
| cf. | | *confer*, compare |
| *CBQ* | | *Catholic Biblical Quarterly* |
| CC | | Continental Commentaries |
| CCWJCW | | Cambridge Commentaries on Writings of the Jewish and Christian World 200 BC to AD 200 |
| CE | | Common Era |
| CEB | | Commentaire évangélique de la Bible |
| CEV | | Contemporary English Version |

## Abbreviations

| | |
|---|---|
| ch(s). | chapter |
| col(s). | column(s) |
| CSCO | Corpus Scriptorum Christianorum Orientalium |
| *CurBS* | *Currents in Research: Biblical Studies* |
| *CurTM* | *Currents in Theology and Mission* |
| Dan | Daniel |
| *DCH* | *The Dictionary of Classical Hebrew*. Edited by David J. A. Clines. 8 vols. Sheffield, 1993–2011 |
| Deut | Deuteronomy |
| diss. | dissertation |
| DJD | Discoveries in the Judaean Desert |
| *DPL* | *Dictionary of Paul and His Letters*. Edited by G. F. Hawthorne et al. Downers Grove, 1993 |
| *DSSSE* | *The Dead Sea Scrolls Study Edition*. Edited by Florentino García Martínez and Eibert J. C. Tigchelaar. 2 vols. Leiden, 1997–1998 |
| e.g. | *exempli gratia*, for example |
| ed(s). | editor(s), edited by |
| EDSS | *Encyclopedia of the Dead Sea Scrolls*. Edited by Lawrence H. Schiffman and James C. VanderKam. 2 vols. Oxford, 2000 |
| *EgT* | *Église et théologie* |
| Eng. | English |
| Eph | Ephesians |
| ESEC | Emory Studies in Early Christianity |
| esp. | especially |
| ESV | English Standard Version |
| et al. | *et alii*, and others |
| etc. | *et cetera*, and the rest |
| ETL | *Ephemerides theologicae lovanienses* |
| *EvRT* | *Evangelical Review of Theology* |
| *EvT* | *Evangelische Theologie* |
| Exod | Exodus |
| *ExpTim* | *Expository Times* |
| Ezek | Ezekiel |
| f(f). | and the following one(s) |
| *FoiVie* | *Foi et Vie* |

# Abbreviations

| | |
|---|---|
| *FZPhTh* | *Freiburger Zeitschrift für Philosophie und Theologie* |
| Gal | Galatians |
| GAP | Guides to Apocrypha and Pseudepigrapha |
| Gen | Genesis |
| *Gen. Rab.* | *Genesis Rabbah* |
| Hab | Habakkuk |
| HALOT | *The Hebrew and Aramaic Lexicon of the Old Testament.* Edited by Ludwig Köhler et al. 5 vols. Leiden, 1994–2000 |
| HBS | Herders Biblische Studien |
| *HBT* | *Horizons in Biblical Theology* |
| Heb | Hebrews |
| Hos | Hosea |
| HTKAT | Herders theologischer Kommentar zum Alten Testament |
| HTKNT | Herders theologischer Kommentar zum Neuen Testament |
| *HTR* | *Harvard Theological Review* |
| i.e. | *id est*, that is |
| IBHS | *An Introduction to Biblical Hebrew Syntax.* Waltke, Bruce K. and M. O'Connor. Winona Lake, 1990 |
| ICC | International Critical Commentary |
| idem | the same |
| *Int* | *Interpretation* |
| Isa | Isaiah |
| JB | Jerusalem Bible |
| *JBL* | *Journal of Biblical Literature* |
| Jer | Jeremiah |
| JETS | *Journal of the Evangelical Theological Society* |
| *JJS* | *Journal of Jewish Studies* |
| Job | Job |
| *Jos. Asen.* | *Joseph and Aseneth* |
| Josh | Joshua |
| JPS | Jewish Publication Society |
| JPSTC | JPS Torah Commentary |
| *JRH* | *Journal of Religious History* |
| *JSJ* | *Journal for the Study of Judaism in the Persian, Hellenistic and Roman Periods* |

## Abbreviations

| | |
|---|---|
| JSJSup | Supplements to the Journal for the Study of Judaism |
| JSNT | *Journal for the Study of the New Testament* |
| JSNTSup | Journal for the Study of the New Testament Supplement Series |
| JSOT | *Journal for the Study of the Old Testament* |
| JSOTSup | Journal for the Study of the Old Testament Supplement Series |
| JSP | *Journal for the Study of the Pseudepigrapha* |
| JSPSup | Journal for the Study of the Pseudepigrapha Supplement Series |
| JSS | *Journal of Semitic Studies* |
| Jub. | *Jubilees* |
| KJV | King James Version |
| KUSATU | *Kleine Untersuchungen zur Sprache des Alten Testaments und seiner Umwelt* |
| L.A.B. | *Liber antiquitatum biblicarum (Pseudo-Philo)* |
| Lad. Jac. | *Ladder of Jacob* |
| LCL | Loeb Classical Library |
| Lev | Leviticus |
| LHBOTS | Library of Hebrew Bible/Old Testament Studies |
| lit. | literally |
| LXX | Septuagint (the Greek OT) |
| m. Ned. | *Mishnah Nedarim* |
| Mic | Micah |
| Migration | On the Migration of Abraham |
| MS(S) | manuscript(s) |
| MT | Masoretic Text |
| n(n). | note(s) |
| NA27 | *Novum Testamentum Graece.* Nestle-Aland, 27th ed. |
| NAB | New American Bible |
| NAC | New American Commentary |
| NASB | New American Standard Bible |
| NCBC | New Century Bible Commentary |
| NEB | New English Bible |
| NEBKAT | Neue Echter Bibel: Kommentar Zum Alten Testament Mit Der Einheitsübersetzung |

## Abbreviations

| | |
|---|---|
| Neh | Nehemiah |
| *Neot* | *Neotestamentica* |
| NETS | New English Translation of the Septuagint |
| NIB | The New Interpreter's Bible |
| NICOT | New International Commentary on the Old Testament |
| *NIDOTTE* | *New International Dictionary of Old Testament Theology and Exegesis.* Edited by Willem VanGemeren. 5 vols. Grand Rapids, 1997 |
| NIGTC | New International Greek Testament Commentary |
| NIV | New International Version ©2011 |
| NJB | New Jerusalem Bible |
| NKJV | New King James Version |
| NLT | New Living Translation |
| *NovT* | *Novum Testamentum* |
| NovTSup | Supplements to Novum Testamentum |
| NRSV | New Revised Standard Version |
| NSBT | New Studies in Biblical Theology |
| NT | New Testament |
| *NTS* | *New Testament Studies* |
| Num | Numbers |
| OT | Old Testament |
| OTL | Old Testament Library |
| OTP | *Old Testament Pseudepigrapha.* Edited by J. H. Charlesworth. 2 vols. New York, 1983 |
| p(p). | page(s) |
| PAST | Pauline Studies |
| Phil | Philippians |
| *Prelim. Studies* | *On the Preliminary Studies* |
| Prov | Proverbs |
| *PRSt* | *Perspectives in Religious Studies* |
| Ps (*pl.* Pss) | Psalm(s) |
| *Pss. Sol.* | *Psalms of Solomon* |
| *RB* | *Revue biblique* |
| REB | Revised English Bible |
| *ResQ* | *Restoration Quarterly* |

# Abbreviations

| | |
|---|---|
| Rev | Revelation |
| rev. | revised (by) |
| *RevQ* | *Revue de Qumran* |
| Rom | Romans |
| *RRef* | *La revue réformée* |
| *RTR* | *Reformed Theological Review* |
| *SBJT* | *Southern Baptist Journal of Theology* |
| SBL | Society of Biblical Literature |
| SBLDS | Society of Biblical Literature Dissertation Series |
| SBLSymS | Society of Biblical Literature Symposium Series |
| *SCJ* | *Stone-Campbell Journal* |
| *SEÅ* | *Svensk exegetisk årsbok* |
| Sir | Sirach/Ecclesiasticus |
| *SJOT* | *Scandinavian Journal of the Old Testament* |
| SNTSMS | Society for New Testament Studies Monograph Series |
| *Spec. Laws* | *On the Special Laws* |
| STDJ | Studies on the Texts of the Desert of Judah |
| StPB | Studia Post-Biblica |
| Syr. | Syriac |
| *T. Job* | *Testament of Job* |
| *T. Jud.* | *Testament of Judah* |
| *T. Levi* | *Testament of Levi* |
| TDNT | *Theological Dictionary of the New Testament.* Edited by G. Kittel and G. Friedrich. Translated by G. W. Bromiley. 10 vols. Grand Rapids, 1964–1976 |
| TDOT | *Theological Dictionary of the Old Testament.* Edited by G. Johannes Botterweck, Helmer Ringgren, and Heinz-Josef Fabry. Translated by John T. Willis, Douglas W. Stott, and David E. Green. 15 vols. Rev. ed. Grand Rapids, 1974-2006 |
| *Tg. Neb.* | *Targum of the Prophets* |
| *Tg. Neof.* | *Targum Neofiti* |
| *Tg. Onq.* | *Targum Onqelos* |
| *Tg. Ps.-J.* | *Targum Pseudo-Jonathan* |
| Tg(s). | Targum(s) |
| *ThTo* | *Theology Today* |

## Abbreviations

| | |
|---|---|
| *TJ* | *Trinity Journal* |
| Tob | Tobit |
| trans. | translation, translated by |
| *TTJ* | *Trinity Theological Journal* |
| *TTKi* | *Tidsskrift for Teologi og Kirke* |
| *TynBul* | *Tyndale Bulletin* |
| *TZ* | *Theologische Zeitschrift* |
| USB4 | *The Greek New Testament*, United Bible Societies, 4th ed. |
| v(v). | verse(s) |
| vol(s). | volume(s) |
| *VT* | *Vetus Testamentum* |
| VTSup | Supplements to Vetus Testamentum |
| Vulg. | Vulgate |
| WBC | Word Biblical Commentary |
| WEC | Wycliffe Exegetical Commentary |
| *WTJ* | *Westminster Theological Journal* |
| WUNT | Wissenschaftliche Untersuchungen zum Neuen Testament |
| *ZAW* | *Zeitschrift für die alttestamentliche Wissenschaft* |
| Zech | Zechariah |
| *ZKT* | *Zeitschrift für katholische Theologie* |
| *ZNW* | *Zeitschrift für die neutestamentliche Wissenschaft und die Kunde der älteren Kirche* |

# 1 INTRODUCTION

## The Juxtaposition of the Blessing of Abraham and the Spirit in Galatians 3:14

A SHORT EPISTLE BUT a key focal point of many scholarly debates—this description of the epistle to the Galatians was true not only during the Reformation, but also in contemporary scholarly discussions on Paul and his theology, especially on the topic of justification.[1] Many aspects of the letter have been studied, but of particular relevance for this research is the area of biblical intertextuality.[2] Despite the short length of the epistle, Galatians has a relatively high number of OT quotations and allusions. Abraham and his biblical and theological significance are especially prominent, and because of this, Galatians has also become an important resource in the study of Paul and Scripture as well as the *Rezeptionsgeschichte* of Abraham.[3]

---

1. Luther's formulation of his doctrine of justification by faith is informed substantially by his exegesis on Galatians. He wrote a commentary on Galatians first in 1519, and then again in 1535, in which he states that the later commentary was intended "to set forth the doctrine of justification as clearly as possible" (Luther, *Lectures on Galatians*, 27:87). This epistle is also a major subject of contention in contemporary discussions on Paul sparked off mainly by Sanders, *Paul and Palestinian Judaism*.

2. The term "intertextuality" here refers to the comparative study of literature in terms of "inter-literature relationships, inter-literature parallelism as well as trans-literature connections" (Tschuggnall, "'Das Wort ist kein Ding,'" 160). Although the term "intertextuality" may have been connected initially with radical postmodernism and its denial of the role of the author in interpretation, this term is now used more broadly without its original connotation. In line with this development, I am using the term "intertextuality" to refer specifically to the interactions between the Pauline writings, Scripture, and the Second Temple Jewish literature.

3. Some of the recent works include: Baumbach, "Abraham unser Vater," 37–56;

# The Blessing of Abraham, the Spirit, and Justification in Galatians

The highest concentration of OT quotations and allusions occurs in Galatians 3 and 4, especially in Gal 3:6–13, where six scriptural citations are compacted within a short span of eight verses.[4] It is no wonder that Gal 3:6–13 has received so much attention from such a considerable number of scholars.[5]

In arguing that justification is by faith rather than by works of the law, Paul cites the example of Abraham in Gal 3:1–14. He starts by questioning the Galatians about whether they have received the Spirit based on the works of the law or by faith (Gal 3:1–5). Next, he claims that since Abraham is justified by faith (Gal 3:6; cf. Gen 15:6), all those who are "of faith" (ἐκ πίστεως) are blessed along with Abraham (Gal 3:7–9; cf. Gen 12:3; 18:18).

Paul contends that all who rely on the works of the law are cursed and that the crucifixion of Christ has brought about redemption from the curse of the law (Gal 3:10–13). Following the scriptural citations in Gal 3:6–13, an interesting phenomenon can be observed in Gal 3:14. Paul concludes his arguments in Gal 3:1–14 with two ἵνα clauses in Gal 3:14:

1. ἵνα εἰς τὰ ἔθνη ἡ εὐλογία τοῦ Ἀβραὰμ γένηται ἐν Χριστῷ Ἰησοῦ ("in order that the blessing of Abraham might come to the Gentiles in Christ Jesus")

2. ἵνα τὴν ἐπαγγελίαν τοῦ πνεύματος λάβωμεν διὰ τῆς πίστεως ("in order that we might receive the promise of the Spirit by faith")

Paul juxtaposes these two clauses, intertwining the main themes of Gal 3:1–5 and Gal 3:6–9 in a climax.[6] Grammatically, these two ἵνα clauses may be purpose or result clauses, while structurally, they may be in a coordinate or a subordinate relationship.[7] Regardless of how these issues

---

Bethune, "Abraham, Father of Faith"; Calvert-Koysis, *Paul, Monotheism and the People of God*; Hansen, *Abraham in Galatians*; Harrisville, *Figure of Abraham*; Longenecker, *Triumph of Abraham's God*; Oeming, "Der Glaube Abrahams," 16–33.

4. (1) Gen 15:6 in Gal 3:6; (2) Gen 12:3 in Gal 3:8; (3) Deut 27:26 in Gal 3:10: (4) Hab 2:4 in Gal 3:11; (5) Lev 18:5 in Gal 3:12; and (6) Deut 21:23 in Gal 3:13.

5. E.g., Bekken, "Abraham og Ånden (Abraham and the Spirit)," 265–76; Caneday, "'Redeemed from the Curse,'" 189–209; Martyn, "Habakkuk 2:4 and Leviticus 18:5," 465–73; Silva, "Abraham, Faith, and Works," 251–67; Sprinkle, *Law and Life*; Wakefield, *Where to Live*; Willitts, "Context Matters," 105–22; Wisdom, *Blessing*.

6. Longenecker, *Galatians*, 123; Silva, *Interpreting Galatians*, 221.

7. Wallace points out that, due to Semitic influence, the ἵνα clause may sometimes be both purpose and result (Wallace, *Greek Grammar*, 472–73). See also Moule, *Idiom*, 142. The term "juxtaposition" is sometimes used for the purposes of contrast

## Introduction: The Juxtaposition of the Blessing of Abraham

are decided, it is clear that there is some kind of relationship between the reception of the Spirit and the fulfillment of the Abrahamic promise.[8] How did Paul arrive at this juxtaposition? Perhaps there was "something within the realm of Jewish expectations that *did* associate the Spirit with the promises of Abraham?"[9] How are these two motifs related to justification?

On the surface, the blessing of Abraham and the promise of the Holy Spirit do not seem to be directly related in the OT. The blessing of Abraham in Genesis is related to land, posterity, and the blessing for the nations in a covenantal context, but there is no mention of the Spirit.[10] Although the phrase "blessing of Abraham" does not appear directly in the prophecies of the promise of the Spirit, a few of the passages in these prophecies allude to the language used in the Abrahamic covenant.[11]

There seems to be a development and some kind of relationship between the two theological motifs that invite further investigation. The following questions still remain: (1) Was there an understanding in the Latter Prophets and in early Judaism that associated the Spirit with the blessing of Abraham and which might lead Paul to relate the two?[12] (2) If there is such a traditional association, how has Paul further developed the relationship? (3) If there is no such traditional association, how does Paul derive the relationship between the two?

This study will seek to answer the questions above and to articulate the relationship between the Abrahamic blessing and the promise of the Spirit in Gal 3:14 by tracing the development and association of these two theological motifs through the OT and the Second Temple literature, how this development may have influenced Paul in his juxtaposition of these two motifs in Gal 3:14, and how their relationship would shed light on Paul's overall argument in Galatians and his theology of justification.

---

or comparison. However, in the case of Gal 3:14, these two clauses are correlated or coordinated, rather contrasted. Most commentators understand these two ἵνα clauses in Gal 3:14 to be coordinating. A few are inclined to see them as subordinating (e.g., Harrisville, *Figure of Abraham*, 10; Duncan, *Galatians*, 103).

8. For a discussion on juxtaposed ἵνα clauses in the Pauline letters, see pp. 53–56 below.

9. Hays, *Faith of Jesus Christ*, 182; emphasis in original.

10. Gen 12:1–3; 15:1–21; 17:1–14; 22:15–18; cf. 26:3–5; 28:13–15.

11. See, e.g., Isa 44:2–3 and Ezek 36:26–28.

12. I am using the term "early Judaism" to refer to the various forms of Jewish belief from the third century BCE until the destruction of the temple in 70 CE.

## History of Research

In this survey on the history of research, we shall begin by first looking at scholars who regard the blessing of Abraham to be the promise of the Spirit. Second, we will proceed to those who think that, while the two are not the same, there is some kind of relationship. Finally, we will look at those who hold that there is no relationship between the two. We will be evaluating the views of these scholars as we go through the history of research. Some of the views may be dismissed in the course of this evaluation, while others will need to be dealt with in more detail in later chapters.

### Interpreters Who Identify the Blessing with the Spirit

Despite the amount of literature on Galatians 3, many interpreters do not address the issue of the relationship between the blessing of Abraham and the promise of the Spirit in Gal 3:14.[13] Nonetheless, as early as 1519, Martin Luther understood the bestowal of the Spirit as part of the content of the Abrahamic blessing.[14] Since then, most modern interpreters have taken a similar stance, even to the extent of equating the blessing of Abraham with the promise of the Spirit.[15]

In spite of this, not many of these interpreters are able to articulate clearly or convincingly why Paul has supposedly identified the Spirit with the blessing of Abraham. Lagrange and Betz explain that Paul may have identified the two on the basis of the experience of the Galatians.[16] However, Paul's argument from Scripture in Gal 3:6–13 suggests that there might also be some scriptural grounds on which he bases the association.

Cosgrove claims that both the early church and Hellenistic Judaism have a tendency to treat "all the divine promises as extensions of the

---

13. Hays lists a number of prominent NT interpreters who did not address this issue at all, such as Lightfoot, Zahn, Lietzmann, Bonnard, Oepke, Bligh, and Lührmann (Hays, *Faith of Jesus Christ*, 181n53).

14. Luther, *Lectures on Galatians*, 27:263. First, Luther explains that the blessing of Abraham consists of the promise that "he should be the father of many nations." Second, he notes that "the Holy Spirit was promised to Abraham when the blessing of faith was promised to him."

15. E.g., Burton, *Galatians*, 177; Ridderbos, *Galatia*, 128; Bruce, *Galatians*, 168; Cosgrove, *The Cross and the Spirit*, 50; Hansen, *Abraham in Galatians*, 126; Eckstein, *Verheißung und Gesetz*, 152; Martyn, *Galatians*, 323; Lambrecht, "Abraham and His Offspring," 526; Heckel, *Der Segen*, 148–49; Marshall, *New Testament Theology*, 233; Schreiner, *New Testament Theology*, 477.

16. Lagrange, *Galates*, 74; Betz, *Galatians*, 152–53.

## Introduction: The Juxtaposition of the Blessing of Abraham

promise to Abraham."[17] Therefore, the promise of the Spirit in the prophetic tradition is also identified as the blessing of Abraham.[18] However, the evidence from the early church and Hellenistic Judaism that Cosgrove cites to support his assertion is not convincing.[19]

## Interpreters Who Associate but Not Identify the Blessing with the Spirit

The fact that Paul juxtaposed the two themes does not necessarily mean that they are *equated*. The two could be related in other ways, as some scholars suggest. For example, (1) according to Hays, it may be the two effects resulting from Christ's redemption (Gal 3:13);[20] or (2) as Fee argues, it may be that the reception of the Spirit is the way by which the blessing of Abraham is fulfilled.[21] Fee notes that even though the experience of the Spirit is associated with the blessing of Abraham in Gal 3:1–14, the promise of the Spirit in Paul should probably be understood in the prophetic tradition of Jeremiah and Ezekiel.[22] However, Fee stops short of explaining how the blessing of Abraham might be related to the promise of the Spirit and the new covenant in Jeremiah and Ezekiel.

Williams and Hong explain that the promise of numerous descendants, which is one of the elements of the Abrahamic blessing and implied in Gal 3:6, is fulfilled by means of receiving the promised Spirit.[23] According to Williams, the receiving of the sonship is closely connected

---

17. Cosgrove, *The Cross and the Spirit*, 105.

18. Ibid., 104–5. Earlier in his book, Cosgrove explicitly states that "the blessing of Abraham is above all the gift of the Spirit," and "Paul identifies the promise (explicitly) and the blessing (by implication) with the gift of the Spirit (3:14)" (idem, 50).

19. The evidence that Cosgrove cites from the early church to support the notion of "promise by extension" are Acts 7:17; 13:32; 26:6 (Cosgrove, *The Cross and the Spirit*, 105). However, he does not specify which Hellenistic Jewish sources he refers to, which perhaps could be those he cited pp. 90–101. Acts 13:32 and 26:6 depict Paul referring to the "good news that . . . God promised to the fathers," and that he was on trial "because of my hope in the promise made by God to our fathers" (ESV). In view of Rom 4:1–25; 15:8–9; Gal 3:8, the promise Paul refers to in Acts 13:32; 26:6 is specifically the Abrahamic promise, not any other divine promise. Similarly, in Acts 7:17, the promise refers unambiguously to the Abrahamic promise to multiply the descendants.

20. Hays, "Galatians," 262.

21. Fee, *God's Empowering Presence*, 394–95. Fee explains that "the Spirit is the way the promised blessing made to Abraham has been realized."

22. Fee, *God's Empowering Presence*, 395.

23. Williams, "Promise in Galatians," 714–16; Hong, "Does Paul Misrepresent the Jewish Law?," 172.

## The Blessing of Abraham, the Spirit, and Justification in Galatians

with God's sending of the Spirit (Gal 4:4–5), and the Spirit also works to "create" the sons of Abraham (Gal 4:28–29).[24] With the inclusion of the Gentiles as children of Abraham and children of God by faith, the Abrahamic promise to bless the nations is also fulfilled through the Holy Spirit.[25]

There are two main problems with this view of the Spirit as the fulfillment of the Abrahamic promise. First, in Galatians, Paul attributes the status of sonship to faith in Jesus Christ (Gal 3:7, 26–29; 4:4–5), not to the Spirit. Second, this view neglects the OT context of the promise of the Spirit and its possible influence on Paul's theology in his juxtaposition of the Abrahamic blessing with the promise of the Spirit.[26]

Hays proposes that a "partial" answer may be found in Paul's use of an early Christian collection of scriptural *testimonia* concerning the messianic seed.[27] He postulates that Isa 44:3 might have been one of the Scriptures in the *testimonia* that associated the blessing of Abraham with the promise of the Spirit.[28] The LXX of Isa 44:3 reads: ἐπιθήσω τὸ πνεῦμά μου ἐπὶ τὸ σπέρμα σου καὶ τὰς εὐλογίας μου ἐπὶ τὰ τέκνα σου ["I will place my Spirit upon your seed and my blessings on your descendants"]. Based on the parallel between πνεῦμα ("Spirit") and εὐλογία ("blessing") in Isa 44:3, Hays claims that "although Paul does not cite this passage, it probably underlies and surely illuminates Gal 3:1–14."[29] However, he admits that there is a problem, as the passage is addressed to Jacob instead of Abraham.[30] Although the language of "blessing" and "descendants" may faintly allude to the Abrahamic promise, Hays has not shown how the "blessing" in Isa 44:3 is related to Abrahamic promise.[31]

---

24. Williams, "Promise in Galatians," 715.

25. Ibid., 716; Hong, "Does Paul Misrepresent the Jewish Law?," 173. Both Williams and Hong also attempt to explain how the element of the land in the Abrahamic promise is fulfilled by the gift of the Holy Spirit. However, an evaluation of such a discussion regarding the land element would be beyond the scope of this study.

26. This is reflected in Williams's statements below: "the promise of many descendants is, at the same time, the promise of the Spirit. . . . In other words, Paul reads beyond the explicit words of scripture to the implicit meaning that for him they contain" (Williams, "Promise in Galatians," 716).

27. Hays, *Faith of Jesus Christ*, 182–83.

28. Ibid., 183.

29. Hays, "Galatians," 261.

30. Hays, *Faith of Jesus Christ*, 182.

31. I shall discuss in detail the relationship between the blessing of Abraham and Isa 44:3 in ch. 4 below.

## Introduction: The Juxtaposition of the Blessing of Abraham

On the other hand, Sze-kar Wan points out that Paul's juxtaposition of the two motifs could be influenced by the Hellenistic-Jewish mysticism that is reflected in Philo.[32] While Wan rightly draws attention to the importance of studying the interactions between Paul and contemporary Jewish thought, the evidence he puts forth does not seem to be conclusive. Wan contends that the promise of Abraham functions in both Philo and Paul as a "vital link between the patriarch and his descendants."[33] According to Wan, the content of the Abrahamic land promise for Philo is the "Wisdom of God" that is given by the divine Spirit, and Philo understands that all proselytes who convert to monotheism are Abraham's descendants.[34] Thus, in this way, the Spirit is related to the Abrahamic promise in Philo. However, when Paul juxtaposes the blessing of Abraham with the promise of the Spirit, he specifically refers to the Abrahamic promise of blessings for the nations, not the land promise, and the content of the promise is the "gospel preached ahead of time to Abraham" (Gal 3:8). Also, for Paul, all who believe in Christ, not those who adhere to monotheistic faith, are descendants of Abraham by faith (Gal 3:7–9). Although Wan admits that the content of God's promise in Philo is different from that of Paul, he argues that the manner by which both appropriated Abraham shows that there might have been "a great deal more contact" between the two than most scholars would assume.[35]

Wan's conclusion is doubtful for the following reasons. (1) While Philo and Paul may be interpreting the same Abraham narrative, the similarity in the manner by which Abraham is appropriated is more formal than actual, since the content is starkly different. (2) The verbal parallels in Galatians 3 are nearer to the OT than to Philo. (3) Paul's interest is historical while Philo's interest is mystical.[36]

---

32. Wan, "Abraham and the Promise of Spirit," 209.

33. Ibid., 224.

34. Wan, "Abraham and the Promise of Spirit," 217–19. Wan infers the content of the Abrahamic promise, specifically the land promise in Gen 15:18, as the "Wisdom of God" from Philo, *Heir* 96–99, 313–16 and that such wisdom is given to Abraham by the divine Spirit (Philo, *Virtues* 212, 217). Wan also argues that when Philo speaks of Abraham as the founder of "the Jewish people" (τὸ τῶν Ἰουδαίων ἔθνος; Philo, *Virtues* 212), he "refers not simply to his fellow-Jews but to all who hold the right belief of God regardless of ethnicity. Gentiles can become 'Jewish' by means of adherence to monotheism" (Wan, "Abraham and the Promise of Spirit," 219–20).

35. Wan, "Abraham and the Promise of Spirit," 223–24.

36. Smith, "Pauline Literature," 278.

## The Blessing of Abraham, the Spirit, and Justification in Galatians

More recently, Morales has proposed that Paul's association of the Spirit and the blessing of Abraham could reflect an early Jewish tradition found in the *Testament of Judah*, which connects the Spirit with blessings and Abraham.[37] *Testament of Judah* 24 speaks of the restoration of Israel after their judgment, which is meted out in the form of the covenantal curses described in Leviticus 26 and Deuteronomy 28–30, and their subsequent repentance. At that time, a messianic figure will appear, and "the heavens will be opened upon him to pour out the spirit as a blessing of the Holy Father. And he will pour the spirit of grace on you" (*T. Jud.* 24:2–3b).[38] According to Morales,

> Following this description, the text proceeds to depict the resurrection of the patriarchs Abraham, Isaac, and Jacob, and to promise a kingdom to the sons of Israel (TestJud 25,1–2). Though the text does not explicitly speak of a "promise," it does seem to present this outpouring of the Spirit as the fulfillment of the promise to Abraham, intriguingly reinterpreting it in terms of resurrection. If one of the underlying presuppositions of Paul's argument in Gal 3,10–14 is Christ's resurrection and the eschatological life that it brings—as seems likely—and if the *Testament of Judah* represents a tradition that may have been available to Paul, then the connection between the Spirit and the promise to Abraham begins to make more sense.[39]

Morales argues that the tradition of associating the Spirit with blessing in *T. Jud.* 24 is not necessarily Christian, as it can be traced to Isa 44:3 and is also apparent in the *Word of the Luminaries* (4Q504).[40]

However, Morales's argument is not convincing. First, the association of the Spirit with blessing only implies that the tradition preserved in *T. Jud.* 24 associates the Spirit with Israel's redemption from the covenantal curses and the restoration of blessing. The text of *T. Jud.* 24:2—25:2 still does not show how the Spirit is associated with the *blessing of Abraham*. Second, the provenance of the *Testament of Judah*, whether Jewish with Christian interpolations or Christian using Jewish tradition, is hotly contested.[41] In either case, even if a Jewish tradition is preserved in *T. Jud.* 24:2–3; 25:1–2, it is difficult to discern in its present Christian form,

---

37. Morales, "Words of the Luminaries," 155–57.
38. *OTP* 1:801.
39. Morales, "Words of the Luminaries," 277.
40. Morales, *The Spirit and the Restoration of Israel*, 69–73.
41. On the provenance of the *Testament of Judah*, see p. 136n2 of ch. 5 below.

## Introduction: The Juxtaposition of the Blessing of Abraham

whether the interpretation of the Spirit and its association with blessing or Abraham, if any, is a Jewish tradition available to Paul or a Christian tradition influenced by Paul. Third, it is not clear from the text how the Spirit is connected with the Abrahamic blessing for the nations through the resurrection of Abraham, and Morales has also not shown how Paul would have associated the resurrection of Abraham (*T. Jud.* 25:1) with the "underlying presupposition" of the resurrection of Christ in Gal 3:10–14.

## Interpreters Who Do Not Relate the Blessing with the Spirit

There are also scholars who argue that the Holy Spirit is not related to the blessing of Abraham. In his commentary on Galatians, Calvin thinks that Paul is not referring to the Holy Spirit here, but to "the spiritual promise," received by faith, in contrast to ceremonial law and physical descent.[42]

Following Calvin's lead, Harrisville argues that πνεύματος should be understood as a "descriptive genitive" and the phrase τὴν ἐπαγγελίαν τοῦ πνεύματος should thus be translated as "spiritual promise." Even if it refers to the Holy Spirit, the promise of the Spirit should be understood to refer to the prophecy in Joel that is fulfilled at Pentecost, not to the Abrahamic promise.[43]

He gives two further reasons why the Holy Spirit is not referred to here.[44] First, Harrisville argues that the two ἵνα clauses are dependent and not coordinate. According to Harrisville, a coordinate reading would require a strict parallel between the two ἵνα clauses, and thus, τὰ ἔθνη ("the nations") would become the implied subject of the verb λάβωμεν ("we might receive"). Harrisville argues that this is not possible, as λάβωμεν includes Paul himself, who is not a Gentile. Second, nowhere else in Paul's letters is it indicated that the Spirit is the content of the promise. On the contrary, Rom 4:13 identifies the content of the Abrahamic promise as ὁ κόσμος ("the world").

Harrisville's arguments are not convincing for the following reasons. First, the blessing of Abraham consists of progeny, land, and blessing for the nations. The Spirit is somewhat related to the eschatological fulfillment of progeny (cf. Gal 4:6), although there is a difficulty in accounting for the land.[45] Second, even if the two ἵνα clauses are dependent and not

---

42. Calvin, *Galatians*, 56.
43. Harrisville, *Figure of Abraham*, 11.
44. Ibid., 10–11.
45. I am using the term "eschatological" in this study to refer to the expectation

coordinate, it only implies that the two are not *equated*; they are still *related*. Third, it is unlikely that the genitive τοῦ πνεύματος is purely descriptive ("spiritual promise") because the gift of the Spirit is mentioned in Gal 3:1–5 and 4:6–7. Paul continues to argue that all who believe in Christ are Abraham's true children (Gal 3:29). Therefore, it is more likely that, in Gal 3:14, Paul sees the reception of the Spirit as related to, though not equated with, the promised blessing made to Abraham in some ways. Nonetheless, the gift of the Spirit should not be understood as the "fulfillment" of the Abrahamic blessing. Rather, Christ is the one who brings about the fulfillment by his vicarious death of the cross (Gal 3:13–14, 16–19).

Kwon also argues strongly against the prevailing understanding of the Spirit as being equated with the content of the blessing of Abraham, to the extent that he denies any relationship at all between the two. He puts forth several reasons why he thinks that "promise of the Spirit" is not related at all to "the Abrahamic promise."[46] (1) Paul does not explicitly claim that the Spirit is the fulfillment of the Abrahamic promise. Many scholars have equated the "promise" in Gal 3:14 with the "promise" in Gal 3:16 onwards only on the basis of their proximity. (2) The association of the Spirit and the Abrahamic promise is unattested in any other contemporary literature. On the contrary, the Jews of Paul's time understood the Abrahamic promise as the promise of the land in an eschatological and universal sense. (3) The alternation between the singular and plural forms of ἐπαγγελία "promise" in Gal 3:16–22 indicates that Paul could not have the singular "promise of the Spirit" in mind. (4) Galatians 3:18 clearly identifies the "inheritance" with the content of God's promise to Abraham. (5) The Spirit is not involved in Paul's discussion of the Abrahamic promise in Gal 3:15–29. Although Paul relates sonship to the gift of the Spirit in Gal 4:7, the notion of the Abrahamic promise is not in view. (6) Paul explicitly mentions the world, that is, the eschatological land as the content of the Abrahamic promise.

---

of "a period in which Yhwh triumphs over evil, redeems his people Israel, and finally rules the world in peace and salvation" that is present in the latter prophets (Arnold, "Old Testament Eschatology," 25). This era is marked by the restoration of Israel from the exile, the renewal of the covenantal relationship with Yahweh, the rule of Yahweh or a Davidic king, the punishment of the wicked (both Gentiles and unfaithful Jews), and the conversion of some pagans to Yahweh as his people (Arnold, "Old Testament Eschatology," 27–29). The NT writers believed that this era was inaugurated by the first coming of Jesus Christ, and it will be consummated at the second coming of Christ (cf. Acts 3:21) (Rowland, "The Eschatology of the New Testament," 57, 59, 68–70).

46. Kwon, *Eschatology in Galatians*, 109–14.

## Introduction: The Juxtaposition of the Blessing of Abraham

Instead, Kwon argues that Paul's understanding of the Spirit is influenced by the prophetic writings in Jeremiah and Ezekiel.[47] Nonetheless, although Kwon describes how the promise of the Spirit in the prophets is reflected in other Pauline letters, he does not explain how Paul understands it in Galatians. Indeed, Kwon offers strong exegetical reasons why the promise of the Spirit should not be understood to be the content of the Abrahamic promise. However, while it may be true that the promise of the Spirit should not be equated with the blessing of Abraham, Kwon has gone too far in denying any relationship between the two. A detailed analysis and critique of Kwon's arguments will come in chapters 2 and 6, but in brief here, Kwon has unduly restricted the Abrahamic promise to the land promise. He has neglected the elements of progeny and blessing for the nations in the Abrahamic promise, both of which are prominent motifs in Paul's argument in relation to the Spirit in Gal 3:7—4:7. Also, it does not follow that if the contemporary Jewish literature does not link the Spirit with the Abrahamic promise, Paul would then also not have linked the two. It is certainly possible that Paul can differ from his contemporaries in his reading of Scripture. Furthermore, although Kwon argues that Paul's concept of the promise of the Spirit is influenced by Jeremiah and Ezekiel, he has neglected the covenantal context in which the bestowal of the Spirit occurs in these prophetic texts. Since the new covenant in Jeremiah and Ezekiel is developed from the Abrahamic and Mosaic covenants, there must be some kind of relationship between the bestowal of the Spirit and the Abrahamic covenant, as we shall see in our study below.

From our survey above, we observe that neither the scholars who equate the blessing of Abraham with the promise of the Spirit nor those who argue for some kind of connection, though not equation, between the two motifs have provided a clear and persuasive explanation of their relationship. The arguments of those who advocate no relationship between the two at all are also not convincing. Therefore, in this study, we shall take up the task of investigating and explaining the relationship between the two motifs and why Paul has juxtaposed them in Gal 3:14.

---

47. Ibid., 116.

# The Blessing of Abraham, the Spirit, and Justification in Galatians

## Methodology and Approaches

### Criteria for Detecting Quotations and Allusions

In order to trace the development of the Abrahamic blessing for the nations and the promise of the Spirit in the OT, Second Temple literature, and in Paul, it is necessary for us to establish the criteria by which we can identify quotations/citations or allusions of the scriptural texts related to these two motifs.[48] An explicit quotation occurs when "an author indicates that the words that follow are not his or her own but are taken from another source."[49] They may or may not be introduced by an introductory formula, but there may be other markers.[50] There is usually close verbal correspondence with the source text, but changes are also possible. The changes may be explained as follows: (1) unintentional changes, such as citing from a different *Vorlage* or imprecision due to citing from memory[51] and (2) intentional changes, which includes the author's own translation of the source text, paraphrasing, and grammatical changes (e.g., syntax, inflection, tense, mood, voice, etc.), in order to fit the new context in which it is cited.[52]

An "allusion" is "a figure of speech that makes indirect extratextual references."[53] The entry in *A Handbook to Literature* defines "allusion" as:

> A figure of speech that makes brief reference to a historical or literary figure, event, or object ... It seeks, by tapping the knowledge and memory of the reader, to secure a resonant emotional

---

48. I am using the two terms—"citation" and "quotation"—interchangeably.

49. Moyise, "Quotations," 15. Hughes offers a similar definition: "a quotation [is] a phrase which is marked, explicitly or implicitly, as referring to the words of a speaker who is not the implied speaker of the composition. The identity of the referent may or may not be known. The words may or may not be quoted verbatim" (*Scriptural Allusions*, 44). See also Schultz, *Search for Quotation*, 211–15; Porter, "Further Comments," 107–8. Porter proposes two separate categories for quotations: (1) formulaic quotation and (2) direct quotation. He classifies "paraphrase" as an indirect citation, rather than a quotation. However, for the purpose of this study, it suffices to include all three under the same category of "quotation."

50. Schultz, *Search for Quotation*, 211–12; Hughes, *Scriptural Allusions*, 44; Moyise, "Quotation," 15.

51. Unintentional changes are difficult to determine, unless it can be established, e.g., that the citation reflects a *Vorlage* represented by certain Qumran manuscripts or the LXX compared with the MT.

52. Schultz, *Search for Quotation*, 212; Moyise, "Quotation," 16–17.

53. Porter, "Allusions and Echoes," 30.

effect from the associations already existing in the reader's mind ... The effectiveness of the allusion depends on a body of knowledge shared by writer and reader.[54]

Porter notes several significant elements in the definition above:

(1) reference may be to historical or literary entities, including people, events, or objects; (2) reference is indirect, as opposed to quotation or paraphrase, both of which are direct; (3) the allusion is intentional on the part of the author toward the reader; (4) allusion may occur without the knowledge of the reader; and (5) allusion is most effective when there is a body of shared knowledge between the author and reader.[55]

Therefore, the main difference between a quotation and an allusion is that the former refers to a specific discourse (either speech or text) directly, while the reference of the latter is indirect. Allusions are also not limited to discourses, but refer more broadly to people, events, or objects.

More recently, the term "echo" is also used in describing intertextual phenomena in general literary studies, and it is brought to the attention of biblical scholars by Hays.[56] Although Harmon thinks that the term "echo" should be distinguished from "allusion," other scholars seem to use them interchangeably.[57] For example, Hollander refers to "echo" as a "mode of allusion," and Hays uses the term "allusive echo."[58] Harmon defines "echo" as "a complex, subtle, and multifarious acoustic phenomenon involving a faint but perceptible repetition inside a work or between works."[59] His definition does not provide sufficient details to distinguish between an "allusion" and an "echo," except for the level of subtlety—how obvious the indirect reference is. This distinction is apparently also Hays's

---

54. Harmon, *A Handbook to Literature*, 14.

55. Porter, "Allusions and Echoes," 30–31.

56. Hays, *Echoes of Scripture*.

57. Harmon contends, "Although usage has never been precise, *allusion* ought to be distinguished carefully from outright QUOTATION, obvious ECHO, and direct or annotated REFERENCE" (Harmon, *A Handbook to Literature*, 14; emphasis in original).

58. Hollander, *Figure of Echo*, 20. Hollander's synonymous use of the terms is reflected in the title of his book. Nonetheless, Hollander states that "allusions" are intended by the author, but "echoes" may or may not be intended (Hollander, *Figure of Echo*, 64). See also Porter, "Allusions and Echoes," 36.

59. Harmon, *A Handbook to Literature*, 171.

understanding.⁶⁰ However, the level of subtlety is not only determined by how obviously the author indicates the hints and markers, but it also depends on how familiar the reader is with the intertextual reference. For this reason, Hays clarifies that he makes "no systematic distinction between the terms."⁶¹ On the contrary, Porter disagrees with Hays's undistinguished use and proposes that the two terms may be distinguished as follows: "allusion is concerned to bring an external person, place, or literary work into the contemporary context, whereas echo does not have the specificity of allusion but is reserved for language that is thematically related to a more general notion or concept."⁶² The definition of "echo" is far from being settled in scholarly discussion. Therefore, I shall be using the term "allusion" predominantly in this study for consistency.

The criteria for identifying quotations and allusions are similar.⁶³ It is necessary for both the criteria below to be fulfilled in order to determine a quotation or an allusion. (1) *Verbal and syntactical correspondence* with the source text. However, there can be flexibility in terms of paraphrase and grammatical changes. (2) *Contextual awareness or parallels*. There need to be indications that the author is aware of or refers to or draws parallels to the context of the source text, from which he or she quotes or alludes to. For example, if the context of the apparent allusion to the Abrahamic blessing for the nations also mentions other elements of the Abrahamic blessing, such as numerous descendants and land, it will strengthen the case for the allusion. For the promise of the Spirit, if the context of the apparent allusion discusses the issue of obedience to the Torah or the covenantal relationship with Yahweh, it will then strengthen the case for the allusion. The quotation or allusion can also reflect the author's interpretive use of the source text.

There are other criteria proposed by various scholars. However, not all of them are as useful. For example, Hays lists "recurrence" as his third "test" for echoes.⁶⁴ This test will work if the same quotation or allusion occurs multiple times in the same document, but it will not help for cases of

---

60. Hays, *Echoes of Scripture*, 29. Hays states that "in general . . . *allusion* is used of obvious intertextual references, *echo* of subtler ones" (emphasis in original).

61. Ibid.

62. Porter, "Allusions and Echoes," 39–40.

63. The criteria proposed by various scholars regarding quotations and allusions overlap. See, e.g., Hays, *Echoes of Scripture*, 29–32; Thompson, *Clothed with Christ*, 30–36; Ciampa, *The Presence and Function of Scripture*, 24–25; Schultz, *Search for Quotation*, 222–27; Berkley, *Broken Covenant*, 60–64; Sprinkle, *Law and Life*, 14–16.

64. Hays, *Echoes of Scripture*, 30.

single occurrence.⁶⁵ The criterion of "conceptual similarities" may also be subsumed under "contextual parallels."⁶⁶ Therefore, we are left with these two main criteria, as proposed by Schultz.⁶⁷

## Dynamics of Intertextuality

Before we trace the development of the Abrahamic blessing for the nations and the promise of the Spirit in the OT, Second Temple literature, and in Paul, it is necessary for us to look into the mutual relationship and interaction of these texts with each other. First, this study is primarily concerned with Paul's understanding of the Hebrew Scriptures, specifically, (1) why Paul juxtaposes the blessing of Abraham with the promise of the Spirit in Gal 3:14, and (2) what relationship Paul could have seen between the two motifs. Therefore, I am concerned with Paul as a reader of Scripture, and I will not deal with the impact of Paul's quotations and allusions in Galatians on the original readers. Although a study on the effect of Paul's use of Scripture on the original readers is important in its own right, it is not the focus of this study.⁶⁸ Second, since Paul reads the Scripture that is available to him in its final literary form, I will also not be dealing with historical-critical issues pertaining to the OT.

Third, as Paul, like any human, is historically and culturally influenced in his interpretation, it is necessary to study carefully the mutual interactions between Paul and the theological and social "climate" of his time. Watson reminds us that three bodies of texts, namely Scripture, Pauline texts, and non-Christian Jewish texts, are engaged in a "three-way conversation . . . an interaction instead of a unilinear movement."⁶⁹

---

65. Porter, "Use of the Old Testament," 83. Porter also notes that Hays's fourth to seventh tests "are less criteria for determining echoes than they are attempts to establish the interpretation of these echoes."

66. For those who propose "conceptual similarities" as a criterion, see, e.g., Thompson, *Clothed with Christ*, 32; Berkley, *Broken Covenant*, 63–64.

67. Schultz, *Search for Quotation*, 222–27. See also Hughes, *Scriptural Allusions*, 52–54.

68. Porter notes that "although investigation of an audience-oriented approach has merit in establishing the shared assumptions and biblical knowledge of the audience . . . it is questionable whether it provides the proper basis for establishing the author's use of the Old Testament" ("Use of the Old Testament," 95). For scholars who use the audience-oriented approach for their analysis of the use of the OT in the NT or in early Jewish literature, see, e.g., Stanley, *Arguing With Scripture*, 38–61; Hughes, *Scriptural Allusions*, 48–50.

69. Watson, *Paul and the Hermeneutics of Faith*, 4–5.

### The Blessing of Abraham, the Spirit, and Justification in Galatians

Paul is not unilaterally influenced by Scripture or by contemporaneous non-Christian Jewish exegetical methods and theology. Therefore, canonical interpretation is necessary in order to understand the theological development of the blessing of Abraham and the promise of the Spirit in the OT itself, as well as Paul's appropriation of the two motifs through his reading of the OT.[70] While there may be commonalities between Paul and early Judaism, there are also differences.[71] Thus, the starting point in understanding Paul's interpretation of the OT should be his own letters and not early Jewish methods, although the non-Christian Jewish sources may be brought into the discussion where they are meaningful or necessary.[72]

On another note, early Judaism is variegated.[73] Multivalent readings of the same passage of Scripture are common in the Second Temple literature. Instead of trying to derive from these divergent sources a single "contemporary Jewish" reading as a foil for the Pauline reading, these sources will be read in their own right to reflect their uniqueness, so that the comparison with the Pauline reading will be meaningful and fruitful.[74] Nonetheless, it is still viable to note the commonalities among the various Second Temple literature readings of the Abrahamic blessing for the nations and the promise of the Spirit for comparative purposes, as long as their distinctiveness is not neglected at the same time.

Fourth, a number of motifs in Galatians pertaining to this study, such as justification, the Spirit, and the Abrahamic promise, are also present in Romans (see esp. Romans 3–4; 8). Scholars are divided as to whether Galatians and Romans should be interpreted in light of each other.[75] As our study pertains to understanding Paul's argument in Galatians, I shall

---

70. "Canonical interpretation" is used here to refer to the interpretation of Scripture that (1) focuses on the theological purpose of the final literary form of each book in the canon; and (2) is sensitive to the theological development of the various motifs in the two testaments in light of the Christ event.

71. Ellis, *Paul's Use of the Old Testament*, 53.

72. Hübner, *Biblische Theologie*, 1:259. Hübner argues that Paul's exegetical method will not be clearly understood if Jewish methodology is taken to be the key to understanding. See also Koch, *Die Schrift als Zeuge*, 202.

73. The variety and complexities of early Judaism are strongly put across in Carson et al., *Justification and Variegated Nomism, Vol. 1: The Complexities of Second Temple Judaism*.

74. Watson, *Paul and the Hermeneutics of Faith*, 3.

75. For scholars who insist that Romans and Galatians should be interpreted in their own right, see, e.g., Bruce, *Galatians*, 2; Kuula, *The Law*, 2:24–25; Stanton, "Law of Moses," 99–100. For those who interpret the two epistles in light of each other, see, e.g., Martyn, *Galatians*, 488; Childs, *Reading Paul*, 122.

*Introduction: The Juxtaposition of the Blessing of Abraham*

be interpreting Galatians primarily in its own right. Nonetheless, in discussions concerning Paul's broader theology in relation to Galatians, his other epistles will be cited to highlight the similarities and differences with Galatians.

## Overview

This study will begin with a detailed exegesis of Gal 3:1–14 in chapter 2, so that we may situate Paul's discussion on the blessing of Abraham and the promise of the Spirit in its historical and literary context. As Paul specifically refers to the element of the blessing for the nations in the Abrahamic blessing (Gen 12:3b) in Gal 3:8, 14, we shall pay special attention to this element and its development. Therefore, in chapter 3, we shall examine the blessing of Abraham (Gen 12:2–3) in the context of Genesis, where it first occurs in the OT, and its relationship with the primeval narrative in Genesis 1–11, as well as its development in the rest of Genesis and the Pentateuch. Next, in chapter 4, we shall trace how the Abrahamic blessing for the nations is further developed in other texts of the OT. Chapter 4 will also examine the promise of the Spirit in the prophets and whether it has any relationship with the Abrahamic blessing for the nations. The objective of chapters 3 and 4 is to provide us with a framework of how Paul might have understood the Abrahamic blessing for the nations and its relationship with the promise of the Spirit.

Subsequently, in chapter 5, we shall survey the Second Temple literature to see how these various kinds of literature understand the Abrahamic blessing for the nations and the promise of the Spirit, and if they exhibit any relationship between the two. The purpose of chapter 5 is to help us have a feel of the theological "climate" during Paul's time and to provide us with a background of how Paul might be interacting with contemporary thought.

Finally, in chapter 6, we shall consolidate our findings in chapters 2 to 5, so as to propose the reason for Paul's juxtaposition of the blessing of Abraham and the promise of the Spirit in Gal 3:14, as well as to articulate the relationship between the two motifs. We will also discuss why our proposed relationship between the blessing of Abraham and the promise of the Spirit in Gal 3:14 would enhance the understanding of Galatians and the theological implications arising from such an interpretation, especially with regard to justification.

# 2 Justification by Faith

## *The Context of Galatians 3:14*

This chapter seeks to provide a contextual and exegetical overview of Gal 3:1–14. First, we shall look into the main theme surrounding Gal 3:1–14 and the function of Gal 3:1–14 in Galatians in order to situate Paul's discussion of the blessing of Abraham and the promise of the Spirit within its historical and literary context. Second, we shall examine key issues in Gal 3:1–14 pertaining to the understanding of Paul's association of the blessing of Abraham with the promise of the Spirit. In this overview, we shall see that the blessing of Abraham is not equated with the promise of the Spirit, as it is often supposed. Neither is it unrelated, as Harrisville and Kwon claim.[1] As an overview, this chapter will raise questions about these key issues but will not seek to answer them in detail. These questions will then prepare us to look into the OT and Jewish background that might have influenced Paul in his association of the blessing of Abraham with the promise of the Spirit. At the end of this study, in chapter 6, we shall revisit the issues we have raised here. Then, we will consolidate our investigation of the OT and Jewish background and formulate the relationship between the blessing of Abraham and the promise of the Spirit in Gal 3:14.

So much has been written on Gal 3:1–14 that it would be impossible to address every exegetical issue in this passage for our study.[2] For example, the significance of the reference to "faith" and "the works of the

---

1. On the supposed equation and non-relation of the blessing of Abraham and the promise of the Spirit in Gal 3:14, see the history of research on pp. 4–11 above.

2. The areas of study and literature involved in this passage are very broad, spanning rhetorical analysis, Paul's use of the OT (including specialized studies on each of the OT quotations in Gal 3:6–13), and topical studies such as justification, Paul and the law, the Spirit, Abraham, etc. See, e.g., Williams, "Justification and the Spirit," 91–100; Boers, *Justification of the Gentiles*; Morland, *Rhetoric of Curse*; Amadi-Azuogu, *Paul and the Law*; Philip, *Pauline Pneumatology*.

law" (ἔργα νόμου) continue to be hotly contested.³ The literature and discussions on these two topics alone are overwhelming, and each constitutes a separate topic by itself. For the purpose of this study, I shall only address the key exegetical issues in Gal 3:1–14 that are pertinent to our study of the blessing of Abraham and the promise of the Spirit. Other issues will be discussed only to the extent that is necessary for this study.

## JUSTIFICATION BY FAITH AS THE CONTEXT OF GALATIANS 3:1–14

Paul's letter to the Galatians was sparked primarily by controversy when some people who had come to the Galatians advocated that Gentile Christians needed to observe the Jewish law in addition to their faith in Christ (Gal 2:15–21; 3:3), specifically with regard to, but not limited to, accepting circumcision (Gal 5:1–6; 6:12–13; cf. 4:8–11).⁴ Their message was contrary to Paul's gospel (cf. Gal 1:6–9), and they had apparently cast doubts on the authenticity of Paul's gospel message. In response, Paul defended the authenticity of his gospel in four ways: (1) his apostolicity was instituted by God himself and not by people (Gal 1:1); (2) his gospel message was revealed by Christ himself and not received from people, including the other apostles (Gal 1:11–24); (3) the leaders at Jerusalem concurred with his gospel message and his mission among the Gentiles (Gal 2:1–10); and (4) his gospel message was supported by Scripture (Gal 3:6—4:31).⁵ Paul was very anxious (cf. Gal 4:19–20) for the Galatians because they were apparently deserting his gospel message and defecting to the teaching of these "trouble-makers" (Gal 1:6–7). Their future hope was in jeopardy should they continue in their present apostasy (cf. Gal 3:3–4; 5:2–7).⁶

---

3. Briefly, the debate over the significance of faith in our passage hinges on "the faith of Jesus Christ." Does the phrase refer to the human "faith in Jesus Christ," or Christ's faith, i.e., "the faithfulness of Jesus Christ"? The dispute on "the works of the law" revolves around whether the phrase refers to the stipulations of the Jewish law in general or specifically to the Jewish laws that mark out ethnicity. For a concise discussion on both these issues in Galatians, see Silva, "Faith Versus Works of the Law," 217–48.

4. Paul uses the terms "trouble-makers" (ταράσσοντες; Gal 1:7; 5:10) and "agitators" (ἀναστατοῦντες; Gal 5:12) to describe them. For a detailed discussion on who these opponents might be, see the introductions of standard commentaries and Porter, *Paul and His Opponents*.

5. See also Bruce, *Galatians*, 19–20.

6. Kwon, *Eschatology in Galatians*, 31–50. Kwon rightly points out the future

# The Blessing of Abraham, the Spirit, and Justification in Galatians

Therefore, Paul began the letter in defense of his apostolic authority and the truth of the gospel (Gal 1:1—2:14). Then he proceeded to argue his case that for both Jews and Gentiles alike, justification is by faith in Jesus Christ and not by the works of the law (Gal 2:15–21). I am taking the phrase διὰ πίστεως Ἰησοῦ Χριστοῦ (Gal 2:16) to mean "by faith in Jesus Christ," rather than "by the faithfulness of Jesus Christ," because I would argue that Paul is contrasting the human "doing" of the law with human "believing in Christ" in Gal 2:15—3:14. The antithesis would not work if the "doing" of the law is contrasted with "the faithfulness of Christ." This is especially clear in (1) Gal 2:16, where Paul insists that "we know that a person is justified by works of the law but by faith in Jesus Christ, so *we have believed in Christ Jesus* (εἰς Χριστὸν Ἰησοῦν)" (ESV, emphasis added);[7] and (2) Gal 3:2, 5, where the "faith" in the work/faith antithesis almost undoubtedly refers to human believing.[8] I also understand the phrase ἐξ ἔργων νόμου ("by works of the law," Gal 2:16) to refer to observing the stipulations of the law in general, rather than restricting its reference only to laws that mark out Jewish identity.[9] This is because, while circumcision (Gal 5:5; 6:12), food laws (Gal 2:11–14), and festival observances (Gal 4:10) may have sparked the controversy at Galatia, Paul is likely to have a broader perspective in mind. This is evident from his references to the law as a whole (Gal 3:10; 5:3, 14) and his accusations that his opponents had not kept the law (Gal 6:13).[10]

Quite a number of scholars note that Gal 2:15-21 forms a summary and transition between his autobiographic defense of the authenticity of his gospel (Gal 1:11—2:14) and his main argument of the letter—the defense of his gospel from the experience of the Spirit and Scripture (Gal 3:1—4:31).[11] In Gal 2:15-21, Paul begins by stating that there are Jewish

---

element of justification present in the letter of Galatians and Paul's concern to warn his readers of the perils of apostasy with a future eschatological outlook.

7. See also Eckstein, *Verheißung und Gesetz*, 18.

8. For a full discussion, see, e.g., Hays, "ΠΙΣΤΙΣ and Pauline Christology," 35–60; and Dunn, "Once More, ΠΙΣΤΙΣ ΧΡΙΣΤΟΥ," 61–81; Achtemeier, "Apropos the Faith of/in Christ," 82–92; Ulrichs, *Christusglaube*; Dunn, "ΕΚ ΠΙΣΤΕΩΣ," 351–66; Bird and Sprinkle, *Faith of Jesus Christ*.

9. See also Martyn, *Galatians*, 261; Eckstein, *Verheißung und Gesetz*, 122; Watson, *Paul and the Hermeneutics of Faith*, 334–35.

10. For detailed discussions, see, e.g., Dunn, *New Perspective on Paul*, 1–88, 111–30, 207–20, 375–88, 407–22; Moo, "'Law,' 'Works of the Law,' and Legalism in Paul," 73–100; Schreiner, "'Works of Law,'" 217–44; Hofius, "'Werke des Gesetz,'" 271–310; Bachmann, "Keil oder Mikroskop?," 69–134.

11. Due to the transitional nature of Gal 2:15-21, some scholars begin a new

*Justification by Faith*

Christians besides himself who know that (εἰδότες ὅτι) justification is by faith in Christ and not by the works of the law (Gal 2:15-16a).[12] The participle εἰδότες (Gal 2:16a) may be understood as circumstantial ("we who are Jews by birth . . . *know*")[13] or causal ("*because* we know").[14] Whichever way the participle is taken, there is a *semantic causal relationship* between the main clause and the participial clause: Jewish Christians, who share the same convictions as Paul regarding justification, believed in Jesus Christ in order to be justified (Gal 2:16b) *because* they know that a person is not justified by the works of the law but by faith in Jesus Christ (Gal 2:16a). Paul reiterates the basis of justification by faith again in Gal 2:16c: "because (ὅτι) by the works of the law, no one will be justified."[15]

Next, Paul substantiates his thesis in Gal 2:16 with two sets of evidence: the evidence of the Galatians' experience of the Spirit (Gal 3:1-5) and the evidence from the Scriptures (Gal 3:6-14).[16] Various motifs brought up in Gal 3:1-14 are further elaborated in Gal 3:15—6:10.[17] Thus, Gal 3:1-14 constitutes the primary substantiation of his fundamental as-

---

section at Gal 3:1 (e.g., Betz, *Galatians*, viii, 114; Matera, *Galatians*, vi, 98). Other scholars take Gal 2:15 as the beginning of Paul's argument on justification by faith (e.g., Bruce, *Galatians*, 57; Fung, *Galatians*, 112). However, scholars differ as to where the main part of the letter that is linked to Gal 2:15-21 ends; some end the section at Gal 4:31 or 5:1 (e.g., Betz, *Galatians*, viii; Bruce, *Galatians*, 57), while others at Gal 5:12 (e.g., Fung, *Galatians*, vi; Matera, *Galatians*, vi). I have taken Gal 4:31 as the ending point of Paul's appeal to the Scriptures. Nonetheless, Paul's argument on justification wraps up only at Gal 5:12. I will demonstrate in ch. 6 that the rest of the letter, from Gal 5:1—6:10, is also integral to Paul's argument in Gal 3:1-14.

12. Richard Longenecker notes that the ὅτι following εἰδότες in Gal 2:16a probably functions as a *recitativum* and "signals that what follows could even be set in quotes as something widely affirmed" (*Galatians*, 83).

13. Longenecker, *Galatians*, 83.

14. Wallace, *Greek Grammar*, 631n47.

15. The ὅτι in Gal 2:16c has a causal function as well as introducing a possible quotation of or allusion to Ps 142:2 LXX (Longenecker, *Galatians*, 88; Silva, "Galatians," 790).

16. See also Betz, *Galatians*, 19; Longenecker, *Galatians*, 98.

17. The various motifs in the primary substantiation (Gal 3:1-14) that are later elaborated in the secondary substantiation (Gal 3:15—6:10) include the Abrahamic promise in relation to the law (Gal 3:15-19), the purpose the law (Gal 3:20-26), sonship of Abraham and of God (Gal 3:27—4:7), enslavement to pre-conversion beliefs and the law (Gal 4:8—5:1), the promise of the Spirit in relation to justification (Gal 5:2-12), and the fulfillment of the law (Gal 5:13—6:10). See also Bachmann, *Sünder oder Übertreter*, 110-51; Rainbow, *Way of Salvation*, 181-82; Longenecker, *Galatians*, 97.

## The Blessing of Abraham, the Spirit, and Justification in Galatians

sertion in Gal 2:16 that justification is by faith in Christ Jesus and not by works of the law. The elaborations in Gal 3:15—6:10 may be seen as the secondary substantiation of Paul's thesis. Paul ends this section on justification with a warning to the Galatians against coming under the law (Gal 2:15—5:12) and an admonition to them to continue living their lives by faith through the Spirit (Gal 5:5—6:10). Paul contends that it is only through the Spirit by faith in Jesus Christ that a person is empowered to live a godly life efficaciously (Gal 5:13—6:10).

Paul mentions the Holy Spirit for the first time in the letter in Gal 3:2, where he appeals to the experience of the Spirit as grounds of his argument that justification is by faith and not by the works of the law (Gal 2:16).[18] At the end of his argument from Scripture (Gal 3:6-12), Paul concludes by stating the purpose(s) of Christ's redemptive work on the cross with two ἵνα clauses, which connect the blessing of Abraham with the promise of the Spirit (Gal 3:13-14). Therefore, we shall delineate Gal 3:1-14 as the primary passage for our study because it forms a subsection within Paul's overall argument on justification by faith (Gal 2:15—5:12), where both the Abrahamic promise and the Holy Spirit play key roles in his argument.[19]

In pitting "by faith" (διὰ/ἐκ πίστεως) against "by works of the law" (ἐξ ἔργων νόμου) in Gal 2:15—3:14, Paul closely relates "being justified" (the passive of δικαιόω)[20] to two other concepts: (1) receiving the Spirit (Gal 3:2-3, 5, 14); and (2) inheriting the Abrahamic promise (cf. Gal 3:29; 4:6-7), which includes "becoming children of Abraham" (Gal 3:7; cf. 3:26, 29) and "partaking in the blessing of Abraham" (Gal 3:8-9, 14).

Considering the relationship between Gal 2:15-21 and the rest of Galatians, we may conclude that Gal 3:1-14 is situated within Paul's lengthy argument on justification by faith in Christ as the means of becoming true

---

18. See also Betz, *Galatians*, 130; Bruce, *Galatians*, 149; Longenecker, *Galatians*, 102.

19. I shall use the terms "blessing of Abraham," "Abrahamic blessing," "Abrahamic promise," and "God's promise to Abraham" interchangeably in this study. Although the term "Abrahamic promise" does not appear in Genesis, the promissory aspect of the blessing is evident in the establishment of the covenant (Gen 15:18; 17:7) and the oath that was sworn (Gen 22:16-18). There is an instance in Josephus where he refers to the Abrahamic "blessing" as "promise" (*Ant.* 1.236). This also seems to be Paul's understanding, as he begins with the "blessing of Abraham" in Gal 3:8, 14 and then speaks of the "promise(s)" God made to Abraham in Gal 3:16-29. See also Cosgrove, *The Cross and the Spirit*, 94-95.

20. All the δικαιόω verbs in Gal 2:15—3:29 are in the passive with implied divine agency (2:16 [3x], 17; 3:11, 24) except for 3:8, where the active form is used with God as the subject.

children of Abraham (Gal 2:15—5:12).²¹ It functions as the main substantiation of Paul's assertion in Gal 2:16 that justification is by faith and not by the works of the law.

Some scholars in recent years have argued that Paul's primary focus in Galatians is not justification by faith but life in the Spirit.²² While it is true that an overemphasis on justification by faith in Galatians may obscure its teaching on the Spirit, playing down justification by faith in favor of the Spirit in Galatians does not do justice to the letter. The language of justification is just as pervasive in the letter as the language of the Spirit.²³ Both justification by faith and life in the Spirit are Paul's answer to the controversy at Galatia: do Gentile Christians need to observe the Jewish law? No, Gentile Christians do not need to observe the law because (1) righteousness before God (i.e., justification) is by faith in Christ Jesus and not by the works of the law (Gal 2:15—3:25); and (2) the reception of the Spirit by faith is the evidence of justification before God (Gal 3:2-5; 5:5).²⁴ As both Bruce and Williams note, justification cannot be understood and experienced apart from the Spirit.²⁵

---

21. See also Hahn, *Kinship by Covenant*, 244-45, who argues that sonship is the "centerpiece and unifying theme of Galatians 3-4" and "sonship is significant not merely for its own sake but because it embodies the fulfillment of God's promise and covenant oath regarding the *inheritance* of Abraham's 'seed.'" I would add that Paul presents "justification by faith in Christ Jesus" as the *means* by which sonship is established (cf. Gal 3:24-29). Some scholars even argue that Gal 2:15-21 is a summary of the essential points of the whole letter (see, e.g., Longenecker, *Galatians*, 83; Hays, "Galatians," 236).

22. For those who argue that life in the Spirit is the main emphasis of Galatians, see, e.g., Cosgrove, *The Cross and the Spirit*, 2, 85-86; Fee, *God's Empowering Presence*, 368-69; Garlington, *Galatians*, 138-39.

23. The δικαιο- word group appears with high concentration in Gal 2:15—5:4, a total of 13 times: 2:16 (3x); 2:17; 2:21; 3:6; 3:8; 3:11 (2x); 3:21; 3:24; 5:4; 5:5. The reference to the Holy Spirit also appears with high concentration in Gal 3:1—6:10, a total of 17 times: 3:2; 3:3; 3:5; 3:14; 4:6; 4:29; 5:5; 5:16; 5:17 (2x); 5:18; 5:22; 5:25 (2x); 6:1; 6:8 (2x).

24. The reception of the Spirit is a sign of being justified before God (Gal 3:2-5; 4:6), and the work of the Spirit brings forth righteousness, life, and true obedience (5:5; 5:16—6:10). We will further examine the relationship between justification and the Spirit in ch. 6.

25. Bruce, "Spirit," 36; Williams, "Justification and the Spirit," 98. Bruce: "[Galatians's] teaching on the Holy Spirit is so interwoven with its teaching on justification by faith that the one cannot be understood without the other, any more than in real life the justifying grace of God can be experienced apart from the Spirit." Williams: "Justification and the Spirit: in Paul's mind one necessarily implies the other, and to claim the one without evidencing the other would be to misapprehend the nature of

## The Blessing of Abraham, the Spirit, and Justification in Galatians

### EVIDENCE OF JUSTIFICATION BY FAITH

### Evidence by Experience of the Holy Spirit

#### *Paul's Rhetorical Techniques and the Effects of His Argument in Galatians 3:1–5*

Galatians 3:1–5 provides the first set of evidence Paul adduces to substantiate his assertion that justification is by faith and not by works of the law. In this section, Paul uses a series of five rhetorical questions in order to remind the Galatians strongly that they should know from their former experience that they had received the Spirit by faith, not by works of the law. The rhetorical technique that Paul employs here shows affiliation with the contemporary rhetorical practices of his day. Betz proposes that Paul uses the technique of *interrogatio*. The feature of this technique is that the answer to every question is self-evident and undeniable.[26] In the case of the Galatians, the undeniable evidence is how they had received the Spirit.

On this point of undeniable evidence, Pelser suggests that the technique of dissociation is also used. This technique "forces the readers to choose between mutually exclusive alternatives"—ἐξ ἔργων νόμου ("by works of the law") or ἐξ ἀκοῆς πίστεως ("by hearing of faith") (Gal 3:2, 5)—and both Paul and the Galatians know very well that the latter is the only answer.[27] Eckstein rightly observes the rhetorical effects of Paul's questions: "based on the experience and discernment of the Galatians, they would have to admit that they have received the Spirit (and with it, justification and new life; cf. Gal 2:16, 19) solely by faith . . . and by no means on the basis of Torah observance."[28]

#### *Paul's Rhetorical Questions in Galatians 3:1–5*

Paul's first question may be paraphrased as: "O, you foolish Galatians! Who has bewitched you regarding the significance of Christ's crucifixion, which I had vividly proclaimed to you before your eyes?" (Gal 3:1) How could the Galatians have turned away from the truth of the gospel, which Paul so clearly preached to them? For Paul, it is almost as if the Galatians

---

Christian life."

26. Betz, *Galatians*, 130. The extensive ancient literature that Betz cites clearly shows the parallel between Paul and the contemporary rhetoric in this technique.

27. Pelser, "Persuasive Device in Galatians," 395.

28. Eckstein, *Verheißung und Gesetz*, 93.

*Justification by Faith*

had been placed under a spell that blinded them to the obvious truth.[29] He also uses the verb "bewitched" (βασκαίνω) to characterize his opponents as malicious sorcerers whose teachings seem plausible but fallacious.[30] Paul's preaching had clearly portrayed (προγράφω)[31] Christ's crucifixion and its significance.[32] How could they have forgotten or missed the truth? The Galatians had to be rebuked for their foolishness.

Next, Paul poses his second question: "This is the only thing I want to learn from you: did you receive the Spirit by works of the law or by hearing of faith?" (Gal 3:2) The antithesis of faith and works in relation to justification earlier (Gal 2:15–21) is now tied in with the reception of the Spirit. Two issues need to be addressed here. The first issue is the phrase ἐξ ἀκοῆς πίστεως (lit. "hearing of faith"). The ambiguity of the phrase arises from questions about both the meaning of the nouns and by their relationship.[33] The lexical and grammatical possibilities give rise to

29. See also Lemmer, "Mnemonic Reference to the Spirit," 373. Lightfoot explains that the word "bewitched" (βασκαίνω), which Paul uses metaphorically here, is derived from the popular belief in the blighting power of the evil eye cast by the sorcerer (*Galatians*, 133). For more discussion on the background of the "evil eye," see Elliott, "Paul, Galatians, and the Evil Eye," 262–73; Longenecker, "'Until Christ Is Formed in You,'" 93–97; Eastman, "The Evil Eye and the Curse of the Law," 69–87.

30. Betz, *Galatians*, 131; Neyrey, "Bewitched in Galatia," 73. Betz cites a number Greek sources, from which he concludes that "bewitched" (βασκαίνω) was commonly used "to characterize opponents and their sophistic strategies." Neyrey suggests that Paul is using a common practice of accusing one's rivals of sorcery or demonic influence.

31. NIV: "clearly portrayed"; NRSV: "publicly exhibited." προγράφω can mean (1) written beforehand (e.g., Rom 15:4; Eph 3:3); or (2) set forth for public notice (BDAG 867). Betz draws the parallel of the ancient orator whose goal "was to deliver his speech so vividly and impressively that his listeners imagined the matter to have happened right before their eyes" (Betz, *Galatians*, 131). Therefore, it is likely that Paul was referring to his vivid recount of the passion of Christ, and προγράφω should thus be more appropriately rendered as "clearly portrayed."

32. Certainly, the Christian *kerygma* of the crucified Christ is not just a narration of his crucifixion story but also an exposition of the significance of his death and resurrection (Acts 2:22–36; 1 Cor 1:17; 15:1–4; 1 Pet 2:24; cf. Gal 3:1 NLT: "the meaning of Jesus Christ's death was made as clear to you"). This is further confirmed by Paul's elucidation of the significance of Christ's crucifixion in Gal 3:13. In view of this, it is unlikely that Paul means his suffering from persecution displayed the crucified Christ; contra Davis, "Meaning of προεγράφη," 194–212.

33. ἀκοή may refer to "the act of hearing" or "that which is heard (i.e., the message/proclamation)" (BDAG 36). πίστις may refer to the "state of believing on the basis of the reliability of the one trusted" or "that which is believed (i.e., the Christian body of faith or the gospel)" (BDAG 818, 820). The fluidity of the genitive can be seen in the alternative renderings listed in (1) to (4) above: qualitative/attributive genitive for (1); objective genitive for (2); attributed genitive for (3); and genitive of product for (4).

alternative renderings such as: (1) hearing with faith or faithful hearing;³⁴ (2) hearing the gospel;³⁵ (3) believing what is heard (i.e., the gospel);³⁶ or (4) the message/proclamation which produces faith.³⁷

Given the antithesis of faith and works in Gal 2:15—3:14, it is more likely that πίστις here refers to human faith rather than the Christian gospel.³⁸ As for the meaning of ἀκοή, whether it refers to "the act of hearing" or "that which is heard" remains debatable.³⁹ The more important issue here is to highlight Paul's contrast between human works and faith. Whichever way ἀκοή is taken, the emphasis on human faith can still be brought across with renderings such as "hearing with faith" (as "the act of hearing") or "believing the message" (as "that which is heard"). Recent scholarly discussions mainly concentrate on debating whether ἀκοὴ πίστεως should be rendered as "hearing with faith" or "message which produces faith."

According to Hays and Martyn, Paul is contrasting human works with divine initiative, as seen in Gal 3:5 where God is emphasized as the one who gives the Spirit and performs miracles. The contrast is not between two human alternatives—work and believe. Therefore, ἀκοὴ πίστεως should refer to "the message that evokes faith."⁴⁰ However, if

---

34. E.g., NASB; ESV; Burton, *Galatians*, 147; Lindsay, "Hearing of Faith," 85–86. It is interesting that Burton renders ἀκοὴ πίστεως as "hearing (of the gospel) accompanied by faith."

35. E.g., Calvin, *Galatians*, 48; Bligh, *Galatians in Greek*, 127; Bruce, *Galatians*, 149. Lietzmann renders ἀκοὴ πίστεως as "das Hören der Glaubensbotschaft" ("hearing the proclamation of faith," i.e., hearing the gospel) (Lietzmann, *Galater*, 18).

36. E.g., NIV; NLT; NRSV; Sanders, *Paul and Palestinian Judaism*, 482; Longenecker, *Galatians*, 103.

37. E.g., Betz, *Galatians*, 133n50; Eckstein, *Verheißung und Gesetz*, 86–88; Martyn, *Galatians*, 286–89; Hays, *Faith of Jesus Christ*, 128–32.

38. Silva, "Faith Versus Works of the Law," 236; Hunn, "ΠΙΣΤΙΣ ΧΡΙΣΤΟΥ," 29.

39. Scholars favoring either ἀκοή as "the act of hearing" (e.g., Lindsay, Williams) or "that which is heard" (e.g., Eckstein, Hays, Martyn) usually appeal to other Pauline usages of ἀκοή (typically Rom 10:16–17; 1 Thess 2:13) to support their arguments (see p. 26n34 above and pp. 26n40, 27n42 below for bibliographic references). Evidence from other Pauline usage is inconclusive. Paul's use of ἀκοή in Rom 10:16 clearly refers to "proclamation/message (i.e., what is heard)," but its use in Rom 10:17 (as well as 1 Thess 2:13) as "the act of hearing" or "the message/proclamation" is debatable (see also Moo, *Romans*, 665–66n27). On the other hand, Hunn argues that the point Paul is making in Rom 10:16–17 is not the same as that in Galatians. Therefore, the context of Galatians alone should be used to determine the meaning of ἀκοή (Hunn, "ΠΙΣΤΙΣ ΧΡΙΣΤΟΥ," 26).

40. Hays, *Faith of Jesus Christ*, 128–32; Martyn, *Galatians*, 286–89. Their argument

we consider the parallel use in Gal 3:5 and its relationship to the faith of Abraham in Gal 3:6,⁴¹ the evidence would favor the contrast between two human alternatives—doing and believing.⁴² After all, Paul cites Gen 15:6 in Gal 3:6 in order to emphasize that *Abraham believed*. Although "hearing with faith" may be more in line with Paul's antithesis of human doing and believing in Gal 2:15—3:14, while "the message/proclamation which produces faith" may shift the focus away from human believing, the latter does not exclude human faith as a response either. "Hearing with faith" also presumes the gospel message as its object of hearing. The bottom line is still the indisputable fact that the Galatians received the Spirit *by faith* (ἐκ πίστεως) and not by works of the law (ἐξ ἔργων νόμου).

The second issue here is the meaning of the preposition ἐκ. Recently, Garlington argues that, other than Gal 3:13, Paul uses the preposition ἐκ in a partitive sense (i.e., denoting source or belonging) consistently in Gal 2:15—3:29.⁴³ According to Garlington, διά is used in an instrumental sense,⁴⁴ while ἐκ is used consistently in a partitive sense, but not likely in an instrumental sense.⁴⁵ Hence, the crux of the matter in Gal 3:2–5 is "*Who possess the Spirit: is it the law-people or the faith-in-Christ-people?*" and the preposition ἐκ stresses the origin, as well as embracing the partisan sense, rather than the instrumental sense.⁴⁶

---

presupposes that πίστις Χριστοῦ in Gal 2:16 refers to "the faithfulness of Christ" (Hays, *Galatians*, 251; Martyn, *Galatians*, 251), and thus their emphasis on divine initiative. Their arguments also presume ἀκοή in Rom 10:16–17 to mean "that which is heard." They also express their concern that the interpretation of the "faith/works" antithesis as two human alternatives would cause some Christians to misunderstand "faith" as being meritorious. On the problem of misunderstanding "faith" as meritorious, see p. 40n102 below.

41. καθώς in Gal 3:6 links the comparison of Abraham with the preceding context and forms the scriptural grounds of Paul's argument (Lightfoot, *Galatians*, 136; Silva, *Interpreting Galatians*, 219–20; cf. BDAG 493).

42. See also Williams, "Hearing of Faith," 87; Silva, "Faith Versus Works of the Law," 235; Hunn, "ΠΙΣΤΙΣ ΧΡΙΣΤΟΥ," 25–30.

43. Garlington, "Paul's 'Partisan ἐκ,'" 567–89.

44. E.g., διὰ πίστεως Ἰησοῦ Χριστοῦ, "through faith in Jesus Christ" (Gal 2:16) (Garlington, "Paul's 'Partisan ἐκ,'" 573).

45. E.g., ἐξ ἐθνῶν ἁμαρτωλοί "sinners belonging to the ranks of the Gentiles" (Gal 2:15); οἱ ἐκ πίστεως "those who belong to the 'faith-party'" (Gal 3:7, 9); ὅσοι ἐξ ἔργων νόμου "whosoever belongs to the 'works-of-the-law party'" (Gal 3:10) (Garlington, "Paul's 'Partisan ἐκ,'" 570, 581–82, 587). Garlington argues that each of these phrases in Gal 2:15—3:29 is to be understood in a partitive sense, rather than in an instrumental sense.

46. Garlington, "Paul's 'Partisan ἐκ,'" 577, 579 (emphasis in original).

Garlington's argument is based on his understanding of Gal 2:15–16, where he submits that, "it is ἐξ ἐθνῶν ἁμαρτωλοί ["sinners from the Gentiles"] that sets up the antithesis of a justification ἐξ ἔργων νόμου versus one ἐκ πίστεως Χριστοῦ."[47] Hence, Garlington paraphrases Gal 2:15–16 as:

> We who are Jews by birth and not sinners *belonging to the ranks of the Gentiles* [ἐξ ἐθνῶν]; we know that a person is not justified *by belonging to the arena of Torah-works* [ἐξ ἔργων νόμου], but through faith in Jesus Christ [διὰ πίστεως Χριστοῦ]. Even we have believed in Christ Jesus in order to be justified *within the realm of Christic faith* [ἐκ πίστεως Χριστοῦ] not *within the orb of Torah-works* [ἐξ ἔργων νόμου], because no person will be justified *by remaining within the sphere of Torah-works* [ἐξ ἔργων νόμου].[48]

Garlington's study has its merits in drawing our attention to the partitive sense in Paul's use of ἐκ in Gal 2:15—3:29. While the use of ἐκ in Gal 2:15; 3:7, 9, 10 is clearly partitive, his argument in favor of a partitive sense and against an instrumental sense in places such as Gal 2:16; 3:2, 5, 8 is not as convincing.[49] The contrast between ἐξ ἔργων νόμου and διὰ πίστεως Χριστοῦ in Gal 2:16a is paralleled by the contrast between ἐκ πίστεως Χριστοῦ and ἐξ ἔργων νόμου in Gal 2:16b. Διὰ πίστεως Χριστοῦ ("by faith in Jesus Christ") is clearly instrumental, just as Garlington notes, but ἐκ πίστεως Χριστοῦ can also be construed as causal (i.e., because of faith in Jesus Christ).[50] In other words, a person is justified due to (ἐκ) his or her faith in Jesus Christ, because faith is the instrument (διά) by which a person is justified. Hence, the causal sense of ἐκ overlaps with the instrumental sense of διά in some ways. The parallel use of διὰ πίστεως with ἐκ πίστεως and their semantic overlap are seen most clearly in Rom 3:30: "since there is one God, who justifies the circumcised by faith [ἐκ πίστεως] and the uncircumcised through faith [διὰ τῆς πίστεως]."[51] If Paul used διὰ πίστεως and ἐκ πίστεως interchangeably in Romans, it is

---

47. Garlington, "Paul's 'Partisan ἐκ,'" 573.

48. Ibid., 570 (emphasis in original).

49. Ibid., 579–80.

50. BDAG 296. Other instances of ἐκ that is used in the causal/instrumental sense include Luke 16:9; 2 Cor 13:4; Rev 8:11; 16:10.

51. See also Rom 4:2: "For if Abraham was justified by works [ἐξ ἔργων], he has something to boast about, but not before God," where Paul clearly uses ἐξ ἔργων in a causal/instrumental sense.

*Justification by Faith*

very unlikely that his use of these two prepositions in Galatians is as distinct as Garlington claims it to be. Furthermore, Garlington's paraphrase of the first and third occurrences of ἐξ ἔργων νόμου in Gal 2:16 above with the word "by" also betrays his subconscious understanding of ἐκ here in the causal/instrumental sense. The partitive sense in Gal 3:7, 9, 10 is derived from the causal/instrumental sense in Gal 2:16; 3:2, 5, because the "faith-in-Christ-people" and the "works-of-the-law-people" are marked by their different understanding with regard to the means by which they are justified. Therefore, while it is correct to deduce that, in Gal 3:2–5, it is the "faith-in-Christ people" who received the Spirit, rather than the "law-people," the preposition ἐκ here nonetheless denotes cause/instrument.[52]

"You are so foolish! After beginning with the Spirit, are you now trying to be perfected by the flesh?" (Gal 3:3) Paul continues his scathing rebuke and interrogation with the third question. There are two sets of contrast here—πνεῦμα/σάρξ (Spirit/flesh) and ἐνάρχομαι/ἐπιτελέω (beginning/finishing). The use of σάρξ ("flesh") here is a double entendre. Flesh is not only contrasted with the divine power of the Spirit as human effort, but it also depicts the circumcision that Paul's opponents had demanded.[53] Hays notes that such a demand may be derived from a tradition in the Mishnah, which "links circumcision explicitly to perfection in the light of [Abraham's circumcision in] Genesis 17."[54] ἐνάρχομαι and ἐπιτελέω are also used together in Phil 1:6 to depict God's work in the believer's life from the beginning to its completion. As Bruce puts it, the completion has to be "achieved on the same plane as the inception."[55] The Galatians are utterly foolish to think that they are to complete their Christian life on a different basis apart from the Spirit.

Paul presses the Galatians further with the fourth question, "Have you experienced (πάσχω)[56] so much for nothing—if indeed it was in

---

52. On the instrumental sense of ἐκ in Paul's language of justification, see Cosgrove, "Justification in Paul," 658–62.

53. Dunn, *Galatians*, 155; Hays, "Galatians," 252.

54. Hays, "Galatians," 252, citing *m. Ned.* 3:11.

55. Bruce, *Galatians*, 150.

56. Although the word πάσχω usually has the meaning of "suffer," there are also instances where it is attested as neutral "experience" (BDAG 785). In the immediate context of Gal 3:2–5, it seems more likely that it refers to the Galatians' experience of the work of the Spirit in their lives (Longenecker, *Galatians*, 104; Dunn, *Galatians*, 156; Martyn, *Galatians*, 285). For those who understand πάσχω negatively as "suffer," see, e.g., Luther, *Lectures on Galatians*, 27:250–51; Lightfoot, *Galatians*, 135; Bruce, *Galatians*, 150; Eastman, *Recovering Paul's Mother Tongue*, 109n70.

vain?" (Gal 3:4) Surely the Galatians have experienced the Spirit's work in their lives before (cf. Gal 3:5). Having received the Spirit by faith and not by works of the law, how could the Galatians not arrive at the conviction that the paradigm of faith is the way to justification, both at their conversion and for their continuation of Christian life (cf. Gal 3:2–3)?[57] Were these experiences really in vain? Hopefully this was not the case (Gal 3:4).[58]

Finally, Paul asks, "So then, does God give you the Spirit and work miracles among you on the basis of your works of the law or your hearing with faith?" (Gal 3:5) The continuous aspect of the present participles ἐπιχορηγῶν ("give/supply") and ἐνεργῶν ("work") implies God's continuous and sustained action among the Galatians.[59] God's gift of the Spirit is not only at conversion but also for the continuation of the Christian life in the Spirit. In this last question, Paul recapitulates his second question (Gal 3:2) but puts the emphasis now on God's continuous work among the Galatians.

## Evidence from Scripture

### Structure of Galatians 3:6–14

In this section, a catena of quotations from Scripture (Gal 3:6–13)[60] forms the second set of evidence to support Paul's assertion in Gal 2:15–21 that justification is by faith and not by works of the law. The antithesis of faith and works in relation to justification in Gal 2:15–21 is now tied in with

---

57. See also Dunn, *Galatians*, 156–57, who notes, "The point here ... is to remind the Galatians of a range of experiences which should have been enough to demonstrate that they were indeed recipients of the eschatological Spirit and that the way they had come into these experiences remained the pattern of life in the Spirit."

58. Gal 3:4b: εἴ γε καὶ εἰκῇ, "if it is really in vain." Lightfoot notes that "εἴ γε leaves a loophole for doubt, and καί widens this, implying an unwillingness to believe on the part of the speaker" (Lightfoot, *Galatians*, 135).

59. Bruce, *Galatians*, 151; Dunn, *Galatians*, 157.

60. (1) Gen 15:6 in Gal 3:6; (2) Gen 12:3 in Gal 3:8; (3) Deut 27:26 in Gal 3:10: (4) Hab 2:4 in Gal 3:11; (5) Lev 18:5 in Gal 3:12; and (6) Deut 21:23 in Gal 3:13. Many scholars plausibly suggest that a number of these citations (e.g., Deut 27:26; Lev 18:5) and the circumcision of Abraham (cf. Genesis 17) may have been used by Paul's opponents to prove that Gentile Christians need to observe the Jewish law in order to become "children of Abraham." See, e.g., Barrett, "Allegory of Abraham," 6–7; Fung, *Galatians*, 137; Longenecker, *Galatians*, 109–10; Dunn, *Galatians*, 159. In Gal 3:6–14, Paul counters his opponents' interpretation by presenting his arguments on how these Scriptures should actually be understood.

the sonship of Abraham (Gal 3:7) and the partaking of the Abrahamic blessing (Gal 3:8-9, 14).

On the one hand, the first set of evidence from experience in Gal 3:1-5 is linked to the second set (Gal 3:6-13) by the adverb καθώς (Gal 3:6), which compares the experience of the Galatians and Abraham with regard to justification by faith.[61] Therefore, some scholars begin the new paragraph at Gal 3:7.[62] On the other hand, Gal 3:6 also serves to introduce the new section in which Paul sets forth his evidence from Scripture. Thus, other scholars begin the new paragraph at Gal 3:6 instead.[63] It seems more likely that Gal 3:6 functions as a janus, concluding Gal 3:1-5 as well as introducing a new section, Gal 3:7-14.[64]

Silva suggests that the structure of Gal 3:6-14 may be understood as a series of five theses with a biblical citation as each of its grounds.[65] Although Silva's proposed structure may be useful for us to see the various logical elements and Paul's use of Scriptures in his arguments in Gal 3:6-14, Silva admits to a number of weaknesses in his structure. First, the structure does not show the relative importance of each thesis in the argument.[66] Second, certain parallel structures may be obscured.[67]

A number of scholars have proposed another form of structure in Gal 3:6-14—the chiasmus.[68] Although scholars differ with respect to

---

61. See p. 27n41 above.

62. E.g., USB4; NIV; ESV; Bruce, *Galatians*, 57; Fung, *Galatians*, vii.

63. E.g., NA27; CEV; NRSV; Dunn, *Galatians*, 21; Martyn, *Galatians*, 296; Hays, "Galatians," 199.

64. See also Silva, *Interpreting Galatians*, 220, who notes that Gal 3:6 "clearly functions as a bridge between the two paragraphs."

65. Silva, *Interpreting Galatians*, 220-22. According to Silva's proposed structure, the theses statements in Gal 3:6-14 are: (1) 3:5 (implied); (2) 3:7, 9; (3) 3:10a; (4) 3:11a; (stated premise in 3:12a, the grounds of this premise in 3:12b) and (5) 3:13a. 3:14 forms the conclusion of the section.

66. Silva, *Interpreting Galatians*, 221-22. Silva explains that it may be argued that the first thesis and its grounds (Gen 15:6) provide the overarching point while the second through the fifth thesis are subordinate arguments. Or perhaps, the second thesis may be a corollary of the first, and the fourth as a corollary of the third (Silva, *Interpreting Galatians*, 222n8).

67. Silva, *Interpreting Galatians*, 221-22n8. Silva gives, as examples, a number of such obscured parallels: (1) the word κατάρα ("curse"), which brackets 3:10 and 3:13; and (2) the structural similarity of Hab 2:4 and Lev 18:5.

68. E.g., Bligh, *Galatians*, 238-39; Ebeling, *Truth of the Gospel*, 165; Lührmann, *Galatians*, 59; Gignac, "Citation de Lévitique 18,5," 381-82; Wakefield, *Where to Live*, 136.

## The Blessing of Abraham, the Spirit, and Justification in Galatians

specific details in their proposed chiastic structure, the general thematic parallels are obvious. The chiastic structure below is a summary of the various proposals:

> **Faith**—basis of justification (Gal 3:6; cf. Gen 15:6)
>> **Blessing**—promised beforehand to Abraham (Gal 3:7–9; cf. Gen 12:3)
>>> **Curse**—threat of curse (Gal 3:10; cf. Deut 27:26)
>>>> **Life**—the possible way by faith (Gal 3:11; cf. Hab 2:4)
>>>> **Life**—the impossible way by the law (Gal 3:12; cf. Lev 18:5)
>>> **Curse**—removal of curse (Gal 3:13; cf. Deut 21:23)
>> **Blessing**—fulfilled in Christ (Gal 3:14a; allusion to Gen 12:3)
> **Faith**—basis of reception of the Spirit (Gal 3:14b)

The chiastic structure has the advantage of helping us see the parallel themes within Gal 3:6–14. In this way, it helps to supplement what is lacking in Silva's structure. In view of the chiasmus, Wakefield argues that the crux of Paul's argument centers on "life."[69] Wakefield argues that Paul's focus here is not soteriology (life vs. death) but "where to live" (hence the title of the book), a choice between "a life of blessing, characterized by the Spirit and righteousness and faith, and a life under curse, characterized by the law." Wakefield's observation is valuable in the sense that it helps to highlight the aspect of life in relationship with other important concepts in Galatians such as the Spirit, righteousness, and faith, a neglected area of study in Gal 3:1–14. However, such a chiastic structure obscures the keyword πίστις ("faith") and its verbal cognate πιστεύω ("believe"), which runs through Gal 3:6–14, even in the sections on "blessing" and "life."[70] In emphasizing "life" as the crux of the matter here, Wakefield has subordinated the aspects of justification and faith under "life." The pervasiveness of the language of righteousness and faith in this passage shows its importance in Gal 3:1–14. The concept of "life/living" is secondary and is only brought up in Gal 3:21 and more fully developed in Gal 5–6. Following Paul's argument from Gal 2:15—3:14, the emphasis here is still on justification (right standing before God), which is primarily soteriological. Therefore, contrary to Wakefield, I would argue that the primary focus here is still "faith" as the means to justification.[71]

---

69. Wakefield, *Where to Live*, 144.

70. πιστεύω ("believe") appears in Gal 3:6 while πίστις ("faith") appears in nearly every verse in Gal 3:7–14, except in Gal 3:10, 13.

71. We will further examine the nature of justification as described in the letter of Galatians in ch. 6 below.

## Justification by Faith

The complexity of Paul's arguments in Gal 3:6–14 defies any single structure that claims to be exclusive.[72] Both Silva's proposed structure and the chiastic structure provide different perspectives in understanding the connection between the blessing of Abraham and the promise of the Spirit in Gal 3:14. Thematically, the parallel between the reception of the Spirit (Gal 3:14b) and the justification of Abraham (Gal 3:6) focuses on faith as the means or basis of justification. Another parallel may be seen between the Abrahamic promise to bless the nations (Gal 3:8) and its fulfillment in Christ (Gal 3:14a). These two thematic parallels warn us against equating the Abrahamic blessing with the reception of the Spirit. This non-equation is also supported by other exegetical and biblical theological reasons, as we shall see in this study.[73]

Within this second set of evidence from Scripture, the following three subsections may be discerned. First, Gal 3:6–9 forms the subsection where Paul argues positively why justification is by faith, using Abraham's faith (Gal 3:6; cf. Gen 15:6) and the Abrahamic promise to bless the nations (Gal 3:8; cf. Gen 12:3) as grounds of the argument. The emphasis is on faith as the means of justification, as Abraham was justified by faith (Gal 3:6), and the Abrahamic promise was given because the Scripture foresaw that God would "justify the Gentiles by faith" (Gal 3:8). Therefore, those who are "of faith" (ἐκ πίστεως) are the true children of Abraham (Gal 3:7) and partake in the blessing together with Abraham (Gal 3:9). In this manner, Paul closely connects justification with partaking in the blessing of Abraham and becoming the true children of Abraham. Second, Gal 3:10–12 forms a subsection in which Paul argues negatively why justification cannot be brought about by the works of the law. The main point is that all who rely on the works of the law are under the curse of the law because they are not able to or have not obeyed the stipulations of the law in one way or another. Therefore, justification cannot be by the works of the law. Third and finally, Gal 3:13–14 forms the culmination of Paul's argument in Gal 3:1–14. Galatians 3:13 puts forth Christ's redemptive work on the cross as the solution to the curse of the law (cf. Gal 3:10). The two purposes of Christ's redemptive work are then stated in

---

72. In his discussion on the discourse and literary structure of Galatians, Silva wisely reminds us "to appreciate that no outline of Galatians . . . can claim to be the only valid one. Different analyses serve different purposes and will succeed in highlighting different features found in the text" (Silva, *Interpreting Galatians*, 96). Subsequently, he applies this same principle to his proposed structure of Gal 3:6–14 (Silva, *Interpreting Galatians*, 222).

73. See especially pp. 34–59 below, as well as chs. 4 and 6 below.

Gal 3:14, forming the climax of the whole argument in Gal 3:1–14.[74] The first purpose clause links Christ's redemptive work on the cross with the fulfillment of the Abrahamic promise to bless the nations (Gal 3:8).[75] The second purpose clause links Christ's redemptive work with the promise of the Spirit, referring back to Gal 3:1–5, where the crucified Christ and the reception of the Spirit by faith are mentioned initially.

Just as Silva marveled, "it is difficult not to be impressed, on the one hand, by the care and effectiveness with which these various themes have been interwoven and, on the other hand, by the glaring gaps in the argumentation."[76] This study will attempt to narrow one of these gaps— why Paul would have juxtaposed "the blessing of Abraham" with "the promise of the Spirit" in Gal 3:14.

## Justification and the Blessing of Abraham

In Gal 3:6–9, Paul supports his assertion that justification is by faith using the Abrahamic promise as grounds of his argument. The citation of Gen 15:6 in Gal 3:6 serves as the scriptural support of Paul's proof from experience (Gal 3:1–5).[77] "Just as Abraham believed [ἐπίστευσεν] God and it was reckoned to him for righteousness [εἰς δικαιοσύνην]" (Gal 3:6),[78] the Galatians received the Spirit by believing the message (ἐξ ἀκοῆς

---

74. Longenecker, *Galatians*, 123; Silva, *Interpreting Galatians*, 221. Silva notes that six crucial concepts are brought together in these two purpose clauses in Gal 3:14: (1) Abraham (3:6–9); (2) Christ (3:1, 13, mentioning the crucifixion); (3) the Gentiles (3:8); (4) the promise/blessing (3:8–9); (5) the reception of the Spirit (3:2, 5); (6) faith (3:2, 5, 6–9, 11–12).

75. Contra the common interpretation, which sees the promise of the Spirit as the fulfillment of the Abrahamic promise (e.g., Silva, *Interpreting Galatians*, 177; Fee, *God's Empowering Presence*, 394).

76. Silva, *Interpreting Galatians*, 221.

77. Paul's citation of Gen 15:6 is essentially the same as the LXX. There are slight differences between the LXX translation and the MT, but they do not affect the overall meaning of Gen 15:6 (see Silva, "Galatians," 793–94 for details).

78. There is an ambiguity of the second clause in Gen 15:6 MT: ויחשבה לו צדקה ("he reckoned it to him [as] righteousness"). Gaston and Oeming suggest that the subject of this clause should be Abraham instead of God (Gaston, "Abraham and the Righteousness of God," 39–68; Oeming, "Genesis 15:6," 182–97). Thus, it is Abraham who reckoned God as righteous. Nonetheless, their views have not gained scholarly acceptance and have been refuted by scholars such as Johnson, "Who Reckoned Righteousness to Whom?," 108–15; Wenham, *Genesis 1–15*, 330; Moberly, "Righteousness of Abraham (Gen 15:6)," 106–8. At any rate, Paul follows the tradition in the LXX in interpreting God as the subject of this clause.

πίστεως) they heard (Gal 3:5), an evidence that they have already been justified (δικαιόω) before God by faith.

In the Jewish tradition, Abraham's faith was always tied with his obedience, especially with the test of sacrificing Isaac.[79] In fact, 1 Macc 2:52 and 4Q225 2 I, 7–12 cite Gen 15:6 explicitly, closely associating the righteousness reckoned to Abraham with him being found faithful when he was tested.[80] In Sir 44:19-20, Abraham is even said to have obeyed the law of God.[81] In this regard, Paul runs against the grain of the common Jewish tradition by emphasizing Abraham's faith, not his obedience, as the reason that God reckoned Abraham as righteous.[82]

Although Paul does not elaborate on the nature of Abraham's faith here as he does in Romans 4, it is clear from the context of Gen 15:1-6 that Abraham believed God would give him countless descendants, as God had promised him earlier (Gen 13:16; cf. Gen 12:2). The parallel here is more than just an analogy of Abraham's faith. It is closely related to the Abrahamic promise in Gal 3:7-9 and deeply rooted in redemptive history.[83]

The main thesis of Gal 3:6-13 is stated in 3:7: "Therefore, you should know that the ones who rely on faith, these people are the children of Abraham."[84] The string of quotations in Gal 3:8-13 serves to justify Paul's

79. E.g., Sir 44:19-20; 1 Macc 2:52; *Jub.* 17:15-18; 4Q225 2 I, 7-12. For a survey of the use of Gen 15:6 during the Second Temple period, see Oeming, "Der Glaube Abrahams," 16-33.

80. 1 Macc 2:52 NRSV: "Was not Abraham found faithful when tested, and it was reckoned to him as righteousness?" 4Q225 2 I, 7-12: ". . . And [Abraham] be[lieved] [in] G[o]d, and righteousness was accounted to him. A son was born af[ter] this [to Abraha]m, and he named him Isaac. Then the Prince of Ma[s]temah came [to G]od, and he accused Abraham regarding Isaac. And [G]od said [to Abra]ham: 'Take your son, Isaac [your] onl[y one whom] you [love] and offer him to me as a whole burnt-offering' . . ." (VanderKam and Milik, "Jubilees," 147).

81. Sir 44:19-20 NRSV: "Abraham was the great father of a multitude of nations, and no one has been found like him in glory. He kept the law of the Most High, and entered into a covenant with him; he certified the covenant in his flesh, and when he was tested he proved faithful."

82. This does not imply that Paul divorces obedience or works from faith (cf. Gal 5:6; 1 Thess 1:3; Rom 1:5), but rather, in the context of Galatians, he opposes the idea that obedience to the law is the means by which a person is justified before God.

83. See also Hahn, "Genesis 15:6 im Neuen Testament," 99; Hansen, "Genesis 15:6 in Galatians," 70; Silva, "Galatians," 793. See also pp. 61-67 below on the redemptive history depicted in Genesis and pp. 183-88 below on how Paul understands its significance in Christ.

84. γινώσκετε ("know") may be either imperative or indicative. Richard Longenecker argues that it should be taken as indicative, as γινώσκετε ἄρα ὅτι ("therefore,

thesis in 3:7.⁸⁵ The dispute here is: who are the true children of Abraham? In view of the Jewish tradition that associates Abraham closely with his obedience to the law and circumcision, Paul's opponents in Galatia may have very likely advocated that Gentile Christians need to be circumcised and to obey the law in order to be included in the covenant as children of Abraham.⁸⁶ Therefore, Paul refutes such a notion here by stating his thesis that it is those who rely on faith (οἱ ἐκ πίστεως) who are truly Abraham's children (Gal 3:7-9), not those who rely on the works of the law (ὅσοι ἐξ ἔργων νόμου; Gal 3:10-12). The motif of sonship of Abraham, together with the motifs of the sonship of God and heirship by extension, continues to be developed further in Gal 3:16—4:7.

As Silva proposes, the citation of Gen 12:3 in Gal 3:8b serves as the grounds to Paul's thesis that "therefore, you should know that those who are of faith are children of Abraham . . . so that (ὥστε) those who are of faith are blessed with the faithful Abraham" (Gal 3:7, 9).⁸⁷ However, ὥστε introduces an inference based on not just the quotation in 3:8b but also

---

you know that") "is a typical disclosure formula in ancient Hellenistic letters that serves more to remind readers of what is known rather than to exhort" (Longenecker, *Galatians*, 114). Longenecker's argument is plausible given its parallel with the Greco-Roman epistolary form and function, as well as Paul's statements in Gal 2:16 and 3:1-5, which assume that both the Jewish and Gentile Christians should know that justification is by faith in Jesus Christ and not by works of the law. Nonetheless, whether γινώσκετε is taken to be imperative or indicative does not affect the semantic relationship of Gal 3:7 with the other clauses in Gal 3:6-13 as the main thesis. We will also provide a more nuanced relationship between justification and becoming true children of Abraham in ch. 6.

85. See also Betz, *Galatians*, 138; Eckstein, *Verheißung und Gesetz*, 95. Betz notes that the first and last scriptural quotations are positive proofs, while the second, third, and fourth quotations serve "to exclude the opposite alternatives, especially the Torah, as a way to salvation." Contra Silva, *Interpreting Galatians*, 221-22, who thinks that the theses in Gal 3:7-13 are subordinate to the implied thesis in Gal 3:5 and the citation of Gen 15:6. The quotations are namely Gen 12:3 (3:8); Deut 27:26 (3:10); Hab 2:4 (3:11); Lev 18:5 (3:12); Deut 21:23 (3:13).

86. Betz, *Galatians*, 7; Longenecker, *Galatians*, 109-12; Dunn, *Galatians*, 9-11; Martyn, *Galatians*, 117-26; Hays, "Galatians," 185-86. Bruce notes that there is evidence that some Jews insisted that circumcision was necessary in order to be admitted into the commonwealth of Israel (e.g., Josephus, *Ant.* 20.34ff.; Philo, *Migration* 92). However, Bruce points out that in Josephus, *Ant.* 20.34ff., there was also another school of Jewish thought which do not insist on circumcision for the proselytes. He also cites the debate between the schools of Shammai and Hillel (*b. Yevamot* 46a), in which some members of the latter advocated that the initial rite of baptism was sufficient apart from circumcision (Bruce, *Galatians*, 28-29).

87. Silva, *Interpreting Galatians*, 220.

on the foresight of the Scripture in proclaiming the gospel beforehand to Abraham (Gal 3:8a).[88] Therefore, the whole of Gal 3:8 functions as the grounds for Paul's assertion in Gal 3:7 that οἱ ἐκ πίστεως ("those who are of faith") are children of Abraham, with the inference in Gal 3:9 as an *inclusio* with Gal 3:7.[89]

Paul's citation of Gen 12:3 in Gal 3:8 is ἐνευλογηθήσονται ἐν σοὶ πάντα τὰ ἔθνη ("all the nations will be blessed in you"). Some scholars suggest that this is a conflation of Gen 12:3 and 18:18, while others argue that it is a conflation of Gen 12:3 and 22:18.[90] The use of τὰ ἔθνη ("the nations"; cf. Gen 18:18; 22:18) instead of αἱ φυλαί ("the families"; cf. Gen 12:3b) and the omission of τῆς γῆς ("the earth") reveal Paul's rhetorical intention to connect the Abrahamic promise of blessing for the nations with the issue of Gentiles and the Jewish law. Nonetheless, such a change is legitimate linguistically.[91] Given Paul's reference to the "seed" (σπέρμα) in Gal 3:16 (cf. Gen 22:18), he could have the whole context of Genesis 12–22 in mind. Paul seems to be applying the concept of the Abrahamic promise within the larger narrative context of Genesis, paying special attention to Genesis 12 and 22, rather than considering only two individual verses by themselves in his conflation.[92]

---

88. The quotation is a subordinate clause to the main verb προευηγγελίσατο ("proclaimed the gospel beforehand"), forming the premise of the Scripture's foresight. See also Wakefield, *Where to Live*, 161, who notes that, syntactically, the quotation cannot stand alone but "supplies the content of the direct discourse 'pre-proclaimed' to Abraham."

89. Note the parallels in Gal 3:7, 9 indicated by οἱ ἐκ πίστεως ("those who are of faith") and Ἀβραάμ ("Abraham").

90. Gen 12:3b LXX: ἐνευλογηθήσονται ἐν σοὶ πᾶσαι αἱ φυλαὶ τῆς γῆς, "all the families of the earth will be blessed in you"; 18:18: ἐνευλογηθήσονται ἐν αὐτῷ πάντα τὰ ἔθνη τῆς γῆς, "all the nations of the earth will be blessed in him"; 22:18: ἐνευλογηθήσονται ἐν τῷ σπέρματί σου πάντα τὰ ἔθνη τῆς γῆς, "all the nations of the earth will be blessed in your seed." For those who think the quotation is a conflation of Gen 12:3 and 18:18, see, e.g., Lightfoot, *Galatians*, 137; Burton, *Galatians*, 160; Wisdom, *Blessing*, 140n58; Stanley, *Arguing With Scripture*, 123n24. For those who argue for a conflation of Gen 12:3 and 22:18, see, e.g., Fung, *Galatians*, 138–39; Collins, "Galatians 3:16," 81–83. On the other hand, Hays thinks that it is a conflation of all three verses ("Galatians," 256).

91. Fung, *Galatians*, 139; Stanley, *Arguing With Scripture*, 123n24; Silva, "Galatians," 793–94.

92. We will revisit the issue of how Paul reads the Genesis narrative in relation to the Abrahamic blessing for the nations in ch. 6.

## The Blessing of Abraham, the Spirit, and Justification in Galatians

According to Paul, the content of the promise is the gospel preached ahead of time (προευηγγελίζομαι) to Abraham (Gal 3:8).[93] The promise was given to Abraham because the personified Scripture foresaw God's original intention to justify the Gentiles by faith.[94] The gospel was not an invention of human origin (cf. 1:11–12), but it is already prophesied in the Scripture.[95] From this understanding, Paul infers (ὥστε) that those who rely on faith are blessed with the believing Abraham (Gal 3:9).[96] For Paul, the promise that Gentiles will be blessed in Abraham is inextricably related to the gospel.

The Gentiles who will be blessed "in" (ἐν) Abraham in Gal 3:8 (cf. Gen 12:3) are now blessed "with" (σύν) Abraham in Gal 3:9. A number of questions arise from Paul's inference in Gal 3:9. On what basis does Paul draw the conclusion that it was God's original intention to justify the Gentiles *by faith*? In what way are the Gentiles blessed "in" Abraham? How are those who rely on faith blessed together "with" Abraham? What is this "blessing"? Is the "blessing" Abraham received in the Genesis narrative the same as the "blessing" that those who rely on faith receive? These questions will be addressed in detail later in chapter 6.

In brief, while God's original intention to justify the Gentiles may be seen in the Abrahamic promise (Gal 3:8; cf. Gen 12:3), the means of justification is not clear from the promise itself in the Genesis narrative. "Faith" as the means of justification is inferred in two ways. First, the Gentiles are blessed "in Abraham" because of their faith "in Jesus Christ." The redemptive work of Christ has caused the blessing of Abraham to come

---

93. Gal 3:8: προϊδοῦσα δὲ ἡ γραφὴ ὅτι ἐκ πίστεως δικαιοῖ τὰ ἔθνη ὁ θεός, προευηγγελίσατο τῷ Ἀβραὰμ ὅτι ἐνευλογηθήσονται ἐν σοὶ πάντα τὰ ἔθνη, "Because the Scripture foresees that God will justify the Gentiles by faith, it proclaimed to Abraham beforehand that 'all the nations will be blessed in you.'" The second ὅτι in Gal 3:8 introduces the promise as the indirect discourse of προευηγγελίσατο. See also Dunn, *Galatians*, 166; Wisdom, *Blessing*, 142–43.

94. Richard Longenecker explains that the Scripture's foresight is a figure of speech for the divine foresight and notes a parallel expression in the rabbinic writings personifying the Torah, citing Strack and Billerbeck, *Kommentar zum Neue Testament*, 3:538 (Longenecker, *Galatians*, 115). The participle προϊδοῦσα ("foreseeing") is more likely causal than circumstantial (contra Longnecker, *Galatians*, 115), because the divine foresight is the basis on which Paul links the promise to the gospel. See also Burton, *Galatians*, 160; Wakefield, *Where to Live*, 162.

95. This concept is also evident in Rom 1:2.

96. τῷ πιστῷ Ἀβραάμ (Gal 3:9) may be rendered as "Abraham who had faith," "the believing Abraham," or "the faithful Abraham." Although the former two would bring across the parallel with those who rely on faith (οἱ ἐκ πίστεως) more clearly, whichever way it is rendered does not substantially affect Paul's argument here.

upon the Gentiles (Gal 3:13–14). Christ is rightfully the "seed" referred to in the Abrahamic promise who brings the promise to fulfillment (Gal 3:16–18; cf. Gen 22:18). As long as individuals are in Christ, they are children of Abraham (Gal 3:27–29). Being children of Abraham, they are therefore (1) heirs to the promise of blessing made to Abraham and (2) also children of God by extension (Gal 3:29—4:7). In this way, the Gentile believers inherit the Abrahamic promise and are blessed "with" Abraham. Second, God justifies on the basis of faith, because the paradigm of faith is the same for the case of Abraham in the past as it is now (Gal 3:6; cf. Gen 15:6).[97] Therefore, those who respond to God in faith like Abraham are likewise justified and blessed "with Abraham" (Gal 3:6, 9).[98] Paul also argues against "works of the law" as a means of justification. Since the Abrahamic promise was made before the law, the means to justification cannot be "by the works of the law" (Gal 3:17–24). Paul therefore concludes that it can only be "by faith" in Christ.

On the point regarding the Gentiles being blessed "in Abraham," Hays argues that "the blessing is given to the Gentiles not in consequence of *their* faith, but in consequence of *Abraham's*; the blessing that God confers upon Abraham is extended vicariously to all nations. The Gentiles are blessed not on the analogy of Abraham, but 'in' him."[99] He supports his assertion further with Gen 22:18, which states that "in your offspring shall all the nations of the earth be blessed, because you have obeyed my voice" (ESV).[100] "This blessing," Hays claims, "is not said to be contingent upon anything that the Gentiles might do in the future. If it can be said to be

---

97. This concept of Abraham's justification by faith as paradigm is also apparent in Rom 4:1–16. Although Paul's doctrine of justification has its primary focus on the Abrahamic promise from a redemptive-historical perspective (Gal 3:8; cf. Gen 12:2) and the parallel drawn from Gen 15:6 in Gal 3:6 is thus more than an analogy of Abraham's faith, such a focus does not necessarily preclude Paul also using Abraham's justification by faith as a paradigm.

98. Johnson, "The Paradigm of Abraham," 195; Williams, "Justification and the Spirit," 95; Dunn, *Galatians*, 162–67; Dumbrell, "Abraham and the Abrahamic Covenant," 22. These interpreters above do not distinguish between the meaning of the phrase "in Abraham" and "with Abraham." To be blessed "in/with Abraham" is to be justified like Abraham. Dunn claims that both "in" and "with" Abraham are overlapping categories in rendering the Hebrew ב (cf. MT Gen 12:3: בך, "in you") (Dunn, *Galatians*, 166). Furthermore, citing BDB and BAGD, Dunn notes that the semantic range of "son of" in Hebrew and also in Greek can denote "[sharing] in a particular quality or characteristic" (Dunn, *Galatians*, 162–63). Therefore, the Gentile believers are "sons of Abraham" because they share the same quality of faith as Abraham.

99. Hays, *Faith of Jesus Christ*, 173–74 (emphasis in original).

100. Ibid., 175.

## The Blessing of Abraham, the Spirit, and Justification in Galatians

contingent upon anything at all, other than God's grace, it is contingent, in the Genesis story, upon Abraham's obedient faith."[101]

While it is true that the figure of Abraham functions as more than an analogy of faith in Galatians, Hays's interpretation is questionable.[102] Abraham's justification in Gen 15:6, which Paul refers to, is not in any way accomplished vicariously for the justification of the Gentiles in the future.[103] Neither is the justification of Abraham an event in which Christians participate in the future in order to be justified. Gentile believers are justified and blessed "in Abraham" not because of Abraham's faith, but because of their faith "in Jesus Christ," the "seed" of Abraham who had fulfilled the Abrahamic promise of blessing for the nations (Gal 3:14, 16–18, 22–24; cf. Gen 22:18).

From the context of Gal 3:6–9, it seems that Paul is referring to justification as the blessing.[104] However, the question remains: is justification the blessing promised to Abraham in the Genesis narrative? On what basis does Paul conclude that justification is the blessing? We shall return to these questions again in chapter 6. In the meantime, we will continue to work with the assumption that Paul understands the justification of the Gentiles by faith as the Abrahamic blessing for the nations.

### Justification and the Law

After supporting his assertion positively that justification is by faith with the paradigm of Abraham and the Abrahamic promise in Gal 3:6–9, Paul

---

101. Ibid., 176.

102. The presupposition behind Hays's interpretation of the vicarious nature of Abraham's obedience in effecting the Abrahamic promise for the nations lies in his thesis that the emphasis of justification should be on "the faithfulness of Jesus Christ," rather than the believer's "faith in Jesus Christ." Hays is concerned that the emphasis on the exercise of human faith will be misunderstood to mean that "Christians are saved by their own Herculean faithfulness . . . by our own cognitive disposition or confessional orthodoxy" (Hays, "ΠΙΣΤΙΣ and Pauline Christology," 55). However, Paul's antithesis of faith and works in Galatians precludes the idea of faith as being meritorious for justification. In his zeal to avoid the possibility of misunderstanding the act of faith on the part of the believer as meritorious, Hays has unduly suppressed the human exercise of faith in Jesus Christ as a necessary response to the gospel, a vital point of argument in Paul. See also Dunn, "Once More, ΠΙΣΤΙΣ ΧΡΙΣΤΟΥ," 68–69; Silva, "Faith Versus Works of the Law," 233–34.

103. See also Johnson, "Paradigm of Abraham," 194.

104. Betz, *Galatians*, 142; Hays, *Faith of Jesus Christ*, 176; Siker, *Disinheriting the Jews*, 37.

turns his attention in Gal 3:10–12 to refute the idea that obedience to the law can bring about justification. Paul gives three reasons as to why it is futile to depend on the works of the law.[105] (1) All who are ἐξ ἔργων νόμου (lit. "of the works of the law") are under a curse because they are unable to keep or have not kept the covenant stipulations in one way or another (Gal 3:10; cf. Deut 27:26).[106] Hence, there is no way of avoiding the curse. (2) It is evident that no one can be justified before God by the law because "the righteous shall live by faith" (Gal 3:11; cf. Hab 2:4). Covenantal relationship with God is based on faith (as seen in the case of Abraham), not by the works of the law. (3) Furthermore, the law is not ἐκ πίστεως (lit. "of faith") but about "doing," as seen in Lev 18:5—"the one who does these things shall live by them" (Gal 3:12; cf. Lev 18:5).[107] Those who rely on observance (i.e., "doing") of the law for their justification would fail, as witnessed by Israel's failure historically. Paul argues further that the only way to be set free from the curse of the law is through Christ, because he took the curse upon himself (Gal 3:13; cf. Deut 21:23). Therefore, Paul concludes that the means of justification cannot be the works of the law, but faith in Jesus Christ.

Three issues arise from Paul's statement in Gal 3:10. First, who are ὅσοι ἐξ ἔργων νόμου (lit. "whosoever who are of the works of the law")? Second, why are they under a curse? Third, what kind of curse are they under? These questions are pertinent in order for us to understand the nature of the blessing of Abraham as opposed to the nature of the curse in Paul's argument, which we shall investigate further in chapter 6.

As Stanley notes, "Whereas Paul's own statement appears to pronounce a 'curse' upon anyone who would attempt to live by the Jewish Torah, the biblical text to which he appeals clearly affirms the opposite: its 'curse' falls not on those who *do* the Law, but on those who *fail* to do it."[108] Traditionally, some interpreters have tried to explain the apparent *non se-*

---

105. As this study primarily deals with the blessing of Abraham and the promise of the Spirit, I shall only deal with the issues regarding the "works of the law" and the "curse of the law" as far as they relate to this study. A detailed discussion on these two topics and the scriptural quotations in Gal 3:10–12 is beyond the scope of this study.

106. See p. 43n117 below on how various scholars understand the ways that those who are ἐξ ἔργων νόμου ("of the works of the law") have not kept the covenant stipulations (i.e., the law).

107. On "doing" as the requirement of the law, see Silva, "Faith Versus Works of the Law," 243; Westerholm, *Perspectives Old and New on Paul*, 304. See below on the use of Lev 18:5 in Gal 3:12.

108. Stanley, "'Under a Curse,'" 481.

*quitur* by supplying an unstated premise. These interpreters understand ὅ σοι ἐξ ἔργων νόμου to be those who seek to achieve righteousness before God by keeping the law.[109] Hence they explain that Paul cites Deut 27:26[110] with an implied premise that it is impossible to keep the law perfectly.[111] Thus those who rely on the works of the law to gain God's acceptance are under the curse of the law.

The implied premise of the impossibility to keep the law perfectly has been vigorously debated in recent scholarship.[112] The scholars who disapprove the implied premise usually claim that neither Judaism during Paul's time nor the Mosaic law requires perfect obedience for righteousness and that forgiveness for transgressions is provided through repentance and the sacrificial system. Philippians 3:6 is frequently cited as evidence that Paul saw his former life as "blameless" regarding the righteousness of the law. Therefore, Paul could not have implied that it was impossible to fulfill the

---

109. E.g., Thomas Aquinas, *Galatians*, 80–81; Burton, *Galatians*, 164–65; Lietzmann, *Galater*, 19; Schoeps, *Paul*, 177; Mußner, *Galaterbrief*, 224–26; Longenecker, *Galatians*, 118.

110. Deut 27:26 MT: ארור אשר לא־יקים את־דברי התורה־הזאת לעשות אותם, "cursed is the one who does not establish the words of this law to do them"; LXX: ἐπικατάρατος πᾶς ἄνθρωπος ὃς οὐκ ἐμμενεῖ ἐν *πᾶσιν* τοῖς λόγοις τοῦ νόμου τούτου τοῦ ποιῆσαι αὐτούς, "cursed is every person who does not remain in *all* the words of this law to do them"; Gal 3:10b: ἐπικατάρατος πᾶς ὃς οὐκ ἐμμένει πᾶσιν τοῖς γεγραμμένοις ἐν τῷ βιβλίῳ τοῦ νόμου τοῦ ποιῆσαι αὐτά, "cursed is every one who does not remain in *all that are written in the book* of the law to do them." Paul's citation is basically similar to the LXX, which has the word πᾶς ("all") added to it. Jerome first noted that the Samaritan Pentateuch also attests to the word "all" (כל), just as the apparatus in the *BHQ* shows (Jerome, *The Epistle to the Galatians* 2.3 cited in Edwards, *Galatians*, 39). However, Paul replaces τοῖς λόγοις ("the words") in LXX with τοῖς γεγραμμένοις ἐν τῷ βιβλίῳ ("the things written in the book"), a phrase that is similarly found in Deut 28:58; 30:10. This change in Paul may reflect his intention of including a broader context of the curses from Deuteronomy 27–28, as well as the Mosaic law as a whole (cf. Deut 30:10) (Caneday, "Redeemed from the Curse," 195; Hays, "Galatians," 258; Silva, "Galatians," 797).

111. So Burton, Lietzmann, Schoeps, Mußner, and Longenecker. Also Calvin, *Galatians*, 53; Luther, *Lectures on Galatians*, 26:253–54.

112. For those against the implied premise, see, e.g., Fuller, "Paul and the Works of the Law," 28–42; Dunn, *Galatians*, 170–74; Scott, "'For As Many As Are of Works of the Law,'" 188–89; Cranford, "Possibility of Perfect Obedience," 242–58; Garlington, "Role Reversal," 97; Young, "Who's Cursed," 79–92; Kuula, *The Law*, 1:67–69; Hays, "Galatians," 257. For those who defend the implied premise, see, e.g., Schreiner, "Is Perfect Obedience to the Law Possible?," 151–60; idem, "Paul and Perfect Obedience to the Law," 245–78; Das, *Paul, the Law, and the Covenant*, 145–70; idem, *Paul and the Jews*, 143–48. For a summary of these two positions, see Moyise, *Evoking Scripture*, 63–77.

law. However, Dumbrell points out that the sacrificial system under the Mosaic covenant is no longer efficacious ever since Christ's atoning sacrifice on the cross.[113] Das also argues that "Jewish literature from Paul's era typically balanced the demand of God's Law for perfect obedience alongside God's gracious election and mercy toward a special people."[114] Blamelessness with regard to the law should also be distinguished from perfect obedience, as early Judaism understood that "the righteous were typically sinners who availed themselves of God's mercy and election even while falling short of the perfect measure toward which they were striving."[115]

Scholars who deny the implied premise offer a variety of explanations about why those who rely on the law are cursed.[116] Even so, most of these scholars would agree that the essential point is that disobedience to the covenant stipulations of the Mosaic law incurs the curse of the law.[117] Those who rely on the works of the law are under a curse because they have disobeyed the law in one way or another. Nonetheless, from the text of Galatians itself, it is most likely that "not keeping the whole law" is the result of "being under the curse" (cf. Gal 5:3, 14; 6:13).[118] Given that ὅσοι ἐξ ἔργων νόμου ("those who rely on the works of the law") is contrasted with οἱ ἐκ πίστεως ("those who rely on faith"), the former primarily refers to Paul's opponents, those who follow their teachings, and others who hold a similar view, not to Jews as a whole or generally to people who try

---

113. Dumbrell, "Abraham and the Abrahamic Covenant," 23.

114. Das, *Paul and the Jews*, 145.

115. Ibid., 147.

116. For a summary and critique of these various views, see, e.g., Schreiner, "Is Perfect Obedience to the Law Possible?," 151–60; Scott, "For As Many As Are of Works of the Law," 189–94; Das, *Paul, the Law, and the Covenant*, 145–70; Westerholm, *Perspectives Old and New on Paul*, 375n66.

117. E.g., the following explanations have the common point that disobedience to the covenant stipulations of the law incurs the curse of the law. (1) By advocating the keeping of the law as a means of distinguishing themselves as the covenant people of God from the Gentiles, these people are breaking the covenant because God's original intention is to include the Gentiles as his people by faith and not by works of the law (Dunn, *Galatians*, 170–74; Wisdom, *Blessing*, 155). (2) Israel as a whole failed to obey the Torah and was exiled as a result of the curse of the law. Those who identify themselves with the deuteronomic covenant by relying on the works of the law will also come under the deuteronomic curses (Wright, *Climax of the Covenant*, 137–56; Scott, "For As Many As Are of Works of the Law," 214–17; Hays, "Galatians," 258–59).

118. After we have examined the Pentateuch and the prophets in chs. 3 and 4, we will use the results of our investigation to reexamine the issue of the implied premise of Gal 3:10 in ch.6.

to earn their salvation by good conduct.[119] These opponents not only advocate the observance of the Jewish law, they depend on such observance for righteousness and life (cf. Gal 3:21; 5:4).[120] Their insistence that Gentile believers need to receive circumcision (Gal 6:12) shows that they do not regard uncircumcised Gentile believers as the people of God.

In Deuteronomy, the curses refer to the judgment for covenant disloyalty through natural disasters and foreign invasion, resulting in death, expulsion from the land into exile, and the scattering of the people among other nations (Deut 28:15–68).[121] It is not clear in the context of Galatians itself how Paul understands the nature of the curse that "those who rely on the works of the law" are under (Gal 3:10) and from which Christ redeemed "us" (Gal 3:13). However, in Pauline thought, transgressing the law is sin, and it incurs the wrath and judgment of God (cf. Rom 2:5, 12). It also results in death (Rom 6:23). Therefore, the curse in Gal 3:10, 13 may be understood as the judgment of God meted out on transgressors.[122]

Regarding Paul's use of Hab 2:4 in Gal 3:11 for his argument, two issues need to be addressed: (1) the semantic relation of the two ὅτι clauses in Gal 3:11;[123] and (2) the context of Habakkuk in relation to Paul's use. First, δῆλον ("it is evident"; Gal 3:11) may be related to the ὅτι of the former clause or the latter clause.[124] If it is related to the former clause, the citation of Hab 2:4 becomes the grounds of the first clause ("*it is evident that* no one is justified before God by the law, *because* 'the righteous shall live by faith'").[125] If it is related to the latter clause, the citation becomes the conclusion of the premise in the first clause ("*because* no one is justified

---

119. Braswell, "'The Blessing of Abraham,'" 77; Silva, "Faith Versus Works of the Law," 225–26. Silva notes that Paul would not have indiscriminately characterized his fellow-Jews as people not characterized by faith, given the high regard he has for Abraham and David (cf. Romans 4). The "works of the law" in the context of Galatians are also specific to the works of the Jewish law (i.e., Torah).

120. Silva, "Faith Versus Works of the Law," 224. See also Eckstein, *Verheißung und Gesetz*, 23, 122.

121. Craigie, *Deuteronomy*, 342.

122. See also Eckstein, *Verheißung und Gesetz*, 123–24.

123. Gal 3:11: ὅτι δὲ ἐν νόμῳ οὐδεὶς δικαιοῦται παρὰ τῷ θεῷ δῆλον, ὅτι ὁ δίκαιος ἐκ πίστεως ζήσεται.

124. Burton, *Galatians*, 166; Hanse, "ΔΗΛΟΝ," 299–303; Wright, *Climax of the Covenant*, 149n42; Wakefield, *Where to Live*, 163n98.

125. Virtually all major English versions (e.g., NASB; NRSV; NKJV; NIV; NLT) and most commentators take this view (e.g., Burton, *Galatians*, 166; Bruce, *Galatians*, 157; Longenecker, *Galatians*, 118; Dunn, *Galatians*, 174).

before God by the law, *it is evident that* 'the righteous shall live by faith'").[126] However, given that the other scriptural citations in Gal 3:6–13 function as the grounds of the assertions, it is more likely that Hab 2:4 functions as the grounds, rather than the conclusion, of Paul's assertion in Gal 3:11a.[127]

Second, if Paul cites Hab 2:4 as the grounds to support his assertion that no one can be justified before God by the law, what is the logic of his argument? The problem seems to be acute because of the words אמונה ("faithfulness/faith") and חיה ("to live"), as well as the personal pronoun, used in Hab 2:4.[128] אמונה usually means "faithfulness," rather than "faith."[129] "Faithfulness" to God may also involve the idea of obedience to

---

126. Hays, "Galatians," 259; Wakefield, *Where to Live*, 162–67.

127. See also Das, *Paul, the Law, and the Covenant*, 165–66n59. The citation of Hab 2:4 as the premise is further supported by a number of interpreters who note that the argument in Gal 3:11–12 is syllogistic, where "no one is justified by the law before God" (Gal 3:11a) forms the conclusion with the major and minor premises in Gal 3:11b-12. See, e.g., Aquinas, *Galatians*, 81–83; Bligh, *Galatians*, 262; Morland, "Expansion and Conflict," 258; Bachmann, "Zur Argumentation von Galater 3.10–12," 536–40.

128. Hab 2:4 MT: וצדיק באמונתו יחיה, "but the righteous shall live *by his faithfulness*"; LXX: ὁ δὲ δίκαιος ἐκ πίστεώς μου ζήσεται, "but the righteous shall live *by my faithfulness*"; Gal 3:11b: ὁ δίκαιος ἐκ πίστεως ζήσεται, "the righteous shall live *by faith*." The MT has the third person pronominal suffix ("his"), the LXX has the first person possessive pronoun ("my"), and Paul does not have any personal pronoun at all. There are also variant readings in other Greek texts such as LXX, MSS A and C (ὁ δὲ δίκαιος μου ἐκ πίστεώς ζήσεται, "but *my righteous one* shall live by faith"); 8HevXIIgr, col. 12 ([δίκ]αιος ἐν πίστει αὐτοῦ ζήσετ[αι], "a [right]eous person [shall] live *in his faith*"); Aquila (δίκαιος ἐν πίστει αὐτοῦ ζήσεται, "a righteous person shall live *in his faith*"); and Symmachus (δίκαιος τῇ ἑαυτοῦ πίστει ζήσεται, "a righteous person shall live *by his own faith*"). The μου in the LXX is most likely due to a scribal error of reading י instead of ו. From Koch's analysis of the various manuscripts and recensions of the LXX, it is likely that Paul had deliberately left out the personal pronoun, rather than citing from a source that did not have it (Koch, "Der Text von Habbakuk 2:4b," 68–85). It is likely that Paul omits the personal pronoun in order to avoid the confusion regarding the reference of faith arising from the different reading in MT and LXX. See also Silva, "Galatians," 801.

129. *HALOT* 1:62–63; *DCH* 1:312–13. Although אמונה primarily means "faithfulness, fidelity, or steadfastness," the context of Habakkuk does not preclude having "faith" in God—trusting in God's faithfulness that he is not condoning the wickedness of the Chaldeans and will bring judgment upon these invaders in due time. Therefore, there need not be a dichotomy between "faith" and "faithfulness." See also Robertson, *Habakkuk*, 179–81; Sanders, "Habakkuk in Qumran, Paul and the Old Testament," 113; Bellis, "Habakkuk 2:4b," 373–74, 384; Watson, *Paul and the Hermeneutics of Faith*, 160–61; Silva, "Galatians," 802.

God's commands.¹³⁰ So, does חיה refer to how a person should live the present life, or how a person shall gain life?

Habakkuk 2:4 occurs within the context of God's response to Habakkuk's complaint that God should use the unrighteous Chaldeans to punish Israel, who are comparatively more righteous than the Chaldeans (Hab 1:12–17). God assures Habakkuk that he is not condoning the Chaldeans, but in due time he will punish them for their wickedness (Hab 2:5–20). In contrast to the arrogance of the unrighteous Chaldeans, the righteous among the Israelites shall trust God and look to him for their deliverance (cf. Hab 3:13, 18), so that they may survive the invasion and live by his faith/faithfulness (Hab 2:4).¹³¹ Therefore, חיה in Hab 2:4 refers to receiving life in the future through deliverance, rather than the conduct of life.¹³²

From the context of Habakkuk, the inference may be drawn that the righteous are characterized by their faith/faithfulness in contrast to the unrighteous, and that they receive future life by their faith/faithfulness. In this sense, Paul's use of Hab 2:4 to mean "the righteous shall live by faith" is latent in the context of Habakkuk. Paul is citing Hab 2:4 in order to emphasize that the righteous will receive life by faith, and that their lives

---

130. Silva, "Galatians," 802. The association of מונה ("faithfulness") with obedience to the law is also seen in the Qumran pesher of Habakkuk (1QpHab VIII, 1–3): "Its interpretation concerns all those who observe the Torah [עושי התורה] in the House of Judah, whom God will save from the house of judgment on account of their tribulation and their fidelity to the Righteous Teacher [ואמנתם במורה הצדק]") (Horgan, "Habakkuk Pesher," 174–75). Although the pesherist interprets אמונה as "*faith in* the Righteous Teacher," he nonetheless understood Hab 2:4 to refer to "those who observe the Torah."

131. For the interpreters who understand חיה ("to be alive") as referring to "surviving" the invasion of the Chaldeans, see Moberly, "אמן," *NIDOTTE* 1:430; Garlington, "Role Reversal," 99. While חיה in the Qal stem usually means "to be alive" in a physical sense, it may also imply a futuristic element. See Brensinger, "חיה," *NIDOTTE* 2:110 and also the discussion on Lev 18:5 below. Some interpreters argue that the personal pronoun refers to the reliability of the vision and hence the faithfulness of God, who is the source of the vision (e.g., Janzen, "Habakkuk 2:2–4," 61; Robertson, *Habakkuk*, 111; Haak, *Habakkuk*, 59; Andersen, *Habakkuk*, 214). However, in view of the fact that the closest antecedent of the personal pronoun is צדיק ("the righteous") and that "the faith/faithfulness of the righteous one" makes good sense in the context, it is less likely that the antecedent should be the vision (Robertson, *Habakkuk*, 177). Even if it refers to the vision and God's faithfulness behind it, it still does not preclude the faith in God that the righteous needs to exercise.

132. The conduct of life is expressed in the Hebrew Bible using הלך ("to walk"), e.g., Deut 8:6; 1 Sam 8:3; 2 Kgs 21:21–22; Ps 128:1; Prov 2:13; Jer 7:23. See also Merrill, "הלך," *NIDOTTE* 1:1032–35.

are also characterized by "faith," rather than by the works of the law.¹³³ This concept is also in line with Abraham's case, where his covenantal relationship with God is also built upon faith (cf. Gal 3:6–9).

In contrast, Paul argues, the law is not characterized by faith, but rather by doing, because Lev 18:5 states that "the one who does them shall live by them" (Gal 3:12).¹³⁴ Once again, as in Paul's use of Hab 2:4 in Gal 3:11, what is Paul's logic of argument in his use of Lev 18:5? Does "live by them" (ζήσεται ἐν αὐτοῖς) refer to justification by the law?¹³⁵ Or to the manner by which a person should live?¹³⁶

Leviticus 18:5 occurs within the context of the Holiness Code (Leviticus 17–26).¹³⁷ The key theme of this section is that Israel is to be set apart from the other peoples as holy to God (Lev 20:26). They shall not emulate the abominable lifestyle of either the Egyptians or the Canaanites (Lev 18:1–5). If they do, they shall be punished by expulsion from the land

---

133. This emphasis of "faith" is also evident in the way Paul is citing Heb 2:4 in Rom 1:17, where the element of "faith" is emphasized in the expression ἐκ πίστεως εἰς πίστιν (see also Dunn, *Galatians*, 174). In Paul's citation of Hab 2:4, there is also the question of whether ἐκ πίστεως is modifying the subject ("*the one who is righteous by faith* shall live") or the verb ("the one who is righteous *shall live by faith*"). For those who take the former view, see, e.g., Bruce, *Galatians*, 161; Fitzmyer, "Habakkuk 2:3–4 and the New Testament," 241. In view of the syntactical similarity with Lev 18:5, which Paul cites in Gal 3:12b as a contrast to Hab 2:4, it is more likely that ἐκ πίστεως modifies the verb (Silva, "Galatians," 801–2; Sprinkle, *Law and Life*, 139).

134. Lev 18:5b MT: אֲשֶׁר יַעֲשֶׂה אֹתָם הָאָדָם וָחַי בָּהֶם, "which if the person does them, he shall live by them"; LXX: ἃ ποιήσας ἄνθρωπος ζήσεται ἐν αὐτοῖς, "which by doing, the person shall live by them"; Gal 3:12b: ὁ ποιήσας αὐτὰ ζήσεται ἐν αὐτοῖς, "The one who does these things shall live by them." The relative clause in Lev 18:5 has become an independent clause in Gal 3:12, and ἄνθρωπος ("person") has been omitted in Gal 3:12. Sprinkle notes that Paul's citation has exactly the same form as Philo, *Prelim. Studies* 86. In view of this, and given the widespread use of Lev 18:5 in the OT and early Judaism, Sprinkle suggests that Lev 18:5 may have become a familiar expression during Paul's time (Sprinkle, *Law and Life*, 134–35). Perhaps the omission of ἄνθρωπος not only reflects Lev 18:5 as a free-standing formula (ὁ ποιήσας αὐτὰ ζήσεται ἐν αὐτοῖς), but also has the purpose of matching it with the parallel expression in Hab 2:4 (ὁ δίκαιος ἐκ πίστεως ζήσεται). See also Stanley, *Paul and the Language of Scripture*, 244–45.

135. E.g., Bruce, *Galatians*, 163; Martyn, *Galatians*, 314–15; Hays, *Faith of Jesus Christ*, 133–34.

136. E.g., Dunn, *Galatians*, 175–76; Young, "Who's Cursed," 89; Bryant, *Risen Crucified Christ*, 177; Wisdom, *Blessing*, 189; Wakefield, *Where to Live*, 174; cf. Avemarie, "Paul and the Claim of the Law," 141.

137. Hartley, *Leviticus*, 249; Joosten, *Holiness Code*, 5–6; Milgrom, *Leviticus 17–22*, 1319.

(Lev 18:24–30), natural disasters, and enemy invasion (Lev 26:14–39). Nonetheless, restoration is possible through repentance (Lev 26:40–45). On the other hand, if Israel is obedient, they shall be blessed with agricultural abundance and victory over their enemies (Lev 26:1–13).[138] The rewards for obedience and punishments for disobedience in Leviticus 26 also reflect a common tradition with the deuteronomic blessings and curses (Deut 27:9—29:1).[139] Israel is to observe the commands of Yahweh; and "the person who does these things shall live by them" (Lev 18:5). Therefore, the concept of וחי בהם ("shall live by them") most likely refers to the assurance of quality life in the future as an outcome of their obedience.[140] Such a concept of future life as a result of obedience continues to be developed in the rest of the OT and is further developed in early Judaism to include even eschatological life.[141]

In line with the thought of Leviticus, the rest of the OT, and early Judaism, Paul is using Lev 18:5 to contrast with Hab 2:4 as an alternative way of receiving life.[142] The way of receiving life by obeying (i.e., "doing") the law would fail, as witnessed historically in Israel.[143] Thus, all who seek jus-

---

138. We shall look into the nature and relationship of the Sinai covenantal blessing and the Abrahamic blessing in detail in ch. 6.

139. Although there are similarities between Leviticus 26 and Deuteronomy 27–28, there are also substantial differences. These differences lead scholars to conclude that they are drawn from the same tradition but are developed independently (Hartley, *Leviticus*, 459; Joosten, *Holiness Code*, 200–2).

140. It is possible that חיה ("to live") refers to the manner of life, given its parallel with הלך ("to walk/live") in Lev 18:4. In this case, the preposition ב would denote manner—to live *according to* them. However, in the parallel but antithetical phrase in Lev 18:29 ("For everyone who does any of these abominations, the persons who do them shall be cut off from among their people"; ESV), "shall be cut off" is the *result* of doing any of the abominations. Therefore, "shall live" in Lev 18:5 is more likely to be the *result* of observing the statutes of Yahweh. In this case, the preposition ב would be instrumental—the person shall live *by means of* doing these things (Levine, *Leviticus*, 119; Milgrom, *Leviticus* 17–22, 1522; Sprinkle, *Law and Life*, 31–34). Nonetheless, the concept of a resultant future life does not preclude the manner of life that the people ought to live in order to receive quality life as a reward.

141. In both Ezek 20:1–32 and Neh 9:29, Israel is depicted as having failed to obey the commandments of Yahweh. As a result, they forfeited the covenantal blessing of life and were punished (Sprinkle, *Law and Life*, 34–44). See also pp. 122–30 below on the allusion to Lev 18:5 in Ezekiel and its function therein. For the use of Lev 18:5 during the Second Temple period, see Willitts, "Context Matters," 110–17; Gathercole, "Torah, Life, and Salvation," 126–45; Avemarie, "Paul and the Claim of the Law," 127–29; Sprinkle, *Law and Life*, 53–130.

142. Sprinkle, *Law and Life*, 138–42.

143. Hays and Martyn think that Paul regards Lev 18:5 as a false promise (Martyn,

tification by the works of the law would end up being cursed (cf. Gal 3:10). Paul gives two main reasons why the way of receiving life by obedience to the law would fail.[144] First, the law could not give life and righteousness (Gal 3:21). Rather, the law was added to identify sin as conscious transgression or to exert a constraint on human sin (Gal 3:19).[145] The law serves only as a guardian temporarily, so that "we," both Jews and Gentiles (cf. Gal 3:28), may be justified by faith when Christ comes (Gal 3:24).[146] Second, human beings, enslaved by sin and by the "elementary principles of the world" (cf. Gal 1:4; 4:8-9; 5:1), do not have the ability to fulfill the law adequately (cf. Gal 5:3; 6:13). Thus, they are also unable to avoid or overcome the curse of the law (Gal 3:10).[147] In view of this, Paul continues to argue that only by faith in Jesus Christ can people be delivered from the curse of the law and be justified before God (Gal 3:13-14).

---

*Galatians*, 332; Hays, *Faith of Jesus Christ*, 192). Sprinkle has rightly pointed out that the promise can only be false if the conditions have been met, but the promise of life is not delivered. Since "it is unlikely that Paul believes that the conditions of the Lev 18:5 have been sufficiently accomplished . . . it is more likely that Paul understands Lev 18:5 as a conditional offer that has not been, or cannot be, met" (Sprinkle, *Law and Life*, 145).

144. For a summary and evaluation of the various explanations of why the Lev 18:5 promise fails, see Sprinkle, *Law and Life*, 142-52.

145. Gal 3:19 states that the law "was added because of transgressions" (τῶν παραβάσεων χάριν προσετέθη). Based on Rom 4:15 ("because the law brings wrath. And where there is no law there is no transgression," NIV), where the context is very similar to here, some understand this statement to mean that the law was added to identify human sin as conscious transgression (e.g., Longenecker, *Galatians*, 138-39; Matera, *Galatians*, 128). In view of the "disciplinarian" role of the law in Gal 3:23-25, others think that it means that the law poses a constraint on human sin (e.g., Hays, "Galatians," 266). These are the two most possible interpretations of the phrase. For an evaluation of other options, see Hays, "Galatians," 266.

146. The παιδαγωγός was usually a slave during the Greco-Roman period who was charged with the supervision and conduct of one or more sons in the family. The responsibility of the παιδαγωγός ceased once the son reached maturity (Longenecker, *Galatians*, 148; Williams, *Galatians*, 102-3). Thus, the law is portrayed here as having a supervisory as well as a temporary role.

147. Sprinkle insists that, in the context of Galatians, Paul opposes Lev 18:5 as an inadequate way to attain life not because of the inability to obey the law perfectly due to sin, but rather, because of enslavement to the "powers of this age" (Sprinkle, *Law and Life*, 150). It is commendable that Sprinkle points out another important factor in Galatians that contributes to human inability to observe the law adequately. The language of imprisonment of humans under sin, which is condemned by the law, is clear in Gal 3:22-23; cf. Gal 1:4.

The Blessing of Abraham, the Spirit, and Justification in Galatians

CHRIST'S CRUCIFIXION AND JUSTIFICATION BY FAITH

## The Efficacy of Christ's Crucifixion

Galatians 3:13–14 serves as the summary of the evidence put forth by Paul in his argument on justification by faith (Gal 3:1–12).[148] Not only does the experience of the Galatians with regard to the reception of the Spirit show that justification is by faith (Gal 3:1–5), the Scripture also testifies similarly (Gal 3:6–12). Works of the law cannot bring about justification, but only lead to condemnation under the curse of the law. However, "Christ redeemed us from the curse of the law by becoming a curse for us—for it is written, 'Cursed is everyone who is hanged on a tree'" (Gal 3:13 ESV; cf. Deut 21:23). Why is the death of Christ on the cross vicarious and redemptive? Who are the "us" that Christ has redeemed? We shall look into these questions in the two sections below.

### Redemption from the Curse of the Law

Redemption from the curse of the law is accomplished by means of Christ "becoming a curse on our behalf" (Gal 3:13). Paul cites Deut 21:23 to explain that Christ took the curse upon himself when he died on the cross.[149] How is Deut 21:23 related to the redemptive effect of Christ's crucifixion?

In Deut 21:22–23, there is an injunction against leaving the corpse of an executed criminal hanging on a tree overnight so as not to defile the land.[150] This is because such a person is accursed by God (Deut 21:23b).

---

148. Dumbrell, "Abraham and the Abrahamic Covenant," 26. The asyndeton in Gal 3:13 indicates its break from the previous sentences, which have a series of connectives. See also Longenecker, *Galatians*, 121.

149. Deut 21:23b MT: קללת אלהים תלוי, "he who is hanging is *a curse of God*"; LXX: κεκατηραμένος ὑπὸ θεοῦ πᾶς κρεμάμενος ἐπὶ ξύλου, "everyone who is hung on a tree is *cursed by God*"; Gal 3:13b: *ἐπικατάρατος* πᾶς ὁ κρεμάμενος ἐπὶ ξύλου, "everyone who is hung on a tree is *cursed*." Paul's citation follows the LXX more closely than the MT, with the exception of changing the participle κεκατηραμένος to the adjective ἐπικατάρατος and the omission of ὑπὸ θεοῦ ("by God"). The former is stylistic, while it is more difficult to determine whether the latter is significant. Scholars have offered various reasons for these two differences. Nonetheless, it is most likely that Paul had made these changes to link Deut 21:23 to his citation of Deut 26:27 in Gal 3:10 (Wilcox, "Upon the Tree," 197). For a survey of the various proposals about the omission, see Wilcox, "Upon the Tree," 86–87; Silva, "Galatians," 797. For the history of interpretation of how the Hebrew construct chain קללת אלהים ("cursed of God") is understood, see Caneday, "Redeemed from the Curse," 197.

150. The capital punishment here generally refers to any violation of covenantal

## Justification by Faith

The body of the criminal is hung after execution as a warning against breaking covenantal laws that are punishable by death.[151] Although it is not elaborated in the context of Deuteronomy, such hanging of the corpse also averts the wrath and judgment of God (Num 25:4; cf. 2 Sam 21:1–14).[152]

There is also a tradition in the early church that associates Christ's crucifixion with "hanging on the tree" (Acts 5:30; 10:39–40; 13:29; 1 Pet 2:24).[153] In emphasizing the sinless nature of Christ, the early church thus understands Christ's death as being vicarious for sinners (1 Cor 15:3; 1 Pet 2:24; cf. 2 Cor 5:21).[154]

In line with the Deuteronomy context and the early church tradition, Paul understands that Christ's crucifixion ("being hung on a tree") involved taking upon himself the curse of the law vicariously for transgressors, and by doing so, he averted the wrath and judgment of God.[155]

---

stipulations that is punishable by death (Craigie, *Deuteronomy*, 285). Contra Garlington, who thinks that it only refers to the rebellious son in Deut 21:18–21 (Garlington, "Role Reversal," 104). As both Deut 21:23 and 27:26 deal with covenantal violations, the curse in both contexts is the same. Contra Brondos, "The Cross and the Curse," 22.

151. Craigie, *Deuteronomy*, 285; Caneday, "Redeemed from the Curse," 199–200; Driver, *Deuteronomy*, 248; Nelson, *Deuteronomy*, 262; Biddle, *Deuteronomy*, 326. Interpreters usually note that the corpse is not cursed because it is hanging upon a tree. Rather, hanging upon a tree is a graphic sign of the person being accursed by God because of covenant violation.

152. Caneday, "Redeemed from the Curse," 200–1. Contra Hamerton-Kelly, "Sacred Violence and the Curse of the Law," 114–15. The judgment came in the form of plagues in Num 25:8–9 and famine in 2 Sam 21:1, 14. Hamerton-Kelly argues that in 2 Sam 21:1–14, the victims that were hung were the ransom paid to the Gibeonites. It is, therefore, human justice that requires the victims, not divine justice. However, he fails to relate the vengeance of God that caused the famine (2 Sam 21:1) with the wrath of God that was turned away after hanging the corpses of the sons of Saul (2 Sam 21:14).

153. In the traditional Jewish understanding of Deut 21:22–23, the corpse is hung on a tree after the death of the criminal, rather than hanging as the means of execution (Craigie, *Deuteronomy*, 285; McConville, *Deuteronomy*, 332). In the Qumran literature, 4QpNah 3–4 I, 7–8 and 11QTa LXIV, 6–13 may provide evidence of associating hanging as a means of execution with Deut 21:23. However, the allusion to Deut 21:23 in 4QpNah is unclear due to a lacuna. Although 11QT[a] LXIV, 6–13 clearly alludes to Deut 21:23, it is not entirely clear if it refers to hanging as a means of execution (Wilcox, "Upon the Tree," 88–90; Caneday, "Redeemed from the Curse," 198–99). Nonetheless, Bruce notes that "the hanging (impalement, crucifixion) of *living* men was not a traditional Jewish mode of execution though it was common among surrounding nations . . . But whether it was a corpse or a living person that was hanged, the principle of Deut 21:22f. was equally applicable in Jewish law" (Bruce, *Galatians*, 165; emphasis in original).

154. Caneday, "Redeemed from the Curse," 206–9.

155. The concept that God's wrath is averted by Christ's death on the cross is also

## The Blessing of Abraham, the Spirit, and Justification in Galatians

Therefore, Christ is able to redeem people from the curse of the law by his death on the cross (Gal 3:13).

### The Objects of Redemption

Interpreters are divided over whether the first person plural ("us") in Gal 3:13 should be inclusive (both Jewish and Gentile Christians) or exclusive (only Jewish Christians).[156] Those who take the inclusive view argue that since the first person plural ("we") in Gal 3:14 is inclusive, it is likely that "us" in Gal 3:13 is also inclusive. Those who take the exclusive view usually think that the "curse of the law" applies only to the Jews. Some who take the exclusive view go a step further and even claim that the redemption of the Jews is a precondition of the salvation extended to the Gentiles.[157]

Two important arguments tip the scales in favor of the inclusive reading. First, the enslaving power of sin is universal over both Jews and Gentiles such that both Jews and Gentiles alike would qualify as transgressors until Christ came (Gal 3:22–23; 4:3–4; 8–9).[158] Thus, the curse of the law would apply to both Jews and Gentiles alike. Second, although Paul uses the first person plural in Gal 2:15-16 to refer to Jewish Christians, including himself, his use of the first person plural in Gal 3:24—4:7 and his switch to second person plural are inclusive of both Jewish and Gentile Christians.[159] If the sonship of God is applicable to all Jews and Gentiles

---

apparent elsewhere in Paul such as Rom 5:9-10; 1 Thess 1:10; 5:9 (Schreiner, *New Testament Theology*, 363).

156. For the inclusive view, see, e.g., Dalton, "'We' in Galatians," 38; Das, *Paul and the Jews*, 124; Dunn, *Galatians*, 176. For the exclusive view, see, e.g., Donaldson, "Curse of the Law," 97; Hays, "Galatians," 261–62; Hong, "Does Paul Misrepresent the Jewish Law?," 178. However, Donaldson became skeptical of his own position later (*Paul and the Gentiles*, 191–92).

157. Hays claims that "Isaiah holds forth the vision of God's final redemption and restoration of Israel as a prelude to the gathering of the Gentiles to worship the one true God" (Hays, "Galatians," 261). However, in the examples that Hays cites (Isa 2:2-4; 60:1-22), it is not clear if the restoration of Israel is prior to or contemporaneous with the gathering of the Gentiles. Donaldson had argued earlier that Paul is reflecting a first-century Jewish "strand of eschatological expectation that anticipated a massive turning of the Gentiles to Yahweh as a consequence of the end-time redemption of Israel," as Tob 14:5-7 indicates (Donaldson, "'Curse of the Law,'" 98–99). However, Donaldson eventually abandoned his earlier position in view of Rom 11, where Paul seems to have perceived the restoration of Israel as yet to happen in the future (Donaldson, *Paul and the Gentiles*, 192–93).

158. Eckstein, *Verheißung und Gesetz*, 152.

159. See also Mußner, *Galaterbrief*, 271.

## Justification by Faith

who believe in Christ (Gal 3:26-28; 4:5-7), it follows that the redemption of Christ should also apply to both Jewish and Gentile believers (Gal 3:13; cf. Gal 1:4). Therefore, it is more likely that the "we" in Gal 3:13 is inclusive.

### The Purpose of Christ's Redemption

In Gal 3:14, Paul states the two purposes of the redemption from the curse of the law that Christ accomplished by his crucifixion: first, "in order that the blessing of Abraham might come to the Gentiles in Christ Jesus" (Gal 3:14a) and second, "in order that we might receive the promise of the Spirit by faith" (Gal 3:14b). Clearly, these two purpose (ἵνα) clauses in Gal 3:14 tie the reception of the Spirit in Gal 3:2-5 to the blessing of Abraham in Gal 3:6-9 chiastically.[160] In this section, we will analyze Gal 3:14 in detail to see if Paul equates the blessing of Abraham with the promise of the Spirit, as commonly assumed.

#### The Grammatical Relationship between Juxtaposed ἵνα Clauses

Before we investigate the relationship between the blessing of Abraham and the promise of the Spirit in Gal 3:14, it is necessary for us to look into other instances where Paul juxtaposes two ἵνα clauses in order to discern whether there are any regular patterns in his usage. In the Pauline letters, other than Gal 3:14, juxtaposed ἵνα clauses occur in Rom 7:13; 1 Cor 4:6; 2 Cor 12:7b; Gal 4:4-5; Eph 5:25-27a; Tit 2:3-5.[161] We will begin with the occurrences in other Pauline letters before coming back to discuss Gal 4:4-5 and apply our findings to Gal 3:14.

Paul affirms that it is not the law, which is good, but his own sinful nature that brings death in Rom 7:13: "Therefore did that which is good become [a cause of] death for me? May it never be! Rather it was sin, in order that [ἵνα] it might be shown to be sin by effecting my death through that which is good, so that [ἵνα] through the commandment sin would become utterly sinful" (NASB). The first ἵνα clause restates the function of

---

160. See p. 32 above on the structure of Gal 3:6-14.

161. I am taking Ephesians and Titus to be written by Paul. A detailed defense of my position is beyond the scope of this study. For arguments for Pauline authorship of Ephesians and the Pastoral Epistles, see, e.g., Hoehner, *Ephesians*, 2-60; Knight, *The Pastoral Epistles*, 4-6, 21-52; Mounce, *Pastoral Epistles*, cxviii-cxxix. Even if we do not consider these two disputed epistles, the conclusions drawn from the remaining undisputed epistles are still the same.

the law in defining what sin is (cf. Rom 7:7), while the second ἵνα clause emphasizes how the law shows the extent of the "sinfulness" of sin. Moo thinks that the second clause elaborates on the first, while Dunn regards the two clauses as "doubling and reemphasis."[162] The two clauses are clearly related in Rom 7:13, and the second clause may be seen as an amplification of the first.[163] Yet, it is difficult to determine with certainty whether the two clauses are coordinate or the second clause is subordinate to the first.

Scholars seem to agree that the second ἵνα clause is subordinate to the first in 1 Cor 4:6: "Now these things, brethren, I have figuratively applied to myself and Apollos for your sakes, so that [ἵνα] in us you may learn not to exceed what is written, so that [ἵνα] no one of you will become arrogant in behalf of one against the other" (NASB).[164] The second clause appears to be the consequence of the first clause and the ultimate purpose of the main clause.[165] The case seems to be also similar in 2 Cor 12:7 and Titus 2:3–5.[166] The context of Eph 5:25–27 also shows that the second clause is a consequence of the first, that is, the presentation of the pure and holy bride is a consequence of her being cleansed.[167]

From Paul's use of juxtaposed ἵνα clauses outside of Galatians, we may make two important observations. First, the second clause usually

---

162. Moo, *Romans*, 452–53; Dunn, *Romans 1–8*, 387.

163. Cf. Cranfield, *Romans*, 1:354; Barrett, *Romans*, 145.

164. See, e.g., Hooker, "'Beyond the Things,'" 128; Conzelmann, *1 Corinthians*, 86 n. 15; Kuck, *Judgment and Community Conflict*, 212; Barrett, *First Corinthians*, 107; Garland, *1 Corinthians*, 136.

165. Robertson and Plummer, *First Corinthians*, 81.

166. 2 Cor 12:7: "Because of the surpassing greatness of the revelations, for this reason, to keep me from exalting myself, there was given me a thorn in the flesh, a messenger of Satan to [ἵνα] torment me—to [ἵνα] keep me from exalting myself!" (NASB). See also Barrett, *Second Corinthians*, 314, who notes that the second ἵνα clause after the main clause (ἐδόθη μοι σκόλοψ τῇ σαρκί, "there was given me a thorn in the flesh") is dependent on the first. Titus 2:3–5: "Older women likewise are to be reverent in their behavior, not malicious gossips nor enslaved to much wine, teaching what is good, so that [ἵνα] they may encourage the young women to love their husbands, to love their children, [to be] sensible, pure, workers at home, kind, being subject to their own husbands, so that [ἵνα] the word of God will not be dishonored" (NASB).

167. See also Best, *Ephesians*, 544–45; Hoehner, *Ephesians*, 757. Eph 5:25–27: "Husbands, love your wives, just as Christ also loved the church and gave Himself up for her, so that [ἵνα] He might sanctify her, having cleansed her by the washing of water with the word, that [ἵνα] He might present to Himself the church in all her glory, having no spot or wrinkle or any such thing; but that she would be holy and blameless" (NASB).

explicates the first clause. Second, with the possible exception of Rom 7:13, the content of the two clauses is related but not equated.

Now we shall turn our attention to Gal 4:4–5. The syntactical structure and content of Gal 3:13–14 and Gal 4:4–5 are very similar:

|  | Gal 3:13–14 | Gal 4:4–5 |
|---|---|---|
| Main clause | Χριστὸς ἡμᾶς ἐξηγόρασεν ἐκ τῆς κατάρας τοῦ νόμου γενόμενος ὑπὲρ ἡμῶν κατάρα, | ἐξαπέστειλεν ὁ θεὸς τὸν υἱὸν αὐτοῦ, γενόμενον ἐκ γυναικός, γενόμενον ὑπὸ νόμον, |
|  | Christ redeemed us from the curse of the law by becoming a curse for us, | God sent his son, who is born of a woman and born under the law, |
| First ἵνα clause | ἵνα εἰς τὰ ἔθνη ἡ εὐλογία τοῦ Ἀβραὰμ γένηται ἐν Χριστῷ Ἰησοῦ, | ἵνα τοὺς ὑπὸ νόμον ἐξαγοράσῃ, |
|  | in order that the blessing of Abraham may come to the Gentiles/nations in Christ Jesus, | in order to redeem those under the law, |
| Second ἵνα clause | ἵνα τὴν ἐπαγγελίαν τοῦ πνεύματος λάβωμεν διὰ τῆς πίστεως. | ἵνα τὴν υἱοθεσίαν ἀπολάβωμεν. |
|  | in order that we might receive the promise of the Spirit by faith. | in order that we might receive the adoption of sonship. |

The observation that ἵνα clauses are often related in Paul but not equated is confirmed further in Gal 4:4–5. Christ's redemption from the law is certainly not the same event as the adoption. The two may be related as two separate consequences of God sending his son, or the adoption may be regarded as a result of the redemption.[168] In the former case, the two clauses would be independent, and the second clause would then not be explicating the first. In the latter case, the second clause would explicate the first. The latter is more likely, as the adoption would not be possible apart from the redemption. Thus, Gal 4:5 most likely confirms the first

---

168. For those who see the two i3na clauses in Gal 4:5 as independent of each other, see, e.g., Lightfoot, *Galatians*, 166; Lagrange, *Galates*, 103; Matera, *Galatians*, 150. For those who understand the second clause as explicating the first, see, e.g., Mußner, *Galaterbrief*, 270; Betz, *Galatians*, 208; Bruce, *Galatians*, 197; Dunn, *Galatians*, 217; Martyn, *Galatians*, 390.

observation from other Pauline letters that the second clause explicates the first.

From our investigation of the juxtaposed ἵνα clauses in the Pauline writings, we can conclude that there is predominant pattern of the second clause explicating the first, and that the content of the two clauses is related but not equated. However, there seem to be also exceptions. Galatians 4:5 is a disputed case with regard to the former, and Rom 7:13 may be an exception to the latter. Therefore, although syntax alone is not decisive for us to determine the relationship between the blessing of Abraham and the promise of the Spirit in Gal 3:14, the results of our investigation favor some relationship between the two and show that the two are not likely to be equated. The context of Galatians will still be the key to understand the relationship between these two motifs.

## *The Relationship and Distinction between the Blessing of Abraham and the Promise of the Spirit*

From Paul's argument, it is clear that one of the purposes (ἵνα) of Christ's redemption from the curse of the law is to fulfill the Abrahamic blessing for the nations (Gal 3:13–14).[169] This blessing refers to being justified by faith before God by believing in Christ Jesus and thereby becoming Abraham's offspring (Gal 3:6–9; cf. 3:24, 29). For Paul, all three elements in the Abrahamic blessing (Gen 12:2–3, 7; cf. Gen 26:3–4; 28:13–14), namely numerous descendants, land, and blessing for the nations, are fulfilled "in Christ Jesus."[170] All who are "in Christ" are Abraham's offspring, regardless of their ethnicity, social status, or gender (Gal 3:27–29). Such a broad spectrum of offspring certainly fulfills the promise of numerous descendants beyond what can be achieved by physical descendants alone.[171] The inclusion of the Gentiles as children of Abraham by faith "in Christ" is thus also the fulfillment of the blessing for the nations (Gal 3:8, 14, 28).

All who are Abraham's offspring "in Christ" are heirs to the inheritance (Gal 3:29; 4:4–7; cf. 3:18). Although the term "inheritance" primarily

---

169. Contra Kwon, *Eschatology in Galatians*, 122–25, who insists that *"Christ is not the fulfiller of the Abrahamic promise but its original co-recipient"* (cf. Gal 3:16–19) (*Eschatology in Galatians*, 124; emphasis in original).

170. Contra Kwon, *Eschatology in Galatians*, 102–7, who argues that the Abrahamic promise(s) in Gal 3:16–29 only refers to the "land" promise. On the elements of the Abrahamic blessing, see also pp. 73–75 below.

171. On the promise of numerous offspring beyond physical descendants in Genesis, see pp. 77–78 below.

refers to "land" in Jewish thought,[172] it has also been spiritualized as "inheriting eternal life" in some early Jewish literature.[173] This spiritualized inheritance can also be seen in the NT (e.g., Eph 1:11–14; Heb 3–4; 11:8–16).[174] However, in Rom 4:13, the inheritance seems to be universalized more than being spiritualized. Therefore, for Paul, the "land" promise (i.e., "inheritance") in the Abrahamic blessing is also fulfilled "in Christ."[175] Although Christ is the fulfillment of the Abrahamic promise, there is still an already and not yet element regarding the inheritance. The heirship of believers to the inheritance has been inaugurated in Christ (Gal 3:29; 4:4–7), but there is still an eschatological component to the inheritance (Gal 5:21; 6:7–9).[176] The basis of the believers' future hope is still through the Spirit by faith in Christ (cf. Gal 5:5–6).

As Kwon notes, Paul does not state explicitly that the Spirit is the fulfillment of the Abrahamic blessing.[177] In the discussion of the Abrahamic promise in Gal 3:15–29, the Spirit does not come into the picture.[178] Even when the Spirit is associated with "sonship" in Gal 4:6, it refers to the sonship of God rather than the sonship of Abraham.[179] The Spirit is not portrayed as the agent by which believers become "sons of God."[180] Rather,

---

172. Herrmann, "נחלה and נחל in the OT," *TDNT* 3:769–76; Wright, "נחל," *NIDOTTE* 3:77–81 See also Dunn, *Galatians*, 186.

173. E.g., 1 *En.* 40:9; *Pss. Sol.* 14:10; *T. Job* 18:6–7.

174. See also Heckel, *Der Segen*, 152–53, who notes that the term "inheritance" in early Christianity is an extensive expression for the reception of the eschatological salvation.

175. As mentioned previously, a detailed discussion on the fulfillment of the "land" promise in the Abrahamic blessing is beyond the scope of this study.

176. Contra Kwon, *Eschatology in Galatians*, 130–54, who argues that Christ is not the fulfillment of the Abrahamic promise. Although Kwon is right that the realization of the inheritance is yet future in Galatians, Christ has still fulfilled the promise by inaugurating the heirship of believers.

177. Kwon, *Eschatology in Galatians*, 109.

178. See ibid., 110–11.

179. Although the "sonship of God" is an extension of the "sonship of Abraham" (cf. Gal 3:25, 29), it is noteworthy that the "sonship" in Gal 4:6 refers specifically to the "sonship of God," not to the "sonship of Abraham."

180. Contra Williams, who argues that in Gal 4:28–29, "the work of creating sons of Abraham is the work of the Spirit" ("Promise in Galatians," 715). In Gal 4:29, the one "born according to the Spirit" more likely refers to Isaac, who was "born through promise" (Gal 4:23), rather than believers in Christ. In view of the parallel between Gal 4:23 and Gal 4:29, "the one born according to the Spirit" would mean "the one born according to the promise uttered through the Holy Spirit" (Fung, *Galatians*, 214n49). Therefore, Gal 4:29 does not imply that the Spirit is the agent by which believers in Christ become "children of Abraham."

the Spirit attests to the "sonship"—*because* [ὅτι] you are sons, God sent the Spirit of his Son into our hearts crying out, 'Abba, Father'" (Gal 4:6).[181] In Galatians, the status of "sonship" is consistently attributed to faith in Christ Jesus (Gal 3:26–29; 4:4–5; cf. Gal 3:7).

The conferring of sonship seems to be simultaneous with the reception of the Spirit (cf. Gal 3:2, 14, 26). There is no clear indication in Galatians that the latter is the cause of the former. What is clearly stated in both Rom 8:14–17 and Gal 4:4–6 is the role of the Spirit as witness to the sonship of the believer.[182] Even if ὅτι in Gal 4:6 is taken to be causal, it need not mean that the reception of the Spirit is chronologically sequential to the conferring of sonship. Rather, the focus here is on the witness of the Spirit as an affirmation of the status of sonship. Given that Paul speaks of these two events in either order in Rom 8:14–15 and Gal 4:6, Richard Longenecker argues that "Paul is not here setting out stages in the Christian life, whether logical or chronological. Rather, his emphasis is on the reciprocal relation or correlational nature of sonship and the reception of the Spirit."[183] These two events are neither identical nor related in a cause-and-effect way, but rather they are coterminous and inseparable.[184]

Therefore, although "the promise of the Spirit" is juxtaposed with "the blessing of Abraham" in Gal 3:14, there is no clear evidence from the context of Galatians that the former should be equated with the latter, or seen as a fulfillment of the latter. This exegetical conclusion is in accord with our investigation above that juxtaposed ἵνα clauses in Pauline usage are usually not equated, although they are related. The question remains: is there a relationship, then, between "the blessing of Abraham" and "the promise of the Spirit"? Or is there no relationship between the two at all,

---

181. See also Lightfoot, *Galatians*, 169; Fung, *Galatians*, 184; Dunn, *Galatians*, 220. ὅτι in Gal 4:6 may be taken to be demonstrative—"(to show or prove) that" (e.g., NEB/REB; Moule, *Idiom*, 147; Zerwick, *Biblical Greek*, §419; Dunn, *Galatians*, 220), or causal (e.g., NASB; NIV; NLT; NRSV; NKJV; ESV; Lightfoot, *Galatians*, 169; Bruce, *Galatians*, 198; Fung, *Galatians*, 184).

182. There has been considerable debate on the function of the Spirit in relation to "sonship." Based on Rom 8:14–17, some scholars argue that the Spirit makes believers God's sons by adoption (e.g., Hodge, *Romans*, 266; Cranfield, *Romans*, 1:397; Obeng, "Abba, Father," 363; Fee, *God's Empowering Presence*, 566; Moo, *Romans*, 502). This interpretation has been rightly questioned by a number of scholars on various grounds. See, e.g., Morris, *Romans*, 313; Murray, *Romans*, 296; Byrne, *Sons of God*, 100; Scott, *Adoption as Sons of God*, 261n143; Burke, *Adopted into God's Family*, 72–99, 140–43.

183. Longenecker, *Galatians*, 173.

184. Scott, *Adoption as Sons of God*, 260–61; Burke, *Adopted into God's Family*, 142–43.

*Justification by Faith*

as Harrisville and Kwon have argued?[185] We also noted earlier that the covenantal context in which the promise of the Spirit occurs in the prophetic tradition also implies that there must be some relationship between the Spirit and the Abrahamic, Sinai, and new covenants. Thus, rather than equating the promise of the Spirit with the Abrahamic promise in Gal 3:14, we need to understand this promise in the prophetic tradition and ascertain its relationship with the blessing of Abraham through further research.[186]

## Conclusion

We have seen in this chapter that Paul's discussion of the blessing of Abraham and the promise of the Spirit is set in the context of his argument that justification is by faith, and not by works of the law (Gal 2:15—5:12). After his preliminary assertion in Gal 2:15-21, Paul sets forth two sets of evidence in order to support his thesis in Gal 2:16 that "a person is not justified by the works of the law but through faith in Jesus Christ" (ESV). In response to Paul's rhetorical questions in the first set of evidence by experience (Gal 3:1-5), the Galatians had to admit that indeed, they had received the Spirit by faith and not by works of the law. The reception of the Spirit by faith is an undeniable evidence that they had been justified by faith.

In the second set of evidence (Gal 3:6-13), Paul cites five scriptural quotations to support his earlier assertion in Gal 2:16. On the positive side (Gal 3:6-9), Paul argues that the paradigm of justification by faith has its basis in the Torah, as seen in the case of Abraham (Gal 3:6; cf. Gen 15:6). The Scripture foresaw the justification of Gentiles by faith in the Abrahamic promise of blessing for the nations (Gal 3:8; cf. Gen 12:3). On the negative side, Paul argues that no one can be justified before God by the law (Gal 3:10-12). Although there seems to be a way to obtain life and righteousness by doing the works of the law (Gal 3:12; cf. Lev 18:5), this

185. Harrisville, *Figure of Abraham*, 10-11; Kwon, *Eschatology in Galatians*, 109-14.

186. Other scholars who propose that "the promise of the Spirit" in Gal 3:14 should be understood in the prophetic tradition of Isaiah, Jeremiah, and Ezekiel include Fee, *God's Empowering Presence*, 395; Hays, "Galatians," 261; Kwon, *Eschatology in Galatians*, 115-17. However, as we have seen in the history of interpretation in ch. 1, these scholars either have not elaborated how the promise of the Spirit in the context of prophetic tradition is related to the Abrahamic blessing or they deny the relationship altogether.

avenue fails. The enslaved human nature is unable to fulfill the stipulations of the law in one way or another, causing them to come under the curse of the law (Gal 3:10; cf. Deut 27:26). On the contrary, the life of the righteous is characterized by faith and they shall receive life by faith (Gal 3:11b; cf. Hab 2:4). Only by faith in Jesus Christ, who accomplished the work of redemption when he was cursed on our behalf in his crucifixion, can people be delivered from the curse of the law and be justified before God (Gal 3:13–14). Christ is the fulfillment of the Abrahamic promise of blessing (Gal 3:14a). The promise of numerous descendants, blessing for the nations, and inheritance are all fulfilled "in Christ."

I have argued that the promise of the Spirit should not be equated with the Abrahamic promise or taken as the fulfillment of the Abrahamic blessing. Rather, the promised Spirit is likely to be understood in the prophetic tradition of Isaiah, Jeremiah, and Ezekiel in relation to the Abrahamic, Sinai, and new covenants. Therefore, in chapters 3 and 4, we shall examine carefully the blessing of Abraham in Genesis, its development in the other OT texts, and the promise of the Spirit in the prophets, so as to (1) investigate the relationships among the Abrahamic, Sinai, and new covenants and (2) determine if there is any relationship between the promise of the Spirit and the blessing of Abraham in the prophetic tradition. Subsequently, we will reexamine Galatians in chapter 6 to see if Paul's understanding of the promise of the Spirit reflects any elements of the prophetic tradition or has any relationship with the blessing of Abraham.

# 3     The Beginning of the Blessing of Abraham

*Genesis and the Rest of the Pentateuch*

IN ORDER TO UNDERSTAND the relationship between Christ's redemption and the fulfillment of the Abrahamic blessing for the nations in Gal 3:13-14 (cf. Gen 12:2-3), it is necessary for us to trace the theological development of the Abrahamic blessing in the OT from its beginning in Genesis. The call of Abraham in Gen 12:1-3 plays a prominent role in the book of Genesis. This divine call initiates the promise to bless Abraham for the first time in Genesis—specifically the establishment of a great nation, which entails descendants and land, and the blessing for other nations through Abraham. The motifs of this promise continue to be developed in the rest of Genesis as well as the Pentateuch.[1] Therefore, in this chapter, we shall seek to interpret Gen 12:1-3 in its narrative context in relation to the primeval history in Genesis 1-11 as well as its development in the rest of the Pentateuch.

## THE RELATIONSHIP OF GENESIS 12:1-3 TO THE PRIMEVAL NARRATIVE

### Thematic and Structural Links

Although it is common to divide the book of Genesis into the primeval history (chs. 1-11) and patriarchal history (chs. 12-50), the patriarchal narrative is inextricably related to the primeval narrative thematically and

---

1. Clines, *Theme*, 48-65; Wenham, *Genesis 1-15*, 268; Alexander, *From Paradise to the Promised Land*, 98-99; Kaiser, *Promise-Plan*, 52-100. Developments of the Abrahamic promise in the Pentateuch may be seen, e.g., in: (1) the reiteration of the promise in Gen 26:3-5; 28:13-14; (2) the beginning of the fulfillment of the promise of numerous descendants in Exod 1:7 and Num 23:10; and (3) the imminent fulfillment of the promise of inheriting the land in Deut 1:8.

## The Blessing of Abraham, the Spirit, and Justification in Galatians

structurally.[2] Thematically, *Leitwörter* ("keywords") such as "land" (אֶרֶץ, אֲדָמָה), "descendants" (זֶרַע), "nations" (גּוֹיִם), "name" (שֵׁם), "greatness" (גָּדַל), "blessing" (בָּרַךְ), and "curse" (אָרַר) are found throughout the book of Genesis.[3] The repetition of these keywords not only links the two narrative sections but also points to the theme of Genesis, which shall be discussed further below.[4]

Structurally, the תּוֹלְדוֹת formula serves as a literary marker not only to mark the beginning of a new section but also to link the preceding narrative to the new section.[5] Hieke observes that each תּוֹלְדוֹת section schematically comprises: (1) the תּוֹלְדוֹת formula, mentioning an "ancestor" who is the genealogical basis of the following events; (2) a short recapitulation of the preceding events in the narrative and/or genealogical form; (3) the progress of the narrative account; and (4) a notice of conclusion.[6] Therefore, the תּוֹלְדוֹת formula at Gen 11:27 not only introduces

---

2. Westermann, *Genesis 1–11*, 585. According to Westermann, this tradition of dividing Genesis into chs. 1–11 and chs. 12–50 goes back as far as the Masoretes and the Midrash.

3. Mathews, *Genesis 1—11:26*, 51; Wenham, *Genesis 1–15*, 268. Buber defines *Leitwort* (lead word or keyword) as "a word or word root that is meaningfully repeated within a text or sequence of texts or complex of texts" and notes that "those who attend to these repetitions will find meaning of the text revealed or clarified, or at any rate made more emphatic" (Buber, "Leitwort," 114).

4. Following Clines's definition, "theme" here refers to "plot with the emphasis on conceptualized meaning," the dominant idea of the whole literary work (*Theme*, 19–24). This definition differs from Martin Noth's, who allows for multiple themes but does not emphasize their coherence into a single dominant idea (*Pentateuchal Traditions*, 46–62). As such, I would use the term "motif" to denote the multiple prominent topics that are developed in the Pentateuch and "theme" to denote the dominant idea.

5. Grüneberg, *Abraham*, 124 and Mathews, *Genesis 1—11:26*, 33. The תּוֹלְדוֹת marker in Genesis could serve as an introduction to, either a genealogy (Gen 5:1; 10:1; 11:10; 25:12; 36:1, 9) or a new section of narrative (Gen 2:4; 6:9; 11:27; 25:19; 37:2) (Hamilton, *Genesis 1–17*, 2–3). It focuses on a particular individual and his immediate children, without having to deal with the details of all the other relatives (Alexander, "Genealogies," 258–59).

6. Hieke, *Die Genealogien*, 243. Hieke also asserts that Genesis is a narrative that progressively focuses the development of Israel among humankind, with סֵפֶר תּוֹלְדֹת אָדָם ("the book of the generations of Adam"; 5:1) as the title of Genesis. Therefore, he argues that the general distinction between a "primeval history" and a "patriarchal history" as the overall structure of the book of Genesis is not right (Hieke, *Die Genealogien*, 250–51). However, given that the narrative begins with broad strokes of history from Genesis 1–11 and narrows the focus on the ancestors of Israel from Genesis 12 onwards, it is not unreasonable generally to divide the book of Genesis into "primeval history" and "patriarchal history," as long as the link and coherence between

*The Beginning of the Blessing of Abraham*

the Abraham narrative, but it is also linked to an ongoing account of the descendants of Shem after the dispersion of the nations (cf. 11:26).[7]

## Pattern of Narrative Cycles

Developing the work of von Rad and Westermann, Clines has shown that the primeval narrative exhibits a recurring sequence of "sin-speech-mitigation-punishment."[8] Four main cycles have been observed in the primeval narrative pertaining to: (1) Adam, (2) Cain, (3) Flood, and (4) Babel.[9] The recurring cycles also indicate the intensification of sin, but each cycle is always accompanied by the extension of God's grace.[10] Clines also proposes that the theme of Genesis 1–11 can be summarized by the overarching pattern of creation-uncreation-re-creation. The primeval narrative begins with the creation account (Genesis 1–2), followed by the escalation of sin resulting in the undoing of the creation, culminating in the flood (Genesis 3–7), then by re-creation after the Flood (Genesis 8–11), although the tendency for humans to sin remains the same as before the Flood.[11] Kruger also points out that the later re-creation never reached the

---

the two sections are well articulated in terms of their place within the overall scheme of the tdlwt markers.

7. Grüneberg, *Abraham*, 124–26.

8. Clines, *Theme*, 66–70. Von Rad had earlier observed a pattern of sin-punishment-forgiveness, while Westermann had noted that there is always a divine speech between the sin and the punishment (Rad, *Genesis*, 152–53; Westermann, "Arten," 52–53). In addition, Clines observes that the element of mitigation is present before the judgment and is significant in the pattern of the narratives.

9. Von Rad includes "the sons of God" episode as one of the cycles, while Westermann includes both "the sons of God" and "Canaan" in the list. However, they were unable to identify clearly the execution of the punishment in these episodes (Rad, *Genesis*, 152–53; Westermann, "Arten," 53). Therefore, I have only listed the four main cycles identified by von Rad, Westermann, and Clines.

10. Clines, *Theme*, 70. Clines summarizes von Rad's earlier observation of intensification as a movement: (1) from disobedience to murder, to reckless killing, to titanic lust, to total corruption and violence, to the full disruption of humanity; (2) from expulsion from the garden to expulsion from the tillable earth, to the limitation of human life, to the near annihilation of mankind, to the "dissolution of mankind's unity"; and (3) from withholding immediate death for Adam and Eve, to the protective mark on Cain and to the preservation of the human race through Noah (Rad, *Genesis*, 152–53). For Clines's justification that the sin and punishment of Babel can be understood as more severe than the Flood, see Clines, *Theme*, 75–76.

11. Clines, *Theme*, 80–82. Parallels to Genesis 1 cited by Clines include: (1) the distinction of the firmament being obliterated (7:11; cf. 1:6ff.) and returning to the

same heights of quality (טוב) as the first creation account (Genesis 1).[12] This parallel and reversal literary structure brings across the theological thrust of the "downward trend of mankind . . . away from God's original intention."[13]

It is interesting to note that the element of mitigation and divine grace for the Babel narrative is not immediately apparent. Two proposals have been made regarding the element of grace in the Babel narrative. First, Clines suggests that the Table of Nations (Genesis 10) has been deliberately dischronologized and placed before the Babel narrative as the element of divine grace in the narrative pattern.[14] According to Clines, although the dispersion may be seen negatively as a judgment on sin, it may also be seen positively as the divine intervention to fulfill the mandate of "filling the earth" (cf. Gen 9:1–7) and thus be part of the divine blessing (Gen 9:1). Longman also takes Genesis 10 as the token of grace, but he understands it as God's grace to split human languages into language groups instead of individual unique dialects or completely silencing their voices.[15]

Second, the element of mitigation and divine grace in the Babel narrative is found in the calling and blessing of Abraham.[16] Not only is Gen 12:1–3 central to the development of the patriarchal narrative, it is also central to the hope of reconciliation between humanity and God after repeated disobedience in a downward spiral of alienation in the primeval narrative. The divine initiative to make Abraham into a great nation and to make his name (שם) great (Gen 12:2) stands in stark contrast to the humanly initiated attempt by the nations, which was thwarted by God, to make a name (שם) for themselves (Gen 11:4).[17]

---

watery formlessness of תהו ובהו; (2) the sequence of destruction is similar to the sequence of creation (7:21); (3) renewed separation of sea and land (8:3, 17, 13); and (4) renewed creational mandate (8:17; 9:1–7; cf. Gen 1:28).

12. Kruger, "Subscripts," 438.

13. Ibid., 445.

14. Clines, *Theme*, 74.

15. Longman, *Genesis*, 121. Longman explains that the grace of God is found in the fact that, although humans can no longer use the same language to communicate with *all* others, communication, while severely impaired, is still possible. There are still "some who speak the same language, and translation remains a possibility to speak to those outside of our own language group."

16. Rad, *Problem of the Hexateuch*, 65–66; idem, *Genesis*, 153–54; Wolff, "Kerygma," 86. Von Rad and Wolff are among the earliest to make such a connection. Clines takes both the Table of Nations and the patriarchal narrative (even the Pentateuchal narrative) as the element of mitigation of the Babel narrative (Clines, *Theme*, 84–85).

17. Alexander, *From Paradise to the Promised Land*, 120; Grüneberg, *Abraham*,

In the midst of the intensification of sin and alienation, a ray of hope may still be seen in the linear genealogies of the primeval narrative.[18] These linear genealogies, introduced by the תולדות formula, establish the main line of descendants in the primeval narrative and trace the line of hope to Abraham. They seek to show continuity with and the legitimacy of the last descendant in the genealogy.[19]

The line of Seth, in which people began to call on the name of the Lord (Gen 4:25–26), is contrasted with the line of Cain, in which terror reigns by the time of Lamech (Gen 4:17–25). The line of Adam, succeeded by Seth, eventually leads to Noah, through whom the human race is preserved in the Flood (Gen 5:1–32). The line of Noah (Gen 6:9–10) is succeeded by the line of Shem (Gen 11:10–26), eventually leading to Abraham, through whom all the families of the earth receive the blessings of Yahweh (Gen 12:3b).

## Divine Blessings in Genesis 1:26–28 and Genesis 12:2–3

The divine promise of blessing in Gen 12:2–3 is a reassertion of God's original intention to bless humankind (cf. Gen 1:28; 9:1).[20] Clines notes the parallels between the promise of blessing to Abraham in Gen 12:2–3 and the creational blessing and mandate in Gen 1:26–28:[21]

---

139; Hamilton, *Genesis 1–17*, 372. Alexander also notes a possible allusion to the "men of renown" (אנשי השם) in Gen 6:4.

18. The deep genealogies (more than two generations) in the primeval narrative (Genesis 1–11) are mostly linear except for Genesis 10, which is segmented. See also Hamilton, *Genesis 1–17*, 3.

19. Hess, "Genealogies," 248; Alexander, "Genealogies," 259; Hopkins, "First Stories," 40–41; Hieke, *Die Genealogien*, 317. See also Berthoud, "Le thème," 263–64. On the other hand, segmented genealogies in Genesis have different functions. Generally, they perform one or more of the following functions: (1) to link the relative kinship of Israel with the neighboring nations; (2) to close a previous linear genealogy by the subdivision of the last generation; and (3) for those introduced with a תולדות formula, to mark the descendants of the unelected son(s) from the line of elected son (Hieke, *Die Genealogien*, 318; Levin, "Genealogies," 33–34; Andersen, "Genealogical Prominence," 254–55; Westermann, *Genesis 1–11*, 529; Johnson, *Biblical Genealogies*, 77).

20. Clines, *Theme*, 85–86; Wenham, *Genesis 1–15*, li–lii, 275.

21. Clines, *Theme*, 85.

| Gen 1:26–28 | Gen 12:2–3, 7 |
|---|---|
| • The multiplication of the human race | • The multiplication of the descendants |
| • The filling of the earth and subduing it | • The promise of the land |
| • The divine-human relationship in which humans are created in the image of God | • The intimate relationship of God with Abraham |
| • God blessed the man and the woman | • God blessed Abraham |

In fact, some scholars have noted that Adam's commission to be fruitful and multiply (Gen 1:28) has been passed on not just to Noah (Gen 9:1–7), but also to Abraham and his descendants.[22] When God established his covenant with Abraham in Genesis 17, he had promised to *multiply* Abraham greatly and to make him exceeding *fruitful* (Gen 17:2, 6), a reminiscence of Gen 1:28.[23] This is further supported by Yahweh's reiteration of the Abrahamic promise to Jacob in which his descendants shall be so numerous as to spread out across the earth (Gen 28:14: ". . . to the west and to the east and to the north and to the south . . .") and in which he is commanded to "be fruitful and multiply" (Gen 35:11).[24]

Clines's suggestion that the mitigation element of the Babel story is the dispersion of the people, which is linked with the creational mandate to fill the earth as participation in divine blessing, is perhaps more probable than the language groups in Genesis 10 suggested by Longman.[25] Nonetheless, considering the plot of the narrative as a whole and the function

---

22. Smith, "Structure and Purpose in Genesis 1–11," 318; Cohen, *Be Fertile and Increase*, 28–31, 39; Wright, *Climax of the Covenant*, 21–26; Beale, *Temple*, 94–96. Besides contemporary scholars, Beale also mentions two sources of Jewish tradition (*Midrash Tanhuma Genesis* 3:5; *Tanhuma Yelammedenu* 2:12) that apply the commission in Gen 1:28 to Noah and Abraham. Beale notes further that, although there are many similarities between Adam's commission and the promise to Abraham, the differences are: (1) the sovereignty over all the earth is expanded to include "unregenerate human forces arrayed against it," and thus the language of "possessing the gate of their enemies"; (2) the blessing for the nations alludes to "a renewed human community bearing God's image"; and (3) the commission has become a promise and its commission implied in the imperatives (Beale, *Temple*, 113–14).

23. Wenham, *Genesis 16–50*, 21–22.

24. See also the promise made by God regarding Isaac (Gen 17:20) and Isaac's blessing on Jacob (Gen 28:3).

25. See p. 64 above.

of both the linear and the segmented genealogies in Genesis, it is more likely that the mitigation element of Babel lies in the Abrahamic promise at the beginning of the patriarchal narrative. This is further confirmed by the close connection between genealogy and blessing, in which the linear genealogies linking Adam to Abraham connect God's original intention to bless humankind to the promise of divine blessing for Abraham.[26]

Thus, the patriarchal narrative in Genesis 12–50 is inextricably related to the primeval narrative in Genesis 1–11. Their relationship is not only evident in the thematic link of *Leitwörter* and in the structural link of the תולדות formula, it is also apparent in the pattern of the narrative cycles in the primeval narratives. The Abrahamic blessing in Gen 12:1–3 serves as the mitigation element of the Babel narrative. Furthermore, parallels between the divine blessing in Gen 1:26–28 and the Abrahamic blessing in Gen 12:1–3 and its reiterations in the patriarchal narrative connect the Abrahamic blessing with God's original intention to bless humankind. Having established the relationship of Gen 12:1–3 with Gen 1–11, the following sections shall discuss the structure of Gen 12:1–3 and its reiterations in the rest of Genesis.

## The Blessing of Abraham in Genesis 12:1–3

### The Structure and Syntax of Genesis 12:1–3

The call of Abraham entails a command from God to leave his homeland, his kindred and his father's household and go to a land that God will show him (Gen 12:1). It is followed by God's promise to him in Gen 12:2–3. For the sake of reference, vv. 2–3 are listed and labeled below:

| | | |
|---:|:---:|:---|
| ואעשך לגוי גדול | 2aα (1) | "I will make you a great nation" |
| ואברכך | 2aβ (2) | "I will bless you" |
| ואגדלה שמך | 2bα (3) | "I will make your name great" |
| והיה ברכה: | 2bβ (4) | "You shall be a blessing" |
| ואברכה מברכיך | 3aα (5) | "I will bless those who bless you" |
| ומקללך אאר | 3aβ (6) | "I will curse the one who curses you" |
| ונברכו בך כל משפחת האדמה: | 3b (7) | "All the families of the earth will be blessed in you" |

---

26. See also Hieke, *Die Genealogien*, 257–60.

## The Blessing of Abraham, the Spirit, and Justification in Galatians

Scholars typically note that the promise consists of seven clauses, as listed above, although the way these clauses are demarcated varies.[27] Two main ways of demarcation have been suggested. (1) Some interpreters suggest that Gen 12:1-3 consists of two parts (vv. 1-2bα and vv. 2bβ-3), each beginning with an imperative.[28] (2) Others maintain the unity of the four clauses in v. 2.[29]

The key factor causing the difference in demarcation lies in how the syntax of וֶהְיֵה ("and you shall be") in v. 2bβ is understood.[30] Those who understand וֶהְיֵה as having only imperatival force would usually see v. 2bβ as a new section, while those who see it as having the force of purpose or consequence would usually group the first four clauses together. Most interpreters would not dispute that the cohortatives following the first imperative in v. 1 have the force of purpose or consequence.[31] Grammati-

---

27. Various reasons for the presence of seven clauses have been proposed: (1) a feature suggesting perfection (e.g., *Gen. Rab.* 17.4; Cassuto, *Genesis: Part II*, 312); (2) a holy number in the OT (e.g., Wenham, *Genesis 1-15*, 270); and (3) a penchant of literary style in grouping materials into heptads (e.g., Hamilton, *Genesis 1-17*, 371, referring to Gordis, "Heptad," 19).

28. Janzen, *Genesis 12-50*, 15; Williamson, *Abraham*, 228-29; Carroll Rodas, "Blessing the Nations," 21. See also Mathews, *Genesis 11:27—50:26*, 107. Mathews explains that the first group of three promises conveys God's resolve to bless Abraham and his family and the second group of three promises pertains to Abraham's mediation of the blessing for the world of nations. See also Ruprecht, "Vorgegebene," 183-84, who understands the first part of the promise as "I will bless you" (v. 2aβ) (explicated by v. 2aα and v. 2bα), and the second part as "you shall be a blessing" (v. 2bβ) (explicated by v. 3a and v. 3b). Nonetheless, Ruprecht thinks that v. 2bβ ("you shall be a blessing") is a consequence of v. 2bα ("I will make your name great") and does not bear an imperatival force (Ruprecht, "Vorgegebene," 180-81).

29. Westermann, *Genesis 12-36*, 149. Westermann partitions it into three parts (vv. 2, 3a, and 3b) in accordance with its function in the patriarchal story. He explains that there is a gradual progression from Abraham (v. 2) to the effect on those who accept him (v. 3a) and eventually the effect on all the families of the earth (v. 3b). Wenham also does not demarcate the promise before the second imperative in v. 2bβ (Wenham, *Genesis 1-15*, 269).

30. The Samaritan Pentateuch reads וִיהִי. Therefore, *BHS* and some commentators propose to emend it by repointing it to וִיהִי: (e.g., Skinner, *Genesis*, 244; Speiser, *Genesis*, 85). By doing so, שֵׁם ("name") possibly becomes the subject. However, this emendation is unnecessary as (1) MT, LXX, and the Vulg. all have second person forms; and (2) וִיהִי in the Samaritan Pentateuch is an imperative influenced by Aramaic (Grüneberg, *Abraham*, 147). Cassuto adds that "no one with a sound feeling of Hebrew language could concur in such 'amendments.'" He cites Zech 8:13 as a parallel passage in support of the MT reading (Cassuto, *Genesis: Part II*, 314).

31. Joüon, *Grammar*, 2:§116b; *IBHS*, §34.6. Grüneberg notes that there is no separate form attested for the cohortative with pronominal suffixes. The context and the

cally, however, the second imperative following the first could be either juxtaposed or indicate purpose.³² If it is juxtaposed, וִהְיֵה will bear an imperatival force and delineating v. 2bβ as a new section may be plausible.

However, it is better to group the first four clauses as a unit and not demarcate v. 2bβ as a new section. First, v. 2a and v. 2b are parallel. The causative nuance of גדל ("great") is apparent in both v. 2aα and v. 2bα, while the root of ברך ("bless") appears in both v. 2aβ and v. 2bβ. All four clauses are directed at Abraham using the second person, while v. 3 is directed to others in relation to Abraham.³³ Demarcating v. 2bβ as a new section would obscure its parallel nature with v. 2aβ.

Second, it is more likely that v. 2bβ bears consequential force, rather than being a simple juxtaposition with the imperative in Gen 12:1.³⁴ In order to determine the force of וִהְיֵה ("and you shall be") in v. 2bβ, it is necessary to consider the meaning of ברכה ("a blessing").³⁵ Most scholars take ברכה to mean that Abraham's name will be a paradigm of blessing, in which Abraham's name is invoked in a blessing.³⁶ Others take it to mean that Abraham is a source of blessing to others.³⁷ Based on his

---

parallel to v. 2bα would render the first two verbs as also having cohortative force (Grüneberg, *Abraham*, 143).

32. Grüneberg, *Abraham*, 145. According to Grüneberg, examples of simple juxtaposition are: Gen 17:1 and Isa 66:10. Examples of consequence or purpose are Gen 45:18 and 1 Sam 28:22 respectively.

33. Scholars who have observed the poetic characteristics (such as parallelism, rhyme, and chiasmus) in Gen 12:1–3 include: Cassuto, *Genesis: Part II*, 315; Mathews, *Genesis 11:27—50:26*, 109; Wenham, *Genesis 1-15*, 276; Westermann, *Genesis 12-36*, 146.

34. See also Sarna, *Genesis*, 89, 358n5. Cohortatives, imperatives, and jussives can all carry the same force of purpose or consequence after an initial imperative (Joüon, *Grammar*, 2:§116h; Merwe et al., *Biblical Hebrew*, 171–72).

35. ברכה ("a blessing") usually refers to the words uttered in a blessing or the prosperity caused by such a blessing. See *DCH* 2:272–73; *HALOT* 1:161 for examples. There are also instances in which a person or a group of people is called a ברכה. See p. 70n38 below on the meaning of the latter use.

36. E.g., Cassuto, *Genesis Part II*, 314; Grüneberg, *Abraham*, 146; Ruprecht, "Vorgegebene," 180; Wenham, *Genesis 1–15*, 276; Sarna, *Genesis*, 89. Their argument is based on Gen 48:20, where the names of Ephraim and Manasseh are invoked in blessings as a paradigm of blessing because the two of them have been so signally blessed.

37. Mitchell, *Meaning of BRK*, 30; BDB 139; Rad, *Genesis*, 160. Those who take וִהְיֵה ("and you shall be") to be imperatival would therefore understand the phrase to mean that God commanded Abraham to be a blessing to others, i.e., a source of blessing for others. See Carroll Rodas, "Blessing the Nations," 22n14; Alexander, "Abraham Re-Assessed," 12–13n10.

lexical studies, Grüneberg has shown convincingly that when a person or a group of people are called a ברכה, they are either "a byword of blessing" or that they are "signally in receipt of blessing," and he argues that "ברכה does not describe a person as a source of blessing."[38] Therefore, Grüneberg argues that in Gen 12:2, ברכה should mean either "recipient of blessing" or "formula of blessing."[39] In view of Grüneberg's lexical conclusion, והיה ברכה (v. 2bβ) means that Abraham will be notably a recipient of God's blessing as a result of being blessed by God (v. 2aβ).

Therefore, the four clauses in v. 2 are related to one another in the following manner. ואברכך ("and I will bless you") in verse 2aβ forms the most basic component of the promise.[40] The effect of the blessing is that Abraham becomes a great nation (v. 2aα), and his name also becomes great (v. 2bα).[41] As a result, Abraham will be notably a recipient of God's blessing (v. 2bβ).[42] והיה ("and you shall be") in v. 2bβ also bears a

---

38. Grüneberg, *Abraham*, 119–21. Grüneberg notes Ps 37:26; Prov 10:7; Isa 19:24; Ezek 34:26; Zech 8:13 as the instances when a person or a group of people are called a ברכה ("a blessing"). In all these contexts, these people are a ברכה because they have been blessed by God. Especially in Isa 19:24, Ezek 34:26; Zech 8:13, the form is similar to Gen 12:2. They are seen as being notably blessed by God, but the contexts do not indicate that they become a source of blessing to others.

39. Grüneberg, *Abraham*, 121, 146.

40. The centrality of ברך ("bless") is evident as the root appears five times in vv. 2–3.

41. See also Ruprecht, "Vorgegebene," 180; Westermann, *Genesis 12-36*, 149–50. Nonetheless, the blessing for Abraham also entails material blessing (Mathews, *Genesis 11:27—50:26*, 113) and spiritual blessing, which is reflected by the assurance of God's presence with Abraham and his descendants (e.g., Gen 26:24; 28:15; 39:2-3, 21–23). Although v. 2aα and v. 2bα are logical consequences of v. 2aβ, the first promise is nevertheless v. 2aα. This sequence is probably intended to highlight the effect of the blessing being well beyond the life of Abraham, not just extending to and directed to Israel as a nation, but also to the other nations (cf. Grüneberg, *Abraham*, 162; Westermann, *Genesis 12-36*, 149).

42. The consequential force of v. 2bβ stems from the cumulative effects of the first three clauses (v. 2aα, v. 2aβ, and v. 2bα), not just v. 2bα (contra Ruprecht, "Vorgegebene," 180). As a result of being blessed by God, Abraham becomes a paradigm of blessing because of his greatness (both in posterity and reputation). Although Ruprecht sees the first and third clauses as the direct consequence of the second clause ואברכך ("and I will bless you"), he takes v. 2bβ as a direct consequence of v. 2bα based on his presupposition that והיה ברכה means a byword of blessing in which Abraham's name is invoked (cf. Gen 48:20). See also v. 2bβ LXX: καὶ ἔση εὐλογητός ("and you shall be blessed"). Apparently, the Septuagint also understood the force of והיה as consequential, as it renders the predicate with an adjective εὐλογητός ("blessed") rather than with a noun εὐλογία ("blessing").

*The Beginning of the Blessing of Abraham*

consequential force from the first imperative לְךָ ("go") in v. 1.[43] As discussed above, the Abrahamic promise in Gen 12:1–3 is the mitigation of the judgment at Babel and the alienation of humankind from God in the primeval narrative, and it serves as the means by which God's original intention to bless all humankind is reinstated. God commands Abraham to leave his homeland and his father's household so that he may be blessed by God (v. 2), and in order that God may accomplish his ultimate purpose to bless all humankind through him (v. 3). Verse 2bβ may thus be seen as consequential to the first imperative in v. 1 rather than a simple juxtaposition. Although ברכה does not refer to Abraham as a *source* of blessing, but as signally blessed, the explication of v. 2bβ in v. 3 clearly portrays Abraham as a *channel* of blessing to others.

The divine promise to Abraham in Gen 12:2–3 may thus be delineated in two sections. The first section contains the first four clauses (12:2), and it pertains to God's blessings for Abraham. The second section contains the next three clauses (12:3), and it has to do with God's blessing for other people in relation to Abraham.

Verses 3a and 3b continue to explicate how other people will receive blessing in relation to him.[44] God will bless those who bless Abraham and will curse the one who disdains him (v. 3a), and all the families of the earth shall be blessed in him (v. 3b).[45] The key issue debated here is the

---

43. Some scholars argue that, although וִהְיֵה ("and you shall be") may have a purposive force in relation to in לְךָ ("go") v. 1, it also retains its imperatival force (Ross, *Creation and Blessing*, 263; see also Carroll Rodas, "Blessing the Nations," 22). If ברכה is taken to mean "a source of blessing," the argument for an imperatival force would work. However, in view of the meaning of ברכה when it refers to a person or a group of people as "recipient(s) of blessing," it is unlikely that the imperatival force is retained, as it is difficult to imagine how a person may be commanded to be a recipient of blessing (see also Grüneberg, *Abraham*, 146).

44. This is the ultimate goal of the command in Gen 12:1 and the climax of the blessings in Gen 12:2–3 (Mathews, *Genesis 11:27—50:26*, 117). On the contrary, Moberly argues that the promise to Abraham is primarily for the benefit of Abraham and his descendants, not for the sake of the nations (Moberly, *Bible, Theology, and Faith*, 125). However, when Gen 12:3b is read in relation to Genesis 1–11, it is clear that while God's promise is for the benefit of Abraham and his descendants, it is primarily God's ultimate purpose of reconciliation in response to the alienation of the whole human race from him. See also Grüneberg, *Abraham*, 244–45.

45. Miller has argued that the disjunctive ו in וּמְקַלֶּלְךָ ("and the one who curses you") excludes the curse from the series of volitions marked by ו consecutives. Therefore, the curse is subordinate, and it is not the purpose of the divine command in v. 1 (Miller, "Syntax and Theology," 473–74). On another related note, Wolff proposes that the singular participle מְקַלֵּל suggests that people who disdain Abraham will be

Niphal נִבְרְכוּ ("be blessed") in v. 3b.⁴⁶ (1) Traditionally, the Niphal has been rendered as passive.⁴⁷ This indicates the divine plan to bless the nations as the ultimate goal. (2) Some scholars have argued for a direct reflexive meaning—"will bless themselves by him."⁴⁸ This would imply that the nations take the initiation to bless themselves by invoking the name of Abraham. (3) More recently, some scholars propose a middle voice here— "will gain/receive/find blessing in you."⁴⁹ This translation claims that the nations will discover their blessings in Abraham.

Traditionally, scholars have generally assumed that the variations in the wording of Gen 12:3b and its reiterations in the Genesis narrative (18:18; 22:18; 26:4; 28:14) are stylistic. Therefore, they assume that the wording of Gen 12:3b and its variations in the reiterations are used interchangeably and are thus synonymous.⁵⁰ However, more recently, some scholars advocate that the Niphal (12:3; 22:18; 28:14) and the Hitpael (22:18; 26:4) bear distinct nuances.⁵¹ I have shown elsewhere that the lit-

---

the exception (Wolff, "Kerygma," 85). However, considering the chiasmus in v. 3a, it would be difficult to ascertain with certainty if the disjunctive ו and the singular reading carry deliberate nuances as proposed above. In the Pentateuch, blessing and curse together as a motif is prevalent, and there is also no lack of people who seek to do harm to Israel (see also Cassuto, *Genesis Part II*, 315; Grüneberg, *Abraham*, 149n36). Furthermore, Wenham notes that without the vowel points, the MT could also be interpreted as a defective spelling of the plural (Wenham, *Genesis 1-15*, 266).

46. This issue has important theological implications, especially regarding the purposes of God in salvation history (Speiser, *Genesis*, 86; Hamilton, *Genesis 1-17*, 374).

47. E.g., LXX; Sir 44:21 LXX; Gal 3:8; KJV; NIV; NASB; NRSV; ESV.

48. E.g., Rashi, *Pentateuch*, 49; Skinner, *Genesis*, 244-45; Westermann, *Genesis 12-36*, 151-52; Moberly, *Bible, Theology, and Faith*, 123; RSV; NJB; NEB.

49. E.g., Wolff, "Kerygma," 79; Mitchell, *Meaning of BRK*, 31-33; Wenham, *Genesis 1-15*, 277-78.

50. E.g., Wenham, *Genesis 1-15*, 277; Westermann, *Genesis 12-36*, 151-52; Hamilton, *Genesis 1-17*, 375-76. The translators of the LXX and Targums also understand the Niphal and Hitpael of ברך in Gen 12:3; 18:18; 22:18; 26:4; 28:14 to be synonymous. The LXX consistently translates all five instances with the future passive (ἐνευλογηθήσονται), while the Targums (*Tg. Neof.*; *Tg. Ps.-J.*; *Tg. Onq.*) consistently render it with the *ithpaal* stem (יתברכון). The *ithpaal* stem in Aramaic is similar to the Hitpael in Hebrew, which can have a reflexive or a passive nuance (Frank, *Grammar*, 18-20).

51. E.g., Grüneberg, *Abraham*, 220, 235, 241; Walton, *Genesis*, 393-94; Carroll Rodas, "Blessing the Nations," 23-24; Frettlöh, *Theologie des Segens*, 296; Williamson, *Abraham*, 228; Flury-Schölch, *Abrahams Segen und die Völker*, 322-26; Benton, "The Niphal and Hitpael of ברך," 1-17. Grüneberg takes the Niphal to be passive in Gen 12:3; 18:18; 28:14 and the Hitpael in Gen 22:18; 26:4 to be "speech action middle," while Walton, Carroll, and Flury-Schölch take Niphal to be passive and the Hitpael

erary context of Genesis indicates that the variations in the wording of the blessing for the nations in Genesis are very likely intentional and that, although the word pairs largely overlap in their meanings, they still bear a slight difference in nuance.[52] Therefore, based on grammatical evidence as well as the literary and narrative context of Genesis, I have also argued that the Niphal of ברך is passive (i.e., the nations "shall be blessed") and the Hitpael of ברך is an indirect reflexive that bears an estimative-declarative force (i.e., the nations "shall regard or declare themselves as blessed" on account of Abraham's offspring).[53] This meaning of the Hitpael overlaps with the Niphal in the passive sense, and it has a slightly difference nuance in the subject's recognition of "being blessed." Such and understanding of the Niphal and Hitpael of ברך is supported by the narrative context of Genesis, which not only repeatedly portrays how other people are blessed or cursed by God on account of Abraham and his descendants (e.g., Abimelech, Laban, Potiphar, Pharaoh, Egypt), but also describes how Laban acknowledges and declares himself to be blessed by Yahweh because of Jacob (Gen 30:27).

Therefore, Gen 12:3 indicates that, through Abraham, all the families of the earth shall be blessed by God. Abraham shall be the means by which God will accomplish his original intention to bless humankind (Gen 1:28) in response to the sin and alienation of humans from God in the primeval narrative.[54]

## The Elements of the Abrahamic Promise in Genesis 12:1–3

The promise to Abraham in Gen 12:2–3, 7 comprises the following basic elements: (1) descendants, (2) land, and (3) blessing for the nations.[55]

---

to be reflexive. Paul Williamson takes the Niphal to be middle and the Hitpael to be "benefactive reflexive." Frettlöh takes the Niphal to be tolerative and the Hitpael to be reflexive. Using cross-linguistic evidence, Benton argues that the Niphal focuses on the resulting state and the Hitpael on the process of the nations being blessed.

52. Lee, "The Niphal and Hithpael of ברך," 279–96.

53. Ibid., 283–94.

54. In view of this relationship of Gen 12:1–3 with the primeval narrative, it is clear that God is the divine agent in the blessing of the nations.

55. Sarna lists seven elements in the Abrahamic promise, each corresponding with the seven clauses in Gen 12:2–3 (Sarna, *Genesis*, 89). However, the first four clauses may be understood collectively as God's blessing directly for Abraham, manifested especially in the form of numerous descendants constituting a nation, resulting in Abraham's fame and him being notably blessed. The last three clauses may also be

Although the promise of the gift of the land to the descendants is only explicit in Gen 12:7, it is implied in Gen 12:1 when God commanded Abraham to leave his homeland to go to the land that God would show him, as well as in Gen 12:2, where the notion of a great nation would entail the land in which the nation dwells.[56]

Clines lists the three elements in the Abrahamic promise as posterity, divine-human relationship, and land.[57] In observing the relationship between the creational blessing and mandate in Gen 1:26–28 and the development of the Abrahamic promise in the patriarchal narrative, Clines thinks that the first element is more appropriately the "divine-human relationship," rather than "blessing." According to Clines, formulations of the relationships between God and the patriarchs or the nation of Israel may be in the form of blessing, God's presence or guidance, and the "self-predication" by God of his relationship with them.[58]

In contrast to Clines, I have listed descendants, land, and blessing for the nations as the three elements of the Abrahamic blessing, for the following reasons. First, the blessing for the nations is explicitly stated as the content of the promise, and it forms the climax of the promise. The relationship of the Abrahamic promise in Gen 12:2–3, 7 with the primeval narrative, as well as the syntactical structure of Gen 12:2–3, clearly shows that the divine initiative of the promise has its climax in the blessings for the nations.[59] The call of Abraham, the promise of divine blessing, descendants, and land are not just primarily for the sake of Abraham and his descendants. Rather, they will be the means by which God will effect his primal intention to bless humankind.[60] Clines has not included the blessing for the nations as one of the elements, possibly because he does not see it being developed in the Pentateuch with the same emphasis as the elements of descendants and land.[61]

---

understood collectively as God's blessing on other people who relate to Abraham, culminating in the blessing for all peoples in the last clause. See pp. 70–72 above.

56. Wisdom, *Blessing*, 27.
57. Clines, *Theme*, 30–38.
58. Ibid., 35–37.
59. See also Alexander, "Abraham Re-Assessed," 13; Hamilton, *Genesis 1–17*, 374; Wenham, *Exploring*, 154; Wisdom, *Blessing*, 27. Wenham basically follows Clines's lists of the elements of the Abrahamic blessing, but he adds the "blessing for the nations" as the fourth element in order to correct Clines's omission (Wenham, *Exploring*, 153–54).
60. On the ultimate universal scope of the blessing, see also Sarna, *Genesis*, 89; Mitchell, *Meaning of BRK*, 30.
61. Cf. Clines, *Theme*, 30.

*The Beginning of the Blessing of Abraham*

Second, the divine-human relationship is not stated explicitly as the specific content of the promise in Gen 12:2–3, 7, only implied and manifested in the promise as blessings. It is more likely that the blessing presupposes a divine-human relationship, rather than the relationship being an element of the promise of blessing in Gen 12:2–3, 7. We will continue to discuss in detail the correlation between blessing and divine-human relationship in chapter 6.

## The Reiterations of the Abrahamic Promise in the Patriarchal Narrative

Reiterations of the Abrahamic promise of blessing (Gen 12:2–3) appear in many forms in the patriarchal narrative. The three elements of the promise of blessings in Gen 12:2–3, namely descendants, land, and blessing for the nations, are not always fully reiterated in each instance. However, the elements of the promise are amplified in some ways in the later reiterations. These reiterations are not only made by God to Abraham, Isaac and Jacob. They also include reiterations by the patriarchs themselves.

Although Paul's quotation of the Abrahamic promise primarily concerns the blessing for the nations (Gal 3:8, 14), it is also necessary to look into how the Abrahamic promise develops in the Pentateuch in its entirety. It is only by doing so that the development of the blessing for the nations can be seen in relation to the development of the other two elements (land and descendants). Nonetheless, more attention will be given to the reiterations concerning the blessing for the nations in Gen 18:18, 22:18, 26:4, and 28:14.

### The Reiterations of the Promise to Abraham

*Genesis 13*

When Abraham came up from Egypt after the famine and settled back in the Negev, a crisis regarding the land arose when it was not able to support grazing for the vast herds and flocks of both Abraham and Lot (Gen 13:1–7). As a result, Lot moved towards the apparently more fertile Jordan Valley in the direction of Sodom and Gomorrah (Gen 13:8–13).

Dispute over the rights to the land and the departure of Lot, a possible heir to the still childless Abraham, created a challenge to the fulfillment of God's promise to Abraham.⁶² Under these circumstances, God assures Abraham of his promise that his descendants will be as countless as the dust of the earth and that the land will be given to him and his descendants forever (Gen 13:14–17).⁶³

## Genesis 15

Despite the first reassurance, the childlessness of Abraham remains unresolved. The possibility of Eliezer of Damascus being Abraham's heir was rejected by God, followed by a reassurance for the second time that his descendants shall be as countless as the stars of the sky (Gen 15:1–5).⁶⁴ After the reassurance, Abraham believed God regarding the promise of a descendant (Gen 15:6).

However, he was also uncertain about the possession of the land (Gen 15:7–8). Therefore, God established a covenant with Abraham with regard to the gift of the land, explaining why the fulfillment of the land promise would be delayed (Gen 15:13–16) and specifying the extent of the land his descendants should possess (Gen 15:18–21).⁶⁵ This covenant in

---

62. Cohn, "Narrative," 6. See also Good, *Irony*, 96.

63. The magnitude of his descendants is amplified with the metaphor of dust, while the nature of the gift of the land is clarified to be everlasting. See also Sarna, *Genesis*, 100, who notes that "the land is given by God to Israel unconditionally and in perpetuity." The extent of the land is also more clearly specified to include all the land that Abraham can see. See also Wenham, *Genesis 1–15*, 298.

64. There is much uncertainty over who Eliezer of Damascus was. Some scholars suggest that Gen 15:2–3 could depict a Nuzi custom whereby a childless man could adopt someone to look after him in his old age. After his death, the adopted "child" would be entitled to the inheritance (Wenham, *Genesis 1–15*, 329; Sarna, *Genesis*, 113; Hamilton, *Genesis 1–17*, 420; Mathews, *Genesis 11:27—50:26*, 164).

65. The countless magnitude of Abraham's descendants is once again assured here but with a different metaphor compared with Gen 13:16. The promise of the land has now been further assured with a covenant for the sake of Abraham, although the certainty of God fulfilling his promise remains the same whether it is a promise or a covenant. The promise of the land is also amplified here with respect to the extent of the boundaries. Some scholars have suggested that the boundaries here were fulfilled during the reign of Solomon (e.g, Wenham, *Genesis 1–15*, 333; Westermann, *Genesis 12–36*, 181; Mathews, *Genesis 11:27—50:26*, 176). However, Wenham suggests that there is still an element of hyperbole here, because in the days of Solomon, although Israel's boundaries approached the limits mentioned here, it is unlikely to have extended as far west as the river of Egypt (Wenham, *Genesis 1–15*, 333; see also Sarna, *Genesis*, 117).

*The Beginning of the Blessing of Abraham*

Genesis 15 has its emphasis in developing the land and posterity elements of the promise in Gen 12:2-3 in relation to the nationhood of Israel.[66]

## Genesis 17

The continued barrenness of Sarah resulted in Sarah's attempt to beget a descendant for Abraham through her maidservant Hagar (Gen 16:1-16). While establishing the covenant of circumcision as a sign of God's covenant with Abraham and his descendants (Gen 17:1-14), God once again emphasized that the descendant should be through Sarah, and he rejected Ishmael as the heir of the promise (Gen 17:15-21).

In conjunction with this third reiteration of God's promise to Abraham, the promise of posterity is not only restricted to Abraham becoming a great nation (Gen 12:2), but it is also amplified: Abraham shall become a father of many nations, and kings shall come from him (Gen 17:5-6). This promise is commonly understood as being fulfilled not just by the nation of Israel, but also by the descendants of Ishmael (Gen 25:12-18), the descendants of Abraham's concubine Keturah (Gen 25:1-5), and the descendants of Esau (Gen 36:1-19, 31-43).[67] Sarah was also given the same promise in Gen 17:16, the fulfillment of which is perhaps understood to be the nation Israel and the descendants of Esau.[68]

However, this promise of becoming "the father of many nations" has dimensions greater than physical descendants.[69] Paul Williamson argues that the metaphorical usage of אב ("father") to portray the idea of counselor, protector, or benefactor in the Hebrew Bible suggests that Abraham's fatherhood here goes beyond genealogical linkage and implies

---

66. Williamson, *Abraham*, 144.

67. Wenham, *Genesis 16-50*, 161, 165; Hamilton, *Genesis 18-50*, 401; Mathews, *Genesis 11:27—50:26*, 202.

68. Some scholars note the parallel promise made to Sarah and conclude that the nations cannot refer only to the descendants of Abraham by Hagar (i.e., the Ishmaelites) and Keturah but has implications beyond physical descendants (Dumbrell, *Covenant and Creation*, 73; Alexander, "Abraham Re-Assessed," 17-18; Watson, *Paul and the Hermeneutics of Faith*, 210). Alexander notes that the concept of "father" in Genesis 17 most probably is not limited to physical descendants but to all who are circumcised, as well as all the nations who are associated with Abraham, because he is a channel of divine blessing to them.

69. This is further supported by the parallel between Gen 17:4-6 and Gen 35:11, where "a nation and a company of nations" shall come from Jacob. Therefore, physical descendants of Abraham as the only referent is not likely for both Gen 17:4-6 and 35:11. See also pp. 83-87 below on Gen 35:11.

that Abraham shall be a spiritual benefactor of many nations, "the mediator of God's blessing to them."[70] Thus, Williamson argues that the covenant in Genesis 17 is related to the one in Genesis 15. The elements of the Abrahamic promise in Gen 12:2-3 in terms of descendants and land, which is developed in Genesis 15, is further expanded in Genesis 17 in terms of nationhood and royal descendants. The element of the blessing for the nations, which is not developed in Genesis 15, is amplified in Genesis 17 in terms of the multinational dimension of Abraham's fatherhood.[71]

## Genesis 18

The fourth reiteration of the Abrahamic promise differs from the first three in that it is found in the self-deliberation of God as to whether he should disclose his plans to destroy Sodom and Gomorrah to Abraham (Gen 18:17-19).

This reiteration has an important implication about how the nations may be blessed through Abraham (Gen 18:18). Mathews notes that the reason for revealing the imminent destruction of Sodom to Abraham is so that the blessing for the nations may be realized through Abraham. This is because (כִּי) he will instruct his descendants to keep the way of the Lord by doing righteousness and justice, so that his descendants will be "a beacon for the nations."[72] However, Mathews does not elaborate on how the descendants of Abraham would be "a beacon for the nations" in the case of the destruction of Sodom and Gomorrah. Could it be that Abraham might instruct Lot, who is part of his household, "to keep the way of the Lord by doing righteousness and justice," so that Lot may act as a beacon for the people of Sodom and Gomorrah? This is unlikely given the fact that Abraham did not have the opportunity to instruct Lot before the destruction of Sodom and Gomorrah.

---

70. Williamson, *Abraham*, 158-60; see also Sarna, *Genesis*, 124. On the significance of אָב, see Wright, "אָב," *NIDOTTE* 1:219-23.

71. Williamson, *Abraham*, 212-14. See also Watson, *Paul and the Hermeneutics of Faith*, 210-11. While it is true that the multinational and royal dimensions of the covenant are not developed in Genesis 15 but in Genesis 17, Paul Williamson reminds us that the element of inheriting the land must not be overlooked (Gen 17:8). Williamson's reminder is a healthy correction to Alexander's and Sailhamer's sharp distinction between the two covenants (Williamson, *Abraham*, 142-43, 211-12; Alexander, "Abraham Re-Assessed," 14-18; Alexander, *From Paradise to the Promised Land*, 143-49; Sailhamer, *Pentateuch*, 156).

72. Mathews, *Genesis 11:27—50:26*, 223.

*The Beginning of the Blessing of Abraham*

Alternatively, Victor Hamilton suggests that the Sodomites, as one of the nations of the earth, are blessed to have Abraham as their intercessor.[73] More importantly, it is through the intercession of Abraham that Lot is spared from destruction (Gen 19:29). Consequently, the descendants of Lot, the Moabite and the Ammonite *nations* (Gen 19:37-38) owed their existence to Abraham indirectly, and thus they are blessed on account of Abraham.[74] Thus, this reiteration in Gen 18:18 uses גויי הארץ ("nations of the earth") instead of משפחת האדמה ("families of the earth"; Gen 12:3), and the Niphal of ברך in Gen 18:18 bears a passive nuance that is consistent with the corresponding Niphal in Gen 12:3b.[75]

Interestingly, Gen 18:19 associates obedience to Yahweh and moral blamelessness with the fulfillment of the Abrahamic promise. Such a relationship is also seen in the covenant obligations in Gen 17:1-14 as well as the later developments in Gen 22:15-18 and 26:3-5 and the rest of the Pentateuch.[76]

## Genesis 22

The final reiteration of the promise to Abraham in his lifetime is situated at the conclusion of the sacrifice of Isaac (Gen 22:17-18). As a result of Abraham's passing of the test by not withholding his only son, the promise is reiterated by God emphatically with an oath, expressed in the infinitive absolute construction כי־ברך אברכך והרבה ארבה את־זרעך ("indeed, I will surely bless you, and I will surely multiply your offspring").[77] The land promise is implicit in the statement that "your offspring shall possess the gates of his enemies" (Gen 22:17). The blessing for the nations through Abraham (ב,בך in 12:3; 18:18) is now expanded to his descendant(s) (בזרעך in 22:18).[78] All three elements of the initial promise

---

73. Hamilton, *Genesis 18-50*, 18.

74. See also Wolff, "Kerygma," 88.

75. Lee, "The Niphal and Hithpael of ברך," 282, 287-88.

76. See pp. 79-81, 82n89, 88-92 below.

77. The metaphor used here recapitulates the stars of the heavens (cf. Gen 15:5) but uses "the sand (חול) of the shore" instead of "the dust (עפר) of the earth" (cf. Gen 13:16).

78. The wording of Gen 22:18 concerning the blessing for the nations alludes to Gen 18:18 in using the phrase גויי הארץ than to Gen 12:3, which uses משפחת האדמה. "Possessing the gates of the enemies" points forward to the defeat of the Canaanite *nations*, and thus גוי is used here (Lee, "The Niphal and Hithpael of ברך," 282). However, the Hitpael of ברך is used here instead of the Niphal in both Gen 12:3 and Gen 18:18.

# The Blessing of Abraham, the Spirit, and Justification in Galatians

in Gen 12:2–3 (descendants, land, and blessing for the nations) are reiterated here, forming an *inclusio* with the initial promise (Gen 12:2–3).[79] As we noted earlier, the Hitpael of ברך is used in Gen 22:18 in contrast to the Niphal in Gen 12:3 and 18:18, and the phrase in Gen 22:18 may be rendered as "all the nations of the earth shall declare themselves as blessed on account of your offspring."[80]

Most interpreters take זרע ("seed/offspring") and the singular pronominal suffix (איביו "his enemies") in Gen 22:17–18 to be a collective singular.[81] The promise of possessing the gates of the enemies may then be understood as being inaugurated at the conquest of Canaan and fulfilled during the monarchichal period.[82] However, Alexander argues that, while the word זרע is usually used collectively in Genesis, it could also refer to a single individual (e.g., Gen 4:25; 21:13).[83] Alexander strengthens his argument by citing Jack Collins's grammatical analysis that the criterion for discerning whether an instance of זרע is singular or collective is in the number of the pronoun that refers to the term.[84] In the case of Gen 22:17, the singular pronoun "his" (the antecedent being זרע) is used as a suffix to the word "enemies" (איביו). Therefore, it is possible that the זרע ("offspring") here refers to an individual descendant of Abraham.[85]

This understanding of זרע ("offspring") as referring to an individual offspring of Abraham has important implications for the fulfillment of the blessing for the nations. It would imply that "all nations of the earth shall [declare themselves to] be blessed" both on account of Abraham's descendants collectively and on account of this individual descendant (והתברכו בזרעך כל גויי הארץ; Gen 22:18).[86] Who, then, can this

---

79. See also Alexander, "Abraham Re-Assessed," 18; Williamson, *Abraham*, 217–20. Paul Williamson also cites other scholars who mention the *inclusio*.

80. Lee, "The Niphal and Hithpael of ברך," 288–95.

81. The collective singular understanding is reflected in many modern English translations, in which the phrase is rendered as "their enemies" (e.g., NASB, NLT, NKJV, NIV, NRSV). Only KJV and ESV translate the personal pronoun as singular, i.e., "his enemies."

82. See also Walton, *Genesis*, 512.

83. Alexander, "Abraham Re-Assessed," 24–25.

84. Collins, "A Syntactical Note (Genesis 3:15)," 139–48; Alexander, "'Seed' in Genesis," 363–67.

85. Alexander, "'Seed' in Genesis," 365. Alexander adds that, although the first זרע ("offspring") in Gen 22:17 definitely refers to a very large number of descendants, the non-conversive ו in the final clause (וְיָרַשׁ) allows the possibility that the referent of the second זרע in Gen 22:17 is different from the first.

86. Alexander thinks that the nations will be blessed through one of Abraham's

individual descendant be? It may perhaps be seen in the Joseph narrative, in which כל־הארץ ("all the earth") came to Joseph to buy grain during the severe famine (Gen 41:57), and in this way, all the families of the earth were blessed because of Joseph. It is also likely, as Alexander argues, that this descendant is connected with the royal line on which the Genesis narrative is focusing.[87]

It is not entirely clear in the context of Genesis why the nations of the earth would declare themselves as blessed on account of Abraham's offspring. However, given the possibility of an individual offspring associated with the royal lineage being referred here, as well as the development of this motif in the later OT, Gen 22:18 may have an eschatological implication awaiting fulfillment beyond the narrative context of the Pentateuch.[88]

## The Reiterations of the Promise to Isaac

After the death of Abraham, God began to bless Isaac (Gen 25:11). The reiteration of the Abrahamic promise is made twice to Isaac (Gen 26:2–5; 26:24). In the first instance, God commanded Isaac not to leave the land of Canaan for Egypt even though there was a famine in the land (Gen 26:1–2). Since it is the first instance of God's reiteration of the Abrahamic promise to Isaac, all three elements of the initial Abrahamic promise in Gen 12:2–3 are mentioned here. As this reiteration clearly refers to the last reiteration to Abraham in Gen 22:15–18, the wording of Gen 26:4

---

descendants, rather than through all of them collectively (Alexander, "Royal Expectations," 203). However, the rest of the Genesis narrative also describes how other people are blessed because of various descendants of Abraham (e.g., Laban through Jacob, the Egyptians and all peoples of the earth through Joseph). Furthermore, the language of possessing the gates of the enemies also points forward to the conquest of Canaan. Therefore, although this reiteration of the Abrahamic promise may have eschatological implications with regard to its referent to an individual (Gen 22:17), it is not necessary to restrict the accomplishment of the blessing for the nations in Gen 22:18 to only one of Abraham's descendants. See also Mathews, *Genesis 11:27—50:26*, 298–99.

87. Alexander, "Genealogies," 267; idem, "Royal Expectations," 202–6. Alexander demonstrates convincingly the interest in tracing the royal line in the Genesis narrative to Judah. Moreover, the association between the Abrahamic promise (including the blessing for the nations) with a Davidic king continues to be developed in the other texts of the OT. See also Williamson, *Abraham*, 250.

88. Scholars who recognize the eschatological trajectory of the Abrahamic promise in Genesis beyond the Pentateuchal narrative include: Childs, *Introduction*, 150–51; Alexander, "Royal Expectations," 187–212; Sailhamer, "Creation," 89–106.

## The Blessing of Abraham, the Spirit, and Justification in Galatians

concerning the blessing for the nations follows Gen 22:18 exactly, using both the phrase גויי הארץ ("nations of the earth") and the Hitpael of ברך.[89]

The Abrahamic promise is now formally passed on to Isaac. The land promise seems to extend beyond Canaan to the surrounding regions, as is indicated by the plural כל־הארצת האל ("all these lands").[90] Furthermore, the basis of God fulfilling the promise is the oath that he made to Abraham when the latter obeyed God's command in the sacrifice of Isaac (Gen 26:3, 5; cf. 22:17–18).

In obedience to God's instruction not to go down to Egypt, Isaac settled in Gerar, where he was blessed by God and became very rich (Gen 26:6–13). The existing inhabitants of Gerar were unhappy to share the land's resources with Isaac and pressured him to leave (Gen 26:14–21). This situation appears to be a threat to the fulfillment of God's promise. Due to the constraints and limitations of the land, the "fruitfulness" of Isaac's household and livestock would be hampered (cf. Gen 26:22). Eventually when he found a place to settle without contention, God appeared to him and assured him of his presence and the promise to bless and multiply him, a reminiscence of his first appearance to Isaac (Gen 26:24; cf. 26:3–4).[91]

## The Reiterations of the Promise to Jacob

### Genesis 28

After receiving the blessing of the first-born from Isaac by unscrupulous means, Jacob had to escape from Esau's wrath by going to Paddan-Aram where his mother's paternal home was (Gen 27:1—28:5). Shortly prior to his departure, Isaac had formally bestowed the Abrahamic promise on Jacob (Gen 28:3–4).[92] It was on his journey from Beersheba towards Haran

---

89. The verbal allusions include "the oath that I swore" (Gen 26:3; cf. 22:16) and "because Abraham obeyed my voice" (Gen 26:5; cf. 22:18b).

90. Wenham, *Genesis 16–50*, 189; Sarna, *Genesis*, 183.

91. See also Sarna, *Genesis*, 186–87.

92. See also Sarna, *Genesis*, 195, who notes that by the act of blessing Jacob, Isaac confirms and recognizes Jacob as "the true heir of the Abrahamic covenant." The phrase ברכת אברהם ("the blessing of Abraham") in Gen 28:4, which LXX translates as τὴν εὐλογίαν Ἀβρααμ, is the only time it appears in the Hebrew Bible. This is also the phrase used by Paul in Gal 3:14 (ἡ εὐλογία τοῦ Ἀβραάμ), the only time it appears in the NT.

that God appeared in Jacob's dream and reiterated the Abrahamic promise to him (Gen 28:10–15).

As with the first reiteration to Isaac, all three elements (land, descendants, and blessing for the nations) of the Abrahamic promise are also reiterated to Jacob in his first encounter with God. The wording of Gen 28:14 concerning the blessing for the nations is the exact replica of Gen 12:3: ונברכו בך כל משפחת האדמה ("and all the families of the earth shall be blessed through you"), with the addition of ובזרעך ("and through your offspring") at the end of the phrase. The form of Gen 28:14 would therefore show the link and continuity of this reiteration with Gen 12:3.[93]

An interesting amplification is made to the promise of descendants in that they will spread out "... to the west and to the east and to the north and to the south..." (Gen 28:14). This description alludes to the creational mandate to fill the earth (Gen 1:28; 9:1–7), and it supports the notion that the mandate has been passed on to Abraham and his descendants. However, Westermann suggests that the mention of the four compass points is more suited to the promise of the land in Gen 13:14.[94] Although the mention of the compass points in Gen 28:14 is reminiscent of Gen 13:14, the difference between the two is that there is a limit to the extent of the land in the latter ("all that you can see"), but the former does not have such a limit. Therefore, the spreading out of the descendants described in Gen 28:14 is more than a description of the extent of the land, but has implications on the universality of Jacob's descendants.

## Genesis 35

After a few decades at Paddan-Aram, Jacob left to return to the land of his fathers at the command of God (Gen 31:3). When Jacob first arrived in the land of Canaan, he dwelt in Shechem (Gen 33:18), but later he moved to Bethel where God had formerly appeared to him (Gen 35:1–7). The massacre at Shechem had triggered fear in Jacob that his household might be exterminated by the inhabitants of the land (Gen 34:30). In response to

---

93. As Gen 28:14 is the last reiteration of the Abrahamic blessing for the nations in Genesis, it is most likely that the wording of Gen 12:3 is replicated here as an *inclusio*. This is further supported by the allusion to the creational mandate to fill the earth (see above), drawing it closer to the language used in the Table of Nations in Genesis 10, where the word משפחה ("family") appears five times. The reiteration in Gen 28:14 also captures the development of the means of blessing from Abraham himself (בובך in Gen 12:3; 18:18) to his offspring (בזרעך) in Gen 22:14 and 26:4.

94. Westermann, *Genesis 12–36*, 455.

this, God appeared to Jacob for the second time at Bethel to reassure him that his descendants would be plentiful and that the land would be given to him and his descendants (Gen 35:9–12).[95]

In this second reiteration of the Abrahamic promise to Jacob, God changes Jacob's name to "Israel" (Gen 35:10) and promises him that "a nation and a company of nations shall come from you, and kings shall come from your own body" (Gen 35:11 ESV). The promise to Abraham that "kings shall come from you" is now also given to Jacob (Gen 35:11; cf. 17:6). The promise that "a nation and a company of nations shall come from you" is also reminiscent of Isaac's blessing to Jacob prior to his departure to Paddan-Aram (Gen 35:11; cf. 28:3).[96] The land promise is also reaffirmed in Gen 35:12.

Walton observes the parallels between the theophanies to Abraham (Genesis 15, 17) and Jacob (Genesis 28, 35):[97]

| Gen 15:7–17 and 28:13–15 | Gen 17:1–8 and 35:10–12 |
|---|---|
| Identification of God as יהוה | Identification of God as אל שדי |
| Ratification of covenant for Abraham and first promise of covenant blessing for Jacob | Indication of acceptance of the covenant with change of name |
| Emphasis on giving of land | Emphasis on many descendants, nations, and kings coming through the patriarch |

While some may understand the fulfillment of Abraham becoming "the father of many nations" to take place through the descendants of Ishmael, the descendants of Keturah, and the descendants of Esau,[98] the fulfillment of Jacob becoming "a nation and a company of nations" is puzzling. The twelve sons of Jacob multiplied to be the twelve tribes of Israel,

---

95. This is the second time that God appeared to Jacob and reiterated the Abrahamic promise. Genesis records a few other times in which God appeared to Jacob: (1) at Paddan-Aram, instructing him to return to his father's land in Canaan (Gen 31:3, 11–13); (2) before he reached the land of Seir, with no specified content of the vision (Gen 32:1); (3) at the brook of Jabbok, where Jacob wrestled with God (Gen 32:24–30); and (4) at Shechem, instructing him to go to Bethel (Gen 35:1).

96. The difference between Isaac's blessing and God's promise here is that עם ("people") is used in the former, while גוי ("nation") is used in the latter. For the significance on the use of these two words, see p. 85n101 below.

97. Walton, *Genesis*, 461. See also Sarna, *Genesis*, 241–42; Williamson, *Abraham*, 168n85; Rapp, *Jakob in Bet-el*, 39–40.

98. See the section on "Genesis 17" above.

but they are still one nation. So what does קְהַל גּוֹיִם ("a company of nations") refer to?

Although Victor Hamilton thinks that גּוֹיִם ("nations") in Gen 35:11 refers to the tribes of Israel, it more likely refers to non-Israelite nations for the following reasons.[99] First, since Abraham as "the father of many nations" (Gen 17:4-6) is a development of the blessing for the nations (Gen 12:3) and it has dimensions beyond the physical descendants of Abraham, Jacob becoming "a nation and a company of nations" (Gen 35:11) should also be understood in the same light.[100] Second, גּוֹיִם is consistently used in the Pentateuch to refer to nations of various ethnicity as political entities.[101]

Therefore, Gen 35:11 states that, although kings will be from the direct descendants of Jacob (מֵחֲלָצֶיךָ, "from your own loin"), both the physical descendants of Jacob as a nation and a multitude of nations will be associated with Israel.[102] While Abraham becoming "the father of many nations" may still possibly be fulfilled through the other physical descendants of Abraham, Jacob becoming "a nation and a company of nations" can only be fulfilled beyond his physical descendants.[103]

---

99. Hamilton, *Genesis 18-50*, 381. For other reasons why Hamilton's proposal is unconvincing, see my arguments in Lee, "Genesis 35:11," 468-70.

100. See the section on "Genesis 17" above.

101. Lee, "Genesis 35:11," 469. Genesis 35:11 alludes to Gen 28:3 and it is reiterated in Gen 48:4, but these two instances has the phrase קְהַל עַמִּים ("a company of people") instead. In the Pentateuch, עַמִּים can include both people of the same race (e.g., Gen 17:14; 25:8; Exod 30:33) or of a different race (e.g., Gen 27:29; Exod 15:14). Although קְהַל עַמִּים in Gen 28:3 and 48:4 may have a broader semantic range and may mean either "a company of people" or "a company of nations," קְהַל גּוֹיִם has a narrower meaning: "a company of nations." Furthermore, קְהַל עַמִּים ("a company of peoples") in Ezek 23:24; 32:3 and קְהַל גּוֹיִם ("a company of nations") in Jer 50:9 refer to the armies formed from a coalition of various ethnic groups or nations (Thompson, *Jeremiah*, 734; McKane, *Jeremiah*, 2:1251, 1259; Lundbom, *Jeremiah 37-52*, 383; Zimmerli, *Ezekiel 1*, 475; idem, *Ezekiel 2*, 154, 159; Block, *Ezekiel 1-24*, 748-52; idem, *Ezekiel 25-48*, 202, 205).

102. See also Alexander, "Abraham Re-Assessed," 17-18; Williamson, *Abraham*, 168-69. It may be argued that the "company of nations" coming from Jacob refers to the two kingdoms of Judah and Israel. However, this is unlikely because the noun קָהָל implies a multitude being assembled (cf. BDB 874; *HALOT* 3:1079-80). Two nations can hardly be regarded as "a multitude of nations." Furthermore, later on in the OT, the prophets look forward to the unification of kingdoms of Israel and Judah at the eschatological restoration (e.g., Jer 3:18; Ezek 37:15-28). Therefore, it is unlikely that the "company of nations" refers to the two divided kingdoms.

103. Nonetheless, I have argued above that even in the case of Gen 17:4-6, Abraham becoming "the father of many nations" has implications beyond his physical descendants (see the section on "Genesis 17" above).

## The Blessing of Abraham, the Spirit, and Justification in Galatians

Both Genesis 17 and 35 are not clear as to how the multinational dimension of the promise is related to Abraham and Jacob. There are also no apparent indications in the Pentateuch, or the history of Israel in the OT, of the fulfillment of "a company of nations" coming from Israel. However, one of the possible ways in which the nations may be related to Jacob is in their subjection to the rule of Israel's king (Gen 49:10; cf. Gen 27:29). It is noteworthy that Gen 49:10 occurs in a prophetic context, indicated by the literary marker—"in the last days" (באחרית הימים; Gen 49:1).[104] Furthermore, when this literary marker is used in the rest of the Pentateuch (Num 24:14; Deut 4:30; 31:29), the context always alludes to the Abrahamic promise.[105] Therefore, considering the non-fulfillment of Jacob becoming "a nation and a company of nations" (Gen 35:11) in the Pentateuch and the history of Israel in the OT and the relationship of Gen 35:11 with Gen 49:10, the promise in Gen 35:11 may then have

---

104. באחרית הימים ("in the last days") in Gen 49:1 may well have eschatological overtones (Sailhamer, "Creation," 92–93; Dempster, *Dominion*, 90). Other than the Pentateuch, באחרית הימים occurs 10 times in the latter prophets in eschatological contexts (Isa 2:2; Jer 23:20; Ezek 38:16; Dan 10:14; Hos 3:5; Mic 4:1, etc.). Three of these instances in the Pentateuch occur in poetic texts (Gen 49:1; Num 24:14; Deut 31:29), in which "the central figure (Jacob, Balaam, Moses) calls together God's people (imperatives) and proclaims (cohortatives) 'what will happen' 'in the last days'" (Sailhamer, "Creation," 92). In most cases, the term באחרית הימים has a "specific eschatological meaning, but in some cases it may simply refer to the distant future. The attempt to understand most of the references in an indeterminate future sense neglects the canonical context" (Dempster, *Dominion*, 90n50).

105. Sailhamer, *Pentateuch*, 405–9; idem, "Creation," 93–104. Sailhamer notes the allusions specific to the Abrahamic blessing for the nations and its association with royal expectations as follows: (1) In Jacob's blessings for his twelve sons, the promise of kings coming from the patriarch is prophesied to come from Judah (Gen 49:10; cf. Gen 17:6; 35:11); (2) In Balaam's oracles, Num 24:9b alludes to Gen 12:3a (cf. Gen 27:29), and Num 23:21, 24; 24:7–9; 17–19 to the prophecy of a ruler from Judah (Gen 49:10); and (3) The MT reading of Deut 32:43 (הרנינו גוים עמו, "rejoice, O nations, his people") may allude to the blessing for the nations (Gen 12:3). Based on MT, Sailhamer thinks that Deut 32:43 shows the broadening of the concept of God's people to include the nations (Sailhamer, *Pentateuch*, 476). However, he has not addressed the problems that arise from the textual variants: 4QDeut[q] reads "rejoice, O heavens, with him" (הרנינו שמים עמו), and the LXX attests to both cola (εὐφράνθητε οὐρανοὶ ἅμα αὐτῷ . . . εὐφράνθητε ἔθνη μετὰ τοῦ λαοῦ αὐτοῦ . . . "Rejoice, O heavens, with him . . . Rejoice, O nations, with his people . . ."). Therefore, while Deuteronomy 32 certainly alludes to the land promise and other motifs in the Pentateuch, the allusion to the blessing for the nations is best taken to be uncertain here. For those favoring the Qumran reading, see *BHQ*; ESV; NLT; CEV; Christensen, *Deuteronomy*, 820; Biddle, *Deuteronomy*, 481–82.

eschatological implications related to the fulfillment of the Abrahamic blessings for the nations.[106]

## Genesis 46

The third reiteration of the Abrahamic promise to Jacob occurred at Beer-sheba, where God instructed him to bring his family to Egypt in order to survive the famine (Gen 46:1–4). In relation to the Abrahamic promise, God assured Jacob that: (1) it is in Egypt that he will make Jacob into a nation (cf. Gen 12:2); and (2) he will bring Jacob back to the land of Canaan (Gen 46:2–4; cf. Gen 12:7).[107]

## The Reiterations of the Promise by the Patriarchs

All three patriarchs recapitulated the Abrahamic promise at some point in their lives. When Abraham's servant asked if he should bring Isaac back to Haran if the prospective wife of Isaac from the clan of Terah was not willing to come to Canaan, Abraham objected firmly, recapitulating the promise that God swore with an oath to give the land of Canaan to his descendants (Gen 24:5–7; cf. 12:1–7; 22:16).

Isaac's first blessing bestowed on Jacob is reminiscent of Gen 12:3. Isaac assents that anyone who curses Jacob shall be cursed, and anyone who blesses him shall be blessed (Gen 27:29).[108] In his second blessing of Jacob, although Isaac prayed that Jacob and his descendants would inherit the blessing of Abraham, he only highlighted the multiplication of offspring and the possession of the land, with the blessing for the nations as only implicit within the blessing of Abraham (Gen 28:3–4). However, it is noteworthy that God's promise that Jacob will become "a company of peoples/nations" in Gen 35:11 and Gen 48:4 is prefigured in Gen 28:3.

While facing the threat of a possible imminent attack from Esau, Jacob prayed to God for protection, holding onto the fact that it was God who commanded him to return to Canaan and onto God's promise that his

---

106. This concept of the nations' subjugation to Israel's king is developed in Psalm 72 in relation to the Abrahamic blessing for the nations (see ch. 4 below).

107. See also Sarna, *Genesis*, 313.

108. Gen 27:29 differs from Gen 12:3 as follows: (1) the plural אֹרְרֶיךָ ("those who curse you") is used here instead of the singular מְקַלֶּלְךָ ("the one who curse you") in Gen 12:3; (2) the active voice in Gen 12:3 is now in passive voice. However, these differences are not significant to the overall meaning of the promise.

descendants should be countless like sand (Gen 32:9–12; cf. 31:3, 28:14). Before giving his blessing to Joseph's sons, Manasseh and Ephraim, Jacob recalls the second theophany at Luz, reiterating the essentials of the promise: (1) the command to be fruitful and multiply; (2) becoming a company of peoples/nations; and (3) the gift of the land as an everlasting possession (Gen 48:3–4). However, he did not mention the promise regarding kings coming forth from him (Gen 48:3–4; cf. 35:9–12), the blessing for the nations, or the other details of the first theophany (Gen 28:13–15).

## The Development of Genesis 12:2–3 in the Pentateuch

The Abrahamic promise in Gen 12:2–3 was only reiterated to Abraham, Isaac, and Jacob. It was not formally passed on to any of the twelve sons of Jacob as it was formally passed on to Isaac (Gen 26:3–4) and Jacob (Gen 28:13–14). Throughout the rest of the Pentateuch (the Joseph story from Genesis 37 to Deuteronomy), the Abrahamic promise is repeatedly expressed as the oath/covenant Yahweh made with Abraham, Isaac and Jacob.[109] In continuity with the Abrahamic covenant, a covenant is now made at Sinai with the twelve tribes of Israel, the people of Israel as a whole, in which they shall be Yahweh's people and he shall be their God (Exod 19:1—20:21; 24:1–11; cf. Gen 17:7–8; Exod 6:7).[110]

Therefore, the covenant at Sinai becomes the focus of the rest of the Pentateuch. Sailhamer summarizes the essence of the Sinai covenant as: (1) God comes to dwell with Israel; (2) Israel is a chosen people; (3) God gives Israel the land; (4) Israel must obey God's will; (5) salvation or judgment is contingent on Israel's obedience.[111]

## The Promise of the Land in the Pentateuch

From the narrative plot of Exodus to Deuteronomy, we can see that the Pentateuch emphasizes the promise of the land.[112] The very reason for the

---

109. Gen 50:24; Exod 6:3–4, 8; 33:1; Lev 26:42; Num 32:11; Deut 1:8; 6:10; 9:5; 29:13; 30:20; 34:4. Yahweh was also addressed as "the God of Abraham, Isaac and Jacob" (Exod 3:6, 15, 16; 4:5; 6:3).

110. See also Lev 11:45; 26:12.

111. Sailhamer, *Pentateuch*, 27.

112. See also Preuss, *Old Testament Theology*, 1:117–20. Preuss notes that "the full arch of the Pentateuchal tradition extends from the promise of the land, to the ancestors, to the Moses group, to Israel coming into existence, and to the realization that

exodus was to begin the fulfillment of the land promise (Exod 2:23–25; 3:7–8). The rest of the Pentateuch describes: (1) the giving of the law, which prescribes how the Israelites should live as the people of God and how they should live in the promised land; and (2) the journey towards the promised land.

Nonetheless, the promise of possessing the land remains unfulfilled at the end of Deuteronomy as a result of the Israelites' rebellion against Yahweh (Num 13–14; Deut 1:19–45). Deuteronomy concludes the forty years of wandering in the wilderness with a covenant renewal in preparation of the conquest of the promised land, which will only begin to be fulfilled in the book of Joshua (Josh 1:6; 21:43–45).[113]

## The Promise of Descendants in the Pentateuch

By the end of Genesis, the promise of descendants is already beginning to be fulfilled. After Jacob settled in Goshen, his descendants were fruitful and multiplied greatly (Gen 47:27). By the time the generation of Joseph and his brothers died, the people were growing exceedingly in numbers, so that the land of Egypt was filled with them (Exod 1:6).[114]

Both the numbering of the Israelites in the wilderness show more than 600,000 males above twenty years old (Num 2:32; 26:51). While looking over the people of Israel camping in the valley, Balaam exclaimed how uncountable the descendants of Jacob were, which is reminiscent of the promise that Jacob's descendants should be like the dust of the earth (Num 23:10; cf. Gen 28:14). In Moses' recounting of the forty years in the wilderness at the beginning of Deuteronomy, he also reminds the Israelites of how God had made them as numerous as the stars of the sky from the seventy persons who went down to Egypt (Deut 10:22).

Although the fulfillment of a vast number of descendants had begun to be realized, other aspects of the promise of descendants have yet to be realized: that the descendant(s) would "possess the gates of the enemies" (Gen 22:18); that they would "spread out to the west and to the east and

---

even these promises had found their fulfillment (Josh. 21:43–45; 23:15—Deuteronomistic) with the reaching and possession of the land" (Preuss, *Old Testament Theology*, 1:119).

113. Waltke and Yu, *Old Testament Theology*, 512–13.

114. See also Waltke and Yu, *Old Testament Theology*, 350, who, noting that Exod 1:1–7 is a janus that connects Exodus to Genesis, claim that the passage "looks back to God's fulfillment of his promise to Abraham to grant him innumerable descendants."

to the north and to the south" (Gen 28:14); and that there would be "a company of nations" coming out of Jacob (Gen 35:11).

## The Blessing for the Nations in the Pentateuch

Among the three elements (i.e., land, descendants, and blessing for the nations) of the Abrahamic promise, the least developed in the Pentateuch is the blessing for the nations. Nonetheless, there is a clear development of this promise in the Joseph narrative. The sovereign hand of God in placing Joseph as governor over the land of Egypt seven years before the great famine was not just to ensure the preservation of the posterity of Jacob, but it was also for the benefit of the other peoples. כל־הארץ ("all [the peoples of] the earth") came to Egypt to buy grain from Joseph because the famine was very severe (Gen 41:57). In this way, כל גויי הארץ ("all the nations of the earth") were blessed in Joseph, the offspring of Abraham.[115]

Christopher Wright argues that the Abrahamic blessing for the nations is developed in Exod 19:4–6, where Israel shall be "a kingdom of priests" if they keep Yahweh's covenant. Israel, as the people of Yahweh,

> would have the historical task of bringing the knowledge of God to the nations, and bringing the nations to the means of atonement with God. The Abrahamic task of being a means of blessing to the nations also put them in the role of priests in the midst of the nations. Just as it was the role of priests to bless the Israelites, so it would be the role of Israel as a whole ultimately to be a blessing to the nations.[116]

Wright continues to explain that in Exod 19:5, covenant obedience is not a condition for Israel to become Yahweh's people or their deliverance from Egypt, but rather a condition for the fulfillment of their role as "a kingdom of priests and a holy nation."[117]

---

115. See also Wenham, *Exploring*, 156. Wenham lists other minor examples where nations are blessed by Abraham, such as Abraham rescuing the people and property of Sodom (Gen 14:11–24) and interceding for Sodom and the people of Gerar (Gen 18:22–33; 20:17).

116. Wright, *Mission of God*, 331. Although Motyer does not think that Israel's priesthood implies her mediatory role among the nations, Wright has demonstrated adequately the parallel between the role of the priests among the Israelites and Israel's priestly role among the nations (Motyer, *Exodus*, 199n8; Wright, *Mission of God*, 330–33).

117. Wright, *Mission of God*, 333.

## The Beginning of the Blessing of Abraham

Deuteronomy continues to portray Israel's responsibility as a light to the nations both positively and negatively, in order to point the nations to the knowledge of Yahweh (Deut 4:6–8; 28:9–10; 29:22–28). This is an important development in the backdrop of the alienation of the whole human race from God (Gen 1–11), although the blessing for the nations through Israel remains unfulfilled from Exodus to Deuteronomy.[118]

Two reasons have been offered as to why the blessing for the nations was not fulfilled in the Pentateuch. Wenham suggests that the blessing of the nations is very little developed in the rest of the Pentateuch not because it has been forgotten, but "because all the nations with whom Israel comes into contact oppose her."[119] On the other hand, Sailhamer proposes that "the covenant at Sinai failed to restore God's blessing to humanity because Israel failed to trust God and obey his will."[120]

Wenham's suggested reason may be one of the possible explanations for the non-fulfillment of the blessing of the nations in the Pentateuch. However, in view of the relationship between the Abrahamic promise in Gen 12:2–3 and the primal divine intention to bless humankind, the blessing of all the nations of the earth through Abraham would entail a fuller and more universal fulfillment in the future beyond the Pentateuchal narrative. Therefore, Wenham has yet to consider the universal scope of the blessing for the nations, and his suggested reason is not likely to be the main reason of the non-fulfillment.

Sailhamer's proposed reason links the fulfillment of the Abrahamic promise closely with covenant loyalty and bears affinity to Christopher Wright's view that the fulfillment of Israel's priestly role to bring blessings to the nations depended on their covenant obedience. Similarly, Wisdom argues that "the continuation of covenant loyalty on the part of Abraham's descendants" will result in "the fulfillment of the promised blessing to all nations" (Gen 18:19).[121] Israel's failure in her covenant responsibilities in the Pentateuch is already apparent in the golden calf incident (Exod 32) and the worship of Baal at Peor (Num 25). Nonetheless, Sailhamer points out that God's promise to restore the original divine blessing would

---

118. Alexander, *From Paradise to the Promised Land*, 265–80.

119. Wenham, *Exploring*, 157. Wenham explains that whoever blesses Israel will be blessed, and whoever curses Israel will be cursed (cf. Gen 12:3a; 27:29b; Num 24:9b). Therefore, the nations had not been blessed because their opposition to Israel is likened to cursing Israel.

120. Sailhamer, *Pentateuch*, 27.

121. Wisdom, *Blessing*, 31.

ultimately succeed because God would "one day give to Israel a heart to trust and obey him" (Deut 30:1–10).[122]

However, Deuteronomy also portrays another perspective on covenant loyalty and the fulfillment of the patriarchal promises. On the one hand, obedience will bring blessings (Deut 28:1–14), and disobedience will bring curses and judgment, resulting in the "reversal" of the fulfillment of the patriarchal promise (Deut 28:15–68). Disobedience will cause the Israelites not to be fruitful and prosperous in their land (Deut 28:18). Their numbers will dwindle to very few, even though they were numerous like the stars before (Deut 28:62). They will also lose the possession of the promised land (Deut 28:63–64). On the other hand, imminent victory in the conquest of the land is not due to their righteousness but to the wickedness of the nations and the faithfulness of God in fulfilling his promise to the patriarchs (Deut 9:4–5).

Therefore, although the failure of Israel may be one of the reasons contributing to the non-fulfillment of the blessing for the nations in the Pentateuch, this promise will still be fulfilled in the future regardless of Israel's loyalty or failure. This would then open up the possibility of God using other means of fulfilling the promise to bless the nations besides the covenant loyalty of Israel. In this manner, the Pentateuch leaves the blessing for the nations as unfulfilled and open to further development.

## Conclusion

Literary devices such as the תולדות formula, the *Leitwörter*, and the narrative cycles of the primeval narrative (Gen 1–11) clearly and inextricably link the patriarchal narrative (Gen 12–50) to the primeval narrative. These thematic and structural links also show that the Abrahamic promise in Gen 12:1–3 is a reaffirmation of God's original intention to bless humankind (Gen 1:28; cf. Gen 9:1).[123] It is a reconciliatory initiative taken by God in response to the persistent alienation of humans from God in the primeval narrative. Therefore, the blessing for the nations by God through Abraham is the climax of the Abrahamic promise. This fundamental element of the Abrahamic promise is not only present in the last reiteration

---

122. Sailhamer, *Pentateuch*, 27.

123. See also Clines, *Theme*, 30, who notes that "the promise or blessing is both the divine initiative in a world where human initiatives always lead to disaster, and a re-affirmation of the primal divine intentions for man."

of the promise to Abraham but also in the first reiteration of the promise to Isaac and Jacob respectively.

I have argued on contextual and grammatical grounds that the force of the Niphal of ברך (Gen 12:3; 18:18; 28:14) is passive, and the Hitpael of ברך (Gen 22:18; 26:4) is estimative-declarative, an indirect reflexive rather than a direct reflexive. Thus, the nations "shall be blessed" by God on account of Abraham (Gen 12:3), and they "shall declare themselves as blessed" by God on account of his offspring (Gen 22:18; 26:4). God is the source of the blessing, while Abraham and his offspring will be the channel by which the blessing is bestowed on the nations.

The Abrahamic blessing for the nations is developed in two important ways in the Genesis narrative. First, the means by which the nations shall be blessed is extended from Abraham to his offspring (זרע) (Gen 22:18; 26:4; 28:14). This offspring very possibly refers to one specific individual, who is associated with the royal line of Judah. This singular interpretation of the offspring (זרע) in Gen 22:18 not only has a grammatical basis, but it is also backed by how Gen 22:18 is developed in other OT texts.

Second, Abraham will not only be the father of the nation of Israel, but also the father of many nations (Gen 17:5–6). Similarly, Jacob will not only become a nation, but also "a company of nations" (Gen 35:11). As this promise of Jacob becoming "a company of nations" is not fulfilled in the Pentateuch or in the history of Israel in the OT, it may thus have eschatological implications in its fulfillment. The Genesis narrative is not entirely clear as to how other nations will be associated with Abraham and Jacob. Nonetheless, there is a hint that these nations may be associated with the patriarchs in their subjugation to the king of Israel, a descendant from the tribe of Judah (Gen 49:10; cf. Gen 27:29).

Although the promise of abundant posterity is beginning to be fulfilled at the end of Genesis, the promise of the land and the blessing for the nations remain unfulfilled in the Pentateuch.[124] With so much of the Abrahamic promise remaining unfulfilled in the Pentateuch, it is no wonder Clines proposes that the theme of the Pentateuch to be "the partial fulfillment—which implies also the partial non-fulfillment—of the promise to or blessing of the patriarchs."[125] Nonetheless, the Pentateuch continually portrays Yahweh, the God of the covenant, as the faithful one who would bring to pass all that he had promised the patriarchs. Therefore, the non-fulfillment of the Abrahamic blessing for the nations in the Pentateuch

---

124. See also Mann, "'All the Families of the Earth,'" 350.
125. Clines, *Theme*, 30.

leaves it open for further development, and the Pentateuch looks forward to the fulfillment of the Abrahamic promise in the future.[126] With this in view, the following chapters will continue to explore the development of the Abrahamic blessing for the nations in other OT texts, early Judaism, and the NT, as well as its relationship with the promise of the Spirit in these three periods. These investigations will then provide the background for us to explore the reason for Paul's association of the Spirit with the blessing of Abraham in Gal 3:14.

---

126. See also Childs, *Introduction*, 151; Sailhamer, *Pentateuch*, 27; Wenham, *Exploring*, 157.

# 4 The Spirit's Role in the Blessing of Abraham

*Development in Other Old Testament Texts*

IN CHAPTER 3, WE have seen that the Abrahamic promise of blessing for the nations remains unfulfilled in the Pentateuch. The open-ended nature of this element of the Abrahamic blessing therefore allows it to be developed further in the OT. In this chapter, we shall examine Ps 72:17 and Jer 4:2, the two major texts that allude to the Abrahamic promise of blessing for the nations in the later OT, as well as Zech 8:13, which might allude to Gen 12:2–3, in order to trace how this motif is further developed.

As this study seeks to understand Paul's juxtaposition of the blessing of Abraham and the promise of the Spirit in Gal 3:14, I will also be tracing the motif of the promise of the Spirit in the prophets in this chapter. The phrase, "promise of the Spirit" (ἡ ἐπαγγελία τοῦ πνεύματος), which appears only in the NT (Acts 2:33; Gal 3:14; cf. Eph 1:13 τὸ πνεῦμα τῆς ἐπαγγελίας, "Spirit of promise"), refers to the promise of the Spirit in the prophets, and the passages in the prophets that mention the promise of the Spirit are Isa 32:15; 44:3; Ezek 36:26–27; 37:14; 39:29; Joel 2:28–29 [MT 3:1–2].[1] We will survey these passages and then focus our attention on Isa 44:3 and Ezek 36:26–27, as these two texts are closely related to the key concepts in Gal 3:1–14.[2]

A major issue in this chapter is: what do these Spirit texts, which are primarily concerned with the restoration of the (Sinai-)covenantal blessings to Israel, have to do with the Abrahamic promise or with the nations? Therefore, we shall begin this chapter by first examining the relationship between the Abrahamic and Mosaic covenants, as well as the new covenant

---

1. Acts 2:33 clearly refers to the event in Acts 2:1–13, which Peter declares to be the fulfillment of the prophecy of the outpouring of the Spirit in Joel (Acts 2:14–21). See also Barrett, *Acts*, 1:149; Fitzmyer, *Acts*, 259; Bock, *Acts*, 131.

2. Some of the key concepts that Isaiah 44 and Ezekiel 36 have in common with Gal 3:1–14 are the restoration of blessings, the Spirit, obedience to the law, and the use of covenantal language.

The Blessing of Abraham, the Spirit, and Justification in Galatians

in Jer 31:31–34. We shall see from our investigation that not only is there continuity in these three covenants, but also that the Abrahamic covenant is the foundation of the Sinai and new covenants. We will also look into the relationship of Israel and the nations as the people of Yahweh, and whether the promises made to Israel in the prophets have anything to do with the destiny of the nations.

## Covenant, Israel, and the Nations

### The Continuity of the Abrahamic, Mosaic, and New Covenants

*The Abrahamic Covenant*

There are two passages in Genesis that speak about Yahweh making a covenant (ברית) with Abraham: Gen 15:7–21 and Gen 17:1–14. In both cases, the covenant was made in response to Abraham's uncertainty regarding the fulfillment of Yahweh's initial promise to him in Gen 12:2–3, 7.[3] The covenant in Gen 15:7–21 regarding the gift of the land is a response to Abraham's uncertainty about whether he would possess the land that was promised to him (Gen 15:8; cf. 12:7; 13:14–17). The covenant in Gen 17:1–14 is in response to Abraham's doubt about the fulfillment of the promise of progeny, manifested in his consent to Sarah's proposal to bear children by Hagar (Gen 16:1–16). As McComiskey puts it, "the major elements of the promise gain the status of covenantal affirmations in Genesis 15 and 17."[4]

It is important to note the specific content of the covenant in Gen 17:1–8. Yahweh declares, "*I will establish my covenant between me and you and your offspring after you throughout their generations for an everlasting covenant, to be God to you and to your offspring after you . . . and I will be their God*" (Gen 17:7–8 ESV; emphasis added). "*Yahweh as the God of Abraham and his descendants, and they as his people*" is the specific content of the covenant, and the covenant is everlasting. The three elements of the Abrahamic promise, namely numerous descendants, land, and blessing for the nations, are affirmed in the divine speech (Gen 17:2–8),[5] while circumcision is the sign of the covenant (Gen 17:10–12).

---

3. See also Dumbrell, *Covenant and Creation*, 54–55, 72; McComiskey, *Covenants of Promise*, 60.

4. McComiskey, *Covenants of Promise*, 61.

5. See pp. 73–75, 77–78 above.

Although ברית ("covenant") does not occur in Genesis 22, Hahn explains that "interpreters both ancient and modern have correctly recognized that the solemn, divine oath of Genesis 22:15–18 ratifies a covenant with Abraham."[6] It is in this covenant that the blessing for the nations is elevated to the level of a covenant obligation with the divine oath.

## The Mosaic Covenant

When Israel was enslaved in Egypt, the reason Yahweh wanted to deliver Israel from Egypt and lead them into the land of Canaan was his covenant with Abraham, Isaac, and Jacob (Exod 6:2–8). By doing so, Yahweh is fulfilling his covenantal promises to take *Israel as his people and be their God*, as well as give them the land of Canaan (Exod 6:7–8; cf. Gen 15:18–21; 17:7–8).[7] Exodus 19–24 tells of the covenant that Yahweh made with the nation of Israel after the exodus. If Israel obeys Yahweh and keeps the covenant, they shall be to Yahweh "a kingdom of priests and a holy nation" (Exod 19:5–6). If Israel is obedient, Yahweh promises to drive out the people of Canaan, so that Israel may possess the land (Exod 23:20–33). The promise to make Abraham into a nation is now fulfilled (cf. Gen 12:2), while the promise to possess the land is at hand (cf. Gen 12:2, 7).

However, the Abrahamic blessing for the nations is not apparent in the Sinai covenant, although there might be a hint of this element in the priestly mediatory role of Israel among the nations (Exod 19:6).[8] Nonetheless, the connection between the priestly role of Israel with the Abrahamic blessing for the nations is not obvious, but indirect. McComiskey argues that the apparent absence of the Abrahamic blessing for the nations in the Sinai covenant "does not imply the abrogation of that element." Rather, the focus of the Sinai covenant is on the nation of Israel, and therefore it only extracts "those elements of the promise that were of particular importance for that time," namely the establishment of the nation of Israel and the gift of the land.[9]

---

6. Hahn, *Kinship by Covenant*, 111.

7. This divine-human relationship between Yahweh and Israel is also repeated in Exod 29:45; Lev 26:12; Deut 26:17–18.

8. Dumbrell, *Covenant and Creation*, 90; Beecher, *Prophets*, 222–25. Whether Israel is to act as an active or passive mediator does not directly pertain to our study. Whichever it may be, Israel will serve as Yahweh's vehicle to point the nations to the knowledge of Yahweh (cf. Deut 4:6–8; 28:9–10; 29:22–28).

9. McComiskey, *Covenants of Promise*, 71.

# The Blessing of Abraham, the Spirit, and Justification in Galatians

Before the second generation of Israelites entered Canaan, God made a covenant with the people of Israel at Moab, other than the one he had made with them at Sinai (Deut 29:1). According to Hahn's analysis, the Sinai covenant is a kinship-type covenant, while the Deuteronomic covenant is treaty-type covenant, in which "[Israel's] *sonship* is emphasized in the former, [and] their *vassalage* is emphasized in the latter."[10] I shall refer to these two closely related covenants as the Mosaic covenant. According to the Mosaic covenantal stipulations, blessings such as the prosperity in the land in terms of the fruitfulness of crops, livestock and human population, and the defeat of enemies, are promised if Israel obeys the covenantal stipulations (Exod 23:20–33; Lev 26:1–13; Deut 28:1–14). These blessings are a sign of Yahweh's favor on his people in the covenantal relationship.[11] On the other hand, if they are disobedient, covenantal curses, the reversal of the covenantal blessings such as defeat by enemies, natural disasters, epidemics, agricultural failure, unsuccessful reproduction of humans and livestock, will certainly come upon Israel (Lev 26:14–39; Deut 28:15–57). Persistent rebellion against Yahweh will incur serious covenantal curses, eventually leading to death, depopulation, and expulsion from the land (Lev 26:27–33; Deut 28:58–68). Nonetheless, restoration of the covenantal blessings is promised when Israel repents (Lev 26:40–45; Deut 30:1–10).

From the above discussion, the continuity between the Abrahamic and Mosaic covenants is clearly established. The Mosaic covenant is closely related to the Abrahamic covenant in terms of the divine-human covenantal relationship, the establishment of the nation, and the gift of the land. The Abrahamic covenant made with the patriarchs is now reconstituted as the Mosaic covenant for the nation of Israel, not as a new covenant *replacing* the former one, but *in continuity* with the patriarchal covenant (cf. Gen 17:7–8; Exod 6:7–8; Lev 26:42; Deut 4:31).[12]

---

10. Hahn, *Kinship by Covenant*, 74 (emphasis in original).

11. We will discuss in detail the correlation between blessing and the divine-human relationship in ch. 6.

12. See also Beecher, *Prophets*, 224; McComiskey, *Covenants of Promise*, 66–72; Dohmen, "Der Sinaibund," 75–78; Williamson, *Sealed with an Oath*, 94. This reconstitution does not mean that both the Abrahamic and Sinai covenants are the same covenant, but rather they are two covenants that are closely related with one another. See also Niehaus, "Theologically Constructed Covenants," 271; idem, "Covenant," 241.

## The New Covenant

In the history of Israel in the OT, there were many more periods of time in which Israel failed to keep the covenant stipulations than when they were faithful to Yahweh. Even in Deut 4:25-31, Moses predicted the Israelites' apostasy, but he also looked forward to their restoration on the basis of Yahweh's faithfulness in keeping the *patriarchal* covenant (Deut 4:31; cf. Lev 26:42). When Israel's apostasy and rebellion against Yahweh became persistent in the later monarchical period, the covenant curses were fully realized through the exile (2 Kgs 17:7-23; 24:1-4). Although the prophets rebuked Israel primarily for breaking the Mosaic covenant and pronounced Yahweh's judgment on Israel, there was always a message of hope in the restoration oracles.

For the purpose of our discussion on the continuity of the covenants, we shall look into Jeremiah's prophecy of the new covenant in Jer 31:31-34:

> 31 Behold, the days are coming, declares the LORD, when I will make a new covenant with the house of Israel and the house of Judah, 32 not like the covenant that I made with their fathers on the day when I took them by the hand to bring them out of the land of Egypt, *my covenant that they broke*, though I was their husband, declares the LORD. 33 But this is the covenant that I will make with the house of Israel after those days, declares the LORD: *I will put my law within them, and I will write it on their hearts. And I will be their God, and they shall be my people.* 34 And no longer shall each one teach his neighbor and each his brother, saying, "Know the LORD," for they shall all know me, from the least of them to the greatest, declares the LORD. For I will forgive their iniquity, and I will remember their sin no more (ESV; emphasis added).

In this restoration oracle, Yahweh promises to make a new covenant with Israel at an indefinite time in the future (Jer 31:31, 33),[13] in order to rectify the broken Mosaic covenantal relationship (Jer 31:32),[14] so that Yahweh

---

13. Dumbrell, *Covenant and Creation*, 174. Dumbrell explains that the phrase, הנה ימים באים ("behold the days are coming") in Jeremiah refers to "an uncertain future, near or remote." Outside of Jeremiah, this phrase (1 Sam 2:31; 2 Kgs 20:17; Amos 4:2; 8:11; 9:13) refers to the indefinite future. See also McKane, *Jeremiah*, 2:817-18; Fischer, *Jeremia 26-52*, 171.

14. Christiansen, *Covenant in Judaism*, 56. Christiansen rightly observes that "Jeremiah's vision of a 'new covenant' has an antecedent of a 'broken covenant'" (cf. Jer 11:10; 31:32). See also Holladay, *Jeremiah 2*, 197; Fischer, *Jeremia 26-52*, 171. The אבות ("fathers") in Jer 31:32 refers to the exodus generation, not the patriarchs.

## The Blessing of Abraham, the Spirit, and Justification in Galatians

will once again be their God, and they shall be his people (Jer 31:33b; cf. Gen 17:7–8; Exod 6:7).[15] Yahweh has to make this new covenant in order to remain faithful to the Abrahamic covenant, which is *everlasting* (Gen 17:7–8). Therefore, this new covenant will also be everlasting (Jer 32:38–40).[16]

Although there is a clear continuity of this new covenant with the Abrahamic and Mosaic covenants, it is also different (Jer 31:31)—different not in an entirely new and unrelated sense, but in the sense of an essential change to an aspect of its nature.[17] Yahweh will now take the initiative to internalize the law in the hearts of the people (Jer 31:33), instead of writing it on tablets or in a book (Exod 24:4–7; 34:1).[18] This divine initiative is necessary in order to solve the problem of the disobedience of the covenantal people, which is the cause of the broken covenant and its curses (Jer 11:1–17).[19] Although the Israelites were expected to keep the law in

---

Therefore, Yahweh is clearly comparing this new covenant with the Sinai covenant. See also Thompson, *Jeremiah*, 580; Keown et al., *Jeremiah 26–52*, 131; McKane, *Jeremiah*, 2:818.

15. Jeremiah clearly alludes to the Abrahamic covenant (Gen 17:7–8) in using the phrases "they shall be my people, and I will be their God" (Jer 31:33; 32:38) and "everlasting covenant" (Jer 32:40). See also McComiskey, *Covenants of Promise*, 82–83; Weinfeld, "Jeremiah," 27.

16. See also Rad, *Old Testament Theology*, 2:214; Schreiner, *Jeremia 25,15—52,34*, 195; Lundbom, *Jeremiah 21–36*, 519; Fischer, *Jeremia 26–52*, 212–13. Lundbom notes that "it is generally agreed that this 'eternal covenant' . . . is the 'new covenant' promised by Yahweh in 31:31–34."

17. See also McKane, *Jeremiah*, 2:818. McKane cites the Jewish scholar Kimchi: "'not like the covenant' does not mean 'not the covenant,' but rather 'the Sinai covenant fundamentally changed.'" On the other hand, Dumbrell notes "the element which will characterize the New Covenant and thus render it 'new' will be its irrefragability. It will not be new because of new conditions which Yahweh will attach to it, nor because it is the product of a new historical epoch, nor because it will contain different promises, . . . but what will make it new is that in the new age *both* partners will keep it" (*Covenant and Creation*, 178; emphasis in original). On the continuity of the Sinai and new covenants, see also Waltke and Yu, *Old Testament Theology*, 438–39.

18. Potter notes that the writing of the law in the heart in Jer 31:33 is in contrast to the sin of Judah engraved in the "tablet of their heart" (Jer 17:1), and he suggests Jeremiah's thought to be: "as long as the Law is written merely on tablets of stone, so long will sin be written on the tablets of the heart. . . . In order for God to forgive he must erase the sin written on the heart and replace it with the Law" (Potter, "New Covenant," 351–52).

19. See also House, *Old Testament Theology*, 319; Hafemann, "The Covenant Relationship," 51–52.

their hearts (Deut 6:6; 30:11–14), they failed to do so.[20] Instead, Israel was persistently rebellious and stubborn in their hearts.[21] Therefore, the divine work in the hearts of the people is necessary to internalize the law (Jer 31:33; cf. Deut 30:6), so that Israel will know Yahweh (Jer 24:7) and fear him (Jer 31:34; 32:39–40; cf. Deut 10:12–13).

What Jeremiah envisions in the new covenant is very much in line with the language in Deuteronomy.[22] On the one hand, he points out the responsibility on the part of the Israelites to circumcise their hearts (Jer 4:4), just like Deut 10:16.[23] "Circumcision of the heart" is used as a metaphor for a heart that is obedient and responsive to Yahweh (cf. Deut 10:16; 30:6).[24] On the other hand, Jeremiah's prophecy of the divine work in human hearts is similar to Deut 30:6. When Moses predicted the apostasy and exile of Israel, he also spoke of how Yahweh would restore his people when the exiles repent and return to Yahweh in obedience (Deut 30:1–6).

---

20. McComiskey, *Covenants of Promise*, 84–85. McComiskey stresses that "it is inadequate to see Jeremiah's contrast between the two covenants solely as expressing the externality of the old covenant as opposed to the internality of the new covenant. The old covenant also had as its ideal an inward orientation of the law... The primary reason for the abrogation of the old covenant was the failure of the people to receive the law into their hearts" (cf. Deut 6:6; 10:16; 30:6). See also McKane, *Jeremiah*, 2:823.

21. E.g., Jer 5:23; 6:28; 7:24; 9:14; 11:8; 13:10; 18:12; 23:17. See especially Jer 11:1–17.

22. Contra Schenker, "Unwiderrufliche Umkehr und neuer Bund," 93–106, who argues that there is a great difference in the thought of Deut 4:25–31; 30:1–14 compared with Jer 31:31–34, in that Deuteronomy depicts obedience to the Torah as achievable by human effort, while Jeremiah proclaims that restoration can only come about through the divine initiative to enable obedience, not by human effort. Although it is true that these two text groups differ in their emphasis, both divine agency and human responsibility are not absent in their larger context. It is too narrow for Schenker to compare only them without acknowledging that similar concepts may still be brought across using different vocabulary, and that concepts not within these specified verses can still be presumed in these verses, because they are present in the larger context of these passages. While it would not be accurate to say that Jer 31:31–34 and Deut 30:1–14 are identical, their overall theology is nonetheless still in line with one another.

23. Jer 4:4a: המלו ליהוה והסרו ערלות לבבכם, "circumcise yourselves to the Lord, and remove the foreskins of your hearts"; cf. Deut 10:16a: ומלתם את ערלת לבבכם, "circumcise the foreskins of your hearts."

24. Carroll, *Jeremiah*, 158; Lemke, "Circumcision," 303–8. Lemke notes that the meaning of this metaphor is further clarified in contexts where "uncircumcision" of the heart and ears are used, depicting "a willful lack of responsiveness to the divine will and covenantal obligation" (Lev 24:41–42; Jer 6:10; 9:25–26 [MT 9:24–25]; Ezek 44:6–9) (Lemke, "Circumcision," 303).

Yahweh will empower the Israelites to obey him with all their hearts and souls by "circumcising" their hearts (Deut 30:6–10). Yahweh's commandments will not be difficult to obey when it is in their mouths and hearts (Deut 30:11–14).

This divine work in the hearts of Yahweh's people, which characterizes the restoration of Israel, continues to be developed in the book of Ezekiel, especially in Ezek 36:26–27.[25] We will discuss Ezek 36:26–27 in detail later in the section on the promise of Yahweh's bestowal of the Spirit.

There is a clear continuity in the Abrahamic, Sinai, and new covenants. While the restoration oracles in the prophets generally speak of Yahweh restoring the Mosaic covenantal relationship and blessings to Israel, the Mosaic covenant is inextricably related to the Abrahamic covenant. Yahweh will restore the (Sinai-)covenantal relationship because of the Abrahamic covenant.

## The Abrahamic Blessing for the Nations in Other Old Testament Texts

Very few OT texts outside the book of Genesis allude to the Abrahamic blessing for the nations (Gen 12:3b). However, there are two texts, namely Ps 72:17 and Jer 4:2, that clearly allude to Gen 12:3b.[26] Zech 8:13 very likely alludes to Gen 12:2–3. We shall examine these three texts below in order to see how the Abrahamic blessing for the nations in Gen 12:3b is developed in the OT outside the Pentateuch. These texts will also shed some light on the relationship of Israel and the nations.

### Psalm 72:17

Psalm 72 is a prayer for the king of Israel that he may reign with righteousness (Ps 72:1–2). There are clear indications that Ps 72:17 alludes to the reiteration of the Abrahamic promise (Gen 12:2–3) in Gen 22:18 (cf. Gen 26:3), as shown in the comparison below:

---

25. See also Hafemann, "Covenant," 51–55.

26. Other than Ps 72:17, Jer 4:2, and Zech 8:13, Wisdom suggests Isa 65:16 as another possible allusion to Gen 12:3b (Wisdom, *Blessing*, 36–42). However, the verbal and thematic parallels argued by Wisdom in Isa 65:16 are far too weak to constitute an allusion to Gen 12:3b. See also Grüneberg, *Abraham*, 211–13 on Isa 65:16.

## The Spirit's Role in the Blessing of Abraham

| Ps 72:17b MT | Gen 22:18a MT | Gen 12:3b MT |
|---|---|---|
| ויתברכו בו כל־גוים יאשרוהו | והתברכו בזרעך כל גויי הארץ | ונברכו בך כל משפחת האדמה |
| may all the nations declare themselves as blessed in him, may they call him blessed | all the nations of the earth shall declare themselves as blessed in your seed | all the families of the earth shall be blessed in you |
| =Ps 71:17b LXX[27] | Gen 22:18a LXX | Gen 12:3b LXX |
| καὶ εὐλογηθήσονται ἐν αὐτῷ πᾶσαι αἱ φυλαὶ τῆς γῆς πάντα τὰ ἔθνη μακαριοῦσιν αὐτόν | καὶ ἐνευλογηθήσονται ἐν τῷ σπέρματί σου πάντα τὰ ἔθνη τῆς γῆς | καὶ ἐνευλογηθήσονται ἐν σοὶ πᾶσαι αἱ φυλαὶ τῆς γῆς |
| all the families of the earth shall be blessed in him, all the nations shall call him blessed | all the nations of the earth shall be blessed in your seed | all the families of the earth shall be blessed in you |

Lexical connections include "name" (שׁם; cf. Gen 12:2), "bless" (ברך), and "nations" (גוים).[28] Structurally, parallels to the patriarchal promises include the use of כל־גוים ("all nations"), the preposition ב ("in/on account of"), and the Hitpael יתברכו ("shall declare themselves blessed").

It is important to note that Ps 72:17 is closer to the reiterations of the Abrahamic promise in Gen 22:18 than to Gen 12:3 itself.[29] This observation is significant, as זרע "seed" in Gen 22:18 very likely refers to an individual descendant of Abraham, rather than to Abraham's descendants collectively.[30] Psalm 72 is not only a royal psalm used during the monarchy, but it also looks forward to an eschatological ideal king who will reign over all the earth (Ps 72:8).[31] In Ps 72:17, the third person pronominal

---

27. The translator of Ps 71:17b LXX had apparently understood this verse as an allusion to Gen 12:3b LXX.

28. See also Wisdom, *Blessing*, 38n87.

29. See also Alexander, "'Seed' in Genesis," 365; Mathews, *Genesis 11:27—50:26*, 298-99; Goldingay, *Psalms*, 2:393. Other interpreters who see Ps 72:17 as an allusion to the Abrahamic blessing for the nations include: Briggs and Briggs, *Psalms II*, 137; Weiser, *Psalms*, 504; Anderson, *Psalms*, 1:526; Kraus, *Psalms 60-150*, 80; Williamson, *Abraham*, 169-70; Wisdom, *Blessing*, 37-39.

30. See pp. 80-81 above on the singularity of זרע ("seed") in Gen 22:18.

31. Williamson, *Abraham*, 169; Beale, *Temple*, 153-54; Bauckham, *Climax*, 321; Kaiser, "Psalm 72," 268-70. Heim points out that the royal psalms do not originate as

suffix of the preposition (בו, "in him") clearly refers to this eschatological ideal Israelite king, a descendant of Abraham, who will reign over all nations (Ps 72:11).[32] Therefore, it is apparent that the "seed" in Gen 22:18 is now identified with this ideal king of Israel.

The connection between the Abrahamic promise and the Israelite monarchy is found in Gen 17:6, 35:11 and 2 Sam 7:9.[33] In Gen 17:6, Yahweh explicitly declared to Abraham that "kings will come forth from you." This promise is then reiterated to Jacob in Gen 35:11 as "kings shall come from your own loins." In 2 Sam 7:9, Yahweh's promise to David to make his name great alludes to the Abrahamic promise in Gen 12:2. Furthermore, the Davidic promise is also everlasting (2 Sam 7:13-16), just like the Abrahamic promises (Gen 13:15; 17:7-8). The motif of the eschatological reign of Israel's king over the whole earth in the royal psalms (Ps 2:8; 72:8-11) is also reminiscent of the development of the Abrahamic promise in Gen 28:14, where Jacob's descendants will extend to the north, south, east, and west, as well as Gen 49:10 (cf. Gen 27:29), where many peoples and nations shall submit to Israel's king.

The translation of יתברכו in Ps 72:17 has generally been either passive ("be blessed") or reflexive ("bless themselves").[34] However, the Hitpael in Ps 72:17 may be better understood as an estimative-declarative

---

"a prediction of a future saviour king," but they refer to the king reigning at the time in its original cultic setting, and "a messianic meaning was given to them only after the disappearance of the Davidic dynasty" (Heim, "Perfect King," 224). Nonetheless, Heim notes that "from the point of view of post-monarchial Judah," Psalm 72 then becomes a model prayer of how the people should pray for the restoration of the kingdom (225). However, Walter Kaiser observes that the language of Psalm 72 "surpassed the capacity of the nation Israel to completely fulfill what was taught," and therefore, both the historical event and the final fulfillment are linked together as a whole event (Kaiser, "Psalm 72," 266, 269-70).

32. This motif of the eschatological reign of the Israelite king over the whole earth is also apparent in Ps 2:8.

33. See also McComiskey, *Covenants of Promise*, 21-23; Alexander, "Royal Expectations," 187-212; Williamson, *Abraham*, 169-70; idem, *Sealed with an Oath*, 144-45. Alexander has shown convincingly that one of the interests of the book of Genesis is to trace the royal line of descendant from Abraham to Judah (Gen 49:8-12), before whom many nations and peoples shall submit in obedience. The books of Samuel and Kings continue to trace the royal line of Judah through David, whose genealogical connection with Genesis is highlighted in the book of Ruth (Alexander, "Royal Expectations," 207 n. 39).

34. Passive: e.g., LXX; ESV; NIV; NRSV; JB; Dahood, *Psalms II*, 179; Wisdom, *Blessing*, 38; Direct reflexive: e.g., RSV; NASB; Briggs and Briggs, *Psalms II*, 137; Kraus, *Psalms 60-150*, 75; Tate, *Psalms 51-100*, 200.

reflexive—"the nations declare themselves as blessed on account of him," the ideal eschatological king of Israel.³⁵ This is because (כִּי) the king rules righteously and delivers the weak and needy from oppression and violence, both in Israel and among the nations (Ps 72:12–14; cf. 72:2–4).³⁶

## Jeremiah 4:2

Jeremiah 3:6—4:4 is a series of the restoration oracles calling Israel to repentance. Allusion to the Abrahamic promise in this passage can be seen as follows. Yahweh promises that, at the time of restoration, Israel will "increase and multiply" in "the land that I gave your fathers" (Jer 3:16, 18; cf. Gen 12:7; 13:14–17; 15:18–21; 26:3–4; 28:13–14). תרבו ופריתם ("you shall increase and multiply") in Jer 3:16 clearly alludes to the reiteration of the Abrahamic promise to Jacob in Gen 35:11, where Yahweh commands Jacob to "be fruitful and multiply" (פרה ורבה). At that time, Jerusalem will be called the "throne of Yahweh," and "all nations shall gather to it ... and they shall no longer walk according to the stubbornness of their evil heart" (Jer 3:17). At the restoration of Israel, "nations shall declare themselves as blessed in him" (Jer 4:1–2).

There are some verbal allusions in Jer 4:2 to the Abrahamic blessing for the nations, as shown below:

| Jer 4:2b MT | Gen 22:18a MT | Gen 12:3b MT |
|---|---|---|
| והתברכו בו גוים ובו יתהללו | והתברכו בזרעך כל גויי הארץ | ונברכו בך כל משפחת האדמה |
| then the nations shall declare themselves as blessed in him, and in him they shall boast | all the nations of the earth shall declare themselves as blessed in your seed | all the families of the earth shall be blessed in you |

The verbal parallels can be seen in the use of the Hitpael והתברכו ("shall declare themselves blessed"), the preposition ב ("in/on account of"), and

---

35. Contra Grüneberg, *Abraham*, 213–15, who argues that the Hitpael should be translated as "all the nations shall use his name to utter a blessing." For details of my arguments, see Lee, "The Niphal and Hithpael of ברך," 288–93, esp. p. 291n37.

36. The כִּי in Ps 72:12 introduces the reason why all nations should serve the ideal king of Israel (Ps 72:11) (see also Goldingay, *Psalms*, 2:389; Tate, *Psalms 51–100*, 221; Kaiser, "Psalm 72," 266). Vv. 12–14 are not just a repetition of vv. 2 and 4. It may be argued from the context that vv. 2–4 refer to God's people Israel and vv. 12–14 to the nations. Contra Briggs and Briggs, *Psalms II*, 135–37; Kraus, *Psalms 60–150*, 79–80.

גוים ("nations").³⁷ Although the preposition ב follows the Hitpael of ברך in all its occurrences in the Hebrew Bible (Gen 22:18; 26:4; Deut 29:18 MT [Eng. 29:19]; Ps 72:17; Isa 65:16 [2x]; Jer 4:2), the combination of the Hitpael of ברך, the preposition ב, and the nations (גוים) as the subject of ברך always alludes to the Abrahamic blessing for the nations (Gen 12:3; cf. Gen 22:18; 26:3; Ps 72:17).

Nonetheless, there is some ambiguity about who the "him" in בו refers to (Jer 4:2). From the context, it likely refers to Yahweh.³⁸ Nonetheless, in the Abrahamic promise, although the nations are blessed "in, or on account of" Abraham and his offspring, they are the channel of the blessing—the means by which the blessing is given—not the source of the blessing; Yahweh is still the divine agent of the blessing (Gen 12:3; 22:18).³⁹ Therefore, "to be blessed on account of Abraham and his offspring" amounts to being blessed by Yahweh.⁴⁰ Because of the other allusions to the Abrahamic promise in the context of Jer 3:6—4:4, as seen above, even if the pronominal suffix to the preposition (בו) refers to Yahweh, and not to Abraham or his offspring, it is still clear that Jer 4:2 is alluding to the Abrahamic promise of blessing for the nations.⁴¹

Although the translation of the Hitpael והתברכו in Jer 4:2 is commonly reflexive ("bless themselves"), and occasionally passive ("are blessed"),⁴² I have shown elsewhere that the Hitpael והתברכו may be

---

37. Scholars who see some degree of allusion to Gen 12:3b; 22:18 include: Bright, *Jeremiah*, 24; Thompson, *Jeremiah*, 213n28; Schreiner, *Jeremia 1—25*, 14, 32; Holladay, *Jeremiah 1*, 128–29; Carroll, *Jeremiah*, 156; Breuer, *Jeremiah*, 32–33; Huey, *Jeremiah*, 79; Lundbom, *Jeremiah 1–20*, 326; Wisdom, *Blessing*, 39; Fischer, *Jeremia 1-25*, 201; Allen, *Jeremiah*, 61. McKane argues that Jer 4:2 is not an allusion to Gen 12:3b or 18:18, because the Hitpael is used here and not the Niphal. Neither does the Hitpael point to an allusion to Gen 22:18 or 26:4, because בזרעך is not the same as בו (McKane, *Jeremiah*, 1:86). However, the allusion need not be restricted to one text, but it may more extensively refer to the notion of the Abrahamic blessing for the nations, which includes Gen 12:3b and its various reiterations in Genesis. Therefore, Jer 4:2 can still be alluding to the concept of the blessing for the nations in Genesis.

38. See also Thompson, *Jeremiah*, 213n28; Holladay, *Jeremiah 1*, 129. On the other hand, the Targum of Jeremiah (*Tg. Neb.*) and LXX take the pronominal suffix to refer to Israel.

39. On the divine agency of the Abrahamic blessing in Gen 12:3, see pp. 69–73 above.

40. See also Thompson, *Jeremiah*, 213n8.

41. Contra Grüneberg, *Abraham*, 218–19.

42. Direct reflexive: e.g., ESV; NASB; NKJV; JB; RSV; Lundbom, *Jeremiah 1–20*, 324; Thompson, *Jeremiah*, 205; Holladay, *Jeremiah 1*, 62; Carroll, *Jeremiah*, 155;

understood more aptly as estimative-declarative ("declare themselves as blessed").[43] Thus, Jer 4:2b may be understood in this way: at the restoration of Israel, the nations will gather to the presence of Yahweh at Jerusalem, and they will "declare themselves as blessed" on account of Yahweh because of the salvation that has come upon them—they shall "no longer walk according to the stubbornness of their evil heart" (Jer 3:17).

The syntax of Jer 4:1-2 seems to indicate that the blessing of the nations (Jer 4:2b) is conditional upon Israel's repentance.[44] However, in Jer 3:17, the gathering of the nations to Yahweh is not portrayed as conditional on Israel's repentance, but rather as an event that will occur at the restoration of Israel. Therefore, the condition in Jer 4:1-2 may be understood as a divinely enabled condition, and Israel's repentance would mark the time of restoration, whereby the blessing for the nations would also take place. Jeremiah looks forward to a time, when in response to the persistent alienation of humans from him since the primeval times, Yahweh's reconciliatory initiative through the Abrahamic blessing for the nations (Gen 12:2-3) will finally be fulfilled at the restoration of Israel.

## Zechariah 8:13

Zechariah 8:1-23 is a restoration oracle that not only deals with Israel, but also the nations. After the pronouncement of judgment on Israel for their sins (Zech 7:8-14), this oracle speaks of a time when Yahweh will once again dwell at Jerusalem. At that time, he will gather his people from

---

Craigie et al., *Jeremiah 1-25*, 63; passive: e.g., NRSV; Huey, *Jeremiah*, 77, 79; Wisdom, *Blessing*, 39.

43. Lee, "The Niphal and Hithpael of ברך," 288-93. Some interpreters who take the direct reflexive reading understand Jer 4:2 to mean that the nations see Israel as a paradigm of blessing, and thus use Israel as a byword of blessing when they bless themselves (e.g., Thompson, *Jeremiah*, 213; McKane, *Jeremiah*, 1:86; Grüneberg, *Abraham*, 218). However, the Hitpael of ברך is more likely to have the nuance of an estimative-declarative reflexive than of a direct reflexive.

44. Carroll, *Jeremiah*, 156; Holladay, *Jeremiah 1*, 126-29; Craigie et al., *Jeremiah 1-25*, 66; Fischer, *Jeremia 1-25*, 200-201. Of the seven verbs in Jer 4:1-2, the first and third verbs are clearly marked by אם, forming the protases—"if you return" and "if you remove your detestable things." Although it is not entirely clear whether the second, fourth, and fifth verbal clauses are apodoses or protases, it is rather clear that the last two verbal clauses regarding the nations are apodoses—"then nations will declare themselves as blessed in him, and they will boast in him." See Holladay, *Jeremiah 1*, 126-27 for an analysis of the seven clauses.

## The Blessing of Abraham, the Spirit, and Justification in Galatians

the farthest ends of the earth,[45] so that they may once again be Yahweh's people and dwell in Jerusalem (Zech 8:1–8). The phrase, "they shall be my people, and I will be their God" (Zech 8:8) and the reference to the people returning to dwell in Jerusalem, which is representative of the promised land, clearly allude to the Abrahamic (Gen 17:7–8) and Sinai (Exod 6:7–8; Deut 30:1–5) covenants.[46]

The restoration of the covenant blessings may be seen in the fruitfulness of the land (Zech 8:12; cf. Lev 26:3–5; Deut 28:1–12). At the time of the invasion and exile, Israel had been a curse (היה קללה, "to be a curse") among the nations (Zech 8:13a). Israel was "a curse among the nations" in the sense that Israel's plight had been an evidence of the covenantal curses and Yahweh's displeasure with them.[47] At the future restoration, Israel shall be a blessing (היה ברכה; Zech 8:13b). Israel will now be seen by the nations as being signally blessed by Yahweh.[48] As a result of the nations' recognizing Yahweh's restored blessings on Israel, "many peoples and strong nations shall come to seek the LORD of hosts in Jerusalem ... saying, '... for we have heard that God is with you.'" (Zech 8:22–23 ESV)

The phrase היה ברכה ("to be a blessing") in Zech 8:13 is an allusion to the Abrahamic blessing in Gen 12:2, where Yahweh promised that Abraham "shall be a blessing."[49] Admittedly, there are no clear verbal allusions to Gen 12:3b, the Abrahamic blessing for the nations, in this passage. Nonetheless, the context of Zech 8:1–23 ties in the restoration with the Abrahamic and Mosaic covenants. Furthermore, the nations (גוים) gathering to Yahweh at the restoration of Israel (Zech 8:20–23), which is similar to Jer 3:17; 4:2, may be a way in which the Abrahamic blessing for the nations is explicated.

Although Zech 8:13 may not allude to the Abrahamic blessing for the nations as clearly as Ps 72:17 or Jer 4:2, it nevertheless has thematic and

---

45. McComiskey explains that the phrase, מארץ מזרח ומארץ מבוא השמש ("from the land of the sunrise to the land of the setting of the sun"), in Zech 8:7 connotes the "farthest reaches of the earth" (McComiskey, "Zechariah," 1141).

46. See also McComiskey, "Zechariah," 1141.

47. Mitchell et al., *Haggai, Zechariah, Malachi and Jonah*, 211; Petersen, *Haggai and Zechariah 1–8*, 308; Smith, *Micah-Malachi*, 237; Meyers and Meyers, *Haggai, Zechariah 1–8*, 423–24; McComiskey, "Zechariah," 1148.

48. Contra Meyers and Meyers, *Haggai, Zechariah 1–8*, 424; Merrill, *Haggai, Zechariah, Malachi*, 227, who think that Israel will be a source of blessing among the nations. היה ברכה means "to be signally blessed," rather than "a source of blessing" (see pp. 69–71 above; Grüneberg, *Abraham*, 117–20).

49. See also Hanhart, *Sacharja*, 517; Merrill, *Haggai, Zechariah, Malachi*, 227; Tidiman, *Zacharie*, 182; Wisdom, *Blessing*, 40–41.

lexical parallels with the Abrahamic blessing in Genesis (cf. Gen 12:2-3; 17:7-8). Therefore, Zech 8:1-23 is still a viable resource for us to trace the development of the Abrahamic blessing for the nations in the OT outside the Pentateuch. Similar to Jer 3:6—4:4, Zech 8:1-23 looks forward to the future restoration of Israel, in which the nations will be drawn to Yahweh, whereby the Abrahamic blessing for the nations is fulfilled.

## Summary

Psalm 72:17, Jer 4:2, and Zech 8:13 develop the Abrahamic blessing for the nations in two streams: (1) the "seed" as a specific individual descendant of Abraham and (2) the eschatological fulfillment of the blessing for the nations. The first stream may be seen in Psalm 72, which develops the Abrahamic blessing for the nations in two important ways. First, the זרע ("seed") in the Abrahamic promise (Gen 22:18) is understood to be the ideal eschatological king of Israel, who will rule over the whole earth (Ps 72:8, 17). Second, under the rule of this eschatological king of Israel, the nations are blessed because he cares and looks after their welfare (Ps 72:9-14, 17). Therefore, all the nations of the earth "shall declare themselves as blessed" on account of this king (Ps 72:17; cf. Gen 12:3b; 22:18).

The second stream of development is seen in Jer 4:2 and Zech 8:13. The contexts of both Jer 4:2 and Zech 8:13 look forward to a time when, at the restoration of Israel, the Abrahamic blessing will be completely fulfilled. Israel will once again be blessed with numerous descendants and the gift of the land (Jer 3:16, 18; Zech 8:4-8). At that time, the blessing for the nations will also be fulfilled, as seen in the gathering of the nations to the presence of Yahweh (Jer 4:2; Zech 8:20-23) and their permanent turning away from evil (Jer 3:17).

## Israel and the Nations as the People of Yahweh

In Gen 35:11, when Yahweh changed Jacob's name to Israel, he promised that Israel would become "a nation and a company of nations." Israel, as the people of Yahweh, will include both the physical descendants of Jacob as a nation and a multitude of nations (cf. Gen 17:4-8). We have seen in chapter 3 that this promise is a development of the Abrahamic blessing for the nations in Genesis. This multinational dimension of Israel as the people of Yahweh continues to be developed in the OT in a variety of ways.

## The Blessing of Abraham, the Spirit, and Justification in Galatians

First, as we have seen, Psalm 72 speaks of the nations being blessed when they come under the rule of the ideal eschatological king of Israel, who is the זֶרַע ("offspring") of Abraham. Although the nations are portrayed as vassals, subjugated under Israel, they are still blessed on account of the righteous rule of the ideal Israelite king, who cares and looks after them in the same way as he treats his own people.

Second, there is a common prophetic tradition that at the eschatological restoration of Israel,[50] nations will gather before Yahweh to seek and worship him (e.g., Isa 2:2-5; 66:18-23; Jer 3:6-4:4; Mic 4:1-4; Zech 8:1-23).[51] In fact, two of these texts, Jer 4:2 and Zech 8:13, actually allude to the Abrahamic blessing, as we have seen.

It is also important to note another related issue here. Concurrent to these salvation oracles regarding the nations, there are also judgment oracles against the nations that have done evil and oppressed Israel (e.g., Isa 14:24—19:15; Jeremiah 46-51; Zech 9:1-8). The relationship between Israel and the nations is also depicted diversely, from subjugation to Israel (e.g., Isa 60:10-16; Mic 7:15-17), to having a relationship with Yahweh that is on the same status as Israel (e.g., Isa 19:24-25; 56:3; Zech 2:11 [MT 2:15]). Based on these diverse depictions in the book of Isaiah, Croatto argues that it is incoherent to read the texts as offering salvation and judgment at the same time. Therefore, he argues that the "nations" in texts such as Isa 2:2-5; 60-62; 66:18-21 refer to the Israelites in the diaspora, rather than non-Israelites.[52] However, judgment against the nations and salvation for the people among the nations who turn to God need not be mutually exclusive or contradictory. For example, while judgment is pronounced on Egypt and Assyria (Isa 14:24-27; 19:1-15), it is also prophesied that there will be Egyptians and Assyrians who will turn to Yahweh despite the judgment (Isa 19:16-25). Rikki Watts has shown convincingly that the diversity reflected in the book of Isaiah is consistent with the diversity depicted in the Abrahamic and Davidic traditions—nations which are against Israel incur judgment from God, while people from other nations, who are in-

---

50. The phrase בְּאַחֲרִית הַיָּמִים ("in the latter days") in Isa 2:2 and Mic 4:1 are commonly understood eschatologically in the ancient versions such as LXX, Tg., Syr., and Vulg. (Wildberger, *Isaiah 1-12*, 88). See also Mays, *Micah*, 96. On the other hand, some scholars point out that the phrase may be used non-eschatologically (e.g., Kaiser, *Isaiah 1-12*, 53; Oswalt, *Isaiah 1-39*, 116). However, the allusion of Isa 66:18-23 to Isa 2:2 points to an eschatological context.

51. Blenkinsopp, *Isaiah 1-39*, 191; Rudman, "Zechariah 8:20-22," 50-54.

52. Croatto, "'Nations,'" 143-61; see also Hollenberg, "Nationalism," 23-36, who holds the same view.

corporated into Israel, can range from those performing menial tasks for Israel to those who are appointed to positions of significant authority.[53] On the other hand, Routledge also shows from the narrative structure of the book of Isaiah that the exaltation of Zion is not an expression of nationalism, but rather functions to reveal God's glory, so that nations may repent and be drawn to God.[54]

Third, and related to the second point above, there are prophetic texts in which other nations are specifically designated as "the people of Yahweh." In Zech 2:11 (MT 2:15), Yahweh declares that when he once again dwells in the midst of Zion, "many nations shall join themselves to the LORD in that day, and shall be *my people*" (ESV; emphasis added). Two passages in the book of Isaiah depict a similar concept.[55] In Isa 56:3–7, the foreigners who join themselves to Yahweh by keeping his covenant need not regard themselves as separated from Yahweh's people.[56] Instead, Yahweh will bring these foreigners to his house, which is called "a house of prayer for all peoples" (Isa 56:7). In Isa 19:18–25, the prophet looks forward to the day when the Egyptians will worship Yahweh in their own land.[57] Not only so, the Assyrians will also worship with the Egyptians (Isa 19:23). "In that day, Israel will be the third with Egypt and Assyria, . . . whom the LORD of hosts has blessed, saying, 'Blessed be Egypt *my*

---

53. Watts, "Echoes from the Past," 481–508. Although Watts focuses his discussion on Isaiah 40–55, his insights are also relevant for the entire book of Isaiah.

54. Routledge, "Narrative Substructure," 183–204. For detailed studies on the relationship of Israel and the nations in the book of Isaiah, see Winkle, "Relationship of the Nations," 446–58; Melugin, "Israel and the Nations in Isaiah 40–55," 246–64; Oswalt, "The Nations in Isaiah," 41–51.

55. See also Willis, "Exclusivistic and Inclusivistic Aspects," 11.

56. The noun used in Isa 56:3, 6 is נֵכָר ("foreigner"), and it is used in the OT to refer to non-Israelites (e.g., Gen 17:12, Exod 12:43). See Blenkinsopp, *Isaiah 56–66*, 136; *HALOT* 2:700; Konkel, *NIDOTTE* 3:108–9.

57. Some scholars think that the cultic centers for Yahweh in the five Egyptian cities were set up by the Jewish diaspora in Egypt, rather than by the Egyptians themselves (e.g., Kaiser, *Isaiah 13–39*, 107–8; Blenkinsopp, *Isaiah 1–39*, 318–19). However, Wildberger points out that the expression—"swearing allegiance" to Yahweh—has to refer "either to Egyptians who had associated themselves with Judaism or to Jewish communities that sought to win proselytes" (Wildberger, *Isaiah 13-27*, 268). Furthermore, there are no good reasons to deny that the Egyptians themselves are not involved in the worship of Yahweh (Isa 19:21). The context of the oracle concerning Egypt (Isa 19:1) makes it clear that the reference to "Egyptians" in the judgment passage (Isa 19:1–17) and the "Egyptians" who will worship Yahweh (Isa 19:21) are consistent.

*people*, and Assyria the work of my hands, and Israel my inheritance'" (Isa 19:24–25 ESV; emphasis added).[58]

With this notion of those nations who have joined themselves to Yahweh by keeping his covenant being called "the people of Yahweh" (cf. Isa 56:3, 6; Zech 2:11 [MT 2:15]),[59] it is therefore reasonable to understand that the covenantal promises made to Israel are also applicable to these nations who turn from their evil ways to worship Yahweh and walk in his ways (cf. Isa 2:3; Jer 3:17; Mic 4:2).[60] With this in mind, we shall now look at the promise of Yahweh's bestowal of his Spirit in the prophets and its relationship with the Abrahamic blessing for the nations.

## THE PROMISE OF YAHWEH'S BESTOWAL OF THE SPIRIT IN THE OLD TESTAMENT

In this section, we shall examine the texts in the prophets that mention the promise of Yahweh bestowing his Spirit on his people. We will specifically

---

58. The epithets, "my people" and "the work of my hands," which are used to describe Israel's relationship with Yahweh (e.g., Isa 5:13; 29:23; 40:1; 45:11; 58:1; 60:21; 64:8 [MT 64:7]), are now used for Egypt and Assyria (see also Watts, *Isaiah 1–33*, 260–61; Groß, "Israel und die Völker," 156). Blenkinsopp notes that, geographically, Assyria, Israel, and Egypt occupy the middle of the known world (as set out in the "Table of Nations" in Genesis 10), "a central zone in which the Abrahamic promise (Gen 12:1–3) attains its fullest instantiation" (Blenkinsopp, *Isaiah 1–39*, 319–20). Wildberger also thinks that Egypt and Assyria probably represent the peoples of the earth (Wildberger, *Isaiah 13–27*, 280). On the relationship of Isa 19:25 with the Abrahamic promise, see also Kaiser, *Isaiah 13–39*, 111; Oswalt, *Isaiah 1–39*, 380–81; Watts, *Isaiah 1–33*, 260.

59. All three texts, Zech 2:11 (MT 2:15) and Isa 56:3, 6, use the same verb לוה in the Niphal ("to join oneself") with a preposition (either אל or על) before the noun יהוה ("Yahweh"). This phrase also occurs in Jer 50:5, where the people of Israel and Judah exhort themselves, "Let us join ourselves to the LORD in an everlasting covenant that will never be forgotten" (ESV). The contexts of Isa 56:3–6 and Jer 50:5 show that the concept of "joining oneself to Yahweh" is closely related to keeping the covenant of Yahweh. See also Petersen, *Haggai and Zechariah 1–8*, 181; Meyers and Meyers, *Haggai, Zechariah 1–8*, 169; McComiskey, "Zechariah," 1064.

60. Isa 2:3 and Mic 4:2 speak of nations who gather before Yahweh at Zion in order that "[God] may teach [them] his ways and that [they] may walk in his paths. For the Torah shall go out from Zion, and the word of Yahweh [shall go out] from Jerusalem." The juxtaposition of the Torah (תורה) and the word of Yahweh (דבר־יהוה) with walking (הלך) in his ways (דרך) clearly alludes to the language of keeping the covenant stipulations (e.g., Exod 19:7; Deut 26:16–17; 28:9; 29:29; 30:10, 16). See also Waltke, "Micah," 680; Brueggemann, *Theology of the Old Testament*, 501–2; Lohfink, "Covenant and Torah," 35; Wildberger, *Isaiah 1–12*, 91.

*The Spirit's Role in the Blessing of Abraham*

look into the reason Yahweh promises to give his Spirit to his people, the function of his Spirit in the lives of his people, and whether the promise of the Spirit is in any way related to the Abrahamic blessing. This inquiry will lay the groundwork for us to investigate further the references to the blessing of Abraham and the promise of the Spirit in the Second Temple literature and in Paul. We will then be able to compare Paul's understanding of the Spirit in Galatians with the OT and see if Paul's juxtaposition of the Abrahamic blessing and the promise of the Spirit is in any way influenced by the OT.

We shall see in the study below that the promise of the Spirit always occurs in the context of Israel's restoration. Two metaphors are used to describe the bestowal of the Spirit—"pouring out of the Spirit" (Isa 32:15; 44:3; Ezek 39:29; Joel 2:28-29 [MT 3:1-2]) and "putting the Spirit within" humans (Ezek 36:26-27; 37:14).[61] As we study these texts below, we will pay special attention to the significance of the two metaphors and the effects resulting from the bestowal of the Spirit.

## Yahweh's Spirit Poured Out on His People

There are four texts (Isa 32:15; 44:3; Ezek 39:29; Joel 2:28-29 [MT 3:1-2]) in the OT that mention the pouring out of Yahweh's Spirit on his people.[62] We shall focus our attention on Isa 44:3, because this text juxtaposes the Spirit with blessing, as in Gal 3:14.[63] We shall see that Isa 44:3 is a key text that sheds light on the relationship between the bestowal of the Spirit and the covenantal blessings. We shall also compare Isa 44:3 with the other three texts (Isa 32:15; Ezek 39:29; Joel 2:28-29 [MT 3:1-2]), so that our understanding of Isa 44:3 may be enhanced through observing the similarities and differences among these four texts.

---

61. Some scholars include Zech 12:10 in the list of passages on the pouring out of the Spirit (e.g., Block, "Gog and the Pouring Out of the Spirit," 268; Hamilton, *God's Indwelling Presence*, 106). However, it is debatable whether the רוח in Zech 12:10 refers to the Spirit of Yahweh (e.g., Mitchell et al., *Haggai, Zechariah, Malachi and Jonah*, 329; Petersen, *Zechariah 9-14 and Malachi*, 121) or the human disposition (e.g., Meyers and Meyers, *Zechariah 9-14*, 335; Merrill, *Haggai, Zechariah, Malachi*, 318-19; McComiskey, "Zechariah," 1088, 1214). As McComiskey explains, חן ("grace") in the OT usually "connotes a positive attitude that may result in favorable action." Therefore, it is more likely that רוח חן ("a spirit of grace") in Zech 12:10 refers to the human disposition, rather than the Spirit of Yahweh.

62. Three different verbs for "pouring" are used in these four texts: ערה ( (Isa 32:15), יצק (Isa 44:3), and שפך (Ezek 39:29; Joel 2:28-29 [MT 3:1-2]). Although the verbs are different, these texts nonetheless bring across the same imagery.

63. See pp. 2, 6 above.

# The Blessing of Abraham, the Spirit, and Justification in Galatians

## Isaiah 44:3

In this subsection, we shall first examine Isa 44:3 in its immediate context. After we have compared Isa 44:3 with Isa 32:15, Ezek 39:29, and Joel 2:28–29 [MT 3:1–2] in the subsequent subsections, we will then return to study Isa 44:3 in the broader context of Isaiah to see if the promise of the Spirit in Isa 44:3 has any connections with the Abrahamic blessing.

In Isa 44:1–5, Yahweh assures his people within the context of disputation with them (Isa 43:22–28).[64] The sin of Israel is the cause of Yahweh's delivering "Jacob to utter destruction, and Israel to reviling" (Isa 43:27–28). Yahweh's reassurances in Isa 44:1–5 mark a sharp contrast with the preceding reproaches:[65]

> 1 But now hear, O Jacob my servant, Israel whom I have chosen! 2 Thus says the LORD who made you, who formed you from the womb and will help you: Fear not, O Jacob my servant, 3 for I will pour water on the thirsty land, and streams on the dry ground; I will pour my Spirit upon your offspring, and my blessing on your descendants, Jeshurun whom I have chosen. 4 They shall spring up among the grass like willows by flowing streams. 5 This one will say, 'I am the LORD's,' another will call on the name of Jacob, and another will write on his hand, 'The LORD's,' and name himself by the name of Israel (ESV).

Despite the judgment on Israel for their sins, Yahweh reassures his people that he will restore them once again.

In Isa 44:3b, Yahweh's Spirit and his blessing are juxtaposed in two cola:

| Isa 44:3b MT | Isa 44:3b LXX |
|---|---|
| אצק רוחי על־זרעך<br>וברכתי על־צאצאיך | ἐπιθήσω τὸ πνεῦμά μου ἐπὶ τὸ σπέρμα σου καὶ τὰς εὐλογίας μου ἐπὶ τὰ τέκνα σου |
| I will pour out my Spirit upon your descendants, and my blessing upon your offspring. | I will place my Spirit upon your descendants, and my blessing upon your children. |

---

64. Brueggemann, *Isaiah 40–66*, 64; Childs, *Isaiah*, 341.

65. Young, *Isaiah*, 3:165. The ועתה ("but now") in Isa 44:1 marks a sharp contrast with Isa 43:22–28.

## The Spirit's Role in the Blessing of Abraham

How, then, is Yahweh's Spirit related to his blessing in this parallel? What does the blessing refer to? Is the Spirit the blessing? We will need to look at the context of Isa 44:3 to determine the answers to these questions.

The parallel of the Spirit with the water in v. 3a and with the blessing in v. 3b may give an impression that the Spirit is the water or the blessing.[66] However, Hebrew poetry seldom depicts parallel cola as having exactly the same meaning; the second colon usually amplifies or heightens the first colon.[67] Therefore, the blessing is not necessarily the Spirit but most likely elaborates on the Spirit. Similarly, the Spirit is not necessarily "the water," but the Spirit that will be poured onto the offspring of Jacob (Isa 44:3b) is an elaboration of the "the water pouring onto the thirsty and the dry land" (Isa 44:3a).

Alter notes that Hebrew poetry frequently switches between literal statements and metaphors in parallelism.[68] Hence, the "thirsty" and "dry ground" in Isa 44:3a can refer to the physical land as well as metaphorically to the people of Israel for the following reasons.[69] First, the masculine substantive adjective צָמֵא ("the thirsty") may refer to individual persons, but it may also refer to the land due to its parallel with the feminine noun יַבָּשָׁה ("dry land").[70] Second, the imagery of drought—"thirsty" and "dry ground"—in Isa 44:3 is reminiscent of the covenantal curses due to disobedience (Lev 26:19–20; Deut 28:22–24). Although the Israelites had been numerous, the covenantal curses, which are incurred by their disobedience, caused their numbers to dwindle (Isa 5:9–14; 6:11; 10:20–22; 32:14; cf. Lev 26:22; Deut 28:62; 1 Kgs 4:20). Nonetheless, Yahweh will restore the abundance of Jacob's descendants when he pours his Spirit on them, and "they shall spring up among the grass like willows by flowing streams" (Isa 44:3–4). Fertility of the land, livestock, and people is a form of covenantal blessings promised by Yahweh (Lev 26:3–5, 9; Deut 28:2–5). It is the Spirit of Yahweh who gives life and vitality (Isa 42:5; cf. Ezek

---

66. E.g., Alexander, *Prophecies of Isaiah*, 161, who thinks that "the *water* of the first [is] clearly identical with the *spirit* of the second" (emphasis in original).

67. Alter, *Art of Biblical Poetry*, 13–26.

68. Ibid., 16–17.

69. Scholars who recognize both the literal and metaphorical referents in the imagery include: Alter, *Art of Biblical Poetry*, 157–58; Baltzer, *Deutero-Isaiah*, 186.

70. Cf. CEV; ESV; NASB; NRSV; NIV; Alter, *Art of Biblical Poetry*, 157; Baltzer, *Deutero-Isaiah*, 184. On the masculine substantive adjective צָמֵא ("the thirsty") as referring to people, see Goldingay and Payne, *Isaiah 40–55*, 1:323–24; Young, *Isaiah*, 3:167). However, contrary to Young, I have argued above that it is not necessary to exclude the physical land even if "the thirsty" could refer to people.

37:1–14).⁷¹ Thus, it is clear that the Spirit is not the blessing in Isa 44:3, but the means of bringing about the covenantal blessings.⁷² The mixed literal and metaphorical imagery in Isa 44:3a switches to a more literal statement in Isa 44:3b, and then to a mixed literal and metaphorical imagery again in Isa 44:4 in the form of a simile.⁷³

More importantly, the restoration of the covenantal blessing is not only regarding the physical increase of the people and the prosperity of the land, but also pertains to the spiritual renewal of the people.⁷⁴ At that time of restoration, the outpouring of the Spirit will vivify the "dried up" spiritual lives of Yahweh's people, and they will acknowledge that they belong to him (Isa 44:5). Therefore, the pouring out of the Spirit on Yahweh's people is the means of bringing about the covenantal blessings of vibrant life and prosperity (Isa 44:3), and it also signifies the ratification and sealing of their covenantal relationship with Yahweh—Yahweh is their God, and they are his people (Isa 44:5).⁷⁵

The "offspring" (זֶרַע) in Isa 44:3 refers generally to the descendants of Jacob at the time of restoration. There is no indication in the context of Isaiah that it should be restricted to refer only to the returning remnant from the exile.⁷⁶ Scholars disagree about whether the people in Isa 44:5 are Israelites or proselytes from other nations.⁷⁷ However, as we have

71. Westermann, *Isaiah 40–66*, 136.

72. See also Hildebrandt, *Old Testament Theology of the Spirit*, 60, 65, who notes that "Isaiah 44:3 shows the harmonious relationship between the promised blessing and its subsequent fulfillment through the work of the Spirit," and "through the Spirit, God brings blessings and restoration to the people of God."

73. On the switch of poetic literary devices in Isa 44:3–4, see also Goldingay and Payne, *Isaiah 40–55*, 1:324. However, in contrast to Goldingay and Payne, who think that Isa 44:3a is a pure metaphor, I have argued above that it is a mixed literal and metaphorical imagery.

74. Other scholars who recognize the imagery of water revivifying the dry land as a metaphor for the spiritual renewal of the people include: Baltzer, *Deutero-Isaiah*, 186; Goldingay and Payne, *Isaiah 40–55*, 1:323; McKenzie, *Second Isaiah*, 64; Oswalt, *Isaiah 40–66*, 166–67; Young, *Isaiah*, 167.

75. See also Hildebrandt, *Old Testament Theology of the Spirit*, 60; Block, "Gog and the Pouring Out of the Spirit," 268–69. Block also notes that "the covenantal context of the pouring out of the Spirit is unmistakable in Isa 44:1–5."

76. Contra Kutsch, "Ich will meinen Geist ausgiessen," 124.

77. For those who think that the people refers only to Israelites, see, e.g., Watts, *Isaiah 34–66*, 144; Brueggemann, *Isaiah 40–66*, 65; Goldingay and Payne, *Isaiah 40–55*, 327. For those who argue that the people refers to proselytes, see, e.g., McKenzie, *Second Isaiah*, 64; Stuhlmueller, *Creative Redemption*, 129n448, 130–31; Westermann, *Isaiah 40–66*, 136.

## The Spirit's Role in the Blessing of Abraham

seen in the discussion of the relationship of Israel and the nations, the two groups are not mutually exclusive.[78] Therefore, the people in Isa 44:5 likely includes both Israelites and proselytes.[79]

### Isaiah 32:15

Similar imagery of pouring out the Spirit as the means of restoring covenantal blessings may be seen in Isa 32:14-18. The desolated land and the deserted city, which were once populated, will once again be fruitful when "the Spirit is poured upon us [the people] from on high" (יערה עלינו רוח ממרום; Isa 32:15a), and the people will then dwell in peace and security (Isa 32:14-18).

The language of the "fertile land" (כרמל), "peace" (שלום), and "security" (מבטח) (Isa 32:15, 18) is certainly reminiscent of the covenantal blessings in Lev 26:3-6 (cf. Deut 28:1-14).[80] There will not only be a transformation of the land, but also a transformation of the people, such that there will be "justice" and "righteousness" in the land (Isa 32:16-17).[81]

### Ezekiel 39:29

Ezekiel 39:25-29 also uses the imagery of the "outpouring of the Spirit" to signify the restored covenantal relationship between Yahweh and Israel.[82] At the restoration of Israel, "they shall forget their shame . . . when they dwell securely in their land with no one to make them afraid" (Ezek 39:26). The language of dwelling "securely" (לבטח) in the land with "no one to make them afraid" (אין מחריד) in Ezek 39:26 is reminiscent of the covenantal blessings in Lev 26:5.[83]

---

78. See pp. 109-12 above.

79. See also Oswalt, *Isaiah 40-66*, 168.

80. Lev 26:3-6a ESV: "If you walk in my statutes and observe my commandments and do them, then I will give you your rains in their season, and the land shall yield its increase, and the trees of the field shall yield their fruit. Your threshing shall last to the time of the grape harvest, and the grape harvest shall last to the time for sowing. And you shall eat your bread to the full and dwell in your land securely [לבטח]. I will give peace [שלום] in the land, and you shall lie down, and none shall make you afraid [אין מחריד]."

81. See also Young, *Isaiah*, 2:400-401; Oswalt, *Isaiah 1-39*, 588; Blenkinsopp, *Isaiah 1-39*, 434-35; Wildberger, *Isaiah 28-39*, 261.

82. Block, "Prophet of the Spirit," 46-48; idem, *Ezekiel 25-48*, 488.

83. See p. 117n80 above.

# The Blessing of Abraham, the Spirit, and Justification in Galatians

Yahweh declares that when he brings back his people from the exile, "they shall know that I am Yahweh their God" (Ezek 39:28). Yahweh had "hidden his face" from Israel because they had transgressed against him (Ezek 39:23–24).[84] In contrast to the previous "pouring out of his wrath" on them in judgment, now, at the restoration of Israel, Yahweh will "pour out his Spirit" upon the house of Israel, and he will no longer "hide his face" from them (Ezek 39:29).[85] Israel's broken relationship with Yahweh will be rectified.[86]

## Joel 2:28–29 (MT 3:1–2)

The outpouring of Yahweh's Spirit in Joel 2:28–29 (MT 3:1–2) also occurs in the context of Israel's restoration (Joel 2:18–27). The language of covenantal blessings in Joel 2:18–27 is clear in the fertility of the land (Joel 2:18–19, 22–26), victory over enemies (Joel 2:20), and the covenantal relationship with Yahweh—Yahweh is their God, and they are his people (Joel 2:27).[87] Yahweh declares in Joel 2:28–29 (MT 3:1–2):

> 28 And it shall come to pass afterward, that I will pour out my Spirit on all flesh, your sons and your daughters shall prophesy, your old men shall dream dreams, and your young men shall see visions. 29 Even on the male and female servants in those days I will pour out my Spirit (ESV).

---

84. Allen explains that the expression "hiding of Yahweh's face" in the prophetic literature "relates to God's punishment of sin" and "implies a break in communication that in this context [of Ezek 39:25–29] is the opposite of covenant intimacy" (cf. Isa 54:7–8; 64:7 [MT 64:6]; Jer 33:5; Mic 3:4) (Allen, *Ezekiel 20–48*, 208–9). Block also notes that Deut 31:16–18 "indicates that the idea of the hidden face of God is closely associated with the notion of divine abandonment" (Block, *Ezekiel 25–48*, 484).

85. Contrast וָאֶשְׁפֹּךְ חֲמָתִי עֲלֵיהֶם, "I will pour out my wrath upon them" (Ezek 36:18; cf. Ezek 7:8; 14:19; 20:8, 13, 21, 33; 22:22, 31) with שָׁפַכְתִּי אֶת־רוּחִי עַל־בֵּית יִשְׂרָאֵל, "I will have poured out my Spirit on the house of Israel" (Ezek 39:29). See also Allen, *Ezekiel 20–48*, 209; Rabinovits, *Yehezkel*, 651. In view of the contrast between the "pouring out of Yahweh's wrath" and the "pouring out of his Spirit," Allen thinks that Ezek 39:29 has a different nuance than Isa 44:3, Joel 2:28 (MT 3:1), and Zech 12:10. However, as we have seen, the outpouring of the Spirit in Ezek 39:29 has essentially the same significance as Isa 44:3 in terms of the restoration of covenantal blessings and the covenantal relationship.

86. See also Eichrodt, *Ezekiel*, 529, who notes that "the outpouring of the spirit . . . serves as a guarantee . . . of the future unbroken fellowship between God and his people."

87. Cf. Lev 26:3–12; Deut 28:1–14. See also Stuart, *Hosea-Jonah*, 258.

## The Spirit's Role in the Blessing of Abraham

וְהָיָה אַחֲרֵי־כֵן ("and it shall be afterwards"; Joel 2:28 [MT 3:1]) functions as a transitional formula, which marks correlation more than sequence, linking Joel 2:28-29 [MT 3:1-2] with Joel 2:18-27.[88] Therefore, the "pouring out of Yahweh's Spirit" is part of the process of restoring the covenantal blessings to Israel.

Yahweh's Spirit will be poured out on כָּל־בָּשָׂר ("all flesh"; Joel 2:28 [MT 3:1]). Scholars are divided over whether "all flesh" refers to Israel or includes Gentiles also.[89] However, since the "pouring out of Yahweh's Spirit" in Joel 2:28a (MT 3:1a) forms an *inclusio* with Joel 2:29b (MT 3:2b), "all flesh" (כָּל־בָּשָׂר) in Joel 2:28a (MT 3:1a) should then be explicated by its parallel in Joel 2:28b-29a (MT 3:1b-2a).[90] The pronominal suffixes ךָ ("your") in 2:28b-29a most likely refer to Israel, the people of Yahweh (cf. 2:27).[91] The significance of "all flesh" is that the Spirit will be given extensively to all of Yahweh's people, regardless of gender, age, and social status.[92]

At first sight, this promise of the bestowal of Yahweh's Spirit seems to exclude people who are not ethnic Israelites. However, as we have noted

---

88. Crenshaw, *Joel*, 163-64; VanGemeren, "Spirit of Restoration," 84-89. The formula אַחֲרֵי־כֵן ("afterwards") in prophetic language usually denotes "an era of God's acts associated with the day of the Lord *after* the judgment of exile or any period of judgment" (VanGemeren, "Spirit of Restoration," 86; emphasis in original). In this sense, וְהָיָה אַחֲרֵי־כֵן ("and it shall be afterwards") in Joel 2:28 (MT 3:1) is related to the period of restoration promised in 2:18-27, which is after the judgment of the locust plague. However, some scholars argue for a primarily temporal understanding of אַחֲרֵי־כֵן. See, e.g., Hubbard, *Joel and Amos*, 68; Finley, *Joel, Amos, Obadiah*, 71; Dillard, "Joel," 294; Treier, "Fulfillment of Joel 2:28-32," 15. However, as VanGemeren notes, the weakness of a primarily temporal reference is that it assumes that the blessings in 2:18-27 are entirely fulfilled before 2:28-32 (MT 3:1-5), which is unlikely because of the "never again" language in 2:19, 26-27 (VanGemeren, "Spirit of Restoration," 88).

89. For those who interpret "all flesh" to refer to Israelites, see, e.g., Allen, *Joel, Obadiah, Jonah, and Micah*, 98; Wolff, *Joel and Amos*, 67; Prinsloo, *Theology of the Book of Joel*, 90; Hubbard, *Joel and Amos*, 69; Finley, *Joel, Amos, Obadiah*, 71-72; Dillard, "Joel," 295; Crenshaw, *Joel*, 165-66; Treier, "Fulfillment of Joel 2:28-32," 16. For those who argue for Gentile inclusion, see, e.g., Kaiser, "Promise of God," 119; VanGemeren, "Spirit of Restoration," 90-92.

90. See also Dillard, "Joel," 295. For those who see the "pouring out of Yahweh's Spirit" forming an *inclusio* in Joel 2:28-29 (MT 3:1-2), see Kaiser, "Promise of God," 114; Prinsloo, *Theology of the Book of Joel*, 89; Barrett, "Pentecost and Other Blessings," 29-30; Treier, "Fulfillment of Joel 2:28-32," 15.

91. Hubbard, *Joel and Amos*, 69; Finley, *Joel, Amos, Obadiah*, 71-72.

92. See also Allen, *Joel, Obadiah, Jonah, and Micah*, 99; Wolff, *Joel and Amos*, 67; Finley, *Joel, Amos, Obadiah*, 72; Crenshaw, *Joel*, 166; Treier, "Fulfillment of Joel 2:28-32," 16.

above, the designation of "Yahweh's people" is not restricted solely to ethnic Israel, but includes people from other nations who have "joined themselves with Yahweh." Therefore, although the promise of the Spirit is made primarily to Israel, the people of Yahweh, in Joel 2:28–29 (MT 3:1–2), the same promise can also be extended to foreigners who have "joined themselves to Yahweh."

### Isaiah 44:3 and the Abrahamic Blessing

Coming back to the outpouring of Yahweh's Spirit in Isa 44:3, is there any relationship between the restoration of the (Sinai-)covenant blessing in Isa 44:1–5 with the Abrahamic covenant? Certainly, there is a relationship.[93] As Blenkinsopp notes, "the Abrahamic blessing runs like a strong undercurrent throughout this entire second part of the book."[94] First, Abraham and Sarah are pointed out as the ancestors (Isa 51:2), and the Israelites are designated as זרע אברהם ("the offspring of Abraham"; Isa 41:8).[95] Second, Yahweh reminds the Israelites that if they had obeyed his commandments, their offspring (זרע) would have been numerous like "sand" (Isa 48:18–19; cf. Gen 22:17; 32:12).[96] Third, when Israel is restored in the future, "the people will be all righteous, like Abraham, and will inherit the land as a mighty nation (Isa 60:21–22; cf. Gen 12:2; 15:6); their descendants will be known among the nations as a people blessed by Yahveh (Isa 61:9)."[97] These allusions to the Abrahamic promise in the book of Isaiah are certainly in line with Lev 26:42 and Deut 4:31, where Yahweh's restoration of the covenantal relationship with Israel is based on his faithfulness in keeping the patriarchal covenant.[98]

---

93. Contra Kwon, *Eschatology in Galatians*, 115n44, who claims that Isa 44:3 "has nothing to do with the *Abrahamic* promise" (emphasis in original).

94. Joseph, *Isaiah 40–55*, 233.

95. Blenkinsopp, *Isaiah 40–55*, 232.

96. Ibid., 233. See also Lev 26:3, 9; Deut 28:2, 11.

97. Blenkinsopp, *Isaiah 40–55*, 233. Cf. Gen 12:2b "you shall be a blessing," where Abraham shall be recognized as signally blessed by Yahweh (see pp. 69–70 above).

98. See also Goldingay, *Message of Isaiah 40–55*, 230, who notes that in Isa 44:3, "following immediately on reference to Jacob-Israel's 'seed,' however, 'blessing' also recalls the promises to Israel's ancestors (esp. Gen. 12.2–3; 22.17–8; 26.3–4; 28:14). They have a particular concern with vitality and fertility, the explicit significance of the reference to Abraham and Sarah's blessing in 51.2. The renewing of the people will be Yhwh's fulfillment of that promise, too."

*The Spirit's Role in the Blessing of Abraham*

## Summary

We can summarize the significance of the "outpouring" metaphor of the bestowal of Yahweh's Spirit as follows. First, the "outpouring" texts always occur in the context of restoration promises to Israel after the judgment of God. This point is common across Isa 32:15, 44:3, Ezek 39:29, and Joel 2:28–29 (MT 3:1–2). Second, the vivifying Spirit is the means by which the vibrant life and prosperity of the covenantal blessings are restored to Israel. This is brought across in the imagery of desolation and drought turning into fruitfulness and vitality (Isa 32:15; 44:3). Just as only an abundant amount of water can make the dry land fruitful, so only a lavish pouring out of the Spirit can restore Israel's "dried up" spiritual life to vibrancy. Third, the outpouring of the Spirit signifies the restoration of Israel's covenantal relationship with Yahweh (see the context of Isa 44:3–5 and Ezek 39:28–29). Fourth, the Spirit will be given extensively to all of Yahweh's people, regardless of gender, age, and social status (Joel 2:28–29 [MT 3:1–2]).

In the book of Isaiah, the restoration of the Sinai-covenantal blessings is ultimately linked to the Abrahamic covenant. At the future restoration of Israel, all the elements of the Abrahamic promise—numerous descendants as a nation, land, blessing for the nations—will be fully realized (Isa 60:21–22; 61:9; 66:18–23).

## Yahweh's Spirit Put Within His People

Another metaphor used to describe the promise of the bestowal of the Spirit is Yahweh's Spirit "put within" his people.[99] Unlike the metaphor of "pouring out," which occurs in various prophets, this metaphor of "putting within" occurs only in Ezek 36:27 and 37:14.[100] As we will not be able

---

99. In the OT, there are a number of individuals who have Yahweh's Spirit in them: e.g., Joseph (Gen 41:38), Joshua (Num 27:18), and David (cf. Ps 51:11 [MT 51:13]). The difference in the book of Ezekiel is that the promise is made to all of Yahweh's people (Ezek 36:27; 37:14). There have been discussions on the work of the Holy Spirit in the lives of OT saints, on whether there is a difference between "coming upon" or "indwelling" of the Spirit, and if the Spirit's indwelling is necessary for the regeneration of OT saints. See, e.g., Block, "Empowered by the Spirit of God," 42–61; Hamilton, *God's Indwelling Presence*. However, as the purpose of this study is to trace the promise of the Spirit in the prophets, we shall not be discussing the work of the Holy Spirit in the lives of OT saints.

100. Although the prepositions used in Ezek 36:27 (בְּקִרְבְּכֶם, "in the midst") and 37:14 (בְּ, "in") are different, the concept of infusion of Yahweh's Spirit is the same in both cases.

to appreciate fully the significance of the metaphor of "putting within" of Yahweh's Spirit without looking at the function of Ezekiel 36-37 in its literary context, we will need to look into how Ezekiel 36-37 is related to the earlier chapters of Ezekiel before we examine Ezek 36:26-27 and Ezek 37:14 in their immediate context. Thereafter, we will consider the relationship of Ezek 36:26-27 and 37:14 with the Abrahamic and Mosaic covenants. As the language used in Ezek 36:26-27 and Jer 31:31-34 is very similar, we will also discuss the relationship between these two passages.

## Literary Context of Ezekiel 36-37

There is a general scholarly consensus on the outline of the book of Ezekiel as follows: (1) The Call of Ezekiel (1:1—3:27); (2) Oracles of Judgment against Israel (4:1—24:27); (3) Oracles of Judgment against the Nations (25:1—32:32); (4) Oracles of Israel's Restoration (33:1—48:35).[101] Israel's sin, especially idolatry, is condemned repeatedly in the messages of judgment in Ezekiel 4-24. Israel had the obligation to keep the covenant stipulations by obeying the "statutes [חֻקּוֹת] and judgments [מִשְׁפָּטִים]" of the law, but they did not (Ezek 5:6-7; 11:12), thereby breaking the covenant (cf. Lev 26:15). As a result of their persistent disobedience throughout their history, Israel has forfeited the covenantal blessings of life and prosperity (cf. Lev 18:5; 26:3-12),[102] and they have now incurred the worst of the covenantal curses—the dwindling of their numbers and expulsion from the promised land (Ezek 20:1-38; 21:1-32; 36:19; cf. Lev 26:14-39; Deut 28:15-68).[103]

While most scholars acknowledge the allusion to Lev 18:5 in Ezekiel 20,[104] it is Sprinkle who has shown convincingly that the two motifs of

---

101. The scholarly consensus is represented in the following: Cooke, *Ezekiel*, 1; Allen, *Ezekiel 1-19*, xxvi-xxxvi; Cooper, *Ezekiel*, 53; Pohlmann, *Ezechiel*, 1:18-19; Block, *Ezekiel 1-24*, vii-x; Block, *Ezekiel 25-48*, vii-viii; Joyce, *Ezekiel*, 61-62.

102. Block, *Ezekiel 1-24*, 635.

103. Wong points out that "violation of the statutes, ordinances and commandments is equivalent to breaking the covenant (Lev 26:15)." He then gives an exhaustive list of the lexical similarities between the book of Ezekiel and Leviticus 26, and he notes that "by appropriating the curse language from Lev 26 within the covenantal framework, Ezekiel actually argues that Israel has suffered or will suffer the covenantal curses (expressed in Lev 26)," because they have violated the covenant (Wong, *Idea of Retribution*, 79-87). Kohn has demonstrated further that the language of both Leviticus and Deuteronomy is clearly present in Ezekiel 20 ("'With a Mighty Hand,'" 159-68).

104. E.g., Cooke, *Ezekiel*, 216; Greenberg, *Ezekiel 1-20*, 366; Allen, *Ezekiel 20-48*,

## The Spirit's Role in the Blessing of Abraham

Israel's disobedience to the "statutes and judgments" of Yahweh and the lack of life therein in the book of Ezekiel have been tied together by the allusions to Lev 18:5 (Ezek 18:9, 17, 19, 21; 20:11, 13, 21, 25).[105] Sprinkle points out that "these motifs are climactically fulfilled in chs. 36–37 where Yahweh causes Israel to obey his 'statutes and judgments' and breathes life into the nation."[106] We shall look into this fulfillment in chs. 36–37 in more detail below.

The first occurrence of restoration promises is in Ezek 11:14-20. After the pronouncement of judgment because of Israel's failure to obey Yahweh's "statutes and judgments" (Ezek 11:1-13), Yahweh promises that he will bring the exiles back to the promised land (Ezek 11:17).[107] In Ezek 11:19-20, Yahweh declares, "I will give them one heart [לב אחד], and I will put a new spirit [רוח חדשה] within them. I will remove the heart of stone from their flesh and give them a heart of flesh, in order that they may walk in my statutes and keep my judgments and observe them. And they shall be my people, and I will be their God."[108]

---

10-11; Block, *Ezekiel 1-24*, 632; Joyce, *Ezekiel*, 150.

105. Sprinkle, "Law and Life," 275-93. Lev 18:5: "And you shall keep my statutes [חקותי] and my judgments [משפטי], which if the person does them, he shall live by them." See pp. 47-49 above on the exegesis of Lev 18:5.

106. Sprinkle, "Law and Life," 275. Rendtorff also argues that the judgments of Ezekiel 20 are fulfilled in Ezekiel 36. The declaration that Yahweh "would pour out his wrath" on the Israelites (Ezek 18:8, 13, 21) and "would scatter and disperse them" (Ezek 18:23), which was not fulfilled then, is now executed in Ezek 36:18, where Yahweh "poured out [his] wrath," and "scattered and dispersed them" (Rendtorff, "Ez 20 und 36,16ff.," 261). Block notes further that "the motif of defilement in 20:7, 18, 26, 31 receives its answer and solution in Yahweh's cleansing in 36:25. The prospect of Israel actually enjoying the covenantal relationship with Yahweh announced in 20:5 is finally realized in 36:28" (Block, *Ezekiel 1-24*, 616).

107. After some of the Israelites had been exiled, those who remained in Jerusalem thought that Yahweh had rejected the exiles, but still favored them (cf. Ezek 11:15). In response to these people, Yahweh made it clear that he has not abandoned the exiles, and he will still judge all who continue in their abominable ways (Ezek 11:14-21). See also Zimmerli, *Ezekiel 1*, 260-62; Greenberg, *Ezekiel 1-20*, 189-90; Allen, *Ezekiel 1-19*, 163-66; Block, *Ezekiel 1-24*, 346-55.

108. While MT attests to the reading "one heart" (לב אחד), the LXX reading of καρδίαν ἑτέρος ("another heart") suggests a Hebrew *Vorlage* with אחר. For scholars who prefer the LXX reading, see, e.g., Zimmerli, *Ezekiel 1*, 230; Tidiman, *Ézéchiel*, 1:167; Allen, *Ezekiel 1-19*, 129n19a. However, given the nuance of "one heart" as "singleness of mind and constancy of conduct" (cf. Jer 32:39 "And I will give them *one heart and one way to fear me* always"), as opposed to its antithesis of a "divided heart" to mean insincerity (cf. Ps 12:2 [MT 12:3]), the MT reading fits the context of Ezekiel 11 better (Greenberg, *Ezekiel 1-20*, 190; Block, *Ezekiel 1-24*, 342, 352-53; Joyce,

123

When רוח ("spirit") is used to refer to the non-corporeal aspect of humans, it may denote a person's disposition, attitude, and inclination or a person's cognitive and volitional faculty.[109] When it is used as a parallel to לב ("heart"), as in Ezek 11:19, both לב and רוח frequently refer to disposition, attitude, volitional or intellectual thinking.[110]

The imagery of a heart transplant brings across the need for a total transformation of the human heart (לב) and the recreation of a new human spirit (רוח),[111] because the רוח ("minds") of the people of Israel were corrupted and filled with evil (Ezek 11:5).[112] Both words, "heart" (לב) and "spirit" (רוח), in Ezek 11:19 refer to the mental faculty of volition. The minds of the people were corrupted, and their renewal would then enable obedience.[113] This is the first instance in which Yahweh declared that when he restores his covenantal relationship with them, he will resolve Israel's problem of disobedience by giving them "one heart and a new spirit." This motif, which we shall discuss further below, is picked up again in the call to repentance in Ezek 18:30–31 and the restoration oracle in Ezek 36:26–27.

## Ezekiel 36–37 and Its Relationship with the Abrahamic and Mosaic Covenantal Blessings

When Jerusalem was destroyed and the people of Israel were deported and dispersed among the nations, they became the "gossip" of the nations, and the name of Yahweh was thus profaned (Ezek 36:2–4, 6, 20–23). This is because the nations attributed the plight of Israel to Yahweh's abandonment

---

*Ezekiel*, 116). The problem of Israel is that they have pursued after idols in their hearts (Ezek 14:3; 20:16), and they have not followed Yahweh with all their hearts, as required by the law (cf. Deut 10:12: "now what does Yahweh your God ask of you, but *to fear Yahweh* your God, *to walk in all his ways* and to love him . . . *with all your heart*").

109. Tengström, *TDOT* 13:388–89; Van Pelt et al., *NIDOTTE* 3:1074–75.

110. Tengström, *TDOT* 13:377; Van Pelt et al., *NIDOTTE* 3:1075. The examples that Van Pelt et al. and Tengström give outside of Ezekiel are Deut 2:30; Ps 51:12, 19 MT [Eng. 51:10,17]; 77:7 MT [Eng. 77:6]; Isa 65:14. See also Wolff, *Anthropology*, 37–38, 51–55.

111. See also Lapsley, *Can These Bones Live?*, 104–5. Lapsley notes that "the language thus suggests that without an act of divine intervention the people are incapable of acting differently than they do."

112. Block, "Prophet of the Spirit," 45; Robson, *Word and Spirit*, 83.

113. In view of the context of Ezekiel 11 and its parallel with לב ("heart"), most scholars agree that the רוח in Ezek 11:19 is anthropological, referring to the human "spirit"—the center of volition and moral will. See, e.g., Zimmerli, *Ezekiel 1*, 262; Block, "Prophet of the Spirit," 45–46; Joyce, *Ezekiel*, 114–16.

## The Spirit's Role in the Blessing of Abraham

of his people and his impotence against Israel's enemies (Ezek 36:2, 13, 20), an insult to the character of Yahweh in terms of his integrity and ability to keep his covenant with Israel.[114] However, the dispersion of Israel among the nations was their own fault. It was the result of Yahweh's judgment on their sins (Ezek 36:16-19), not because Yahweh was impotent against their enemies. Therefore, for the sake of vindicating his own holy name, Yahweh declared that he will restore Israel's prosperity in their own land (Ezek 36:21-38), so that the nations "may know that [he is] Yahweh" (Ezek 36:23, 36). Yahweh made it clear to Israel that it is not for their sake that he is restoring them, and they ought to be ashamed of their ways (Ezek 36:22, 32). By restoring Israel, Yahweh will make himself known among the nations and reveal that he is not impotent and that he has not abandoned his people.

Scholars disagree about whether the recognition formula ("that they may know that I am Yahweh") in the book of Ezekiel, when addressed to the nations, implies a saving knowledge of Yahweh.[115] It is unlikely that there are any salvific connotations in the recognition formulae addressed to the nations in the book of Ezekiel. As Joyce notes, these formulae addressed to the nations always occur in the context of either judgment against the nations or restoration of Israel.[116] Its function is clearly revelatory of Yahweh's character, such as his omnipotence, justice, and faithfulness. For the context of Ezekiel 36–37, the recognition formulae point to the fact that the nations will know that Yahweh is not impotent against Israel's enemies, and he has been faithful in keeping his covenant with Israel—the vindication of Yahweh's name against false charges by the nations. Furthermore, the response of the nations to such knowledge of Yahweh is not addressed at all. John Evans has argued convincingly that unlike the recognition formula used in Isa 19:21, "the recognition formulae in Ezekiel do not lead the reader to expect the nations either to trust in Yahweh and repent, or to experience covenantal blessing." From his study, Evans concludes that "Ezekiel's keynote formula indicates that the subjects of the verb יָדַע will assuredly know Yahweh in the sense of recognizing his powerful presence

---

114. Joyce, *Divine Initiative*, 127; Pohlmann, *Ezechiel*, 2:486; Block, *Ezekiel 25–48*, 347-48; Greenberg, "Salvation of the Impenitent," 265-66.

115. For those who argue for a salvific function of the recognition formula, see, e.g., Reventlow, "Die Völker," 33-43; Rad, *Old Testament Theology*, 2:237; Zimmerli, "Knowledge of God," 88-89; Martens, "Ezekiel's Contribution," 75-87. For those who argue for a purely revelatory function without salvific connotation, see, e.g., Joyce, *Divine Initiative*, 90-97; Strong, "Ezekiel's Use of the Recognition Formula," 115-33.

116. Joyce, *Divine Initiative*, 91.

as God, in his acts and his words . . . as the God of Exodus who enforces the covenant."[117]

The language of restoration in Ezek 36:8–38 is expressed in the various forms of the Mosaic covenantal blessings in Lev 26:3–12 and Deut 28:1–14; 30:1–10.[118] Yahweh shall gather his people, who had been dispersed among the nations, and they shall return to the promised land (Ezek 36:8, 24, 28a; cf. Deut 30:3–5a). The fertility of the land, the livestock, and the people will be restored (Ezek 36:10–12, 29b–30, 33–38; cf. Lev 26:4–5, 9–10; Deut 28:3–6, 8, 11–12; 30:5b, 9).[119] Their covenantal relationship with Yahweh will once again be restored—they shall be Yahweh's people, and he shall be their God (Ezek 36:28; cf. Lev 26:9, 12, 44). The language of "multiplying and being fruitful," as well as the covenantal formula "you shall be my people, and I shall be your God" (Ezek 36:11, 28), alludes to Lev 26:9, 11, which has its origin in the patriarchal promises and covenant in Gen 17:7–8; 35:11 (cf. Lev 26:42, 45).[120]

The restoration of covenantal blessings in the Mosaic covenant is conditional upon the obedience of Israel and their repentance (Lev 26:3, 40–41; Deut 28:1, 9, 13–14; 30:1–2, 10). How then, can the problem of Israel's disobedience be resolved (cf. Ezekiel 11, 20)? Does Israel have the responsibility, as well as the inherent ability, to repent and obey? Is the divine initiation of restoration for the sake of vindicating Yahweh's name (Ezek 36:22, 32) contrary to the condition of Israel's obedience and repentance? The problem of Israel's disobedience and its resolution are addressed in both Jeremiah and Ezekiel.

In Ezek 36:26–27, Yahweh declares how he would resolve the problem of Israel's persistent disobedience: "And I will give you a new heart [לב חדש], and a new spirit [רוח חדשה] I will put within you. And I will remove the heart of stone from your flesh and give you a heart of flesh. And I will put my Spirit [רוחי] within you, and cause you to walk in my statutes and be careful to obey my rules" (ESV). The motif first brought up

---

117. Evans, "Ezekiel's Recognition Formulae," 277, 324. Evans's study involves the use of the recognition formula in Ezekiel in comparison with its use in other parts of the OT.

118. For the allusion to the covenantal language of Leviticus 26 in Ezekiel 36, see Milgrom, "Leviticus 26 and Ezekiel," 59–60; Block, *Ezekiel 25–48*, 333; Wong, *Idea of Retribution*, 85–87.

119. See also Block, *Ezekiel 25–48*, 358 and n. 101, who notes that "the productivity of the land is a natural outgrowth of the normalization of the relationships among God, people, and land."

120. See also Zimmerli, *Ezekiel 2*, 251.

in Ezek 11:19–20 is now revisited and elaborated. A comparison of Ezek 11:19–20 and Ezek 36:26–28 shows their relationship:

| Ezek 11:19–20 MT | Ezek 36:26–28 MT |
|---|---|
| ונתתי להם לב אחד ורוח חדשה אתן בקרבכם והסרתי לב האבן מבשרם ונתתי להם לב בשר: למען בחקתי ילכו ואת־משפטי ישמרו ועשו אתם והיו־לי לעם ואני אהיה להם לאלהים: | ונתתי לכם לב חדש ורוח חדשה אתן בקרבכם והסרתי את־לב האבן מבשרכם ונתתי לכם לב בשר: ואת־רוחי אתן בקרבכם ועשיתי את אשר־בחקי תלכו ומשפטי תשמרו ועשיתם: וישבתם בארץ אשר נתתי לאבתיכם והייתם לי לעם ואנכי אהיה לכם לאלהים: |
| *And I will give to them one heart, and I will put within them a new spirit.* And I will remove the heart of stone from their flesh, and I will give to them a heart of flesh, in order that they may walk in my statutes and keep my judgments and do them. Then they will be my people, and I will be their God. | *And I will give to you a new heart, and I will put within you a new spirit.* And I will remove the heart of stone from your flesh, and I will give to you a heart of flesh. *And I will put my Spirit within you,* and cause you to walk in my statutes and cause you to keep my judgments. Then you will live in the land that I gave to your fathers, and you will be my people, and I will be your God. |

Most scholars understand the רוח in Ezek 36:26 to be anthropological.[121] However, Block argues that the רוח in both vv. 26 and 27 refer to Yahweh's Spirit. He argues that although "the new heart" is anthropological and parallel to "the new spirit" in Ezek 36:26, "the new spirit" is not necessarily anthropological. This is because "synonymity is seldom exact in Hebrew parallelism, and here the terms are associated with different prepositions."[122] Furthermore, the source of the new heart is unspecified, but the new spirit is identified as Yahweh's Spirit.[123] In view of the same motif in Ezek 11:19; 18:31, in which רוח refers to the human spirit, the center of volition, as well as its parallel with לב ("heart"), it is more likely that רוח חדשה ("new spirit") in Ezek 36:26 refers to the human volitional faculty that has been transformed by the רוח of Yahweh. It may be argued that since there was no רוח in the fleshly bodies of the reassembled bones in Ezek 37:8 until Yahweh sent his רוח into them (Ezek 37:9–10, 14), רוח

---

121. E.g., Joyce, *Divine Initiative*, 166; Greenberg, *Ezekiel 21–37*, 730; Robson, *Word and Spirit*, 245.

122. Block, *Ezekiel 25–48*, 355–56.

123. Ibid., 356.

# The Blessing of Abraham, the Spirit, and Justification in Galatians

in Ezek 36:26 should therefore also be divine rather than anthropological. However, there is a shift in meaning of רוח in Ezek 37:8 from "breath of life" to "Yahweh's Spirit" in Ezek 37:14. Thus, a shift in meaning of רוח in Ezek 36:26 from "human faculty of volition" to "Yahweh's Spirit" in 36:27 is also likely.[124]

While Ezek 11:19–20 does not mention the *means* by which "the one/new heart and the new spirit" is accomplished, it is clear from Ezek 36:27 that the infusion of Yahweh's Spirit is the means by which the human spirit—the moral will and volition—is transformed, thereby empowering his people to obey his "statutes and judgments." The gift of his Spirit's indwelling is Yahweh's effective and permanent solution to the problem of disobedience.[125] Only through divinely empowered obedience can the covenantal blessings for Israel be perpetuated and the covenantal curses subverted (cf. Lev 26:3–45; Deut 28:1–68).

The significance of this obedience metaphor of "putting within" of Yahweh's Spirit in Ezek 36:26–27, in terms of its divine initiative, is in line with the obedience metaphor of Yahweh "circumcising the hearts" of his people in Deut 30:6 and "inscribing" his law in the heart of his people (Jer 31:31–34).[126] For Jeremiah, the persistent evil inclination of the heart makes it impossible for the people to obey God by their own ability (Jer

---

124. See also Hals, *Ezekiel*, 270, who notes the shift from "spirit" to "my spirit" in both Ezek 36:26–27 and Ezek 37:9–10, 14.

125. See also Greenberg, "Three Conceptions," 375; idem, "Salvation of the Impenitent," 268–69; Lapsley, *Can These Bones Live?*, 166; Wong, *Idea of Retribution*, 188. Lapsley explains that Yahweh "gives a new mind/spirit/self in order to avoid further repetitions of Israel's history of failure." Wong notes that Yahweh's cleansing and implanting of a new spirit and new heart eliminates the possibility that the people will defile their land again. Greenberg puts it more strongly: "God will no longer gamble with Israel as he did in the old times, and Israel rebelled against him; in the future—no more experiments! God will put his spirit into them, he will alter their hearts (their minds) and make it impossible for them to be anything but obedient to his rules and his commandments," and "because of their enforced obedience to divine laws they would never again be uprooted from their land, but would reside in it forever as God's covenant-partners" (Greenberg, "Three Conceptions," 375; idem, "Salvation of the Impenitent," 268).

126. Other scholars who see a relationship between Ezek 36:26–27 and Jer 31:31–34, or with Deut 30:6, in terms of the divine regeneration of the human heart for obedience include: Cooke, *Ezekiel*, 391; Eichrodt, *Ezekiel*, 502; Zimmerli, *Ezekiel* 2, 248–49; Tidiman, *Ézéchiel*, 2:145; Block, *Ezekiel 25–48*, 354, 356–57; Greenberg, *Ezekiel 21–37*, 735–37; Groß, "Der Mensch als neues Geschöpf," 101–4; Blenkinsopp, *Ezekiel*, 169; McKane, *Jeremiah*, 2:824.

13:23; 17:9).[127] Although this notion is not as explicit in Ezekiel, the metaphor of a "heart of stone" (Ezek 11:19; 36:26) indicates unresponsiveness, obduracy, incorrigibility, and "lifelessness" (cf. 1 Sam 25:37),[128] and the vision of the "very dry" bones implies that only by divine means can Israel's "deadness" be brought to life again (Ezek 37:1-6, 14).[129] Only when Yahweh puts his Spirit within his people Israel will they be able to live again (Ezek 37:14). Therefore, the phrase, "I will put my Spirit within you" in Ezek 36:27 and 37:14 draws together two important aspects of Yahweh's infusion of his Spirit—empowerment for obedience (Ezek 36:26-27) and revivification (Ezek 37:14). As Sprinkle notes, the problem of Israel's disobedience and lack of life, as stated in Ezekiel 20, is resolved in Ezek 36:27 and 37:14 by the "putting within" of Yahweh's Spirit in his people.[130]

Nonetheless, Israel has the responsibility to repent and obey. It is important to note the difference between the ability and the responsibility to repent and obey. Human incapacity to obey does not eradicate a person's responsibility to repent and obey (Ezek 33:10-11).[131] Ezekiel 18:30-31 calls on Israel to "repent and turn from all your transgressions lest iniquity be your ruin. Cast away all the transgressions that you have committed and make yourselves a new heart and a new spirit! Why will you die, O house of Israel?" (ESV; cf. Jer 4:4; Deut 10:16). Therefore, all the more they have to rely on the divine initiative to effectuate obedience.[132] As Joyce points out, human responsibility and divine initiation are so intricately related that both aspects are present and held in tension, although one aspect may be emphasized over the other for rhetorical reasons.[133] Divine empower-

---

127. Vieweger, "Die Arbeit," 26; Lapsley, *Can These Bones Live?*, 58-60.

128. Block, *Ezekiel 25-48*, 355; Greenberg, *Ezekiel 21-37*, 730. Block notes further that the present condition of Israel "can be altered only by direct divine intervention" (Block, *Ezekiel 25-48*, 356). Commenting on Ezek 36:26-27 elsewhere, Greenberg notes that "all hope in the capability of Israel in its present state to live up to its ideal purpose has been lost" (Greenberg, "Three Conceptions," 375).

129. Lapsley, *Can These Bones Live?*, 170.

130. Sprinkle, "Law and Life," 289-92.

131. See also Matties, *Ezekiel 18*, 207-8.

132. See also Allen, "People of God in the Prophets," 161-63, who notes that both Jeremiah and Ezekiel see the solution to the people's disobedience "in an eschatological change wrought by God, so that what his people should do matched what they could do" (Allen, "People of God in the Prophets," 163).

133. Joyce, *Divine Initiative*, 125-29. Joyce concludes from his study that the rhetorical function of the emphasis placed on human responsibility in the first part of the book of Ezekiel (chs. 1-24) stresses that Israel totally deserves the disaster of defeat and exile, while the rhetorical function of the emphasis on divine initiative in the later

ment ensures obedience, but it does not preclude human responsibility in response to carry out the actual observance of Yahweh's "statutes and judgments" (Ezek 36:27).[134] Therefore, the divine initiation of restoration for the sake of vindicating Yahweh's name (Ezek 36:22, 32) is not contrary to the condition of Israel's obedience and repentance. The central truth lies in the fact that "humankind is ultimately impotent without God."[135]

Ezekiel 37:24 also envisions that at the time of restoration, when Israel "shall obey Yahweh's statutes and judgments," they shall also be ruled by a Davidic king.[136] At that time, Yahweh will make "an everlasting covenant of peace with them" (Ezek 37:26; cf. 16:59–63). This association of the establishment of an "everlasting covenant" and the divine empowerment of obedience clearly parallels the juxtaposition of the "new/everlasting covenant" and divine empowerment of obedience in Jer 31:31–34; 32:37–40.[137] Ezekiel 37:24–27 also clearly alludes to the language of covenantal blessings in Lev 26:1–13 and the Abrahamic covenant in Gen 17:7–8.[138] There-

---

part of the book (chs. 33–37) singles out Israel as "the undeserving recipient" of divine favor (Joyce, *Divine Initiative*, 126).

134. Davis, *Swallowing the Scroll*, 116; Matties, *Ezekiel 18*, 207–8; Joyce, *Divine Initiative*, 127.

135. Joyce, *Divine Initiative*, 129.

136. Cf. Isa 11:1–16, which also links the restoration of Israel with the rule of a Davidic king. There are scholars who argue that the Davidic king is the means by which obedience to Yahweh is guaranteed (Ezek 37:24), and some of them hold that Ezek 36:26–27 is elaborated in Ezekiel 37. E.g., Eichrodt, *Ezekiel*, 514; Allen, "Structure," 140; Renz, *Rhetorical Function*, 115–16; Wong, *Idea of Retribution*, 113; Sprinkle, "Law and Life," 291–92. However, Robson rightly notes that, although the Davidic king is associated with the obedience of the people, there is no clear indication that the king is the agent who enables the obedience, whereas it is clearly stated in Ezek 36:27 that it is Yahweh's Spirit who enables obedience. Rather, the king and the obedience of the people are features of the restoration (Robson, *Word and Spirit*, 250–51).

137. For discussions on the relationship of the "new covenant" in Jer 31:31–34 and the "eternal covenant" in Jer 32:38–40 with Ezek 16:59–63; 37:26, see, e.g., Renaud, "L'alliance éternelle," 335–49; Vieweger, "Die Arbeit," 26–29; Block, *Ezekiel 1–24*, 517; Lundbom, *Jeremiah 21–36*, 466–69, 519.

138. The parallels in Ezek 37:24–27 with Lev 26:1–13 include: "dwelling in the land," Yahweh's "dwelling place" (מִשְׁכָּן) among his people, Yahweh "multiplying" (רבה) his people, and the covenant formula of "I will be their God, and they shall be my people" (see also Allen, *Ezekiel 20–48*, 194; Block, *Ezekiel 25–48*, 420–21; Greenberg, *Ezekiel 21–37*, 757; Wong, *Idea of Retribution*, 86, 115–17). Garscha notes that the obedience of the people described in Ezek 37:24b fulfilled the condition of blessings stated in Lev 26:3 (Garscha, *Studien zum Ezechielbuch*, 227). The parallels in Ezek 37:24–27 with Gen 17:1–8 include: "multiplying" (רבה) the descendants, "everlasting covenant" (ברית עולם), the covenant formula of "I will be their God, and they shall

## The Spirit's Role in the Blessing of Abraham

fore, both Jeremiah and Ezekiel share the same prophetic tradition that at the future restoration of Israel, Yahweh will resolve the problem of Israel's disobedience and reestablish the everlasting covenant with Israel, so that Yahweh may restore the covenantal blessings and fulfill the Abrahamic covenant (cf. Lev 26:42; Deut 4:31).[139]

Is there, then, any relationship between the promise to "put Yahweh's Spirit within" his people in Ezek 36:27; 37:14 and the Abrahamic blessing for the nations? Admittedly, the context of Ezekiel 36–37 is clear that the promise is directed to the nation of Israel at their restoration. The salvation of the nations is not in view.[140] As Evans notes, "the idea of the nations' salvation as a part of Yahweh's plan is neither propounded nor contradicted; it is simply absent in Ezekiel."[141] Nevertheless, considering the broader theological framework of the prophetic tradition regarding the "nations who have joined themselves to Yahweh" being regarded also as "Yahweh's people" (Isa 19:25; Zech 2:11[MT 2:15]) and the patriarchal promise of "Israel becoming a nation and a company of nations" (Gen 35:11), it is not unreasonable to understand that the bestowal of the Spirit, which is promised to the nation of Israel as Yahweh's people in Ezek 36:27 and 37:14, can also be extended and applied to a broader definition of Yahweh's people, to include "nations who have joined themselves to Yahweh."

### Summary

The metaphor of the "putting within" of Yahweh's Spirit in his people occurs in the restoration oracles of Israel in Ezek 36:27; 37:14. Israel had been disobedient to the "statutes and judgments" of Yahweh, thereby breaking the covenant and incurring the covenantal curses on the one hand and forfeiting the covenantal blessings of life and prosperity (Ezek 11:1–12; 20:1–39) on the other hand. At the time of restoration, Yahweh will permanently resolve the problem of Israel's obedience and lack of life by "putting his Spirit within his people," so that they may obey his "statutes

---

be my people," and "dwelling in the land forever" (see also Allen, *Ezekiel 20–48*, 194; Block, *Ezekiel 25–48*, 417–18).

139. On the fulfillment of the Abrahamic covenant at the future restoration in Ezek 37:24–27, see also Block, *Ezekiel 25–48*, 420.

140. See also pp. 125–26 above on the issue of whether the recognition formulae addressed to the nations in Ezekiel 36–37 have any salvific connotations for the nations.

141. Evans, "Ezekiel's Recognition Formulae," 284.

and judgments" (Ezek 36:27) and live (Ezek 37:14). It is only by such a divinely empowered obedience through the Spirit that the covenantal blessings may be perpetuated and the covenantal curses subverted. At the time of the future restoration, a Davidic king shall rule over Yahweh's people, and the Abrahamic and Mosaic covenantal promises will be realized permanently (Ezek 37:24–28).

## The Relationship between the Outpouring and the Putting Within of Yahweh's Spirit

From our study of the "outpouring" and "putting within" of Yahweh's Spirit, we can see the respective emphases of these two metaphors, as well as a certain degree of overlap in their significance. Both these metaphors may be described under a broader category—Yahweh's promise to bestow his Spirit on his people as part of the restoration of Israel.[142] The "outpouring" metaphor emphasizes the restoration of the covenantal relationship with Yahweh (Isa 44:1–5; Ezek 39:29) and the lavishness of the gift of the vivifying Spirit (Joel 2:28–29 [MT 3:1–2]; cf. Isa 32:15; 44:3). On the other hand, the "putting within" metaphor stresses the divine empowerment of obedience through the transformation of the human heart and spirit by Yahweh's Spirit (Ezek 36:26–27).

These two metaphors overlap explicitly in portraying the life-giving aspect of Yahweh's Spirit. The vivifying work of the Spirit in the "putting within" metaphor is stated directly in Ezek 37:14, while it is brought across in the "outpouring" metaphor through the imagery of the desolated and dry land turning into fruitfulness and vibrancy (Isa 32:15; 44:3).

Some other aspects also overlap implicitly. Although the extensive gift of the Spirit (cf. Joel 2:28–29 [MT 3:1–2]) is not the emphasis of the "putting within" metaphor, the connotation is nonetheless present in the idea that the Spirit is "put within" the "whole house of Israel" (Ezek 37:11; cf. 36:22). The idea of the restored covenantal relationship with Yahweh is also present in the covenantal formula of "you shall be my people, and I will be your God" in Ezek 36:28. The transforming work of the Spirit in the lives of the people is hinted at in the context of the "outpouring" metaphor in Isa 32:16–17 as well.

---

142. All the texts of the "outpouring" (Isa 32:15; 44:3; Ezek 39:29; Joel 2:28–29 [MT 3:1–2]) and the "putting within" (Ezek 36:27; 37:14) of Yahweh's Spirit occur in the context of the restoration of Israel.

Block argues for a fundamental difference in the meaning of "putting within" in Ezek 36:27; 37:14 and the "pouring out" in Ezek 39:29, in that the former "relates more immediately to the rebirth of the nation, her receiving new life," while the latter "represents a sign and seal of the covenant . . . the divine mark of ownership."[143] On the contrary, Robson argues against Block that there is no significant shift in the meaning of the "pouring out" and "putting within" of Yahweh's Spirit in the book of Ezekiel, because "it is not simply the 'presence' of Yahweh's רוח among the people that assures their future, but the permanent transformation effected by the outpouring." In other words, it was because of their transgressions that Yahweh "hid his face" from his people previously (Ezek 39:23). Now, it is the obedience brought by the Spirit that causes Yahweh not to "hide his face" from his people (Ezek 39:29).[144]

On the one hand, Block is right to highlight the difference in emphasis of the two metaphors in Ezekiel. On the other hand, Robson also rightly points out the overlap of the two metaphors. Therefore, rather than taking the the metaphors of the "outpouring" and "putting within" of Yahweh's Spirit to be either "distinct" or "similar," it may be better to understand that these two metaphors have different emphases, but also overlap in some other aspects either explicitly (e.g., vivification, the means of restoring covenantal blessings) or implicitly (e.g., extensive gift of the Spirit, sign of covenantal relationship, transformation of human lives).

## Conclusion

In this chapter, we have looked into three important aspects of the blessing of Abraham and the promise of the Spirit in the OT outside the book of Genesis. First, we have investigated the relationship between the Abrahamic, Sinai, and new covenants. Second, we have traced how the Abrahamic blessing for the nations is developed in Psalm 72 and in the prophets. Third, we have examined the promise of the bestowal of Yahweh's Spirit in the prophets and its relationship to the Abrahamic, Sinai, and new covenants. The following conclusions are based on the OT texts that we have studied in this chapter.

The Abrahamic covenant was the basis for the establishment of the Sinai covenant (Exod 6:7–8; cf. Deut 9:5). The Abrahamic covenant, which was made with the patriarchs, was reconstituted with the people of Israel,

---

143. Block, "Gog and the Pouring Out of the Spirit," 267–68.
144. Robson, *Word and Spirit*, 253–54, 256–62.

the descendants of Abraham, as the Sinai covenant. In the Sinai covenant, the following elements of the Abrahamic covenant were affirmed: (1) the divine-human relationship with Yahweh as their God, and Israel as his people (Exod 6:7; cf. Gen 17:7-8); (2) the gift of the promised land of Canaan (Exod 6:8; 23:30; cf. Gen 15:18-21; 17:8); (3) the establishment of the populous nation of Israel (Exod 1:7; 19:5-6; cf. Gen 17:2, 6). However, the element of the Abrahamic blessing for the nations (Gen 12:3b) is barely developed in the Sinai covenant, because the focus of the Sinai covenant is the nation of Israel. Nonetheless, the Abrahamic blessing for the nations will come into play again at the eschatological restoration of Israel.

As the Mosaic covenant was broken time and again in the history of Israel by their disobedience and failure to keep the covenantal stipulations, the prophets not only pronounced Yahweh's judgment in terms of the execution of the covenantal curses (e.g., Jer 11:1-17; Ezek 20:1-38; Zech 7:8-14; cf. Lev 26:14-39; Deut 28:15-68), but they also announced that Yahweh would restore his covenantal relationship with Israel after the judgment in terms of a new and everlasting covenant (e.g., Jer 31:31-34; 32:36-44; Ezek 37:26). Yahweh's Spirit, whose bestowal is described by the metaphors of "outpouring" (Isa 32:15; 44:3; Ezek 39:29; Joel 2:28-29 [MT 3:1-2]) and "putting within" (Ezek 36:27; 37:14), is the means by which the covenantal blessings are restored to Israel (cf. Lev 26:1-13, 40-45; Deut 28:1-14; 30:1-10). The vivifying Spirit: (1) restores life and prosperity to the people and their land (Isa 32:15; 44:3; Ezek 37:14); (2) signifies the restoration of the divine-human covenantal relationship (Isa 44:1-5; Ezek 39:29); and (3) empowers the people to obey Yahweh (Ezek 36:27), so that the covenantal blessings may be perpetuated and the covenantal curses subverted permanently. This new and everlasting covenant not only restores the Mosaic covenant, but also ultimately fulfills the Abrahamic covenant (cf. Lev 26:40-42; Deut 4:29-31).

A number of features shall characterize the restoration of Israel, among which two are noteworthy for the purpose of our study. First, there will be people from among the nations who will "join themselves to Yahweh" by keeping his covenant, and they shall thereby also become the people of Yahweh (Isa 56:3-7; Zech 2:11; cf. Isa 19:18-24). These nations shall gather at the throne of Yahweh to worship him and walk in his ways (Isa 2:2-3; 66:18-24; Jer 3:16; 4:2; Zech 8:20-23). Along this trajectory, the covenantal promises made to Israel, including the promise of bestowing Yahweh's Spirit, which is the means by which the covenantal blessings are effected, would thus also be applicable to these nations who have turned

## The Spirit's Role in the Blessing of Abraham

to Yahweh. Among the texts that discuss the nations coming to Yahweh to worship him, Jer 4:2 and Zech 8:10 actually allude to the Abrahamic blessing for the nations. Second, at the time of restoration, a Davidic king shall rule the people (Ezek 37:24–25; cf. Isa 11:1–16).

Although Ezek 37:24–25 does not mention that the Davidic king shall rule over the other nations, yet in another stream of development of the Abrahamic blessing for the nations, Psalm 72 looks forward to a time when the ideal Israelite king shall reign over Israel and all the nations of the earth. Psalm 72:17 clearly alludes to the Abrahamic blessing for the nations (Gen 22:18; cf. 12:3b). The "seed of Abraham" in Gen 22:18 has been identified with this ideal Israelite king. Both Israel and the nations shall be blessed on account of this king (Ps 71:17), because he rules in righteousness and looks after their welfare.

In the oracles regarding the restoration of Israel, the prophets in aggregate looked forward to a time when the covenantal promises and blessings should be fully restored to the people of Yahweh. These blessings are not just the Mosaic covenantal blessings, but more so the Abrahamic covenantal blessings. All the elements of the Abrahamic promise shall be fully realized. Yahweh's people shall have their covenantal relationship with him restored (e.g., Isa 44:5; Jer 31:33; Ezek 36:28; 37:23; Zech 8:8; cf. Gen 17:7–8). They shall possess and dwell in the promised land forever as a mighty populous nation (e.g., Isa 60:21–22; Ezek 37:21–22, 25–26; cf. Gen 12:2, 7; 17:6–8). All the nations of the earth shall be blessed at the future restoration of Israel, when they shall turn from their wicked ways (Jer 3:17) and turn to worship Yahweh (e.g., Isa 2:2–3; 66:18–24; Jer 3:16; 4:2; Zech 8:20–23; cf. Gen 12:3b; 22:18). Yahweh's people shall not only consist of the nation of Israel, but also a multitude of nations (Isa 19:18–24; 56:3–7; Zech 2:11; cf. Gen 17:5–6; 35:11).

With these understandings we have gleaned from the prophets regarding the relationship between the bestowal of the Spirit and the restoration of the Abrahamic and Mosaic covenantal blessings to Israel and the nations of the earth, we shall proceed to investigate how the blessing of Abraham and the promise of the Spirit are being developed in the Second Temple literature and in Paul. The similarities and differences of these two motifs in the OT in comparison with the Second Temple literature and Paul will then help us understand why Paul associates the Spirit with the blessing of Abraham in Gal 3:14.

# 5 The Spirit's Temporary Absence in the Blessing of Abraham

*Development in the Second Temple Literature*

IN THIS CHAPTER, WE shall examine how the motifs of the Abrahamic blessing for the nations and the promise of Yahweh's bestowal of his Spirit were developed in the Second Temple literature.[1] This study seeks to observe how these two motifs are developed in relation to the Gentiles in order to facilitate our investigation of how Paul might have interacted with contemporary thoughts on these two motifs in Gal 3:1-14.[2]

---

1. "Second Temple literature" commonly refers to the Jewish literature between the writings of the Hebrew Bible and the Mishnah, including some books that were written after the destruction of the temple (Collins, "Literature," 53). As this study examines the development and mutual relationship of the Abrahamic blessing for the nations and the promise of the Spirit in the Second Temple literature, a comprehensive study on the Abrahamic blessing pertaining to posterity and land, as well as a general survey of the Spirit in the same period is beyond our scope. Wisdom and Philip have also examined one of these two motifs in the Second Temple period in their respective monographs (Wisdom, *Blessing*, 65-86; Philip, *Pauline Pneumatology*, 77-118). Both works are detailed and commendable in various ways, and I will be interacting with them actively in this study.

2. Although there is an allusion to the Abrahamic blessing for the nations in *T. Levi* 4:4-6 and an allusion to the promise of the Spirit in Ezek 36:26-27 in *T. Jud.* 24:3-4, I will not include the *Testaments of the Twelve Patriarchs* in my discussion. It is debatable whether the work is Jewish with Christian interpolations (Kee, "Testaments of the Twelve," 1:777-78) or Christian using Jewish materials (Jonge, "Testaments of the Twelve," 509). As it is not possible to extract earlier Jewish material in the present form without affecting the overall coherence of the work (Hollander, "Testaments of the Twelve," 73-74), it is best to regard the final form of the work as Christian and leave it out of our discussion. For a survey on the history of research on the date and provenance, see Kugler, *Testaments of the Twelve*, 31-38.

## The Spirit's Temporary Absence in the Blessing of Abraham

## THE ABRAHAMIC BLESSING FOR THE NATIONS IN THE SECOND TEMPLE LITERATURE

### Ben Sira[3]

Yeshua, the son of Eleazar and the grandson of Sira (Sir 50:27), wrote the book of Ben Sira in Hebrew around 195–180 BCE.[4] According to the grandson of Yeshua, who translated the book into Greek, his grandfather composed the book to help others who are less familiar with the Hebrew Scriptures, so that "those who love learning might make even greater progress in living according to the law" (Prologue, NRSV).[5] The last part of the book (Sir 44:1—50:24) is commonly known as the "Praise of the Ancestors," in which the author selects a number of key figures from the Law and the Prophets as exemplars of "godly people whose virtues will not be forgotten," and whose family lines endure "for their sakes" through "God's covenant with them" (Sir 44:10–12).[6] It is in this section that Ben Sira alludes to the Abrahamic blessing for the nations (Sir 44:21).

---

3. The versification of the book of Ben Sira in this section follows the NRSV. For a survey on the differences in chapter and verse enumeration due to transpositions and recensions of the Greek text, see Coggins, *Sirach*, 17–18. The Hebrew text in this section is cited from Beentjes, *Ben Sira in Hebrew*, 78.

4. Skehan and Di Lella, *Ben Sira*, 8–10; Crenshaw, "Sirach," 611; Coggins, *Sirach*, 18–20, 33.

5. As stated in the prologue in the Greek translation, the grandson of Yeshua translated the original Hebrew into Greek around 117 BCE, during the reign of Euergetes (Skehan and Di Lella, *Ben Sira*, 8; Coggins, *Sirach*, 18).

6. Translation taken from Skehan and Di Lella, *Ben Sira*, 497–8. Various suggestions have been given regarding the purpose of the "Praise of the Ancestors": (1) to persuade readers that the rewards of life are promised in both wisdom and the law (Burkes, "Wisdom and Law," 265–67); (2) to encourage readers who were living in a Hellenistic culture to persevere in their ancestral faith (Di Lella, "Praise of the Ancestors," 153, 155, 167; Brown, "God and Men in Israel's History," 214; Whybray, "Ben Sira and History," 138); (3) to describe the canon of the Hebrew Scriptures as "the Law and the Prophets" (e.g., Goshen-Gottstein, "Praise of the Fathers," 235–67). Although the "Praise of the Ancestors" exhibits an understanding of a bipartite division of the Scriptures as "the Law and the Prophets," it can also include the pedagogical and apologetical purpose of the "Praise" (Di Lella, "Praise of the Ancestors," 153; Ska, "L'éloge des pères," 181–93 ; contra Goshen-Gottstein, "Praise of the Fathers," 242, who excludes the latter).

## The Blessing of Abraham, the Spirit, and Justification in Galatians

In Sir 44:19–21 (NRSV), Ben Sira praises Abraham as follows:

> 19 Abraham was the great father of a multitude of nations,
>     and no one has been found like him in glory.
> 20 He kept the law of the Most High,
>     and entered into a covenant with him;
> he certified the covenant in his flesh,
>     and when he was tested he proved faithful.
> 21 Therefore the Lord assured him with an oath
>     that the nations would be blessed through his offspring;
> that he would make him as numerous as the dust of the earth,
>     and exalt his offspring like the stars,
> and give them an inheritance from sea to sea
>     and from the Euphrates to the ends of the earth.

Sir 44:19–20a alludes to Genesis 17, where Abraham is called the "father of many nations" (Gen 17:4, 6), and where God made a covenant with Abraham and his offspring to be their God, with circumcision as the sign of the covenant (Gen 17:7–8, 10–14).[7] Next, Ben Sira alludes to the reiteration of the Abrahamic blessing in Gen 22:16–18 in order to highlight that the blessing for the nations and of numerous descendants was confirmed with an oath as a result of Abraham's obedience (Sir 44:20b–21ab).[8]

It is interesting to note that Ben Sira alludes to Ps 72:8, and he connects it with Gen 22:17–18, just as Ps 72:17 alludes to Gen 22:18.[9] However, while Ps 72:17 interprets the "seed" (זרע) as singular, referring to the ideal king of Israel, who will rule over the whole earth, Ben Sira takes the "seed" (זרע) to be collective, referring to the descendants of Abraham, who are destined to inherit the whole earth.[10] Also, although

---

7. See also Skehan and Di Lella, *Ben Sira*, 505; Marböck, "'Geschichte Israels,'" 184; Crenshaw, "Sirach," 842; Schreiner, "Patriarchen," 439; Reiterer, "Pentateuch," 173; Di Lella, "Praise of the Ancestors," 160.

8. In Sir 44:20b–21b MS B, Abraham's obedience as the grounds for God's oath that he shall have numerous offspring and that "the nations would be blessed through his offspring" is marked by the connective על כן ("therefore"; LXX διὰ τοῦτο). See also Mack, *Wisdom and the Hebrew Epic*, 211, 213; Wisdom, *Blessing*, 66; Di Lella, "Praise of the Ancestors," 160. On the allusion of Sir 44:20b–21b to Gen 22:16–18, see also Skehan and Di Lella, *Ben Sira*, 505; Marböck, "'Geschichte Israels,'" 184; Crenshaw, "Sirach," 842.

9. See also pp. 102–5 above on Ps 72:17. On the allusion of Sir 44:21c to Ps 72:8, see also Skehan and Di Lella, *Ben Sira*, 505; Marböck, "'Geschichte Israels,'" 184; Crenshaw, "Sirach," 842; Schreiner, "Patriarchen," 439. Cf. Sir 44:21c with Ps 72:8 ESV: "May he have dominion from sea to sea, and from the River to the ends of the earth!"

10. On the descendants of Abraham inheriting the whole earth, see also Mack,

the metaphors of the "sand of the seashore" and the "stars in the sky" in Gen 22:17-18 function similarly to describe how numerous Abraham's descendants shall be, Ben Sira understands the metaphor of the "dust of the earth" (cf. Gen 13:16; 28:14) as describing the abundance of Abraham's descendants, and the "stars of the sky" (cf. Gen 15:5: 22:17) as the exaltation (ἀνυψῶσαι, "to exalt") of Abraham's descendants (Sir 44:21b).[11] Although Ben Sira does not elaborate on how the nations shall be blessed by the descendants of Abraham, he clearly ties the blessing for the nations to Abraham's obedience.[12]

In accordance with the Genesis narrative, Ben Sira also mentions that the Abrahamic blessings have been passed on to Isaac and Jacob (Sir 44:21-23; cf. Gen 26:3-5; 28:4, 13-15).[13] It is noteworthy that, although the Hebrew MS B of Sir 44:22 indicates that "the covenant of all his forebears" and "the blessing" have been given to Jacob, Sir 44:22-23a LXX states that "a blessing of all people and a covenant" are given.[14] It is difficult

---

*Wisdom and the Hebrew Epic*, 54; Marböck, "'Geschichte Israels,'" 184.

11. Sir 44:21b NRSV: "that he would make him as numerous as the dust of the earth, and exalt his offspring like the stars." This strophe appears in the LXX but is not attested in the extant Hebrew manuscript fragments, and the Syr. version reads, "that he would make his descendants numerous as the sands of the seashore, and that he would set his descendants above all other nations" (Skehan and Di Lella, *Ben Sira*, 504; Beentjes, *Ben Sira in Hebrew*, 13-19, 78). See also Schreiner, "Patriarchen," 439, who notes the change in the interpretation of the metaphor of the stars to mean that "the people of Israel is significant in the Hellenistic world."

12. A few scholars attempt to elucidate Ben Sira's understanding of how the nations shall be blessed by Abraham's descendants. E.g., (1) Abraham is an asset to the world when his descendants are faithful to God, and thus exert a worldwide influence on others (Reiterer, "Pentateuch," 174); (2) Abraham is the mediator of blessings to the peoples of the world (Marböck, "'Geschichte Israels,'" 184-85). Although Wisdom notes that "the connection between blessing for the nations and Israel's role as inheritor of the whole earth is left unstated," he nevertheless deduces, "It may be that as Israel fills the whole earth, this presence is the blessing for the nations" (Wisdom, *Blessing*, 67). These elucidations are reasonable deductions from the text, but they are nonetheless not spelled out explicitly by Ben Sira himself.

13. See also Mack, *Wisdom and the Hebrew Epic*, 45, 53; Crenshaw, "Sirach," 842.

14. Cf. Sir 44:22 MS B, lit.: "And also he established [the covenant] with Isaac similarly, for the sake of Abraham his father. The covenant of all his forebears [ברית כל ראשון], he has given it, and the blessing [וברכה], he caused it to rest upon the head of Israel" and Sir 44:22-23a LXX, lit.: "And with Isaac he established similarly, because of Abraham his father's sake, a blessing of all people and a covenant [εὐλογίαν πάντων ἀνθρώπων καὶ διαθήκην], he made it rest upon the head of Jacob" (both translations mine). ראשון in MS B means "forebears" (BDB 911; *HALOT* 3:1168). However, the LXX reads ἄνθρωποι ("people"). The LXX also differs from the

to determine with certainty whether the LXX or the Hebrew MS B has the reading closer to the original.[15]

Based on Sir 44:22–23a LXX, Wisdom argues that, because "the promise of blessing for the nations . . . is repeated in Ben Sira's brief account of the continuation of the covenant with Isaac," the repetition "thereby suggests its importance" for Ben Sira.[16] Wisdom's inference is questionable, as he assumes the LXX to be the original reading, and he has ignored the variant reading in the Hebrew text of Sir 44:22. If it could be established that the Hebrew MS B has the original reading, it may be possible to argue that the repetition of the blessing for the nations/peoples in the LXX suggests its importance for Ben Sira's grandson, who translated the Hebrew original to Greek, rather than Ben Sira himself. However, the LXX could also be an unintentional misreading of the Hebrew original. The presence of the variant readings warns us against drawing conclusions on Ben Sira's literary emphasis based on only one of the variant readings. Therefore, it is tenuous to infer any importance in the "blessing of all people" for Ben Sira or his grandson based only on the LXX rendering of Sir 44:22–23a.

In any case, the blessing for the nations is still tied closely with Abraham's obedience, and there is nowhere else in the book of Ben Sira that shows concern for the salvation and well-being of the Gentiles. Given this overall tenor of the book, it is unlikely that Paul's emphasis on the blessing for the nations in Gal 3:6–14 is in any way influenced by the LXX rending of Sir 44:22–23a.[17]

---

Hebrew MS B in that the latter links the phrase, כל ראשון ("all the forebears"), with ברית ("covenant"), while the former links πάντων ἀνθρώπων ("all people") with εὐλογία ("blessing"). Nonetheless, the syntax of the LXX is ambiguous regarding the phrase, "the blessing of all people and the covenant," in that both may be linked with Isaac (e.g., REB), or Jacob (e.g., NRSV), or the blessing may be linked with Isaac and the covenant with Jacob (e.g., NJB).

15. The difficulty in determining the original reading of Sir 44:22–23 lies in the fact that the passage in Hebrew is only extant in MS B, which was recovered from the Cairo Synagogue Genizah and dated from the twelfth century (Skehan and Di Lella, *Ben Sira*, 51–52). Those who follow the Hebrew MS B reading are, e.g., NAB; Skehan and Di Lella, *Ben Sira*, 503; Di Lella, "Praise of the Ancestors," 160. Those who follow the LXX reading are, e.g., NRSV; REB; NJB; Wisdom, *Blessing*, 66.

16. Wisdom, *Blessing*, 66–67.

17. Paul might be aware of both the Hebrew and Greek renderings of Sir 44:22–23, since both texts were in circulation during the first century CE. Hebrew manuscript evidence dated between the the first century BCE and the first half of the first century CE are 2Q18 and 11QPs<sup>a</sup> from Qumran (Skehan and Di Lella, *Ben Sira*, 53). Although there is no extant Greek manuscript dated from the first century CE, the large number

## The Spirit's Temporary Absence in the Blessing of Abraham

### Tobit[18]

The book of Tobit is commonly dated between 225 and 175 BCE.[19] The narrative of the book is set in the eighth century BCE among the eastern Diaspora, and it seeks to instruct the Jews in the Diaspora how they should live, especially in obeying the Mosaic law.[20]

The narrative ends with a song of praise by Tobit, the main character of the book, before his death (Tob 13:1—14:15). In this song, Tobit speaks of Jerusalem, and how many nations will come to Jerusalem with gifts to present to God, the King of heaven (Tob 13:11). All who are against Jerusalem will be cursed, while all who fear and love her will be blessed forever (Tob 13:12, 14).[21] The language of "all nations coming to Jerusalem with gifts" (Tob 13:11) most likely alludes to Isa 2:2-4, 60:3-16 and Mic 4:1-4, and the curse and blessing language in Tob 13:12, 14 to Gen 12:3a, 27:29 and Num 24:9.[22] Although Tob 13:12, 14 does not directly allude to the

---

of manuscripts from the third century CE onwards shows its widespread use after its translation at the end of second century BCE. For a comprehensive list of the extant Greek manuscripts, see Ziegler, *Sapientia*, 7-13. On the other hand, Paul's emphasis on the inclusion of Gentiles in the blessing of Abraham in Galatians may be his response to the lack of concern for the Gentiles in this tradition.

18. Unless otherwise indicated, the versification of Tobit in this section follows the NRSV, and the English translation is taken from Fitzmyer, *Tobit*. The Hebrew/Aramaic texts and their corresponding translation are taken from García Martínez and Tigchelaar, *Dead Sea Scrolls Study Edition*, 1:386-87, 398-99.

19. Moore, *Tobit*, 40-42; Nowell, "Tobit," 976-77; Schüngel-Straumann, *Tobit*, 39; Otzen, *Tobit*, 57; Fitzmyer, *Tobit*, 52. The original language of the book of Tobit is Semitic (either Aramaic or Hebrew), and there are two recensions of the Greek version. For details of the manuscript evidence of the Semitic text of Tobit and its various versions, see Otzen, *Tobit*, 60-66; Fitzmyer, *Tobit*, 3-28; Weeks et al., *Tobit*, 1-59.

20. Levine, "Tobit," 42-51, 64; Otzen, *Tobit*, 2; Fitzmyer, *Tobit*, 31-32; Ego, "Tobit and the Diaspora," 41-54.

21. In the Greek version, the shorter recension has "all who love you shall be blessed [εὐλογημένοι]," while the longer recension has "all who fear you shall be blessed [εὐλογητοί]" (Fitzmyer, *Tobit*, 302). Nevertheless, the concept of "those who love Jerusalem are blessed" is the same in both verses. The antecedent of the second person singular pronoun ("you") in Tob 13:12, 14 is Jerusalem (Tob 13:9). See also Schüngel-Straumann, *Tobit*, 172-74; Fitzmyer, *Tobit*, 311. Contra Wisdom, *Blessing*, 68n10, who thinks that the "you" refers to God.

22. See also Moore, *Tobit*, 280-81; Schüngel-Straumann, *Tobit*, 172; Fitzmyer, *Tobit*, 314-15. Tob 13:12 NRSV: "Cursed are all who speak a harsh word against you; cursed are all who conquer you . . . But blessed for ever will be all who revere you." Both recensions of Tob 13:14 LXX (=Tob 13:12 Eng.) alludes to Gen 12:3a LXX in their use of εὐλογέω/εὐλογητός ("blessed"; cf. εὐλογέω in Gen 12:3a LXX) and ἐπικατάρατος ("cursed"; cf. καταράομαι in Gen 12:3a LXX). The Qumran Aramaic

Abrahamic blessing for the nations in Gen 12:3b ("all the families of the earth shall be blessed in you"), the allusion to Gen 12:3a ("I will bless those who bless you, I will curse the one who curses you") in the context of "many nations coming to Jerusalem" may indicate how the author of Tobit understands the manner by which nations are blessed by their association with Abraham's descendants—those nations who treat Jerusalem and her people well shall be blessed.[23]

## Jubilees[24]

It is now commonly accepted that the book of *Jubilees* was composed in Hebrew around the mid-second century BCE.[25] The genre of *Jubilees* is classified as the "Rewritten Bible," in which the author copies large amounts of passages from the Pentateuch into a new literary framework, usually with minor changes and expansions, in order to address contemporary issues

---

of Tob 13:12 (4Q196 17 II, 15-16) uses the word ארר ("cursed"), which is a cognate of the word ארר ("to curse") in Gen 12:3a MT. However, the second half of Tob 13:12 on the blessing is not preserved in the Qumran fragments. See also Fitzmyer, *Tobit*, 314-15. For a textual comparison of the Greek, Latin, Hebrew, Aramaic, and Syriac of Tob 13:12-14, see Weeks et al., *Tobit*, 310-13.

23. See also Wisdom, *Blessing*, 68n10. Wisdom also thinks that Tob 4:12 alludes to the Abrahamic blessing for the nations. In Tob 4:12-13, Tobit exhorts his son on the importance of endogamy: "Remember, my son, that Noah, Abraham, Isaac, and Jacob, our ancestors of old, all took wives from among their kindred. They were blessed [εὐλογήθησαν] in [ἐν] their children, and their posterity will inherit the land." (Tob 4:12b NRSV). Wisdom asserts that "with the mention of Abraham and his sons which preceded, the use of the future [sic] passive of εὐλογεῖν with the preposition ἐν will almost certainly alert the reader familiar with the Genesis narrative to the third strand of the promise [i.e., blessing for the nations]" (Wisdom, *Blessing*, 67-68). However, I disagree with Wisdom, because (1) the subject of the aorist passive, εὐλογήθησαν ("they were blessed"), is clearly the patriarchs, and not the nations; and (2) there is no mention at all of how nations may be blessed on account of Abraham or his descendants in the context of Tob 4.

24. Unless otherwise indicated, the English translation of the book of *Jubilees* in this chapter is taken from VanderKam, *Jubilees* (1989b).

25. Wintermute, "Jubilees," 2:43-44; Endres, *Biblical Interpretation*, 10; VanderKam, *Jubilees* (2001), 13-21; Segal, *Jubilees*, 319-22. The Hebrew original was later translated into Greek, and from the Greek into Latin, Classical Ethiopic, and possibly Syriac. Some Hebrew fragments of the book have been found at Qumran, but the most complete extant manuscript of *Jubilees* is in Ethiopic. For the textual history of *Jubilees*, see VanderKam, *Jubilees* (1989b), V-XXXIV; idem, *Jubilees* (2001), 13-17.

and to present the author's interpretation of the biblical text as authoritative.[26] As such, *Jubilees* retells Genesis and the first half of Exodus.[27]

The overall contexts, in which the Abrahamic blessing for the nations and its reiterations appear in *Jubilees*, are similar to the contexts of Genesis. However, a closer look reveals some significant differences in the immediate context of the Abrahamic blessing in *Jubilees* compared with Genesis. In Genesis, the divine promise of blessing to Abraham in Gen 12:1–3 is a reassertion of God's original intention to bless humankind (cf. Gen 1:28; 9:1).[28] However, in *Jubilees*, God's blessings on the first pair of humans (Gen 1:28) is absent, but replaced by an expansion on the Sabbath, where God separated "a people for [him]self from among [his] nations" from the descendants of Jacob, so that they may keep the Sabbath (*Jub.* 2:17–21). The promise of blessing made to Abraham for the first time in Genesis is immediately subsequent to the Babel incident and the linear genealogies of Shem and Terah (Gen 11:1–32).[29] On the other hand, *Jubilees* expands the Genesis text substantially by providing a story of Abraham's early life, in which the author relates Abraham's conversion from polytheism to monotheism and emphasizes his zeal and piety towards this monotheistic God (*Jub.* 11:15—12:20). The divine promise of blessing was made to Abraham for the first time in response to his prayer to seek God's guidance (*Jub.* 12:21):

---

26. VanderKam, "Jubilees," 113; Segal, *Jubilees*, 4–5. See also Nickelsburg, "Bible Rewritten," 97–104; Harrington, "Bible Rewritten," 239–40.

27. Nickelsburg, "Bible Rewritten," 97; VanderKam, "Jubilees," 113; idem, *Jubilees* (2001), 11.

28. See pp. 61–67 above.

29. Although Abram's name was changed to "Abraham" only in Gen 17:5 (cf. *Jub.* 15:7), I will use the name "Abraham" throughout this section for the sake of simplicity.

## The Blessing of Abraham, the Spirit, and Justification in Galatians

| Jub. 12:22–23 | Gen 12:1–3 ESV |
|---|---|
| When he had finished speaking and praying, then the word of the Lord was sent to him through me: "Now you, come from your land, your family, and your father's house to the land which I will show you. I will make you into a large and populous people. I will bless you and magnify your reputation. You will become blessed in the earth. *All the nations of the earth will be blessed*³⁰ *in you*. Those who bless you I will bless, while those who curse you I will curse." | Now the LORD said to Abram, "Go from your country and your kindred and your father's house to the land that I will show you. And I will make of you a great nation, and I will bless you and make your name great, so that you will be a blessing. I will bless those who bless you, and him who dishonors you I will curse, and *in you all the families of the earth shall be blessed*." |

Despite the change of the immediate context of the Abrahamic blessing, the wording of the blessing for the nations (*Jub.* 12:23) follows Gen 12:3b rather closely, with the exception of rendering מִשְׁפְּחֹת ("families") as "nations."³¹ The change from "families" to "nations" in *Jub.* 12:23 does not show clearly how the author understood the blessing of the nations. However, while the blessing of the nations is the climax of the Abrahamic promise in Genesis, the change in context and the absence of the divine blessing of Gen 1:28 in *Jubilees* water down such a climax.³²

---

30. All English translations render the Ethiopic verb (*yetbāraku*; "bless") consistently as passive ("be blessed"), except for Wintermute, who translates it as a direct reflexive ("bless themselves") in *Jub.* 12:23; 18:16; 24:11 (Schodde, "Jubilees," 457, 472, 728, 737; Charles, "Jubilees," 48, 63, 78, 87; Wintermute, "Jubilees," 2:81, 91, 103, 109; VanderKam, *Jubilees* [1989a], 73, 109, 152, 176). Wintermute's rendering is likely due to his understanding of the force of the Niphal and Hitpael of ברך ("to bless") in the Genesis MT, rather than warranted by the Ethiopic verb. This is because the form of the Ethiopic word for "bless" (*yetbāraku*) is the same in *Jub.* 12:23; 18:16; 24:11; 27:23 (VanderKam, *Jubilees* [1989a], 76, 105, 134, 152). Furthermore, as the Ethiopic version is most likely translated from the Greek version, it probably reflects the future passive ("will be blessed") in the LXX Genesis texts, rather than the Niphal and Hitpael of the Hebrew Genesis texts. VanderKam confirmed my observations above in a personal email to me dated January 30, 2009. Unfortunately, there are no extant Hebrew manuscript fragments that attest to *Jub.* 12:23; 18:16; 24:11 (cf. VanderKam, *Jubilees* [1989b], VII).

31. There is a textual variant of "fathers" instead of "nations" in some Ethiopic MSS. VanderKam points out that, as all the versions of Gen 12:3 and the Syriac citation show, the correct reading should be "nations" (VanderKam, *Jubilees* [1989b], 73).

32. Scholars who also see the change in context in *Jubilees* compared with Genesis include Müller, "Abraham-Gestalt," 244–46; Balestier-Stengel, "Un aperçu," 61–71. Müller notes that the author of *Jubilees* has a different emphasis from Genesis and uses the primeval narrative of Genesis primarily to emphasize the importance of keeping the Sabbath, the special election of the descendants of Jacob, the solar calendar, and

## The Spirit's Temporary Absence in the Blessing of Abraham

The next reiteration of the Abrahamic blessing for the nations occurs in the context of the sacrifice of Isaac (*Jub.* 18:16; cf. Gen 22:18).[33] While Abraham is tested by God in Gen 22:1–19 in order to find out whether he truly fears God (Gen 22:12), *Jubilees* sets the test of Abraham as a response of God to the challenge of Prince Mastema with regard to Abraham's faithfulness (*Jub.* 17:15–18:16). God already knew Abraham to be faithful (*Jub.* 17:15), and the test was to prove Abraham's faithfulness (*Jub.* 18:16):

| *Jub.* 18:15–16 | Gen 22:16–18 ESV |
|---|---|
| He said, "I have sworn by myself, says the Lord: because you have performed this command and have not refused me your first-born son whom you love, I will indeed bless you and will indeed multiply your descendants like the stars in the sky and like the sands on the seashore. Your descendants will possess the cities of their enemies. *All the nations of the earth will be blessed through your descendants* because of the fact that you have obeyed my command. I have made known to everyone that you are faithful to me in everything that I have told you. Go in peace." | and [the LORD] said, "By myself I have sworn, declares the LORD, because you have done this and have not withheld your son, your only son, I will surely bless you, and I will surely multiply your offspring as the stars of heaven and as the sand that is on the seashore. And your offspring shall possess the gate of his enemies, and *in your offspring shall all the nations of the earth be blessed*, because you have obeyed my voice." |

The wording of the Abrahamic blessing for the nations in *Jub.* 18:16 follows Gen 22:18 closely, and the change in context in this case does not alter the fact that God affirmed his initial promise to bless Abraham (Gen 12:2–3; *Jub.* 12:22–23) because of Abraham's obedience.

God's reiteration of the Abrahamic promise to Isaac for the first time in *Jubilees* 24:8–11 is set in the same context as in Gen 26:1–5, when Isaac settled in the land of the Philistines during a famine:

---

the Jubilean year system. Balestier-Stengel also sees the rereading of Gen 11:27—12:5 in *Jub.* 12 as being set in a context different from Genesis in an attempt by the author to address contemporary issues and to present Abraham as the model of perfect Jew. On the blessing for the nations as the climax of the Abrahamic blessing in Genesis, see p. 74 above.

33. Although the Abrahamic blessing for the nations is reiterated in Gen 18:18, there is no parallel in *Jubilees*.

# The Blessing of Abraham, the Spirit, and Justification in Galatians

| Jub. 24:9-11 | Gen 26:2-5 ESV |
|---|---|
| The Lord appeared to him and told him: ". . . I will be with you and bless you, because I will give this entire land to you and your descendants. I will carry out the terms of my oath which I swore to your father Abraham. I will make your descendants as numerous as the stars of the sky. I will give this entire land to your descendants. *All the peoples of the earth will be blessed through your descendants* because of the fact that your father obeyed me and kept my obligations, commands, laws, statutes, and covenant. Now obey me and live in this land." | And the LORD appeared to him and said, ". . . I will be with you and will bless you, for to you and to your offspring I will give all these lands, and I will establish the oath that I swore to Abraham your father. I will multiply your offspring as the stars of heaven and will give to your offspring all these lands. *And in your offspring all the nations of the earth shall be blessed*, because Abraham obeyed my voice and kept my charge, my commandments, my statutes, and my laws." |

Once again, the wording of the Abrahamic blessing for the nations in *Jub.* 24:11 follows Gen 26:3 closely. Although VanderKam renders the phrase as "all the peoples" in *Jub.* 24:11, all other English translations render the phrase as "all the nations."[34] As the Ethiopic word for "nations" is the same in *Jub.* 12:23; 18:16; 24:11, VanderKam's change to "peoples" in *Jub.* 24:11 is likely to be a stylistic variation.[35]

The immediate contexts of Genesis 26 and *Jubilees* 24 do not clearly show how "all the nations of the earth will be blessed" in Isaac's descendants. However, the story of Isaac cursing the Philistines in *Jub.* 24:27-33, which is not found in the context of Genesis 26, may show the author's antagonism towards the Gentile nations.

As in the case of Genesis, the last instance of the Abrahamic blessing for the nations in *Jubilees* appears in the context where God reiterates the Abrahamic blessing to Jacob for the first time at Bethel when he was on his way to Haran (Gen 28:10-17; *Jub.* 27:19-25):

---

34. Schodde, "Jubilees," 728; Charles, "Jubilees," 78; Wintermute, "Jubilees," 2:103.

35. Cf. VanderKam, *Jubilees* (1989a), 76, 105, 134; idem, *Jubilees* (1989b), 73, 109, 152. The Ethiopic word for "nations" is *'aḥzāb* (VanderKam, *Jubilees* [1989b], 73 notes on 12:23). In a personal email to me dated January 30, 2009, VanderKam confirmed that his rendering of "peoples" in *Jub.* 24:11 instead of "nations" does not reflect a different Ethiopic word.

| Jub. 27:22–23 | Gen 28:13–14 ESV |
|---|---|
| He spoke with Jacob and said: "I am the God of Abraham your father and the God of Isaac. The land on which you are sleeping I will give to you and your descendants after you. Your descendants will be like the sands of the earth. You will become numerous toward the west, the east, the north, and the south. *All the families of the nations will be blessed through you and your descendants."* | And behold, the LORD stood above it and said, "I am the LORD, the God of Abraham your father and the God of Isaac. The land on which you lie I will give to you and to your offspring. Your offspring shall be like the dust of the earth, and you shall spread abroad to the west and to the east and to the north and to the south, and *in you and your offspring shall all the families of the earth be blessed."* |

As before, the wording of the Abrahamic blessing for the nations in *Jub.* 27:23 follows Gen 28:14 rather closely. Although the Ethiopic version of *Jub.* 27:23, whose English translation is shown above, reads "families of the nations," the Latin version reads "families of the earth."[36]

There are a number of examples in Genesis in which "nations are blessed" on account of Abraham and his descendants, either on an individual or on a national basis: (1) Abraham rescued the people and property of Sodom (Gen 14:11–24) and interceded for Sodom and the people of Gerar (Gen 18:22–23; 20:17); (2) Laban acknowledged that he had been blessed by God because of Jacob (Gen 30:27); and (3) Potiphar, Egypt, and "all the earth" are blessed because of Joseph and his storage of food for the severe famine (Gen 39:5; 41:53–57). In the literary framework of *Jubilees*, only (1) and (3) above are included (*Jub.* 13:22–29; 39:3; 42:2–3), but the passage on "all the earth" coming to buy food from Egypt has been omitted (cf. Gen 41:57).

---

36. VanderKam, ed., *Jubilees* [1989a], 282; idem, *Jubilees* [1989b], 176 notes on 27:23, 351. Following Endres, Wisdom suggests that "the change in Jubilees from 'earth' to 'nations' is the one significant modification in this verse, and it appears to make the text refer more directly to gentiles" (Endres, *Biblical Interpretation*, 99; Wisdom, *Blessing*, 71). The inference drawn by them is questionable because they have neglected the alternate reading in the Latin version, which is an independent witness of the Greek version, and have assumed the reading in the Ethiopic version, which was also translated from the Greek version, to be the original in Hebrew or in the Greek version. Furthermore, the oldest extant Latin manuscript is about nine hundred years earlier than the oldest extant Ethiopic manuscript (VanderKam, *Jubilees* [1989b], XVII). Therefore, the Latin version is more likely to be closer to the Greek version than the Ethiopic version. This textual variant warns us against taking the Ethiopic reading definitively in deriving the theological "climate" of Paul's time.

However, from an expansion of the Abraham story, where Abraham summoned all his children and grandchildren from Sarah, Hagar, and Keturah in order to exhort them before he sent his other children away from Isaac (*Jub.* 20:1-13; cf. Gen 25:6), we may infer how the author of *Jubilees* understands the nations to be blessed on account of Abraham. After exhorting his children to keep the commands of the Lord (*Jub.* 20:2-9a), Abraham assured them that if they "do what is right and just before [the Lord]," God will bless them with all kinds of fruitfulness (*Jub.* 20:9). As a result of their prosperity, all the nations of the earth will desire to be like them, and they will bless the descendants of Abraham in the patriarch's name so that they may also be blessed likewise by God (*Jub.* 20:10).[37]

The author of *Jubilees* considers God's blessings on Abraham and his descendants as a paradigm that is desired by all other people. The nations' use of Abraham's name in blessing his descendants, in order that they themselves may be blessed by God, reflects the author's understanding of God's promise to Abraham in Gen 12:3a, "I will bless those who bless you." However, such an understanding of nations actively seeking to be blessed by God like Abraham and the use of Abraham's name as a formula of blessing is not apparent in the narrative context of Genesis.[38] Nonetheless, the key issue in *Jub.* 20:1-13 is Abraham's effort to exhort and motivate his children to keep God's laws, rather than on how the nations may be blessed on account of Abraham and his descendants.[39]

---

37. In *Jub.* 20:10, Abraham said to all his children and grandchildren from Sarah, Hagar, and Keturah, "You will become a blessing on the earth, and all the nations of the earth will be delighted with you. They will bless your sons in my name so that they may be blessed as I am."

38. Nowhere in Genesis do people actively seek to be blessed by God like Abraham or of people using his name as a formula of blessing. How others are blessed on account of Abraham and his descendants is stated as a matter of fact in the narrative (e.g., Potiphar in Gen 39:5) and at most acknowledged (e.g., Laban in Gen 30:27), but these people do not actively seek to be blessed on account of their association with Abraham or his descendants.

39. See also Müller, "Abraham-Gestalt," 251-52, who notes that "the general theme [of *Jub.* 20-21] is a warning against idolatry and impurity, which is supplemented by a requirement to obey God in order to receive his blessing." Contra Wisdom, *Blessing*, 73, who argues with regard to *Jub.* 20:10 that "obedience to the Lord's commandments by Abraham's children thus results in a blessing for those who dwell upon the earth." Although Wisdom admits that "the text of Jubilees does not indicate the nature of this blessing," he thinks "it is possible the author understands that the ubiquitous presence of the descendants of Abraham will mediate blessing for the nations (*Jub.* 19.21b-24)." However, it is clear from the context of *Jubilees* 19-20 that the mention of Abraham and his children "becoming a blessing" (*Jub.*19:17; 20:10) among other people refers to

While the Abrahamic blessing for the nations is intricately related to the original divine intention to bless humankind (Gen 1:28) and forms an integral part of the Genesis narrative, the citing of this element of the Abrahamic promise in *Jubilees* appears to be incidental, even though its wording follows the Genesis texts closely. The author does not seem to be especially concerned with developing the motif of the Abrahamic blessing for the nations. Instead, the author is mainly concerned with using parts of the Genesis narrative to justify (1) the use of a Jubilean chronological system and a solar calendar; (2) the importance of keeping the Torah and the understanding that the Torah was already revealed to the ancestors prior to Moses; (3) the segregation from impure Gentiles;[40] and (4) the preeminence of the priestly line.[41]

## Philo[42]

Philo of Alexandria lived from about 20 BCE to 50 CE.[43] The frequent mention of Abraham in his works and his extensive interpretation of Genesis make him a very important resource in our study on the development of the Abrahamic blessing for the nations during the Second Temple period. Philo cites the Abrahamic blessing for the nations explicitly in *On the Migration of Abraham* (*Migration* 1; cf. Gen 12:3), *Who is the Heir?* (*Heir* 8; cf. Gen 26:4), and *On Dreams* (*Dreams* 1.3; cf. Gen 28:14).[44] He also expounds in detail how the nations are blessed on account of Abraham's descendants in *Migration* 118–122 and *Dreams* 1.175–177.[45] Philo's un-

---

them as a *paradigm* of being specially and signally blessed by God, rather than a *source* of blessing for other people. This understanding is confirmed in *Jub.* 12:23 (cf. Gen 12:2), where God promised that "Abraham will become blessed in the earth."

40. On the general attitude of *Jubilees* towards the Gentiles, see p. 162 below.

41. VanderKam, "Origins and Purposes," 16–19. See also Segal, *Jubilees*, 322–24, who proposes that *Jubilees* sought to explain the origin of the law, the chronological system, and the origin of evil.

42. Unless otherwise indicated, the English translation of Philo's works in this section is taken from Philo, *Works of Philo*, and the Greek texts are quoted from *Philo: With English Translation* (LCL).

43. Williamson, *Philo*, 1; Scholer, "Introduction to Philo," xi.

44. All of Philo's citations of the Abrahamic blessing for the nations (*Migration* 1; *Heir* 2.8; *Dreams* 1.3) follow the LXX verbatim (cf. Gen 12:3; 26:4; 28:14 LXX).

45. Philo's usual practice is to offer both literal and allegorical interpretations of the Scriptures he is discussing. In this section, I will primarily discuss his literal interpretations in the main text and mention his allegorical interpretations in the footnotes. This is because the former explains how other people are blessed by individuals, and it is

derstanding of the significance of Abraham as "the father of many nations" in relation to the Gentiles is found in *Questions and Answers on Genesis* (*QG* 3.42, 44; cf. Gen 17:4, 6).

## On the Migration of Abraham

Philo cites Gen 12:1-3 as the introduction to his work, *On the Migration of Abraham* (*Migration* 1).[46] Throughout the work, Philo interprets various phrases of Gen 12:1-3.[47] When commenting on the phrase, "I will bless those who bless thee, and curse those who curse thee" (*Migration* 109-117; cf. Gen 12:3a), Philo uses Balaam as an illustration. Philo explains that although Balaam seems to have blessed Israel outwardly, God knew that in Balaam's heart, he was actually cursing Israel (*Migration* 115). Therefore, Balaam was judged "to have been an impious man and accursed," even though he appeared to be blessing Israel outwardly (*Migration* 113). Therefore, as Wisdom notes, the intention to bless or curse Abraham or his descendants is "the criterion upon which blessing and cursing will come to other people."[48]

In *Migration* 118-127a, Philo elucidates how "all the tribes of the earth shall be blessed in you."[49] According to Philo, there had been instanc-

---

thus more relevant to our present study. The latter is about how a sound human mind can positively affect its various mental faculties, and it has no bearing on how other people may be blessed as a result.

46. Philo, *Migration* 1: "And the Lord said unto Abraham, 'Depart out of thy land and out of thy kindred, and out of thy father's house, into the land which I will shew thee; and I will make thee a great nation and will bless thee and will make thy name great, and thou shalt be blessed. And I will bless them that bless thee, and them that curse thee I will curse, and in thee shall all the tribes of the earth be blessed" (in Philo, *Philo: With an English Translation*. Translated by Francis H. Colson and George Herbert Whitaker).

47. The phrases that Philo comments on are, e.g., "depart from your land and kindred" (Philo, *Migration* 7-12), "I will make you a great nation" (Philo, *Migration* 53-55), "I will bless you" (Philo, *Migration* 70-72), "I will make your name great" (Philo, *Migration* 86), and "you shall be blessed" (Philo, *Migration* 106-8).

48. Wisdom, *Blessing*, 79. See also Böhm, *Rezeption und Funktion*, 273, who explains Philo's interpretation of "I will bless those who bless thee, and curse those who curse you" in *Migration* 109-117 as "the sincere blessing of a wise man by another person for a reward."

49. Other than the literal interpretation described above, Philo also gives an allegorical interpretation: "This is a pregnant and significant announcement; for it implies that, if the mind continues free from harm and sickness, it has all its tribes [φυλαί] and powers in a healthy condition, those whose province is sight and hearing and all

## The Spirit's Temporary Absence in the Blessing of Abraham

es when people have benefitted from an individual with noble character (*Migration* 120a). Such an individual is righteous and has wisdom, good character, and irresistible power that are given by God for the benefit of others (*Migration* 120b–121a). People benefit when the individual shares all his/her possessions generously with others (*Migration* 121b). Whatever such an individual does not have, he or she will pray to God, and God will unreservedly bless such a righteous person, such that the blessings overflow to others (*Migration* 121b–122).

Both Abraham and Moses are then mentioned as illustrations of how God answered their prayer and how others benefitted as a result of their intercession (*Migration* 122).[50] Philo himself provides a summary statement of his interpretation of "all the tribes of the earth shall be blessed in you" as follows: "We have now, then, said enough about gifts which God is accustomed to bestow on those who are to become perfect, and through the medium of them on others also" (*Migration* 127a).

### Who is the Heir of Divine Things?

In *Who is the Heir?* Philo cites Gen 26:4 to support his argument that Abraham shows his love for God by obeying all of God's commands (*Heir*

---

others concerned with sense-perception, and those again that have to do with pleasures and desires, and all that are undergoing transformation from the lower to the higher emotions" (Philo, *Migration* 119 [Colson and Whitaker, LCL]). The "earth" is interpreted allegorically as the human mind, while the "tribes" are the sensory and emotive faculties of the mind. This interpretation is also similar in Philo, *QG* 4.183 and Philo, *Dreams* 1.177.

50. Philo alludes to Abraham's intercessory prayer for Sodom, and how Lot was spared as a result (Philo, *Migration* 122b; cf. Gen 18:23–32; 19:29; see also Colson and Whitaker, LCL, 203; Böhm, *Rezeption und Funktion*, 274n118), as well as Moses' plea with God to spare the rebellious Israelites, who believed the ill report of the spies (cf. Num 14:11–20; see also Colson and Whitaker, LCL, 201 and the translator's notes in Philo, *Works of Philo*, 265n60).

8–9).[51] However, Philo does not elaborate how "the nations shall be blessed" in this work.[52]

## On Dreams, That They Are God-Sent

In his treatise to explain that certain dreams, in which the dreamer is able to foresee the future, are from God, Philo cites Jacob's dream of the ladder as his example (*Dreams* 1.2–3; cf. Gen 28:12–15).[53] As Philo cites Gen 28:12–15 LXX verbatim, the divine reiteration of the Abrahamic blessing for the nations in Gen 28:14 is also included in *Dreams* 1.3.[54]

Subsequently in *Dreams* 1.176–178, Philo explicates how "all the tribes of the earth shall be blessed in you": "but the wise and virtuous man is not only a blessing to himself, but he is also a common good to all men, diffusing advantages over all from his own ready store" (*Dreams* 1.176).[55]

---

51. See also Böhm, *Rezeption und Funktion*, 275 and n. 122. Philo, *Heir* 8–9: ". . . Abraham displayed his love to his master in the last sentence of the divine oracle given to his son, 'I will give to thee and to thy seed all this land, and in thy seed shall all the nations of the earth be blessed, because Abraham thy father obeyed my voice, and kept all my precepts, and all my commandments, and my laws, and my judgments.' And it is the greatest possible praise of a servant that he does not neglect a single thing of the commandments which his master lays upon him, but that he labors earnestly without any hesitation and with all his vigor, and even beyond his power to perform them all with a well affected mind."

52. See also Wisdom, *Blessing*, 80. Although Philo does not explain how "the nations shall be blessed" when he cites Gen 26:3 in *Heir* 8–9, he gives his interpretation of the blessing for the nations in Gen 26:4 in *QG* 4.183. However, he does not elaborate on the literal meaning in *QG* 4.183 but only gives the allegorical interpretation, which is basically the same as in *Migration* 119 (cf. Gen 12:3b) and *Dreams* 1.175 (cf. Gen 28:14). In *QG* 4.183, Philo interprets the "nations" as the various sensory and emotive faculties of the mind, while the "earth" refers to the person. If the mind is able to control all the senses and emotions ("the nations"), these faculties will become better ("be blessed").

53. Philo, *Dreams* 1.2–3: "Now the second species is that in which our mind, being moved simultaneously with the mind of the universe, has appeared . . . to be under the influence of divine impulses, so as to be rendered capable of comprehending beforehand . . . some of the events of the future. Now the first dream which is akin to the species which I have been describing, is that which appeared on the ladder which reached up to heaven. . . . And Jacob dreamed, and behold a ladder . . . and the Lord was standing steadily upon it; and he said, I am the God of Abraham thy father . . ."

54. Philo, *Dreams* 1.3b: "in thee shall all the kindreds of the earth be blessed, and in thy seed also."

55. As in *Migration* 119 and *QG* 4.183 (see above), Philo also offers an allegorical interpretation: "For if the mind which is in me have been rendered pure by perfect

## The Spirit's Temporary Absence in the Blessing of Abraham

Then, Philo employs two illustrations to show how others are blessed by a wise person: (1) as the sun is the light of all who have eyes, the wise person is light to "all those who partake of a rational nature" (*Dreams* 1.176); and (2) as the burning of aromatic herbs fill "all persons near them with their fragrance," all those people near to the wise people are also influenced and "so become improved in their characters" (*Dreams* 1.178).[56]

## Questions and Answers on Genesis

In the Genesis narrative, the promise of Abraham becoming "the father of many nations" (Gen 17:4-6) is a development of the blessing for the nations (Gen 12:3b).[57] Although the relationship between the two is not as close in Philo's work, his interpretation of Gen 17:4, 6 in *QG* 3.42, 44 nonetheless shows some connection between the two.

Philo offers two literal interpretations for Gen 17:4 (*QG* 3.42).[58] First, it means that each of Abraham's sons shall be a "founder of a nation."

---

virtue, then the 'tribes' [φυλαί] of that which is earthly in me are sharers of its purifying, those I mean which pertain to the senses and to that chiefest container, the body" (*Dreams* 1.177; Philo, *Philo*). In this passage, the "tribes" are interpreted allegorically not only as the sensory faculties, but also as the body.

56. In addition to the point about how people may be blessed by a wise individual, Wisdom concludes from *Dreams* 1.175 that "Philo declares this promise [i.e., the blessing for the nations] means that the Jewish race is a beneficial influence on the world," because Philo applies "the language of Abraham's descendants being multiplied like the sand of the earth both to their increase in number and to their moral influence on the world" (Wisdom, *Blessing*, 81). However, a closer reading of *Dreams* 1.175 shows that "the race of wisdom" (τὸ σοφίας γένος) does not refer to the "race" of Abraham (i.e., his descendants) characterized by wisdom, but rather Philo's allegorical interpretation of "race" as wisdom. It is wisdom (ὁ παιδείας λόγος "trained reason"; Colson and Whitaker, LCL) that restrains sinful and unjust deeds, not the descendants of Abraham. Thus, the one who possesses wisdom inherits "all the parts of the world, penetrating everywhere," and thereby, "the wise and virtuous man is not only a blessing to himself, but he is also a common good to all men, diffusing advantages over all from his own ready store" (Philo, *Dreams* 1.175b-176). It is important to note that Philo speaks of a wise individual who blesses others in this context, and not the Jewish race as a whole.

57. For the relationship between the blessing of the nations and Abraham becoming "the father of many nations" in the Genesis narrative, see pp. 77-78 above.

58. As is his usual practice, Philo also offers an allegorical interpretation of Abraham becoming "the father of many nations" in addition to the two literal interpretations in *QG* 3.42. The "multitude of nations" is interpreted allegorically as the "multifarious inclination of the will in each of our minds," and the "father" is the control of all these inclinations. If a person is able to exercise "supreme authority" in controlling all the

Second, Abraham shall not only love and care for his kindred, but also for all humankind.[59] Philo continues to comment on Gen 17:6 in *QG* 3.44 as follows:

> And that expression, "I will set thee among the nations," was used in order that God might more evidently demonstrate that he was making him worthy to be as a foundation and firm support to the nations through his wisdom, not only to his own nation, but also to all other peoples . . . since the wise man is the redeemer of nations and intercessor for them before God, and since it is he who implores pardon for the sins of his relations.

For Philo, Abraham, as the father of many nations, cares for all humankind and intercedes for them before God.[60] In this manner, the nations are blessed on account of Abraham.

## Summary

Philo cites the Abrahamic blessing for the nations in *Migration* 1 (cf. Gen 12:3); *Heir* 8 (cf. Gen 26:4); *Dreams* 1.3 (cf. Gen 28:14), and he offers his literal interpretation of how "the nations shall be blessed" in *Migration* 118–127; *Dreams* 1.176–178. For Philo, the people of other nations may be blessed on account of a wise individual, when such individuals, who are blessed richly by God due to their righteousness, share their possessions with others, intercede for others, and influence others for the better by their good character. This understanding is also apparent in Philo's exposition on the significance of Abraham as "the father of many nations" in *QG* 3.42, 44 (cf. Gen 17:4, 6).

Philo speaks of such a wise individual in general without specifying their ethnicity. However, given Philo's commitment to his Jewish heritage and beliefs, especially his attention to the law of Moses, and his interest

---

inclinations of the mind, these inclinations will be changed for the better.

59. Philo, *QG* 3.42b: "In the manner of a father, thou shalt be invested with care and supervision of many nations, for a lover of God is by the same token wont to be a lover of mankind, so that he is greatly concerned not only for his countrymen but also for all others at the same time, especially for those who are able to receive the discipline of attention and whose characters are not unpleasant and hard but easily give place to virtue and are submissive to right reason" (In *Philo: With an English Translation*).

60. In mentioning Abraham's intercessory prayers, Philo most likely alludes to Abraham's intercession for Sodom and his nephew, Lot (Gen 18:22–33), as well as his prayer for healing Abimelech's household (Gen 20:17–18). On the allusion to Gen 18:22–33, see also Böhm, *Rezeption und Funktion*, 353–54.

in persuading non-Jews on the universality of the law of Moses, we may assume that such an individual must have been a God-fearing person, who may be either a Jew or a proselyte.[61]

## *The Ladder of Jacob*[62]

The *Ladder of Jacob* is possibly a first-century Jewish work that expands on Gen 28:10–19, in which Jacob dreamt of a ladder connecting earth to heaven with angels of God ascending and descending on it.[63] This literary work not only adds details of the dream that are absent in Gen 28:12–15 (*Lad. Jac.* 1:4–6), it also seeks to explain the significance of the dream and its added details (*Lad. Jac.* 3:1–7:35).[64] Lunt notes that the theme running throughout the six chapters of the *Ladder of Jacob* "appears to be an apocalyptic vision of the future," which explains Israel's sins as the reason of the exile, and looks forward to a time when God will deliver the people.[65]

The divine speech in *Lad. Jac.* 1:9–12 generally follows the wording of Gen 28:13–15, with some alterations:[66]

---

61. On Philo's commitment to his Jewish beliefs and the law of Moses, and his interest in reaching out to non-Jews, see, e.g., Williamson, *Philo*, 2–5, 23–26; Scholer, "Introduction to Philo," xiii; Borgen, *Philo*, 282–87. Ronald Williamson also points out Philo's emphasis on obedience to the Law, rather than ethnicity, as the basis of being accepted by God, for Philo speaks of God's acceptance of proselytes, as well as his rejection and punishment of disobedient Jews.

62. Unless otherwise indicated, the English translation of the *Ladder of Jacob* is taken from Lunt, "Ladder of Jacob," 2:407.

63. The only extant ancient witnesses to the *Ladder of Jacob* are a number of Slavonic manuscripts that date from the fifteenth century CE and later (Lunt, "Ladder of Jacob," 2:402–3). The Slavonic version is likely to have been translated from Greek (Pennington, "Ladder of Jacob," 453; Lunt, "Ladder of Jacob," 2:403; Kugel, *Ladder of Jacob*, 24). Lunt notes the transliteration of Hebrew words in the text, and proposes that the *Ladder of Jacob* probably originated as a Jewish document during the first century CE, but was later redacted by Christians in the Byzantine circles (Lunt, "Ladder of Jacob," 2:402, 404n3). On the basis of observing a number of parallels to the rabbinic traditions and likely allusions to the historical events during the Roman rule of Palestine, Kugel also comes to a similar conclusion as Lunt (Kugel, *Ladder of Jacob*, 24–32; idem, "The Ladder of Jacob," 209 and n. 2). See also Charlesworth, "Ladder of Jacob," 3:609; Orlov, *Apocalypticism*, 401.

64. Most scholars agree that *Lad. Jac.* 7:1–35, found in the longer recension, is a Christian addition (James, *Lost Apocrypha*, 101; Lunt, "Ladder of Jacob," 404; Charlesworth, "Ladder of Jacob," 609; Kugel, "Ladder of Jacob," 227).

65. Lunt, "Ladder of Jacob," 406.

66. As this study focuses on the Abrahamic blessing for the nations, I shall not

## The Blessing of Abraham, the Spirit, and Justification in Galatians

| Lad. Jac. 1:9–12 | Gen 28:13–15 ESV |
|---|---|
| And he said to me, "The land on which you are sleeping, to you will I give it, and to your seed after you. And I will multiply your seed as the stars of heaven and the sand of the sea. *And through your seed all the earth and those living on it in the last times of the years of completion shall be blessed.* My blessing with which I have blessed you shall flow from you unto the last generation; the East and the West all shall be full of your tribe." | And behold, the LORD stood above it and said, "I am the LORD, the God of Abraham your father and the God of Isaac. The land on which you lie I will give to you and to your offspring. Your offspring shall be like the dust of the earth, and you shall spread abroad to the west and to the east and to the north and to the south, and *in you and your offspring shall all the families of the earth be blessed*. Behold, I am with you and will keep you wherever you go, and will bring you back to this land. For I will not leave you until I have done what I have promised you." |

The means of blessing for the nations in *Lad. Jac.* 1:11 is only "through your seed," unlike Gen 28:14, which has "in you and your offspring." Also, the nations are said to be blessed until "the last times."[67] Although God's blessing is said to flow through Jacob until "the last times," it is not clear from the context what the nature of this blessing is.

Wisdom argues from this text that the blessing for the nations is "Israel's blessing flowing to the inhabitants of the earth. The whole world will be filled with Jacob's tribe and this ubiquitous presence may be the author's implicit suggestion concerning the form in which this blessing for all the earth is realized."[68] As Wisdom himself admits, his inference is only "implicit," and the explanation of the significance of the dream in the *Ladder of Jacob* from chapter 3 onwards does not explicate how nations

---

comment on changes made regarding other elements of the Abrahamic promise, such as descendants and land, in *Lad. Jac.* 1:9–12.

67. See also Pennington's translation of *Lad. Jac.* 1:11: "Through your descendants will the whole land be blessed, and those who live in it, until the last times, *even the years of the end*" (Pennington, "Ladder of Jacob," 456; emphasis in original). Lunt's translation may give the impression that the nations will be blessed only "in the last times" (see, e.g., Charlesworth, "Ladder of Jacob," 609). However, Pennington's translation shows that it may also mean that the nations will be blessed in the seed of Jacob throughout the ages until the last times. James's rendering is also similar to Pennington's (James, *Lost Apocrypha*, 97). Nonetheless, Lunt's rendering of *Lad. Jac.* 1:12 clarifies that the blessing will flow from Jacob throughout all generations.

68. Wisdom, *Blessing*, 77.

will be blessed in Jacob's seed.[69] Therefore, it is not clear from the context of the *Ladder of Jacob* how nations will be blessed by the seed of Jacob.

## Other Texts of the Second Temple Literature

*Liber antiquitatum biblicarum*, which is usually dated between 50 CE and 150 CE, belongs to the genre of "Rewritten Bible," and it covers the biblical narrative from Adam to Saul.[70] Although it is a rich source of Jewish traditions of the first century CE, it has no quotations or allusions of the Abrahamic blessing for the nations. Although Wisdom admits that the Abrahamic blessing for the nations is never explicitly quoted or alluded to in *Liber antiquitatum biblicarum*, he nevertheless cites four passages (*L.A.B.* 11.1; 21.5b; 23.12; 51.2-4) as possible references to blessing for the Gentiles.[71] However, a close examination of these texts shows otherwise.

First, in *L.A.B.* 11.1-2, the Torah that God gives through Moses is said to be "a light to the world" by which God shall judge the whole world. The language of blessing is not explicit in the text. As Wisdom himself admits, even if blessing is implicit for the people who obey the law, the mediator is the law, not the descendants of Abraham.[72]

Second, in *L.A.B.* 21.1-5, God reveals to Joshua in his old age that the people of Israel will turn to idolatry, and God will abandon them consequently (*L.A.B.* 21.1).[73] In response, Joshua pleads with God to keep the people from sin and to choose a suitable leader to succeed him, so that they may not be destroyed, and "the nations of the earth and the tribes of the world may learn that you are eternal" (*L.A.B.* 21.5b).[74] In view of *L.A.B.* 21.5b, Wisdom argues that "although the term blessing is not used here, it may be implied that the nations will have the possibility, at least, to give up their devotion to other gods and worship the one true god."[75] However, as Jacobson points out, Joshua's statement in *L.A.B.* 21.5b needs

---

69. Ibid., 76-77n57. As Wisdom also notes that, although there may be hints on how nations will be blessed in Jacob's seed in *Lad. Jac.* 7:14, 33-34, this whole chapter is very likely a Christian addition, and thus it is not likely to reflect Jewish thoughts during the Second Temple period.

70. Jacobson, *Liber antiquitatum biblicarum*, 1:199-213.

71. Wisdom, *Blessing*, 74-76.

72. Ibid., 75.

73. See also Murphy, *Pseudo-Philo*, 100-102.

74. Translation taken from Harrington, "Pseudo-Philo," 2:330.

75. Wisdom, *Blessing*, 75.

to be understood in light of Josh 7:9, for if the Canaanites heard that the people of Israel are destroyed, "what will you do about your great name?" Joshua's plea is concerned with maintaining "God's reputation among the nations," and it functions as a motivation for God to accede to the request.[76] The nations' knowledge of God's nature in *L.A.B.* 21.5b has to do with the vindication of God's name and his eternal promise, and the blessing of the nations is not in view in the context of *L.A.B.* 21.1–5.

Third, *L.A.B.* 23.12–13 is an exhortation to Israel to obey God's law. In order to motivate Israel, the author lists the advantages that Israel will have if they obey.[77] The motif of Israel's fame among the nations due to their obedience is similar to Deut 4:4–6.[78] In both *L.A.B.* 23.12–13 and Deut 4:4–6, the witness of the nations of Israel's blessedness functions as a motivation for Israel to obey, and there is no indication in either context of how these nations would be or could be similarly blessed.

Fourth, in the prayer of Hannah in *L.A.B.* 51.3–6, Hannah addresses the nations, and declares that Samuel will bring the Torah to the nations (*L.A.B.* 51.3–4). Wisdom argues that Hannah's statement that "all will find truth" (*L.A.B.* 51.4a) through her son points toward "a universalism which corresponds to the motif of blessing for the nations."[79] However, as Jacobson points out, the address to the nations and kingdoms at the beginning of the prayer could also be a hymnal convention for rhetorical effect (cf. Mic 1:2; Ps 49:2 MT; 68:33 MT).[80] In any case, the language of blessing is not explicit, and the inference of an implicit blessing mediated through Samuel, a descendant of Israel, is at most indirect.

Scholars have observed that Josephus uses various sources of the Second Temple literature other than the Scriptures in his writings and carefully reworks them.[81] Therefore, although Josephus's *Jewish Antiquities* is written at the end of the first century CE,[82] it might still be a resource in our research, to some extent, on how the Abrahamic blessing for the nations is developed during the Second Temple period. However, in his narratives

---

76. Jacobson, *Liber antiquitatum biblicarum*, 2:684.
77. Murphy, *Pseudo-Philo*, 112.
78. Jacobson, *Liber antiquitatum biblicarum*, 2:727.
79. Wisdom, *Blessing*, 76; similarly Murphy, *Pseudo-Philo*, 191–92.
80. Jacobson, *Liber antiquitatum biblicarum*, 2:1098–99.
81. The various sources used by Josephus include the Hebrew Bible, the LXX, the Aramaic Targums, the Apocrypha and Pseudepigrapha, and Hellenistic Jewish writers such as Philo (Attridge, *Interpretation of Biblical History*, 29–38; Feldman, *Josephus's Interpretation*, 23–30, 51–56).
82. Bartlett, *Jews in the Hellenistic World*, 79; Feldman, *Judean Antiquities*, XVII.

on Abraham, Isaac, and Jacob, Josephus does not cite or comment on the Abrahamic blessing for the nations.[83] The passages in the *Jewish Antiquities* that are parallel to the contexts of the Abrahamic promise in Genesis are: *Ant.* 1.154 (cf. Gen 12:1-6); 1.233-235 (cf. Gen 22:11-18); 1.279-283 (cf. Gen 28:11-15). In the context of his narrative on the sacrifice of Isaac (*Ant.* 1.235), Josephus mentions that "Abraham's race will become many nations" (cf. Gen 17:4, 6) and that when they have taken possession of the land of Canaan by arms, "they would be envied by all men." Wisdom thinks that "they would be envied by all men" is "an oblique reference to the Lord's promise to Abraham to bless the nations."[84] However, there is no hint from the context that Josephus associates his allusion to Gen 17:4, 6 with the Abrahamic blessing for the nations (Gen 12:3b; 22:18) or how the nations may be blessed by "envying" Abraham's descendants. Josephus's silence regarding the Abrahamic promise, especially with regard to land and nationhood, could be due to the sensitivity of Jewish nationalism after the thwarted Jewish revolution of 66-74 CE.[85] Consequently, the element of blessing for the nations in the Abrahamic promise is also left out.[86]

There is also no text in the extant Qumran literature that comments on the Abrahamic blessing for the nations.[87] This phenomenon is not surprising given the attitude of the Qumran community towards Gentiles and proselytes.[88] Wisdom rightly argues that Scott's attempt to associate God's blessings on all three sons of Noah with the Abrahamic blessing for the nations in the Qumran *Commentary on Genesis A* (4Q252 II, 6-8) is tenuous.[89] Scott argues that the "tent of Shem" in which God will dwell (4Q252 II, 7) is to be understood in terms of the "Abrahamic Promise of the Land" (4Q252 II, 8; cf. Gen 12:1).[90] According to Scott, since (1) the land promise, which is explicitly mentioned in 4Q252 II, 8, refers back to the Noahic blessing, and (2) the blessing for the nations in Gen 12:3, though it is not cited in 4Q252 II, 8, should also refer back to the Table of Nations in the Genesis narrative, then "the idea all three sons of Noah are

---

83. See also Wisdom, *Blessing*, 82-86.
84. Ibid., 84.
85. Feldman, *Josephus's Interpretation*, 289.
86. See also Wisdom, *Blessing*, 86.
87. Ibid., 77-78; Heckel, *Der Segen*, 117.
88. On the attitude of the Qumran community towards Gentiles and proselytes, see pp. 170-72 below.
89. Wisdom, *Blessing*, 77n59.
90. Scott, *Paul and the Nations*, 47.

blessed is apparently equated with the promise that, in Abraham, all the families/nations of the earth will be blessed." This inference is certainly far-fetched, because the commentary on Gen 8:13–12:4 in 4Q252 II, 6–10 has no reference to the blessing for the nations (Gen 12:3) at all.

## The Promise of the Spirit in the Second Temple Literature

A number of passages in the Second Temple literature allude to the promise of the Spirit in the prophets, especially with regard to the work of the Spirit in renewing life and restoring covenantal blessings (cf. Isa 44:3; Ezek 37:14), and in enabling obedience (cf. Ezek 36:26–27). The texts that we shall be examining in detail are in *Jubilees* (1:19–25), the Qumran literature—*Thanksgiving Hymns* (1QH$^a$ VIII, 24–25; 29–31; XII, 31–34; XV, 9–10; XX, 14–15), *Words of the Luminaries* (4Q504 1–2 recto V, 10–16), and *Rule of the Community* (1QS III, 6–12; IV, 20–21)—and *Joseph and Aseneth* (8:9; 15:5–7). We will also discuss whether the gift of the Spirit mentioned in the texts above is available for Gentile converts.

### *Jubilees*

*Jubilees* 1:1–29 forms the introduction of the book and sets the background on how Moses received the words of the Lord through an angel when he ascended Mount Sinai to receive the stone tablets (cf. Exod 24:1–18). While Moses was on the mountain for forty days and forty nights, the Lord "showed him what (had happened) beforehand as well as what was to come" (*Jub.* 1:4). When the Lord foretold the future apostasy, exile, and restoration of Israel to Moses even before he brings the people into the promised land, Moses pleaded with the Lord not to allow his people to err or deliver them into the hands of the nations, and to "create for them a pure mind and a holy spirit" so that they may not "be trapped in their sins from now to eternity" (*Jub.* 1:5–21).[91]

However, the Lord did not relent about his threat to bring on the exile, but he assured Moses that he would transform the disposition of his people at the time of restoration after the exile:

---

91. Moses' plea to God to "create a pure heart and holy spirit" in the people clearly alludes to Ps 51:10–11 (MT 51:12–13). See also Philip, *Pauline Pneumatology*, 82; Smith, "'Spirit of Holiness,'" 77.

> 22b I know their contrary nature, their way of thinking, and their stubbornness. They will not listen until they acknowledge their sins and the sins of their ancestors. 23 After this they will return to me in a fully upright manner and with all (their) minds and all (their) souls. I will cut away the foreskins of their minds and the foreskins of their descendants' minds. I will create a holy spirit for them and will purify them in order that they may not turn away from me from that time forever. 24 Their souls will adhere to me and to all my commandments. They will perform my commandments. I will become their father and they will become my children. 25 All of them will be called children of the living God... They will know that they are my children and that I am their father in a just and proper way and that I love them (Jub. 1:22b-25).

In *Jub.* 1:23-24a, the author of *Jubilees* juxtaposes two metaphors of obedience—the circumcision of the heart in Deut 30:1-10 and putting a new spirit within the people in order to effect obedience in Ezek 36:25-27—to bring across how God will permanently resolve the problem of disobedience at the time of restoration.[92] However, while the purification language in *Jub.* 1:23 alludes to Ezek 36:25, the spirit language alludes more to Ezek 11:19-20 than Ezek 36:26-27, in that the holy spirit in *Jub.* 1:23 is not specified as "God's spirit." Nevertheless, it is clear from the text that such a spirit is created by God. Divine initiation and intervention are necessary in order to transform the "contrary nature" and "stubbornness" of the people (*Jub.* 1:22-25). This concept of the necessity of divine intervention in *Jubilees* is in line with the OT prophets (cf. Jer 31:31-34; 32:36-41; Ezek 36:26-27).

A number of scholars have argued that the restoration of Israel was conditional upon their repentance in *Jub.* 1:22-25.[93] However, Lambert has shown convincingly that the author of *Jubilees* leans more towards divine grace and intervention than human agency in repentance. First, Lambert explains that *Jub.* 1:15-25 is an attempt by its author to reconcile the tension between Deut 4:29-31 and 30:1-10, where the former emphasizes human agency in returning to God while the latter stresses the divine initiative in transformation. The intercessory prayer of Moses (*Jub.*

---

92. On the allusion to Deut 30:1-10, see also Davenport, *Eschatology*, 26n3; Smith, "Spirit of Holiness," 77-78. On the juxtaposition of Deut 30:1-10 and Ezek 36:25-27, see also Philip, *Pauline Pneumatology*, 82.

93. Davenport, *Eschatology*, 26; Smith, "Spirit of Holiness," 77-78.

1:19–21) between *Jub.* 1:15–18 (cf. Deut 4:29–31) and *Jub.* 1:22–25 (cf. Deut 30:1–10) resolves the tension by reporting:

> an otherwise unknown conversation purported to have taken place between God and Moses at Sinai: God revealed to Moses a plan for Israel's redemption, Moses protested the absence of divine re-creation, and God revised the original formulation accordingly. Deuteronomy 4:29–31 thus reflects God's initial, abrogated plan; Deut 30:1–10, the revised.[94]

Second, the recognition of sinfulness (*Jub.* 1:22) is not to be equated with "repentance—an expression of contrition or resolution never to sin again."[95] The overall context of *Jub.* 1 seeks to show "Israel's responsibility for its affliction and the deity's for its redemption . . . Israel needed to experience the exile . . . to make quite clear to them their worth and dependence vis-à-vis the deity."[96] While Lambert is correct in showing that *Jub.* 1:15–25 leans toward the necessity of divine intervention and transformation, we must not neglect its author's emphasis in the whole book of *Jubilees* on the timeless nature of the covenantal laws and the human responsibility in fulfilling the covenantal obligations.[97] Nonetheless, *Jub.* 1:22–25 plays the role of recognizing divine enablement for obedience. Such a notion of divine empowerment and human responsibility in *Jubilees* is in line with both Deuteronomy and the prophets.

As with the promise of the Spirit in Ezek 36:26–27, the promise that God will create a holy spirit in his people at the time of restoration in *Jub.* 1:23 is addressed to the nation of Israel, and *Jubilees* does not address the issue of whether Gentile converts may be included in this promise. In fact, not only does *Jubilees* not address the issue of proselytism at all, it is generally antagonistic toward the Gentiles (e.g., *Jub.* 22:16–18; 24:28–33; 30:5–17).[98]

---

94. Lambert, "Did Israel Believe?," 639.
95. Ibid., 645.
96. Ibid., 646.
97. VanderKam, "Origins and Purposes," 18; Segal, *Jubilees*, 323.
98. See also VanderKam, "Origins and Purposes," 18–19; idem, *Jubilees* (2001), 132; Philip, *Pauline Pneumatology*, 83n19.

## Qumran Literature[99]

The Qumran community believed that they were the true eschatological people of God who had received the Spirit of God (e.g., CD III, 13-20; 1QS II, 25-III, 6; 1QH$^a$ VIII, 24-31; 4Q504-506).[100] They were the true "Israel."[101] The Israel that was exiled had gone astray, and the sectarians are the remnant who holds fast to the commandments of God, with whom God established his eternal covenant (CD III, 12-15). The Jews who are contemporaneous to the sectarians, but are outside the sect, are also excluded as the people of God. This is because these outsider Jews do not subscribe to the purification requirements of the sect, and thus they are not included in the covenant of the community (1QS II, 25-III, 6; V, 10-13). We shall look at a number of passages in the *Thanksgiving Hymns* (*Hodayot*), the *Words of the Luminaries* (*Divrei Ha-me'orot*), and the *Rule of the Community* (*Serek Hayaḥad*) that associate the bestowal of God's Spirit with obedience to the law or the blessings of God. Thereafter, we shall also discuss whether it may be inferred from the Qumran literature that proselytes are able to receive the Spirit of God.

---

99. Unless otherwise indicated, the English translation of the Qumran literature in this section is taken from Wise et al., *Dead Sea Scrolls*, and the Hebrew texts are taken from García Martínez and Tigchelaar, *Dead Sea Scrolls Study Edition* (*DSSSE*).

100. Johnston, "'Spirit' and 'Holy Spirit,'" 38-41; Kuhn, *Enderwartung und gegenwärtiges Heil*, 130-39; Vos, *Traditionsgeschichtliche*, 56-60; Deasley, "Holy Spirit," 61-62; Sekki, *Meaning of Ruaḥ*, 90n56, 223; Montague, *Holy Spirit*, 119-22; Kvalvaag, "Spirit in Human Beings," 170-75.

101. Davies, "'Old' and 'New,'" 33. Davies notes that in the Qumran literature, "there are three 'Israels' at play: the sect; the discredited entity of the past, a nation punished by exile; and a continuing, equally discredited entity, the contemporary Jewish society outside the sect."

The Blessing of Abraham, the Spirit, and Justification in Galatians

### Thanksgiving Hymns[102]

It is commonly accepted that the composition of the *Thanksgiving Hymns* (*Hodayot*) dates from the second half of the second century BCE.[103] The earliest of the manuscripts dates from the last quarter of the first century BCE, while the latest and most extensive (1QH[a]) dates from the first century CE.[104]

Although 1QH[a] VIII has many lacunae, it may still be seen from the text that the psalmist acknowledges that there can be no righteousness apart from God (1QH[a] VIII, 24, 29a), and thus relies on God's Spirit, which has been given to the psalmist, (1) to cling to God's covenant, to love God, and to walk/serve in truth and a perfect heart (1QH[a] VIII, 24–25)[105] and (2) to be cleansed (לטהרני) from sin, and brought near to God (1QH[a] VIII, 29b–30).[106] Such an acknowledgement of no righteousness apart

---

102. Early publications of the *Thanksgiving Hymns* uses the old column numbering system of Sukenik, who first transcribed and published 1QH[a] (Sukenik, *Dead Sea Scrolls*, plates 35–58). However, recent translations have adopted the new column numbering system according to Puech's research (Puech, "Quelques aspects," 38–55). E.g., *DSSSE*, 1:147–202; Wise et al., *Dead Sea Scrolls*, 171; Vermes, *Complete Dead Sea Scrolls*, 249. Nonetheless, their respective line numbering of 1QH[a] differs significantly from each other (for more details, see Hughes, *Scriptural Allusions*, 7–8). In this section, I am using the line numbering system of Wise et al., *Dead Sea Scrolls*, 170–205. Whenever the text of 1QH[a] is cited in the footnotes below, the corresponding line numbers in *DSSSE* will be indicated in parenthesis.

103. Puech, "Hodayot," 1:366; Falk, "Psalms and Prayers," 27.

104. Mansoor, *Thanksgiving Hymns*, 7–10; Starcky, "Quatre étapes," 483n8; Knibb, *Qumran Community*, 157; Puech, "Hodayot," 366.

105. Holm-Nielsen, *Hodayot*, 235n10. Holm-Nielsen's reconstruction of ול[התהל]ך ("to walk") is based on 2 Kgs 20:3, but he also acknowledges the possibility of Licht's and Dupont-Sommer's reconstruction of ול[עובד]ך ("to serve").

106. 1QH[a] VIII (formerly XVI), lines 24–25, 29b–31 (lines 14–15, 19b–21 in *DSSSE*):
- 24   And as I come to know all these things [I] will find the proper reply, prostrating myself and [. . .] for my rebellion, seeking a spirit of [. . .]
- 25   encouraging myself by [Your] h[oly] spirit, clinging to the truth of Your covenant, [serv]ing You in truth and a perfect heart, and loving [Your holy name.]
- 29b  I know that no one can be righteous apart from You. And I entreat Your favor by that spirit which You have given [me,] to fulfill
- 30   Your [mer]cy with [Your] servant for[ever,] to cleanse me by Your holy spirit, and to bring me near by Your grace according to Your great mercy [. . .] in [. . .]
- 31   standing [. . .] the place of [Your] wi[ll] which You have chos[en] for those who love You and keep [Your] comma[nd]ments.

## The Spirit's Temporary Absence in the Blessing of Abraham

from God and reliance on God is also clear in 1QH$^a$ XII, 31b–34a, a text that is more complete than 1QH$^a$ VIII.[107] The Spirit of God also keeps the psalmist from stumbling (1QH$^a$ XV, 9–10a)[108] and motivates the psalmist to listen faithfully to God's counsel (1QH$^a$ XX, 14b–15).[109]

God gives the Spirit to the psalmist,[110] and the Spirit purifies (טהר) the psalmist from sin (1QH$^a$ VIII, 30) and enables an obedient and pious life (1QH$^a$ VIII, 25, 30; XV, 10; XX, 15). This concept is most likely influenced by Ezek 36:25-27.[111] The connection between Ezek 36:25-27 with the *Thanksgiving Hymns* is drawn together by the language of "cleansing," "putting within of God's Spirit," and "obedience."[112] The prophecy of the future "cleansing" and "putting within of God's Spirit" in Ezek 36:25-27 is regarded as actualized in the *Thanksgiving Hymns*.

---

107. 1QH$^a$ XII (formerly IV), lines 31b–34a (lines 30b–33a in *DSSSE*):

> 31b I know that man has no righteousness, nor does the son of man walk in the perfect
> 32 way. All the works of righteousness belong to God Most High. The way of man does not last except by the spirit which God created for him,
> 33 to perfect a way for humankind so that they may know all His works by His mighty power and the abundance of His mercies upon all those
> 34a who do His will.

Although the "spirit" in line 32 may refer to the human spirit, rather than God's spirit, the human spirit is nevertheless renewed by God.

108. 1QH$^a$ XV (formerly VII), lines 9–10a (lines 6–7a in *DSSSE*):

> 9 I give thanks to You, O Lord, for You have sustained me with Your strength, and Your holy spirit
> 10a You have spread out over me so that I will not falter.

109. 1QH$^a$ XX (formerly XII), lines 14b–15 (lines 11b–12 in *DSSSE*):

> 14b And I, the Instructor, have known You, O my God, by the spirit
> 15 which You gave me, and I have listened faithfully to Your wondrous counsel by Your holy spirit.

110. 1QH$^a$ VIII, 29; XX, 14b–15a: "the spirit which you have given me"; XV, 9b–10a: "the holy spirit you have spread over me."

111. See also Sekki, *Meaning of Ruah*, 222; Philip, *Pauline Pneumatology*, 86; Smith, "Spirit of Holiness," 91–95. Although Barry Smith notes that the "spirit of holiness" in the *Thanksgiving Hymns* is a "principle of obedience," he does not mention its allusion to Ezek 36:26–27.

112. Cf. Ezek 36:25–27 ESV: "I will sprinkle clean water on you, and you shall be clean [טהר] from all your uncleannesses, and from all your idols I will cleanse [טהר] you. And I will give you a new heart, and a new spirit I will put within you . . . And I will put my Spirit within you, and cause you to walk in my statutes and be careful to obey my rules."

# The Blessing of Abraham, the Spirit, and Justification in Galatians

## Words of the Luminaries

The *Words of the Luminaries* (*Divrei Ha-meʾorot*) is a collection of prayers for the consecutive days of the week. The oldest copy of this work (4Q504) is dated paleographically to about 150 BCE.[113] Although there are indications of a non-Qumranic origin, the *Words of the Luminaries* was nevertheless preserved and used liturgically by the Qumran community.[114]

The form of the prayer on the sixth day of the week (4Q504 1-2 recto V) bears the typical characteristics of a penitential prayer, as listed by Falk: (1) confession of sins, usually in the form of a historical recollection; (2) confession that God's judgment is just; (3) recital of God's mercies in the past; (4) petition for mercy.[115] The thoughts expressed in 4Q504 1-2 recto V 10-16 clearly allude to Deut 30:1-2 and Isa 44:3:[116]

---

**4Q504 1-2 recto V, 10-16**

10 whereby You brought us forth from Egypt while the nations looked on. You have not abandoned us 11 *among the nations* [בגוים]; rather, You have shown covenant mercies to Your people Israel in all 12 [the] lands to *which You have exiled them* [שמה אשר הדחתם]. You have again *placed it* 13 *on their hearts* [להשיב אל לבבם] *to return to You* [לשוב עודך], *to obey Your voice* 14 *[according] to all that You have commanded* [כ]ול אשר] ולשמוע בקולכה צויתה] *through Your servant Moses.* 15 [In]deed, *You have poured out Your holy spirit upon us* [יצקתה את רוח ... עלינו], 16 [br]inging *Your blessings to us* [ברכותיכה לנו]. You have caused us to seek You in our time of tribulation

---

**Deut 30:1-2 ESV**

1 And when all these things come upon you, the blessing and the curse, which I have set before you, and *you call them to mind* [והשבת אל־לבבך] *among all the nations* [בכל־הגוים] *where* the LORD your God *has driven you* [שמה ... אשר הדיחך], 2 *and return to the LORD your God,* [ושבת עד־יהוה אלהיך] you and your children, and *obey his voice in all that I command you* [ושמעת בקלו ככל אשר־אנכי מצוך] today, with all your heart and with all your soul,

---

**Isa 44:3b ESV**

*I will pour my Spirit upon your offspring* [אצק רוחי על־זרעך], *and my blessing on your descendants* [וברכתי על־צאצאיך].

---

113. Baillet, *Qumrân Grotte 4*, 137; Falk, *Daily, Sabbath, and Festival Prayers*, 61; Chazon, "Words of the Luminaries," 2:989; Davila, *Liturgical Works*, 239.

114. Baillet, *Qumrân Grotte 4*, 137; Chazon, "*Divrei Ha-meʾorot*," 3-17; idem, "4QDibHam: Liturgy or Literature?," 447-55.

115. Falk, "Psalms and Prayers," 8.

116. See also Carmignac and Guilbert, *Les textes de Qumran*, 2:307nn13-14; Baillet, *Qumrân Grotte 4*, 147; Philip, *Pauline Pneumatology*, 85; Davila, *Liturgical Works*, 262; Smith, "Spirit of Holiness," 81n18.

The future orientation in Isa 44:3: "I will pour out my Spirit upon your offspring, and my blessings upon your descendants" is taken to be actualized in 4Q504 1–2 recto V, 15–16: "You have poured out Your holy spirit upon us, [br]inging Your blessings to us."[117] The ability to repent and obey all of God's commands is attributed to God's work in their hearts (lines 12–14), which is in line with the context of Deut 30:1–6.[118] Although obedience is not directly attributed to the work of the Spirit, it is nevertheless indirectly linked to the Spirit by the allusion to Isa 44:3 regarding the bestowal of the Spirit, in which the Spirit is understood as the means by which God brings the covenantal blessings back to the people (lines 15–16: ‏[לה]ביא ברכותיכה לנו‎, "[to] bring your blessings to us"). Morales also notes that, by alluding to Isa 44:3, this prayer in 4Q504 1–2 recto V 10–16 "presents Israel's reception of God's holy Spirit and of the blessing as the sign that God has redeemed Israel from the curses of Leviticus and Deuteronomy."[119]

## Rule of the Community

The *Rule of the Community*, or the *Serek Hayaḥad*, originates from about the middle of the second century BCE, at the beginning of the Qumran community.[120] This document not only provides the rules that govern the community members at Qumran but also explains the theological rationale of the group.[121] 1QS, the most complete manuscript of the *Rule of the Community*, was copied approximately between 100 and 75 BCE.[122]

---

117. See also, Smith, "Spirit of Holiness," 81, who notes that "God poured his spirit of holiness on the people *before* they returned to him, so that the spirit of holiness is the cause of their repentance" (emphasis in original).

118. See Deut 30:6 ESV: "And the LORD your God will circumcise your heart and the heart of your offspring, so that you will love the LORD your God with all your heart and with all your soul, that you may live." The reliance on God for the ability to obey is also evident in 4Q504 4, 11–12: "Circumcise the foreskin[s of our heart . . .] . . . again strengthen our heart to do [. . .] [. . . to] walk in Your ways [. . . ]" (Davila, *Liturgical Works*, 248), which is reminiscent of Deut 10:16; 30:6. See also Falk, "Psalms and Prayers," 11.

119. Morales, "The Words of the Luminaries," 270–72.

120. Charlesworth et al., *Rule of the Community*, 2; Knibb, "Rule of the Community," 2:796.

121. Knibb, *Qumran Community*, 77; Charlesworth et al., *Rule of the Community*, 2; Metso, *Serekh*, 1.

122. Charlesworth et al., *Rule of the Community*, 2; Metso, *Textual Development*, 14; Knibb, "Rule of the Community," 794. For bibliography on paleographical and radio-carbon dating of 1QS, see Metso, *Textual Development*, 14n3.

## The Blessing of Abraham, the Spirit, and Justification in Galatians

There are five main sections in the *Rule of the Community*: (1) introduction (1QS I, 1–15); (2) liturgy on the admission into the covenant and its annual renewal (1QS I, 16–III, 12); (3) treatise on the two spirits (1QS III, 13–IV, 26); (4) various rules for the community (1QS V, 1–IX, 26a); (5) concluding hymn (1QS IX, 26b–XI, 22).[123] The section on the liturgy of admission and annual renewal begins as follows: "all who enter the *Yahad's* Rule shall be initiated into the Covenant before God, agreeing to act according to all that He has commanded and not to backslide because of any fear, terror or persecution" (1QS I, 16–17). Those who are unrepentant shall not be initiated into the *Yahad* (1QS II, 25–26). Even the ceremonies of atonement and water purification cannot cleanse such unrepentant people (1QS III, 4–5). This is because:

> 6b only through the spirit [רוח] pervading God's true society can there be atonement for a man's ways, all 7 of his iniquities; thus only can he gaze upon the light of life and so be joined to His truth by His holy spirit [רוח], purified from all 8 iniquity. Through an upright and humble attitude [רוח] his sin may be covered, and by humbling himself before all God's laws his flesh 9 can be made clean. Only thus can he really receive the purifying waters and be purged by the cleansing flow. Let him order his steps to walk faultless 10 in all the ways of God, just as He commanded for the times appointed to him. Let him turn aside neither to the right nor the left, nor yet 11 deviate in the smallest detail from all of His words. Then indeed will he be accepted by God, offering the sweet savor of atoning sacrifice, and then only shall he be a party to the Covenant of the 12 eternal *Yahad* (1QS III, 6b–12).

The word רוח ("spirit") occurs three times in this passage. Scholars are divided over whether the three occurrences of רוח in this passage refer to God's Spirit or the human spirit.[124] It is most likely that the first two instances of רוח refer to God's Spirit, while the third instance refers to

---

123. Although scholars differ slightly in demarcating the sections, these five main sections are apparent in most of them. See, e.g., Knibb, *Qumran Community*, 77; Bockmuehl, "1QS," 387–88; Metso, *Serekh*, 7–14.

124. The options for רוח in 1QS III, 6–8 include: (1) all three instances refer to the human spirit (e.g., Carmignac and Guilbert, *Les textes de Qumran*, 1:30–31nn72, 76; Knibb, *Qumran Community*, 92; Smith, "Spirit of Holiness," 87–89); (2) the second instance refers to God's Spirit, while the other two refer to the human spirit (e.g., Leaney, *Rule of Qumran*, 35; Sekki, *Meaning of Ruah*, 225; Kvalvaag, "Spirit in Human Beings," 172); (3) the first two instances refer to God's Spirit, while the last refers to the human spirit (e.g., Anderson, "Use of 'Ruah,'" 301; Charlesworth et al., *Rule of the Community*, 13);

## The Spirit's Temporary Absence in the Blessing of Abraham

the disposition of the human spirit, for the following reasons. First, Sekki notes that the term רוח קדושה ("holy spirit") in the Scrolls usually refers to God's spirit and rarely refers to the human spirit. According to Sekki's research, if it is used to refer to the human spirit (e.g., CD V, 11; VII, 4), syntactical markers will make this clear. In addition, whenever there is a suffix on קדוש (sg.) in the Scrolls, it always refers to God.[125] In the case of 1QS III, 7, there is a variant reading of רוח קדושו ("his holy spirit") in 4Q225.[126] Therefore, the term רוח קדושה ("holy spirit") in 1QS III, 7 probably refers to God's spirit.[127]

Second, in the final psalm of the *Rule of the Community*, the psalmist confesses that God is the one who can atone (כפר) for "all [his] iniquities" (1QS XI, 14: כול עוונותי, "all my iniquities"; cf. 1QS III, 6b-7a, 7b-8a: כול עוונותו, "all his iniquities"). Although the final psalm may be a later addition to the *Rule of the Community*, it nevertheless reflects the understanding of the redactor that the contents of this psalm are in accord with the beliefs of the community.[128] Therefore, the spirit of the true council that atones (כפר) for all the iniquities of the people (1QS III, 6-7a) and the holy spirit (רוח קדושה) that purifies (טהר) people from all their iniquities (1QS III, 7b-8a) both refer to the spirit of God.

Third, although both 1QS III, 6 and 8 refer to atonement and should be understood together, it is not absolutely necessary to read רוח ("spirit") in both lines as referring to the same thing.[129] On the one hand, 1QS III, 6 emphasizes that it is by God's spirit that all the iniquities of a person can be atoned for, and thus, the purification rite in itself will never be able to cleanse a person who has an unrepentant heart and who rejects the commands of God (1QS II, 25–III, 5). On the other hand, 1QS III, 8 stresses that a person must truly be repentant, shown by a humble and upright attitude (רוח), and submission to all the commands of God.[130] Only then

---

125. Sekki, *Meaning of Ruaḥ*, 75–77.

126. Ibid., 92–93; Charlesworth et al., *Rule of the Community*, 12n57.

127. Nearly all scholars take the רוח in 1QS III, 7 to refer to God's spirit, with the exception of Smith, Knibb, and Carmignac-Guilbert (see p. 168n124 above).

128. On the insertion of the final psalm, see Metso, *Textual Development*, 144–49; idem, *Serekh*, 14. See also 1QS II, 8, which also mentions the atonement of sins by God.

129. Contra Sekki, *Meaning of Ruaḥ*, 106–8; Smith, "Spirit of Holiness," 87–89.

130. Another way to explain how רוח in 1QS III, 6–8 can be understood as both the divine Spirit and human attitude is provided by Vos: "As the Spirit of revelation, the Spirit comes from God. At the same time, however, the Spirit becomes the possession of the community to such an extent, that one could translate רוח in 3,6–8 as 'attitude.'

will atonement be available for him through the Spirit and the purification rites be effective (1QS III, 8–9).[131]

The purification from sin brought about by the sprinkling of water and the Spirit of God in 1QS III, 6–9 is very likely an allusion to Ezek 36:25–27, and it is also reminiscent of 1QH[a] VIII, 30.[132] However, unlike Ezek 36:27, 1QS III, 6–9 does not attribute obedience to God's commands directly to the work of the Spirit. Instead, human responsibility to obey is emphasized (1QS III, 8b, 9b).[133] Nonetheless, at the final visitation of God at the end of the age, God will "purify all the human deeds, and . . . extinguish every perverse spirit from the inward parts of the flesh, cleansing from every wicked deed by a holy spirit" (1QS IV, 20–21).[134] In the *Rule of the Community*, it is at the very end of the age that God's Spirit will bring about complete obedience to his law.

## Proselytes and the Spirit of God in the Qumran Literature

Although Baumgarten notes that the "Qumran writings do not tell us anything specific about the procedure for the conversion of gentiles," he infers that proselytes could possibly enter the Qumran community by

---

Both meanings—divine Spirit and human attitude—are not mutually exclusive . . . Just like the justification and the appropriate change of the pious, God's inspired Spirit and the attitude of the righteous people at Qumran cannot be sharply separated" (Vos, *Traditionsgeschichtliche*, 58).

131. See also Nötscher, "Heiligkeit," 341, who argues that both 1QS III, 6 and 7 refer to God's spirit, who brings about atonement for all iniquities, and 1QS III, 8 as the human spirit, who needs to cooperate, and Vos, *Traditionsgeschichtliche*, 58, who explains that without the presence and work of the Spirit in the life of the person (1QS III, 6–8), the ceremonies of atonement and water purification are ineffective.

132. Leaney, *Rule of Qumran*, 139; Sekki, *Meaning of Ruaḥ*, 107.

133. Nonetheless, such an emphasis on human responsibility to repent and obey is reflective of Ezek 18:30–31.

134. The majority of scholars regard רוח קודש ("the holy spirit") in 1QS IV, 21 as God's spirit, with a few exceptions. For a summary of scholars of both positions, see Sekki, *Meaning of Ruaḥ*, 207nn59–63. The arguments about רוח קדושה ("the holy spirit") in 1QS III, 7 as referring to God's Spirit are also applicable here in 1QS IV, 21. Sekki has also argued convincingly that, compared with the רוח ("spirit") in 1QS III, 15–18, which is the "spiritual capacity unchangeably conditioning man's religious life from birth," 1QS IV, 21 speaks of the רוח "as an eschatological gift of God which is to cleanse [a person] from all evil deeds and to effect a radical change in his inherited spiritual nature. The author of 4:21a, then, is dealing with a traditional biblical concept based on passages such as Is. 44:3, Joel 3:1 and Ezk. 36:25–27" (Sekki, *Meaning of Ruaḥ*, 208).

Torah observance and by undergoing purification.[135] Following Baumgarten, Philip argues, "Presumably, and by inference, we may argue that the proselytes, who are purified from all the transgressions of the law (1QS V, 14) could possibly have entered the community and thus experienced the Spirit."[136] Is this inference plausible?

A number of scholars have noted the inferior status of proselytes compared with ethnic Israelites in the Qumran writings.[137] In the *Damascus Document*, even though there were proselytes living within the Qumran community, they were a separate class, distinct from the priests, the Levites, and the Israelites (CD XIV, 4-6). These proselytes, as Hannah Harrington points out, were most likely Gentile servants of its Jewish members (CD XII, 10-11), who became the sect's communal possessions and adhere to communal regulations (CD XIV, 4-6), but are nonetheless not full-fledged members.[138] Although the *Temple Scroll* permits proselytes in the middle court of the Temple (11Q19 XL, 6-7), the *Florilegium* excludes all proselytes from the Temple in the last days (4Q174 III, 4).[139] Furthermore, in the assembly of the annual review of the sectarians' spiritual standing in the Covenant, the *Rule of the Community* lists only three

---

135. Baumgarten, "Proselytes," 2:701.

136. Philip, *Pauline Pneumatology*, 86.

137. E.g., Schiffman, "Non-Jews," 169-70; Berthelot, "La Notion," 184-86, 193-215; Harrington, "Keeping Outsiders Out," 195-97. Baumgarten himself notes the inferior status of the proselytes and their exclusion from the Temple (Baumgarten, "Proselytes," 700-701). In continuity with the Hebrew Scriptures, the Qumran writings use the term rg to denote non-Israelite "stranger(s)" who are "integrated into Israel" (Berthelot, "La Notion," 171). Berthelot notes that the Qumran usage of this term most frequently refers to a social category rather than a religious category (see also Harrington, "Keeping Outsiders Out," 195; contra Baumgarten, "Proselytes," 700). Although 4Q174 1-3 I, 4 (see above) may bear the connotation of a "proselyte"— a Gentile converted to Judaism—Berthelot points out that, unlike the rabbinic use of the term גר to denote "proselytes," who are ideologically in equal standing as the Jews, the Qumran גר is an inferior group (Berthelot, "La Notion," 214-15). For bibliography on the rabbinic understanding of proselytes, see Harrington, "Keeping Outsiders Out," 195n30.

138. Harrington, "Keeping Outsiders Out," 195-97.

139. See also Knibb, *Qumran Community*, 260. Knibb points out that the exclusion of proselytes from the temple most likely alludes to Deut 23:2-3 and Ezek 44:3, and he explains that "by the use of the biblical passage the temple is already being implicitly identified as the community." He also notes the contrast with CD XIV, 3-6, where proselytes were "assigned a place." Thus, he concludes that the issue in the *Florilegium* has to do with excluding proselytes from full membership in the community.

groups: priests, Levites, and Israelites (1QS II, 19–22).[140] Therefore, it is unlikely that the proselytes were allowed to participate in the initiation rite of the Qumran sectarians, and they were probably not accepted as full members of the Qumran community.[141] Thus, the gift of God's Spirit is only for the Qumran sectarians (1QS III, 6–8), and it is not available for the proselytes.[142] The problem with the inference of Baumgarten and Philip lies with their blurring of the boundaries between the wider circle of the Qumran community and the restrictive circle of Qumran sectarians, who have gone through the initiation rite and regard themselves as the only ones to be in the eternal Covenant of God.[143]

## Summary

We have examined a number of passages from the *Thanksgiving Hymns*, the *Words of the Luminaries*, and the *Rule of the Community* that associate the Spirit of God with blessing and/or obedience to God's commands. In the various Qumran texts we have studied, the promise of the Spirit in the prophets (e.g., Isa 44:3; Ezek 36:26–27) has been regarded as actualized among the Qumran sectarians, but it also has an element of complete realization in the future (1QS IV, 20–21).[144] There is also a strong emphasis on the cleansing function of the Spirit that purifies the community members from all their sin. Both the *Thanksgiving Hymns* and the *Words of the Luminaries* attribute the ability to live piously and to obey God's commands to the work of God in the lives of the sectarians. The former directly attributes the ability of pious living and obedience to the work of the Spirit, which is given to the sectarians, but the latter is unclear re-

---

140. This stands in stark contrast to CD XIV, 4–6, which lists four groups in the community: the priests, the Levites, the Israelites, and the proselytes.

141. See also Berthelot, "La Notion," 215; Harrington, "Keeping Outsiders Out," 196. Contra Baumgarten, "Proselytes," 701.

142. Contra Philip, *Pauline Pneumatology*, 86.

143. The wider circle of the community includes those who have gone through the initiation rite, those who are on probation (1QS VI, 13–23), and the proselytes. On those who are on probation before becoming full members, see Knibb, *Qumran Community*, 119–22; Metso, *Serekh*, 11–12.

144. See also Smith, "Spirit of Holiness," 83. Hur also notes that the Qumran literature regards the Spirit as "the essential (soteriological?) gift in every member of the community," and such an understanding is "basically concerned with, or much influenced by, the references to the future expectation of the Spirit found in Isa. 44.3; Ezek. 36.27; 37.14 (cf. Joel 2.28–29)" (Hur, *Dynamic Reading*, 86).

garding the relationship between obedience and the Spirit. The gift of the Spirit is also understood in the *Words of the Luminaries* as the means by which God's covenantal blessings are restored to Israel. Such emphases on the cleansing and empowerment of God's Spirit for piety and obedience may very well be influenced by Ezek 36:25-27. However, in the *Rule of the Community*, although the cleansing function of God's Spirit is mentioned, human responsibility to obey is stressed, rather than attributing obedience to the work of God's Spirit.

We have also seen that, although there were proselytes living among the Qumran sectarians, they were not regarded as full members. Thus, it is unlikely that proselytes were allowed to be initiated into the covenant or expected to receive the Spirit of God.

## Joseph and Aseneth[145]

According to the majority of contemporary scholarly opinion, *Joseph and Aseneth* is most likely a Hellenistic Jewish work written in Greek approximately between 100 BCE and 100 CE.[146] This work is divided into two parts, chs. 1-21 and chs. 22-29. The first part of the story gives an account of the conversion of Aseneth, the daughter of an Egyptian priest whom Joseph married (cf. Gen 41:45).

---

145. Philip did not include *Joseph and Aseneth* in his discussion, citing uncertainty in dating as his reason (Philip, *Pauline Pneumatology*, 90n49). Late first century CE is usually taken as the *terminus ante quem*, given the high likelihood of the apocryphon's origin during the Egyptian milieu before the severe persecution of the Jews in Egypt (Humphrey, *Joseph and Aseneth*, 30). If this Egyptian provenance is correct, *Joseph and Aseneth* would be relevant to our discussion as a Jewish work contemporaneous to the time of Paul.

146. E.g., Sänger, "Erwägungen," 86-106; Burchard, "Joseph and Aseneth," 2:181, 187-88; Chesnutt, *Death to Life*, 69, 80-85; Humphrey, *Joseph and Aseneth*, 28-37; Inowlocki, *Des idoles mortes*, 23-26. Recently, Kraemer has advocated Christian authorship and a date from the third or fourth century CE onwards (Kraemer, *When Aseneth Met Joseph*, 225-85; see also Penn, "Identity Transformation," 177-83). The arguments presented by Kraemer are not convincing, and the weight of the evidence leans towards a Jewish authorship (Humphrey, *Joseph and Aseneth*, 35-37; Collins, "Joseph and Aseneth," 97-112; Burchard, "Joseph und Aseneth," 74; idem, "Küssen," 323n16). Given the strong stance taken by the Jews during the Second Temple period against mixed marriages with Gentiles (e.g., Ezra 9:1—10:43; Neh 13:1-9, 23-31; *Jub.* 30:1-17; Tob 4:12; Philo, *Spec. Laws* 3.29; Josephus, *Ant.* 8.191-93; 12.187), *Joseph and Aseneth* is most appropriately seen as a Jewish apology for Joseph's marriage to a Gentile woman in Gen 41:45 (see also Philonenko, *Joseph et Aséneth*, 101; Collins, "Joseph and Aseneth," 102-7).

## The Blessing of Abraham, the Spirit, and Justification in Galatians

At the first meeting of Joseph and Aseneth, Aseneth's father instructed her to give Joseph a kiss of greeting (*Jos. Asen.* 8:4). When Joseph refused to let her kiss him for religious reasons, Aseneth became upset and was in tears (*Jos. Asen.* 8:5-8). At the sight of Aseneth's distress, Joseph had compassion on Aseneth, and he prayed:

> Lord God of my father Israel . . . *renew her by your spirit*, and form her anew by your hidden hand, and make her alive again by your life, and let her eat your bread of life, and drink your cup of blessing, and *number her among your people* that you have chosen before all (things) came into being . . . and let her enter your rest which you have prepared for your chosen ones, and live in your eternal life for ever (and) ever (*Jos. Asen.* 8:9; emphasis added).[147]

After Joseph went away, Aseneth mourned and fasted for the next seven days, threw away her idols, repented from her sins, prayed to God on the eighth day for his forgiveness, and sought refuge in the God of Joseph (*Jos. Asen.* 10:1–13:14). When she finished praying, an angel appeared to her and declared:

> "Behold, from today, *you will be renewed* and formed anew and made alive again, and you will eat blessed bread of life, and drink a cup of immortality, and anoint yourself with blessed ointment of incorruptibility . . . And your name shall no longer be called Aseneth, but your name shall be City of Refuge, because *in you many nations will take refuge with the Lord God*, the Most High, and under your wings many peoples trusting the Lord God will be sheltered, and *behind your walls will be guarded those who attach themselves to the Most High God* in the name of Repentance" (*Jos. Asen.* 15:5-7; emphasis added).

Aseneth also received the "spirit of life" (πνεῦμα ζωῆς) and immortality by consuming the honeycomb that the angel gave to her (*Jos. Asen.*

---

147. The English translation and versification of *Jos. Asen.* is taken from Burchard, "Joseph and Aseneth (*OTP*)," 2:177-247, and the Greek text is taken from Burchard et al., *Joseph und Aseneth*. Modern translators usually prefer Philonenko's shorter critical text (Philonenko, *Joseph et Aséneth*, 3-10; e.g., Cook, "Joseph and Aseneth," 465-503; Inowlocki, *Des idoles mortes*, 17-18, 159-86). Nonetheless, most exegetes accept Burchard's longer text as earlier (e.g., Chesnutt, *Death to Life*, 65-69; Bohak, *Joseph and Aseneth*, 105-9; Humphrey, *Joseph and Aseneth*, 17-26). Although some scholars argue for the priority of the shorter text (e.g., Standhartinger, *Frauenbild*, 50-88), most scholars remain unconvinced. See Burchard, "Text von Joseph und Aseneth," 3-34; idem, "Text of Joseph and Aseneth," 83-96, esp. 91n93.

## The Spirit's Temporary Absence in the Blessing of Abraham

16:14).¹⁴⁸ This reception of "the spirit of life" is reiterated when Joseph kissed Aseneth at their second meeting (*Jos. Asen.* 19:11).¹⁴⁹

Holtz argues that *Jos. Asen.* 8:9; 15:5-7, which are cited above, are Christian interpolations because he claims that the language of new creation and rebirth has no appropriate parallel in early Judaism.¹⁵⁰ Holtz also points out that *Jos. Asen.* 15:5 refers to the Christian Eucharist—"eating the blessed bread of life" and "drinking the cup of immortality."¹⁵¹ However, Chesnutt has shown convincingly that "the language of new creation appears often enough in rabbinic sources in connection with proselytism," and that the meal language in the context of *Jos. Asen.* more likely refers to the "whole Jewish way of life" than a ritual meal.¹⁵²

The notion of God's spirit renewing and revivifying the spiritual life of a person is certainly not exclusively Christian. As we have seen in chapter 4, Ezekiel speaks about Yahweh putting his Spirit within his people as a new spirit (Ezek 36:26-27) to revivify their spiritually dead lives (Ezek 37:14), transforming them in order that they may be able to obey his statutes and judgments.¹⁵³ We have also seen in Isa 44:1-5 that the bestowal of Yahweh's spirit signifies the restoration of covenantal relationship (Isa 44:5).¹⁵⁴ In other words, the gift of the Spirit to the people affirms that they

---

148. See also Levison, *Spirit*, 252. Levison correctly observes that, in *Joseph and Aseneth*, "the spirit is associated with entrance into a life of faith" and "the spirit purifies and draws people into the sphere of the faithful."

149. According to *Jos. Asen.* 19:10-11, Joseph gave her three kisses at their second meeting, conferring on her the "spirit of life," "spirit of wisdom," and "spirit of truth." However, chronologically speaking, Aseneth first received the "spirit of life" and attained immortality during the angel's visit before meeting Joseph for the second time (*Jos. Asen.* 16:14). Therefore, Chesnutt notes that "at the literary level it is not surprising that various means would be used to reiterate the principle that immortality is attained by adherence to the Jewish faith" (Chesnutt, *Death to Life*, 138-39).

150. Holtz, "Christliche interpolationen," 484-85.

151. Ibid., 486.

152. Chesnutt, *Death to Life*, 128-35, 173-74, esp. 135, 173; idem, "Meal Formula," 115-21; see also Philonenko, *Joseph et Aséneth*, 60-61. For a list of rabbinic texts listed by Chesnutt where new creation language appears in connection with proselytism, see Chesnutt, *Death to Life*, 173-74.

153. *Jos. As.* 8:9b: "*renew* [ἀνακαίνισον] her *with your Spirit* [τῷ πνεύματί σου] . . . *make* her *alive again* [ἀναζωοποίησον] by your life"; cf. Ezek 36:26; 37:14 NETS: "And I will give you a new heart, and a *new spirit* [LXX: πνεῦμα καινὸν] I will give in you . . . And I will give *my Spirit* [τὸ πνεῦμά μου] into you, and *you shall live* [LXX: ζήσεσθε]."

154. *Jos. As.* 8:9bc: "renew her *with your Spirit* [τῷ πνεύματί σου] . . . number her among your people that you have *chosen* [ἐξελέξω] before all (things) came into

175

belong to Yahweh and they are his people. Therefore, Joseph's prayer—to renew Aseneth by his Spirit and make her alive again so that she may be numbered among God's people—should not be taken as exclusively Christian. The language of *Jos. Asen.* 15:7 clearly alludes to the LXX of Isa 56:3, 7 and Zech 2:15 [Eng. 2:11], where foreigners and nations who have "joined themselves to the Yahweh" are regarded as Yahweh's people.[155] A comparison of the texts is as follows:

---

*Jos. Asen. 15:7*

and your name shall no longer be called Aseneth, but your name shall be *City of Refuge* [πόλις καταφυγῆς], because in you *many nations will take refuge with the Lord* [καταφεύξονται ἔθνη πολλὰ ἐπὶ κύριον] God . . . and behind your walls will be guarded *those who attach themselves to the Most High God* [οἱ προσκείμενοι τῷ θεῷ τῷ ὑψίστῳ] in the name of Repentance . . .

---

Isa 56:3, 6-7 NETS

Let not the alien *who clings to the Lord* [ὁ προσκείμενος πρὸς κύριον] say, "So then the Lord will separate me from his people" . . . And to the aliens *who cling to the Lord* [οἱ προσκείμενοι κυρίῳ] . . . [I will] make them joyful in my house of prayer . . . for my house shall be called a house of prayer *for all the nations* [πᾶσιν τοῖς ἔθνεσιν]

---

Zech 2:11a NETS [LXX 2:15a]

And *many nations shall flee to the Lord for refuge* [καταφεύξονται ἔθνη πολλὰ ἐπὶ τὸν κύριον] on that day and shall become a people to him

---

Zech 2:11a ESV [MT 2:15a]

And *many nations shall join themselves to the LORD* [ונלוו גוים רבים אל־יהוה] in that day, and shall be my people.

---

being"; cf. Isa 44:1-5 NETS: "But now hear, O Iakob my servant and Israel whom *I have chosen* [LXX: ἐξελεξάμην]! . . . I will put *my spirit* [LXX: τὸ πνεῦμά μου] on your offspring . . . This one will say, 'I am the God's,' and this one will call out in the name of Iakob; yet another will inscribe, 'I am God's,' in the name of Israel." See pp. 116-17 above on whether Gentiles are included in Isa 44:5.

155. It is noteworthy that all three texts in the MT, Isa 56:3, 6; Zech 2:15, use the same verb לוה in the Niphal "to join oneself" with a preposition (either אל or על) before the noun יהוה "Yahweh." The familiarity of the author of *Jos. Asen.* with the LXX is well known; see, e.g., Delling, "Der Sprache der Septuaginta," 29-56; Humphrey, *Joseph and Aseneth*, 31-33; Inowlocki, *Des idoles mortes*, 23-24. On the allusion to Isa 56:6; Zech 2:15 LXX, see also Delling, "Der Sprache der Septuaginta," 33; Burchard, "Joseph and Aseneth *(OTP),*" 226 nn. l and p; idem, "Joseph and Aseneth," 103; Evans, "Scripture-Based Stories," 65. See also pp. 111-12 above on Isa 56:3, 6; Zech 2:11 [MT 2:15].

*The Spirit's Temporary Absence in the Blessing of Abraham*

The key difference in *Jos. Asen.* compared with the OT is that God's Spirit is now given to a Gentile convert, a notion that is not explicit in the OT, but may by inferred.[156]

## Other Texts of the Second Temple Literature

Besides *Jub.* 1:22–23; 1QS III, 6–12; 4Q504 1–2 recto V, 15, Philip also includes 4 *Ezra* 6:27–28 as a text possibly influenced by Ezek 36:26–27 in his discussion on the "prophetic expectation of the Spirit in the post-biblical literature."[157] However, there is no indication from the context of 4 *Ezra* 6:26–28 that the change in human disposition occurring at the end of the age is brought about by the Spirit of God. On another related note, Cosgrove lists *Jub.* 1:21; *T. Levi* 18:11; *T. Job* 48:2–3; 1QS IV, 20–21 as examples of Jewish texts that show an "expectation that the Spirit would one day create a people obedient from the heart to God's law."[158] As mentioned above, I will not include the *Testament of the Twelve Patriarchs* in our discussion.[159] As for *T. Job* 48:2–3, it is not clear from the context whether the Spirit is the cause of the "change of heart" that occurred after Job's daughter put on the cord that was given to her. The effect of the "change of heart"—not minding earthly things anymore—is also not a clear allusion to obeying God's law.

In his discussion on the "expectation of the Spirit upon Gentiles in post-biblical literature," Philip cites passages from the *Wisdom of Solomon* and Philo, which he thinks exhibit an understanding of the expectation and present reality of God's Spirit that is available to all humans, Jews and Gentiles alike.[160] However, I do not think these passages cited by Philip are relevant for our discussion for the following reasons. In the *Wisdom of Solomon*, wisdom is used almost synonymously with terms such as "spirit of the Lord," and "holy spirit" (Wis 1:4–7), and it is available to all righteous persons who seek it, even pagan rulers (Wis 1:1–2; 6:12; 7:7).[161] At times Philo refers to a divine spirit (πνεῦμα θεῖον), which is given to all human beings at creation (e.g., Philo, *Creation* 135; *Alleg. Interp.* 1.31–38),

---

156. See pp. 109–12, 131 above on whether the bestowal of the Spirit in Ezek 36:27; 37:14 applies to the nations and on "Israel and the nations as the people of Yahweh."

157. Philip, *Pauline Pneumatology*, 78–88.

158. Cosgrove, *The Cross and the Spirit*, 103.

159. See p. 136n2 above.

160. Philip, *Pauline Pneumatology*, 90–118.

161. Winston, *Wisdom of Solomon*, 100.

through whom humans are given the capacity to know God (Philo, *Alleg. Interp.* 1.37–38). The concept of the divine spirit in the *Wisdom of Solomon* and in Philo as available to all human beings is in continuity with one of the OT concepts with regard to God's Spirit given universally as the power to animate life (cf. Gen 2:7; Job 27:3; 33:4; 34:14–15; Ps 104:29–30) and as the source of wisdom and understanding (cf. Job 32:8; Prov 1:20, 23; 2:6). However, this concept of divine spirit as common grace is different from the promise of God's Spirit in the prophets as special grace, given so that God's people may be revivified from their spiritual deadness and be transformed (cf. Isa 32:15; 44:3; Ezek 36:26–27; 37:14). Unlike the former, the latter concept of God's Spirit as special grace is not universal, but only bestowed on God's people in the context of restoration. Therefore, the issue of whether Gentile converts are able to receive God's Spirit as special grace in the Second Temple literature should not be confused with and discussed together with the concept of the divine spirit as common grace mentioned in the *Wisdom of Solomon* and in Philo.[162]

Philip also argues that, since Abraham is the standard of nobility for all proselytes in Philo, *Virtues* 219, Abraham's experience of the divine spirit (Philo, *Virtues* 217) is also "normative for all proselytes."[163] However, in the context of *Virtues* 212–220, the nobility of Abraham as a standard for proselytes centers in his conversion from polytheism to his belief in the monotheistic God, rather than other details of his life, such as his experience of the Spirit. This may be seen in the parallel drawn from Tamar for proselyte women (Philo, *Virtues* 220–222). Therefore, given the parallel between Abraham and Tamar, the inference that Philip draws from Philo implying Gentile converts are to experience the divine spirit like Abraham is only remotely possible and indirect.

## Conclusion

Wisdom has argued that the Second Temple literature commonly interprets the blessing for the nations as the positive influence on the Gentiles due to the ubiquitous presence of righteous Jews in the world and stresses "the importance of Israel as the mediator of blessing through her occupation

---

162. On the universality of the divine spirit for animating life and giving wisdom, as well as the Spirit given for restoring God's people, see also Montague, *Holy Spirit*, 3–16, 45–60; Hildebrandt, *Old Testament Theology of the Spirit*, 56–59, 91–103.

163. Philip, *Pauline Pneumatology*, 117.

of the whole world."[164] In contrast, the conclusions drawn from this study show otherwise. Although the Abrahamic blessing for the nations is cited explicitly in Ben Sira (Sir 44:21), *Jubilees* (*Jub.* 12:23; 18:16; 24:11; 27:23), Philo (*Migration* 1; *Heir* 8; *Dreams* 1.3), and the *Ladder of Jacob* (*Lad. Jac.* 1:11), it is usually associated with obedience to God's commands and laws, and most of them do not explain specifically how the nations will be blessed on account of Abraham and his descendants—except for *Jubilees* (*Jub.* 20:1-13) and Philo (*Migration* 109-127a; *Dreams* 1.176-178).

In *Jubilees*, when the nations see how Abraham's descendants had been richly blessed with prosperity by God, they use Abraham's name as a formula of blessing to bless Abraham's descendants, so that they may be blessed likewise (*Jub.* 20:1-13). This depiction reveals how the author associates Gen 12:3a ("I will bless those who bless you, and I will curse the one who curses you") with the blessing for the nations in Gen 12:3b. A similar association can also be seen in the book of Tobit, which alludes to Gen 12:3a in Tob 13:12 and interprets it to mean that nations who love or fear Jerusalem are blessed (Tob 13:12, 14). Philo explains how nations shall be blessed on account of Abraham and his descendants in terms of how a God-fearing and wise individual benefits other people. Such individuals share their material possessions with others, successfully intercede for them before God, and improve the character of others by their good influence (*Migration* 118-127a; *Dreams* 1.176-178; cf. *QG* 3.42, 44). Nonetheless, Philo's literal understanding of how the nations are blessed on account of Abraham's descendants is defined religiously, rather than ethnically. For Philo, it is the presence of godly individuals that blesses others, not the presence of Jews in general. Both *Jubilees* and Philo understand the nature of the blessing to be material prosperity, while Philo also includes spiritual and moral benefits. Tobit does not comment on the nature of the blessing.

The primary concern of the books of Ben Sira, Tobit, and *Jubilees*, is to exhort the Jews living in the Hellenistic world to continue to obey the Mosaic law, while the *Ladder of Jacob* provides an apocalyptic message of hope in God's deliverance from the exile due to the sins of Israel. Therefore, their citation of the blessing for the nations in the Abrahamic promise appears to be incidental. It is not further developed in the book of Ben Sira and in the *Ladder of Jacob*, and it is apparently of secondary

---

164. Wisdom, *Blessing*, 86.

concern even when it is developed a little further in the books of Tobit and *Jubilees*.[165]

With respect to the promise of the Spirit in the Second Temple literature, both *Jubilees* and the Qumran community have a common understanding of the Spirit's function to cleanse the people from sin and to empower them to obey God's commands, in order that the problem of disobedience may be resolved permanently at the restoration of Israel (e.g., *Jubilees* 1:23–24a; 1QH$^a$ VIII, 24–30; 1QS III, 6–8).[166] This understanding is most likely derived from Isa 44:3 and Ezek 11:19–20; 36:25–27. However, in contrast to *Jubilees*, which perceives the bestowal of the Spirit to be in the future, the Qumran community views the promise of the Spirit in Isa 44:3 and Ezek 36:25–27 as actualized among them (e.g., 1QH$^a$ XX, 14b–15; 4Q504 1–2 recto V, 10–16), a view shared by *Joseph and Aseneth* (*Jos. Asen.* 15:5–7). Nonetheless, there is still a future element to be fully realized at the end of the age (1QS IV, 20–21). In the allusion to Isa 44:3 in 4Q504 1–2 recto V, 15–16, the Spirit is understood to be the means by which covenantal blessings are restored to Israel. The Spirit as a mark of membership of the people of God is apparent in both the Qumran literature (e.g., 1QS III, 6–12; 4Q504–506) and in *Joseph and Aseneth* (*Jos. Asen.* 8:9; 15:5–7).[167]

Regarding the recipients of the Spirit, there is generally no expectation in the Second Temple literature for Gentile converts to receive the Spirit—with the exception of *Joseph and Aseneth*, in which the Spirit is given to Aseneth, a proselyte woman. The promise of the Spirit cited in *Jubilees* 1:23–24a pertains to the Israelites. Not only does *Jubilees* not comment on proselytism, but it is antagonistic towards the Gentiles. The case is not only similar for the Qumran community, but it is even more stringent. The Spirit can only be received by the sectarians, but not by the non-sectarian Jews or the Gentile converts. Similarly, Philip observes that in the Second Temple literature, "anticipation of the Spirit upon the Gentiles is almost non-existent, and that the promise of the Spirit is on

---

165. See also Heckel, *Der Segen*, 116–17, who notes that both Sir 44:19–23 and *Jub.* 20:1–13; 24:9–11 closely connect the giving and fulfillment of the Abrahamic blessing for the nations with obedience to the Torah, and that in *Jubilees* the blessing for the nations is overlaid by the injunction to separate from Gentiles (*Jub.* 22:16, 20).

166. See also Philip, *Pauline Pneumatology*, 82, 85–87; Wenk, *Community-Forming Power*," 111; Bennema, *Power of Saving Wisdom*, 88. Both Wenk and Bennema observe the cleansing and empowerment function of the Spirit in the Qumran literature, but they do not discuss *Jubilees*.

167. See also Wenk, *Community-Forming Power*, 95–96, 102–5.

the people, only when they become members of the community of God."[168] Nonetheless, Philip thinks that it may be possible to infer from Philo (*Virtues*, 217–219) and the Qumran literature that proselytes may receive the Spirit.[169] In contrast, I have shown above that the inference is only remotely possible in Philo and not plausible from the Qumran literature.

From this study, we can also see that the Second Temple literature that comments on the Abrahamic blessing for the nations and the promise of the Spirit does not associate the two motifs. Even in the case of *Joseph and Aseneth*, where a proselyte woman receives the Spirit and becomes a member of the people of God, the bestowal of the Spirit and the salvation of Gentiles are not related to the Abrahamic blessing for the nations. This phenomenon stands in contrast to the apostle Paul, who juxtaposes the Abrahamic blessing for the nations and the promise of the Spirit in Gal 3:14. In the following chapter, we shall discuss how Paul might have interacted with the OT and the Second Temple literature on these two motifs, as well as explain the reason for his juxtaposition.

---

168. Philip, *Pauline Pneumatology*, 120. However, Philip chooses not to include *Joseph and Aseneth* in his discussion.

169. Philip, *Pauline Pneumatology*, 86, 116–18. See also Wenk, *Community-Forming Power*, 88–92, who holds a similar view as Philip with regard to proselytes receiving the Spirit in Philo.

# 6

# The Spirit's Relationship with the Blessing of Abraham in Galatians

## *Implications on Justification by Faith*

IN CHAPTER 1, WE raised the question of the relationship between the blessing of Abraham and the promise of the Spirit in Gal 3:14, as well as how their relationship would shed light on Paul's overall argument in Galatians and his theology of justification. While a few scholars argue that these two motifs are unrelated, most claim that the promise of the Spirit is the content of the blessing of Abraham. I have argued, however, that the two motifs in Gal 3:14 should not be equated. Nevertheless, there is some kind of relationship between the two. Now that we have examined these two motifs in the OT and the Second Temple literature, we shall proceed to consider how Paul might have interacted with the OT and contemporary Jewish thought in his arguments in Gal 3:1–14. We will then conclude from our discussion in this chapter why Paul associates the blessing of Abraham with the promise of the Spirit in Gal 3:14. We shall also discuss the implications of my proposed understanding of Paul's association of these two motifs for interpreting the book of Galatians and for Pauline studies, especially regarding justification.

I have also argued in chapter 2 that Paul refers to justification as the blessing of Abraham in Gal 3:6–9 and closely associates justification with the reception of the Spirit in Gal 3:1–5. In order for us to understand Paul's association of the Spirit with the blessing of Abraham and their respective relationships with justification, we will first need to examine the nature of blessing in the Abrahamic promise, the Mosaic covenant, and the prophets.

## The Spirit's Relationship with the Blessing of Abraham in Galatians

### THE BLESSING OF ABRAHAM FOR PAUL

It is common among scholars to understand the nature of blessing in Genesis and the Mosaic covenant to refer primarily to the prosperity and well-being of people, specifically in terms of numerous progeny and material wealth as a manifestation of the power of life (e.g., Gen 1:28; 9:1; 24:35–36; 26:12–14; 30:43; 39:5; Lev 26:1–13; Deut 28:1–14).[1] In referring to justification as the blessing of Abraham in Gal 3:6–9, has Paul then "transformed" the OT concept of blessing into "God's saving deeds in Christ," as Westermann claims?[2]

We have seen in chapter 3 that, in Genesis, the blessing of Abraham is God's reconciliatory initiative in response to the persistent alienation of humankind from God ever since the primeval times. It is essentially the turning point in God's plan to reverse the curse on humankind due to the fall (cf. Gen 3:1–19).[3] The blessing of Abraham in Genesis is essentially soteriological—to redeem humankind from the curse of sin and to reconcile humankind to God by restoring their alienated and broken relationship with God. Brueggemann also notes that the call of Abraham "has to do not simply with the forming of Israel but with the re-forming of creation, the transforming of the nations."[4]

From the broader Pauline theology, we know that, for Paul, all have sinned (Rom 3:9, 23), and God's righteousness demands that sinners be judged (Rom 3:19). Sinners can only be redeemed from sin, justified before God, and reconciled to him by faith in Jesus Christ (Rom 3:21–26; 5:1; 2 Cor 5:18–21). Paul asserts that "if anyone is in Christ, he is a new creation" and that "in Christ God was reconciling the world to himself" (2 Cor 5:17–18 ESV). Hence, considering the soteriological nature of the blessing of Abraham (Gen 12:2–3) and its significance in redeeming humankind from sin and restoring their relationship with God, it is no wonder that Paul sees the Abrahamic blessing for the nations in terms of Christ's redemption from the curse (Gal 3:13–14) and refers to the blessing as justification (Gal 3:6–9).[5] Therefore, Paul naturally understands

---

1. E.g., Pedersen, *Israel*, 182; Westermann, *Blessing in the Bible*, 30; Brueggemann, *Reverberations*, 19; Mathews, *Genesis 11:27—50:26*, 113. For a history of interpretation of blessing, see Mitchell, *Meaning of BRK*, 17–27; Leuenberger, *Segen und Segenstheologien*, 45–64.

2. Westermann, *Blessing in the Bible*, 77.

3. Wolff, "Kerygma," 86–87; Scharbert, "ברך," 2:306–7.

4. Brueggemann, *Genesis*, 105.

5. See also Heckel, *Der Segen*, 119–20. For details on how Paul understands all

the verb, "blessed," in the Abrahamic blessing for the nations to be passive (ἐνευλογηθήσονται; Gal 3:8; cf. Gen 12:3; 18:18; 22:18; 26:4; 28:14 LXX)—the nations are blessed by God on account of Christ, the promised offspring of Abraham (Gal 3:8, 13–14, 16).[6]

Nonetheless, how do we reconcile the predominant emphasis on numerous progeny and prosperity in the rest of Genesis and in the Mosaic covenant with the redemptive concept of the Abrahamic blessing in Paul? It is important to note that blessing from God presupposes a positive relationship and solidarity between God and the recipients of the blessing.[7] Therefore, blessings of abundant life, in the form of numerous progeny and prosperity in Genesis and in the Mosaic covenant, are a manifestation of a healthy relationship with God—the source of life and all goodness—while curses stand for a broken relationship with him—the loss of life and goodness.[8] As such, the keeping and breaking of the covenantal relationship with God are marked by blessings and curses respectively (Lev 26:1–39; Deut 28:1–68). Therefore, the nature of blessing in the Abrahamic and Mosaic covenants should not be confined to the outward manifestations of numerous progeny and prosperity, but should be understood as rooted in a positive relationship of the people with Yahweh as their God.[9] Thus,

---

three elements of the Abrahamic promise, namely numerous descendants, land, and blessing for the nations, as being fulfilled in Christ, see pp. 56–57 above. Similarly, Nwachukwu argues that, in the letter of Romans, "the doctrine of justification is developed from the background of themes relating to the creation-covenant scheme. On the basis of this scheme, Paul shows how justification by faith functions as a term of mediation in God's plan to show mercy to all" (Nwachukwu, *Creation-Covenant Scheme*, 177). Contra Cosgrove, *The Cross and the Spirit*, 50–51, who argues that "[Paul] never equates the blessing . . . with justification."

6. See also Heckel, *Der Segen*, 120. On the singular reference of Abraham's offspring in Gen 22:18, see pp. 80–81 above.

7. Scharbert, "ברך," 2:288. Scharbert notes that the blessing is "always a manifestation of an intimate relationship with the one for whom it is intended . . . thus it has to do with God's relationship to his people and his worshippers." Even in cases where the people who are blessed because of Abraham's descendants (e.g., Laban, Potiphar) do not have a direct relationship with Yahweh, it still presupposes that these people must have a positive relationship with the descendants of Abraham in order to be blessed (cf. Gen 12:3a).

8. See also Nowell, "Narrative Context of Blessing," 9–10, who points out that the content of the OT blessings indicates "the abundance and overflow of life" and "the sharing of life" with God, to whom life belongs.

9. See also Grüneberg, *Blessing*, 7, who explains that "the Old Testament does not confine God's activity to a spiritual realm distinct from the physical world, but sees God's hand at work in everything and expects God's favor to be apparent in every aspect of a person's life," and that although the majority of the blessings refer to material

while the Abrahamic blessing for the nations (Gen 12:3b) bears a redemptive purpose of restoring the relationship between God and humankind, such an understanding does not contradict the manifestation of the blessing of abundant life, in the form of numerous progeny and prosperity, depicted in the rest of Genesis and in the Mosaic covenantal blessings.

For this reason, Paul does not seem to distinguish between the blessing and curse language in Genesis and Deuteronomy when he presents the blessing of Abraham as antithetical to the deuteronomic curses in Gal 3:6–14. Thus, it is very likely that he also relates the deuteronomic curses (Gal 3:10, 13; cf. Deut 21:23; 27:26) to the curse of the fall (cf. Gen 3:14–19), in that both are the result of sin and the mark of a broken relationship with God.[10] Therefore, although the "curse of the law" in Gal 3:10, 13 refers directly to the judgment of God meted out on transgressors of the law, it can also extend to the "curse of sin" in more general terms. This is further supported by Paul's understanding that, although Gentiles do not have the Mosaic law, the moral law of God is written in their conscience, such that they are also considered "law-breakers" when they sin and would incur the wrath and judgment of God in the same way as the transgressors of the law (Rom 2:12–16).[11] Thus, Christ's death on the cross redeems both Jewish and Gentile believers (ἡμᾶς, "us"; Gal 3:13) from the curse of the law in order that the blessing of Abraham may come upon the nations (Gal 3:13–14).[12]

In view of the redemptive and reconciliatory purpose of the Abrahamic blessing for the nations in Genesis, it is not surprising to find two of the three allusions to the Abrahamic blessing in other OT texts, namely Jer 4:2 and Zech 8:13, occurring in the context of restoration.[13] Jeremiah 3:6–4:4, Zech 2:10–12, and Zech 8:1–23 look forward to the time of Israel's restoration of its covenantal relationship with Yahweh, at which time na-

---

blessings, "there are some exceptions," such as Deut 28:9, which is a "promise that Israel will be God's holy people."

10. See also Eckstein, *Verheißung und Gesetz*, 166; Heckel, *Der Segen*, 146, who notes that there is an affinity between the abrogation of the curse on humans in the primeval history and the abrogation of sin for Paul.

11. Bruce, *Galatians*, 167.

12. For other exegetical reasons for the inclusive reading of the first person plural in Gal 3:13, see pp. 52–53 above and p. 187 below.

13. Redemption from sin may be seen in Jer 3:17, where the nations shall "no longer walk according to the stubbornness of their evil heart." The reconciliation with God may be seen in Zech 2:11 (MT 2:15), where "many nations shall join themselves to Yahweh, and they shall be [his] people."

tions will also be drawn to Yahweh to worship him. Both Jeremiah and Zechariah understand that the Abrahamic blessing for the nations shall be fulfilled at that time.[14] I have also shown that in Ps 72:17, the Abrahamic blessing for the nations is linked to a specific offspring of Abraham, the ideal eschatological Israelite king.[15] These developments of the Abrahamic blessing for the nations in other OT texts, together with the prophetic texts that associate the restoration of Israel with the rule of a Davidic king (e.g., Isa 11:1–16; Ezek 37:24–27), are very likely the basis of Paul's identification of Christ Jesus, the son of David (cf. Rom 1:3), as the promised descendant and fulfillment of the Abrahamic blessing for the nations (Gal 3:16; cf. Gen 22:18; 26:4).[16]

Christ as the fulfillment of the Abrahamic blessing for the nations is also apparent in Acts 3:25, where Peter proclaims to the Jews within the temple precinct, "You are the sons of the prophets and of the covenant that God made with your fathers, saying to Abraham, 'And in your offspring shall all the families of the earth be blessed.' God, having raised up his servant, sent him to you first, to bless you by turning every one of you from your wickedness" (Acts 3:25–26 ESV).[17] The nature of the Abraha-

---

14. See also pp. 105–9 above.

15. See pp. 102–5 above.

16. Similarly, in Rom 15:8–15, Paul argues that God has fulfilled the patriarchal promises by including the Gentiles as his people through Christ and supports his argument with a series of scriptural citations, including Isa 11:10 (cf. Rom 15:12). The purpose of Paul's argument in Rom 15:8–15, though, is to encourage both Jewish and Gentile believers to live in harmony with each other (Rom 15:4–7) (Käsemann, *Romans*, 384–85; Moo, *Romans*, 873–74; Schreiner, *Romans*, 752; Jewett, *Romans*, 887–92). Both Scott and Heckel also think that Paul's identification of Christ as the promised descendant of Abraham is associated with the messianic interpretation of Ps 72:17 (Scott, *Paul and the Nations*, 129–30; Heckel, *Der Segen*, 146–47). The tradition of Jesus as the fulfillment of the Abrahamic promise and the messianic son of David is also picked up by Matthew, who portrays Jesus as the descendant of Abraham and David (Matt 1:1), the messiah who has already come (Matt 11:2–6; 16:13–18; 27:11, 37), and whose message of salvation is for all the nations (Matt 28:18–20) (see also Pyne, "'Seed,'" 213–14).

17. The major difference between Acts 3:25b and Gen 12:3b; 22:18 LXX is the use of πατριαί ("families") instead of φυλαί ("families"; Gen 12:3b) and ἔθνη ("nations"; Gen 22:18). Nonetheless, πατριά is frequently used to translate מִשְׁפְּחָה ("family"; Gen 12:3b MT) in the LXX (Barrett, *Acts*, 1:212; Léonas, "Acts 3,25–26," 152; Marshall, "Acts," 549). As Peter includes his Jewish audience as those who are blessed in the blessing for the nations (Acts 3:26), it is likely that πατριαί is used instead of ἔθνη, because the latter usually means "Gentiles" at that time (Fitzmyer, *Acts*, 291; Léonas, "Acts 3,25–26," 160; Marshall, "Acts," 549). Regarding the arguments for Gen 12:3; 22:18 as part of the early Christian oral tradition and *testimonia*, see e.g., Dodd,

mic blessing for the nations in Acts 3:25-26 is understood to be the divine act of turning the people away from sin, a concept in line with the redemptive and reconciliatory purpose of the Abrahamic blessing in Genesis and similar to Paul's argument in Gal 3:6-14.[18] However, while Paul focuses on the Gentiles in his citation of the Abrahamic blessing for the nations, the same citation in Acts 3:25 functions to remind the Jews of their need to repent and receive the blessing of restoration through Jesus Christ (Acts 3:19-20).[19] Paul's overall argument is that both Jews and Gentiles need to be justified by faith in Christ (Gal 2:15-16; 3:13-14, 24-29).

In summary, "to be blessed" by God with the blessing of Abraham (Gal 3:6-8; 13-14) is to be redeemed from the curse of sin—the result of both the fall and covenantal violations—and to be reconciled with God as his people—a restoration from both the broken covenantal relationship and the alienation of humanity from God due to the fall. This blessing is for both Jews and Gentiles, and it is made possible by Christ's vicarious death on the cross (Gal 3:13-14).[20] Although Paul focuses on the blessing of Abraham coming to the Gentiles in Gal 3:14 and Acts 3:25 on the Jews, both Paul and Peter understand that the blessing is for both Jews and Gentiles.

Paul's understanding of the Abrahamic blessing for the nations (Gen 12:3; 22:18) stands in contrast to Jewish contemporary thought in two main ways. First, the nature of the blessing for the nations is usually material in the Second Temple literature, although Philo also includes spiritual benefits, such as intercessory prayers and positive moral influence (*Jub.* 20:1-13; Philo, *Migration* 118-127a; *Dreams* 1.176-178).[21] On the other hand, Paul sees the Abrahamic blessing for the nations as a redemptive

---

*According to the Scriptures*, 43-44; Albl, *Scripture Cannot Be Broken*, 193-95.

18. The active infinitive ἀποστρέφειν ("to turn away") in Acts 3:26 may be transitive (i.e., God turning the people away from sin) or intransitive (i.e., the people themselves turning away from sin). The former sees repentance as being enabled by God (e.g., Barrett, *Acts*, 1:214), while the latter sees repentance as a human responsibility and implies that repentance is a condition to receive the blessing (e.g., Schneider, *Apostelgeschichte*, 1:329 n. 124). However, as Barrett argues, the intransitive is usually expressed by the passive or middle in Greek; thus in this case, the active form more likely denotes the transitive (Barrett, *Acts*, 1:214). Nonetheless, divine enablement of repentance does not preclude human responsibility to repent (cf. Acts 3:19; see also Heckel, *Der Segen*, 98-99; Bock, *Acts*, 181-82).

19. See also Léonas, "Acts 3,25-26," 150.

20. See pp. 50-53 above.

21. See pp. 149-55 above.

and reconciliatory act of God.²² Second, the Abrahamic blessing is often tied to obedience to God's commands and laws in contemporary Jewish thought (Sir 44:19–21; *Jub.* 18:15–16; 20:1–13; 24:9–11; Philo, *Heir* 8–9).²³ The blessing for the nations, which is cited along with other elements of the Abrahamic blessing, seems to be included incidentally, and it is of secondary concern in the Second Temple literature.²⁴ In view of prevailing Jewish thought, it is no wonder that the "trouble-makers" (ταράσσοντες; Gal 1:7; 5:10) in Galatia also insist that the Gentile Christians need to observe the Jewish law in addition to their faith in Christ (Gal 2:15–21; 3:3; 4:8–11; 5:1–6; 6:12–13). This is the notion that Paul seeks to correct in the letter of Galatians, in which he insists that it is by faith in Christ, not by obedience to the law, that a person is blessed and reckoned righteous by God and included in God's people (Gal 2:16; 3:6–9; 26–29). What, then, is Paul's view of obedience in the lives of believers? We shall look into this issue of obedience as we discuss the promise of the Spirit and its relationship with the Abrahamic blessing for the nations below.

## The Promise of the Spirit for Paul

We have seen in chapters 4 and 5 that the understanding of the promise of the Spirit in Second Temple literature as a whole is similar to the OT prophets: the Spirit is (1) the means by which covenantal blessings are restored to the people of God (a) by revivifying their lives (Isa 32:15; 44:3; Ezek 37:14) and (b) by empowering them to obey God (Ezek 36:27); and (2) the mark of a restored covenantal relationship with God (Isa 44:1–5; Ezek 39:29). While the promise of the Spirit is in the future in the prophets, it is regarded as actualized among the Qumran community and in *Joseph and Aseneth*. With the exception of *Joseph and Aseneth*, there is no expectation in the Second Temple period that Gentile converts would receive the Spirit.

Paul's pneumatology in Galatians runs along the same lines as the OT and the Second Temple literature in several ways. First, like the Qumran

---

22. The redemptive nature of the Abrahamic blessing for the nations may be seen in Gal 3:13–14, while the reconciliation and restoration of the relationship with God as his people may be seen in Paul's arguments that those who believe in Christ, the promised descendant of Abraham, are the offspring of Abraham and the children of God (Gal 3:7, 16, 24–29).

23. See also Heckel, *Der Segen*, 116–17.

24. See pp. 178–80 above.

community and *Joseph and Aseneth*, the promise of the Spirit is an actualized event (Gal 3:1–5, 14; 4:6). Second, the Spirit received by the believers is a witness to their status as the "children" (υἱοί) of God (Gal 4:6; cf. 3:26) and the heirs of the Abrahamic promise (Gal 3:29; 4:7). Therefore, for Paul, the reception of the Spirit signifies believers' membership in God's people. The Spirit is also the source and perpetuator of the believer's life in Christ (Gal 5:25; 6:8; cf. Gal 3:3).[25] However, the major difference in Paul, compared with the general expectation during the Second Temple period, is that the gift of the Spirit is received only by faith in Christ Jesus, apart from observing the law and regardless of ethnicity (Gal 3:1–5; 13–14, 28–29; 4:6).[26] The three points of difference are: (1) the recipients of the Spirit; (2) the means of reception—faith in Jesus Christ; and (3) the apparent dissociation between obedience to the Torah and the reception of the Spirit (see the antithesis between faith and the works of the law in Gal 3:1–14). So, where did Paul get the idea that Gentile believers in Christ who have received the Spirit need not observe the Jewish law in order to be part of the covenant community of God?

At first sight, the promise of the Spirit in the OT seems to be addressed only to the Israelites (Isa 32:15; 44:3; Ezek 36:26–27; 37:14; Joel 2:28–29 [MT 3:1–2]). However, I have argued in chapter 4 that since the nations who have "joined themselves to Yahweh" are also called "the people of Yahweh" (Isa 56:3–7; Zech 2:11 [MT 2:15]), it is reasonable to understand that the promise of the Spirit made to Israel as the people of God is also applicable to these nations. Therefore, Gentile converts may also receive the Spirit that is promised in the prophets.

---

25. Gal 5:25: "If we live by the Spirit, let us also walk by the Spirit." Fung notes that the Spirit is "the source and sustaining power of believers' spiritual life" and "the regulative principle of the believers' conduct" (Fung, *Galatians*, 275; see also Bruce, *Galatians*, 257; Martyn, *Galatians*, 545). Given that the immediate context of Gal 5:25 deals with how believers ought to live (Gal 5:16–26), it may be possible to understand the phrase "live by the Spirit" to be synonymous with "walk by the Spirit," i.e., both referring to the manner by which believers should live their lives (cf. Longenecker, *Galatians*, 265). However, given Paul's emphasis on the Spirit as the beginning *and* continuation of the believer's life and justification in Christ in Gal 3:3, it is more likely that "live by the Spirit" refers to the principle of the Spirit as the source and perpetuator of life and "walk by the Spirit" as the working out of that life (see also Dunn, *Galatians*, 317). "Reaping eternal life from the Spirit" (Gal 6:8) also points to the Spirit as the source and perpetuator of life.

26. Although the Spirit is given to a Gentile convert in *Joseph and Aseneth* (*Jos. Asen.* 8:9; 15:5–7), it nevertheless, as in *Jubilees* and the Qumran community, does not associate the gift of the Spirit with any messianic expectations.

## The Blessing of Abraham, the Spirit, and Justification in Galatians

Philip argues that Paul's conviction that Gentile Christians receive the Spirit apart from Torah observance is based on his ministry experience at Antioch, where he witnessed Gentile Christians receiving the Spirit apart from the law in the missionary efforts of the Hellenistic-Jewish Christians.[27] According to Philip, Paul was influenced by these Hellenistic-Jewish Christians, who "could accommodate the non-proselyte Gentile into the Christian community" as a result of "the conventional expectation of the pilgrimage of the nations rooted in the Old Testament."[28] However, the prophetic tradition of the eschatological turning of the nations to Yahweh mentions their obedience to the Torah (e.g., Isa 2:2–4; 56:3–7; Mic 4:1–2; Zech 14:16–19). How, then, is their obedience related to their turning to Yahweh? Is there any scriptural basis from which Paul draws his conclusion that the gift of the Spirit and justification are apart from Torah observance?

On the one hand, convictions from experience do play an important role both for the apostles at the Jerusalem Council and Paul. James agreed with the testimony of Peter, Paul, and Barnabas that the Gentile believers had received God's Spirit apart from circumcision and Torah observance (Acts 15:7–14). Paul argues from the experience of the Galatian Gentile Christians that they had received the Spirit by faith in Christ and not by the works of the law (Gal 3:2, 5). Therefore, Philip's argument regarding the origins of Paul's pneumatology based on ministry experience is plausible to a certain extent, but Philip has yet to address the tension apparent in the association of Torah obedience with the pilgrimage of the nations in the OT. It is also important to note that Paul is not only arguing that Gentile believers have received the Spirit apart from Torah observance, but that *both Jewish and Gentile believers* receive the Spirit and are justified apart from Torah observance (Gal 2:15–16; 3:13–14).

On the other hand, Paul not only argues from the experience of the Gentile believers (Gal 3:2, 5), he also gives evidence from Scripture (Gal 3:6–14). James also appealed to Scripture while agreeing with the experience of Peter, Paul, and Barnabas (Acts 15:14–17; cf. Amos 9:11–12). Therefore, there is likely to be some scriptural basis that leads Paul to his

---

27. Philip, *Pauline Pneumatology*, 227.

28. Ibid., 226–27. If Philip had included *Joseph and Aseneth* in his discussion on the expectation of the Spirit during the Second Temple period, he would have an important piece of evidence to support his thesis that Hellenistic-Jews were indeed more open to the concept of Gentile converts receiving the Spirit. See Philip, *Pauline Pneumatology*, 90n49 and also pp. 173nn145–46 above.

conviction that the gift of the Spirit and justification are not based on Torah observance.

Coming back to the promise of the Spirit in the OT, Ezek 36:26-27 proclaims that God will put his Spirit within his people to empower them to "walk in [his] statutes and be careful to obey [his] judgments" at the restoration of Israel. I have argued in chapter 4 that both Jeremiah and Ezekiel speak of the inability of the people to obey God apart from divine empowerment and that this promise in Ezek 36:26-27 (cf. Jer 31:31-34; 32:39-40) is God's permanent and effective solution to the problem of disobedience. At the eschatological restoration of Israel, obedience to the law is not the prerequisite of receiving the Spirit, but rather the *result* of the Spirit's work. As I have argued, although this promise of the Spirit is made to repentant Israelites, it may also be applied to nations who have "joined themselves to Yahweh." Therefore, the nations' obedience to the Torah associated with their eschatological turning to Yahweh is also the *result* of the Spirit's empowerment, rather than the prerequisite for them to become the people of God.

Although Paul does not cite Ezekiel anywhere in Galatians, this prophetic tradition of the divine empowerment to obey through the Spirit is apparent in the second half of Galatians.[29] By themselves, humans are enslaved (Gal 4:3, 8-9; 5:1) and incapable of fulfilling "the whole law" (Gal 3:10; cf. 5:3).[30] It is the work of the Spirit in believers' lives that resists sin and brings forth true obedience and righteousness in accord with the law (Gal 5:13-26).[31] It is the Spirit who ensures believers of the hope of righteousness and eternal life (Gal 5:5-6; 6:8; cf. Ezek 36:26-27; 37:14).[32]

---

29. See also Kruse, "Paul, the Law and the Spirit," 122-23; Rowland, "Eschatology of the New Testament," 62.

30. See the section on "The Implied Premise in Galatians 3:10" below. For scholars who take "the whole law" in Gal 5:3 to refer back to "all that is written in the book of the law" in Gal 3:10, see, e.g., Howard, *Paul*, 16; Barclay, *Obeying*, 64; Martin, "Apostasy," 453.

31. See esp. Gal 5:16 ESV: "But I say, walk by the Spirit, and you will not (οὐ μή) gratify the desires of the flesh." Paul's use of the double negation (οὐ μή) shows his confidence that the believer who is empowered by the Spirit will certainly be able to resist sin (Barclay, *Obeying*, 111; Longenecker, *Galatians*, 245). Nonetheless, Paul does not imply that believers will no longer sin (cf. Gal 6:1), but that in their struggles against sin, they are assured of the victory over sin if they depend on the empowerment of the Spirit.

32. Bruce, *Galatians*, 231-32, 265; Fee, *God's Empowering Presence*, 417-19, 467-68.

## The Blessing of Abraham, the Spirit, and Justification in Galatians

I have pointed out earlier that, in the OT, the divine intervention to transform the human heart and enable obedience through the internalization of the law is not only described as the putting of God's Spirit within his people (Ezek 36:26-27), but also as the "circumcision of the heart"—a metaphor for a heart that is obedient and responsive to Yahweh (Deut 30:6, 8; cf. Jer 4:4; 31:33-34; 32:39-40).[33] These OT concepts are reflected in Paul's use of circumcision language. For Paul, the true significance of circumcision does not lie in the outward circumcision of the flesh, but in the inward transformation of the heart by the Spirit to obey God. These various aspects of circumcision may be seen in Rom 2:25-29, 1 Cor 7:19, Gal 5:6; 6:15, and Phil 3:2-3.[34] Therefore, in line with the prophetic tradition, Paul argues that obedience to the law is not the prerequisite for receiving the Spirit and justification, but rather true obedience to God in accord with the law is the result of the work of the Spirit.[35] This is the way that Paul understands the association of obedience to the law with the eschatological restoration of Israel and the pilgrimage of the nations in the prophetic tradition.

Does Paul, then, also understand the Spirit to be the means by which covenantal blessings are restored to God's people (cf. Isa 44:3; Ezek 36:26-38)? Or is the Spirit the content of the Abrahamic blessing, as many scholars have supposed? What, then, is the relationship between the promise of the Spirit and the blessing of Abraham for Paul?

---

33. See pp. 101-2 above.

34. See esp. Rom 2:29b: "circumcision is a matter of the heart, by the Spirit, not by the letter"; 1 Cor 7:19: "For neither circumcision counts for anything nor uncircumcision, but keeping the commandments of God"; Gal 5:6: "For in Christ Jesus neither circumcision nor uncircumcision counts for anything, but only faith working through love"; 6:15: "For neither circumcision counts for anything, nor uncircumcision, but a new creation" (ESV).

35. See also Sprinkle, *Law and Life*, 201-2. Sprinkle notes that in the Qumran literature, some form of prior obedience must be demonstrated in order to be considered for membership (e.g., CD III, 12), but "for Paul Christian obedience is shaped and generated by Christ and the indwelling Spirit." Sprinkle's observations about the *Damascus Document* is similar to our conclusions about the *Rule of the Community* above, which emphasizes human responsibility in obedience (see pp. 167-70 above).

## The Spirit's Relationship with the Blessing of Abraham in Galatians

### THE RELATIONSHIP BETWEEN THE BLESSING OF ABRAHAM AND THE PROMISE OF THE SPIRIT

We return to Hays's question: was there "something within the realm of Jewish expectations that *did* associate the Spirit with the promises of Abraham?"[36] In chapter 1, we have seen that Wan proposes that Paul's juxtaposition of the two motifs could be influenced by the Hellenistic-Jewish mysticism that is reflected in Philo.[37] Our study on the blessing of Abraham and the promise of the Spirit in the OT and Second Temple literature has shown that Paul has more affinities with the OT tradition than with Philo's mystical and allegorical interpretations of the Abrahamic promise. Even Philo's literal interpretation of the Abrahamic blessing for the nations bears no affinities with Paul's interpretation of the same motif.[38] Therefore, our study has confirmed that Wan's arguments are unconvincing.

Hays proposes that Isa 44:3 is the "partial" answer to his question, but he did not develop his suggestion by showing how the blessing in Isa 44:3 is related to the Abrahamic promise.[39] This study has helped supply this lack by showing that in Isaiah, not only are the Sinai-covenantal blessings fully restored at the eschatological restoration of Israel, but also all the elements of the Abrahamic promise are fully realized.[40] This notion is in accord with Lev 26:42 and Deut 4:31, where Yahweh's restoration of his covenantal relationship with Israel is based on his faithfulness in keep-

---

36. Hays, *Faith of Jesus Christ*, 182 (emphasis in original).

37. Wan, "Abraham and the Promise of Spirit," 217–19, 223–24. For more details on Wan's arguments and the reasons I have listed on why Wan's argument is unconvincing, see p. 7 above.

38. See pp. 149–55 above.

39. Hays, *Faith of Jesus Christ*, 182–83; Hays, "Galatians," 261. While I agree with Hays that Isa 44:3 is a key passage in understanding Paul's juxtaposition of the blessing of Abraham and the promise of the Spirit in Gal 3:14, there is no evidence in the NT corpus to support Hays's suggestion that Isa 44:3 was part of the early Christian *testimonia* (*Faith of Jesus Christ*, 182–83).

40. See pp. 120–21 above. Contrary to Kwon, *Eschatology in Galatians*, 115n44, who asserts that Isa 44:3 "has nothing to do with the *Abrahamic* promise" (emphasis in original). Morales also tries to address Hays's concern that Isa 44:3 speaks of Israel, but not Abraham (cf. Hays, *Faith of Jesus Christ*, 182). He rightly notes the description of Israel as the "seed of Abraham" in Isa 41:8 (cf. Gal 3:29) and God's blessing of Abraham in Isa 51:2 (Morales, *The Spirit and the Restoration of Israel*, 110–11). However, he has only highlighted the lexical links between Israel and Abraham as well as the verbal allusion to the blessing of Abraham in Isaiah, but he has not shown sufficiently the other contextual parallels in Isaiah with the blessing of Abraham in Genesis or the relationship between the covenantal blessing in Isa 44:3 and the blessing of Abraham.

ing the patriarchal covenant. Therefore, we may conclude that the Spirit is not only the means of restoring the Sinai-covenantal blessings in Isa 44:3, but also ultimately the means of realizing the Abrahamic blessing for the nations. The Spirit, who revivifies and signifies the restored relationship between God and his people (Isa 44:3–5), is given to the repentant physical descendants of Jacob (Isa 44:3), and by extension to the foreigners who have "joined themselves to Yahweh" and who need not regard themselves as "separate" from God's people (Isa 56:3–6). The promise in Gen 35:11, which is a development of the Abrahamic blessing for the nations, that Jacob, who was renamed Israel, shall become "a nation and a company of nations," is finally fulfilled at the eschatological restoration of Israel.[41]

While the Second Temple literature does not link the Abrahamic blessing for the nations with the promise of the Spirit, the larger context of Isa 44:3 is very likely to have influenced Paul in juxtaposing "the blessing of Abraham" and the "promise of the Spirit" in Gal 3:14.[42] Paul clearly portrays the Spirit as given to all believers regardless of ethnicity (Gal 3:2, 5; 3:13–14). The Spirit is the source and sustenance of life and the witness to the restored relationship with God (Gal 4:6; 5:25; 6:8). But how is the Spirit the means by which the blessing of Abraham is bestowed upon both Jewish and Gentile believers?

While Isa 44:3 does not spell out the details of how the Spirit is the means by which the covenantal blessings are restored to God's people, Ezek 36:26–27 and 37:14 do. Isaiah 44:3–4 hints at the revivification function of the Spirit by contrasting the metaphors of "thirsty land" and "dry ground" with "spring[ing] up among the grass like willows by flowing streams" (ESV), but Ezek 37:14a spells it out explicitly, "And I will put my Spirit within you, and you shall live" (ESV). The Spirit of God put within his people empowers them to obey the "statutes and judgments" of God's law (Ezek 36:26–27), so that the covenantal curses due to their disobedience may be subverted and the covenantal blessings that come with obedience may be perpetuated.[43]

Similarly, this empowerment of God's indwelling Spirit that is prophesied in Ezek 36:26–27 can be seen Paul's argument in Galatians in the

---

41. Lee, "גוים in Genesis 35:11," 467–82.

42. 4Q504 1–2 recto V, 15–16 understands the Spirit to be the means of restoring blessings to Israel, but it associates the blessing with the Sinai-covenant but not the Abrahamic promise. Although *Jos. Asen.* 8:9, 15:5–7 speaks of the gift of the Spirit to a Gentile convert, it also does not relate it to the Abrahamic blessing for the nations. See pp. 166–67, 173–77, 181 above.

43. See pp. 122–31 above.

following ways. First, believers who "walk by the Spirit" are empowered by the Spirit to overcome sin—the desires of the flesh (Gal 5:16–21)—and to live out their faith in love (Gal 5:6, 22), so that the intention of the law is fulfilled (Gal 5:14). The fulfillment of the law does not mean the carrying out of every stipulation of the law, for Paul argues against the need for Gentiles to observe Jewish laws such as circumcision.[44] Rather, as Barclay argues, it implies "the total realization and accomplishment of the law's demand" when "God's purposes and promises had reached their fulfillment in Christ" (Gal 4:4).[45] Also, as Dunn explains, the "fulfillment" of the law in Rom 8:4; 13:8 and Gal 5:14 refers to accomplishing "the essential requirement . . . which lies behind the individual requirements, the character and purpose which the individual requirements are intended to bring to expression."[46] For Paul, the just requirement of the law in terms of atonement for sins has already been fulfilled by Christ's vicarious sacrifice (Gal 1:4; 3:13; cf. Rom 8:3–4), and the moral requirement of the law, which serves to instruct God's people how to love one another, is fulfilled by those who are empowered by the Spirit of Christ to live out their faith in love (Gal 5:14, 16, 22; cf. Rom 8:4; 13:8–10).

Second, by empowering the believer to fulfill the law through love, the Spirit continues to guard the believer against the "curse of the law" (cf. Gal 3:10), from which Christ has already redeemed believers (Gal 3:13).[47] Wilson argues that the phrase "under the law" in Galatians (Gal 3:23; 4:4–5, 21; 5:18) serves as a shorthand for "under the curse of the law" in Gal 3:10, 13.[48] Therefore, the believer who is "led by the Spirit" is not "under (the curse of) the law" (Gal 5:18).[49] However, Moo argues that "under the law" refers to a broader meaning of "a status of close supervi-

---

44. Kruse, "Paul, the Law and the Spirit," 127–28.

45. Barclay, *Obeying*, 139.

46. Dunn, *Romans 1-8*, 423. See also Moo, "The Law of Christ," 359–60, 371–72.

47. Wilson, *Curse of the Law*, 117–25, 139–42. See also Morales, "Words of the Luminaries," 275–77, who also rightly notes that the outpouring of the Spirit functions as a sign of Israel's redemption from the curses of Deuteronomy in Isa 44:3, 4Q504 1-2 recto V, 15–16, and Gal 3:10–14. However, he has unduly restricted the redemption to Jewish Christians in Gal 3:13. As Morales admits, while his conclusion of the Spirit as the sign of Israel being redeemed from the curse of the law in Jewish tradition is helpful for us to see the connection between the Spirit and the curse of the law in Gal 3:10, 13, it does not help to explain "why Paul includes Gentiles in the blessing" (Morales, "Words of the Luminaries," 275, 277).

48. Wilson, *Curse of the Law*, 30–44. However, Wilson does not address how the promise of the Spirit is related to the Abrahamic blessing for the nations.

49. Ibid., 118–20.

sion and custodial care" by the law, rather than the narrower meaning of being subject to the curse of the law, because Christ is born "under the law" (Gal 4:4), but not subject to its curse. Nonetheless, Moo thinks that "the phrase can occasionally include within it nuances of condemnation. But this is a nuance and not the basic meaning of the phrase."[50] In the case of Gal 5:18, the nuance of condemnation is also included, because those who are under the governance of the law will also come under the curse of the law due to their sin. In this sense, I agree with Wilson that the work of the Spirit in believers' lives guards against the curse of the law.

Third, the Spirit is not only the evidence of present justification (Gal 3:2–5), but also ensures believers of their hope of righteousness (Gal 5:5)— their future justification.[51] The "righteousness" in ἐλπίδα δικαιοσύνης ("the hope of righteousness"; Gal 5:5) is most likely an objective or epexegetic genitive, i.e., the hope which consists of righteousness.[52] Nonetheless, a few interpreters hold to a subjective genitive, i.e., righteousness as the source of the hope or "that for which righteousness hopes."[53] However, the objective/epexegetic genitive is preferred for two reasons. First, the subjective genitive would leave the "hope" without a specific content. The verb ἀπεκδέχομαι ("eagerly await") in Paul's writings is always used in eschatological contexts, and the content of the object is usually specified (e.g., Rom 8:19, 23; 1 Cor 1:7; Phil 3:20).[54] Second, the issue in Galatians has to do with the maintenance and ultimate status of justification (Gal 2:17; 3:3; 5:4).[55] Therefore, the "hope of righteousness" in Gal 5:5 refers to the ultimate future justification that believers hope for and are assured of by the Spirit.[56] We have seen above that Paul regards the blessing of Abraham as justification.[57] In other words, by empowering believers (1) to live

50. Moo, "Law of Christ," 362.

51. See also Kwon, *Eschatology in Galatians*, 200.

52. The objective genitive is reflected in some English versions and most commentaries (e.g., NLT; NIV; Burton, *Galatians*, 278; Guthrie, *Galatians*, 130; Martyn, *Galatians*, 472).

53. E.g., Fung, *Galatians*, 226; Matera, *Galatians*, 182; Fee, *God's Empowering Presence*, 419.

54. Smith, *Justification and Eschatology*, 94–95n71, 119.

55. See also Stanton, "Law of Moses," 104; Rainbow, *Way of Salvation*, 158–61; Garlington, *Galatians*, 161.

56. Other scholars who understand Gal 5:5 as a reference to future justification are, e.g., O'Brien, "Justification in Paul," 90; Dunn, *Galatians*, 269–70; Martyn, *Galatians*, 472; McGrath, "Justification," 518; Marshall, *New Testament Theology*, 233.

57. See pp. 33, 38–39, 183–85 above.

out their faith in obedience so as to fulfill the law and (2) to overcome sin so that believers may be guarded continually against the curse of the law, the Spirit not only ensures the perpetuation of the covenantal blessings of a restored relationship with God, it also ensures the perpetuation of the blessing of Abraham.[58]

As I have mentioned in chapter 2, Gal 3:1–14 is Paul's primary substantiation of his fundamental thesis that justification is by faith in Christ Jesus and not by works of the law (Gal 2:16), and the various motifs brought up in Gal 3:1–14 are then elaborated in Gal 3:15—6:10. Just as Paul elucidates in Gal 3:15—4:31 the various motifs regarding the Abrahamic promise in relation to the law, he also explicates the Spirit and its function in relation to justification and the fulfillment of the law in Gal 4:6-7, 29 and 5:5; 5:16—6:10. The reception of the Spirit as the evidence of the present status of justification is first mentioned in Gal 3:2, 5, and the Spirit in relation to the beginning (ἐνάρχομαι) and completing (ἐπιτελέω) of the status of justification is first hinted at in Gal 3:3. The concept of the Spirit as the evidence of a restored relationship with God and as the means of preventing the covenantal relationship from being broken by disobedience (i.e., subversion of curse and perpetuation of blessing) is inherent in the promise of the Spirit in the prophets (cf. Isa 44:3–5; Ezek 36:26–27), and it is thus latent in Gal 3:14b. These two underlying ideas of the Spirit as evidence and means in Gal 3:14b are then further explicated in Gal 4:6-7, 29 and 5:5, 16—6:10. This understanding helps us to see clearly the integral connection between the so-called "doctrinal" (Galatians 1–4) and "ethical" (Galatians 5–6) sections of the letter of Galatians.

In summary, the relationship between the blessing of Abraham and the promise of the Spirit in Gal 3:14 is as follows. First, the Spirit signifies the reconciled relationship between God and his people, and thus, the reception of the Spirit by those who believe in Christ is the evidence that they have received the blessing of Abraham—their present justification before God. Second, the Spirit ensures the perpetuation of the blessing of Abraham—future justification—by working in the lives of believers to produce true obedience and righteousness, as well as by empowering them to resist sin, so that the law may be fulfilled and the curse of the law may continue to be subverted. While it is common for scholars to note the function of the Spirit as the evidence of present justification, this study has shown further that the Spirit also maintains the status of justification and

---

58. See below for more discussion on the role of the Spirit in present and final justification.

ensures future justification.[59] We will discuss further in detail the role of the Spirit in future justification in the implications section below.

I therefore affirm the assertion of Fee and Kwon that the promise of the Spirit in Gal 3:14 should be understood as the fulfillment of the prophetic promises in Isaiah, Jeremiah, Ezekiel, and Joel.[60] While neither Fee nor Kwon elaborates on how these prophetic promises are understood as fulfilled in the letter of Galatians, our discussion above has filled this gap. On the one hand, Kwon is right in arguing that the Spirit should not be equated with the Abrahamic promise.[61] Indeed, as we have seen, the blessing of Abraham, which is identified as justification in Gal 3:6–9, is not the promise of the Spirit. On the other hand, this study also shows that Kwon is mistaken in denying any relationship between the Abrahamic promise and the promise of the Spirit.[62] Rather, the Spirit is the evidence of receiving the blessing of Abraham, and it perpetuates the blessing. In view of this relationship between the blessing of Abraham and the promise of the Spirit, Fee's statement that "the Spirit is the way the promised blessing made to Abraham has been realized" is correct to a certain extent,[63] but needs to be refined as follows: Christ's substitutionary death on the cross is the way by which the promised blessing made to Abraham has been realized, and the Spirit is the evidence of the blessing and the means by which the blessing is perpetuated (Gal 3:13–14).

## Implications

### The Implied Premise in Galatians 3:10

In chapter 2, we raised the issue about whether there is an implied premise about the impossibility of keeping the law perfectly in Paul's citation of Deut 27:26 in Gal 3:10. At the same time as I argued that Paul's association of the Spirit with the blessing of Abraham in Gal 3:14 may be explained in relation to Isa 44:3–5 and Ezek 36:26–27, I have also shown that Paul's concept of the promise of the Spirit reflected in the letter of Galatians is deeply influenced by the prophets, even though he does not cite them

---

59. For the bibliography of scholars who discuss the function of the Spirit in present justification, see p. 204n84 below.

60. Fee, *God's Empowering Presence*, 395; Kwon, *Eschatology in Galatians*, 115–17.

61. Kwon, *Eschatology in Galatians*, 107–13.

62. Ibid., 109–11.

63. Fee, *God's Empowering Presence*, 394–95.

explicitly. Therefore, in addition to the theology of Deuteronomy and the contemporary Jewish view of the law, the theology of the prophets on human responsibility and ability to keep the law also very likely has an impact on Paul in his arguments in Gal 3:6–14.[64]

Ezekiel repeatedly accuses the people of Israel and Judah of their failure to keep the law ever since the exodus (e.g., Ezek 2:3; 5:6–8; 20:1–32). The same holds for Isaiah and Jeremiah (e.g., Isa 42:24; Jer 11:7–8). Not only did the nation as a whole disobey, but individuals were held accountable for their own actions as well (e.g., Jer 17:10; 18:11–12; Ezek 18:1–32; esp. 18:30).[65] Yahweh's speech in Ezekiel 18 even emphasizes that the individual ought to obey "all [Yahweh's] statutes" (כל־חקותי, "all my statutes" Ezek 18:19, 21).[66]

On the one hand, Deut 30:11–14 portrays that it should not be difficult for the Israelites to obey law.[67] Therefore, Israel's failure to keep the law may be seen as their refusal to keep the law, rather than their inability to keep the law. Indeed, Israel had repeatedly rejected God's law, just like Ezekiel points out again and again (Ezek 5:6; 20:13, 24). However, on the other hand, both Jeremiah and Ezekiel also stress the hardness of the people's hearts ("the heart of stone" in Ezek 11:19; 36:27) and their inability to obey by themselves (cf. Jer 13:23). Their constant refusal had led to the hardening their hearts, which in turn needed divine intervention to change their hearts and enable them to obey the law (cf. Jer 31:33–34; Ezek

---

64. See also Ciampa, "Scriptural Language," 43–44. Ciampa notes that authors may be influenced "not only by passages or books but even by a whole tradition." Ciampa reminds us that in studying Paul's use of the Scripture, we need to take into consideration "the many subtle or intuitive ways in which Scripture may be influencing the argument of the text" (46).

65. As Das points out, "the fate of the nation as a corporate whole cannot be abstracted from the conduct of its individual members. The sin of individual Israelites accrues to Israel as a whole" (*Paul, the Law, and the Covenant*, 152).

66. The requirement to obey "all the statutes" does not imply that the person has the innate ability to perform "all the statutes." Therefore, the person has to depend on God's enablement in order to fulfill the responsibility of keeping "all the statutes." See pp. 100–102, 126–31 above on human inability, human responsibility, and divine empowerment.

67. Deut 30:11–14 ESV: "For this commandment that I command you today is not too hard for you, neither is it far off. It is not in heaven, that you should say, 'Who will ascend to heaven for us and bring it to us, that we may hear it and do it?' Neither is it beyond the sea, that you should say, 'Who will go over the sea for us and bring it to us, that we may hear it and do it?' But the word is very near you. It is in your mouth and in your heart, so that you can do it."

11:20; 36:27).⁶⁸ Hahn notes that Israel's obduracy was already expected in Deut 4:25–31 and 8:1–10, and "Moses alludes to Israel's prideful incapacity (29:4) to keep the law of the Deuteronomic covenant, despite their sworn covenant oath to do so (27:15–26)."⁶⁹ If the people had an innate ability to keep the law adequately, there would be no need for this divine intervention.⁷⁰

Other than the influence of the theology of the prophets, Paul may also have been influenced by the Septuagintal tradition regarding the requirement to obey "all the law." Scholars have noted that the MT of Deut 27:26 does not have the word "all" (כל), but Paul's wording of Deut 27:26 in Gal 3:10 is closer to the LXX in his use of the word "all" (πᾶς).⁷¹ Paul then cites Lev 18:5 ("the one who does them shall live by them") in Gal 3:12 to make his point that the law is not of faith, but requires obedience. Although Paul only cites Lev 18:5b, it is noteworthy that, in the LXX, Lev 18:5a also differs from the MT in its use of the word "all" (πᾶς):

| Lev 18:5a LXX | Lev 18:5a MT |
|---|---|
| καὶ φυλάξεσθε *πάντα* τὰ προστάγματά μου καὶ *πάντα* τὰ κρίματά μου καὶ ποιήσετε αὐτά | ושמרתם את חקתי ואת משפטי |
| And you shall keep *all* my commands and *all* my judgments, and you shall do them | And you shall keep my statutes and my judgments |

---

68. See also Hahn, *Kinship by Covenant*, 82, 249, who notes, "Ezekiel recognized not only the defective aspects of the Deuteronomic covenant, but also its prophecies of eventual self-retirement, divine intervention, and renewal," and "although life through the Deuteronomic covenant was a theoretical possibility (Deut 30:15–19), both God and Moses knew and declared that in fact, death and exile would result (Deut 30:1). Then, there would be a new initiative on God's part: a regathering of the exiles and a supernatural 'circumcision' of their hearts (30:4–6). This new initiative of God involving the cleansing of the heart is what Jeremiah identifies as the new covenant (Jer 31:31)."

69. Hahn, *Kinship by Covenant*, 77.

70. See also McConville, *Grace in the End*, 137, who notes, "These places [Deut 30:6; Hos 14:4; Jer 31:33; 32:39–40] affirm that the answer to Israel's infideltily lies in God himself. He will somehow enable his people ultimately to do what they cannot do in their strength, namely, to obey him out of conviction and devotion of their own hearts."

71. See p. 42n110 above.

In view of Paul's knowledge of the Scriptures, it is very likely that Paul would be familiar with the context of Lev 18:5 LXX. Thus, the addition of the word πᾶς ("all") in the LXX for both Deut 27:26 and Lev 18:5a could very well have influenced Paul in his argument that it is necessary to obey the whole law (cf. Gal 5:3, 14; 6:13).[72]

Therefore, considering the influence of the prophets and the Septuagintal tradition on Paul, his citation of Deut 27:26 in Gal 3:10 might possibly include the premise that "it is impossible to keep the law perfectly" and has reference to individual obedience.[73]

## Justification

Our study has also confirmed my argument earlier that the central issue in Gal 3:1–14 is justification by faith in Christ as the means of becoming the children of Abraham, in which the blessing of Abraham is understood to be justification, while the promise of the Spirit is associated with the evidence and perpetuation of the blessing.[74] In view of the close relationship between justification, the blessing of Abraham, and the promise of the Spirit, three issues arise with regard to Gal 3:1–14 and its broader implications.

First, since the gift of the Spirit marks the beginning of the believer's new life in Christ, and the Spirit continues to sustain and work in the believer's life in Christ, is Paul then primarily arguing about how to obtain life or how to live life in Gal 3:1–14? In his recent monograph, Wakefield argues that Gal 3:1–14 is primarily about "where to live"—in the new age in Christ, or in the old age of the law—rather than how to obtain life—whether or not one is saved, or how.[75] However, Sprinkle has

---

72. See also Das, *Paul, the Law, and the Covenant*, 157n34.

73. The likely influence of the prophets on Paul lends weight to the implied premise of "the impossibility of individuals to keep the law entirely." Contra, e.g., Fuller, "Paul and the Works of the Law," 28–42, who thinks that the curse applies only to legalistic misuse of the law; Wright, *Climax of the Covenant*, 147 and Scott, "For As Many As Are of Works of the Law," 214n89, who think that the issue in Gal 3:10 has to do with Israel's disobedience as a whole and not with the individual.

74. See pp. 183–85, 194–98 above.

75. Wakefield, *Where to Live*, 144–45, 184–88. See also p. 32 above on my interaction with Wakefield regarding the chiastic structure of Gal 3:6–14 and my exegesis of Gal 3:11–12. Wakefield insists that the contrast is not between "a choice of life and death," but rather "a life of blessing" and "a life under curse" (Wakefield, *Where to Live*, 144). Although Wakefield notes that Gal 5:25 and 6:8 may refer to "gaining life," he nevertheless thinks that Gal 3:11–12 follows Gal 2:14, 19–20 in referring to "living life" (*Where to Live*, 170).

## The Blessing of Abraham, the Spirit, and Justification in Galatians

shown convincingly that Hab 2:4 and Lev 18:5 in their original contexts as well as their citation in Gal 3:11–12 are to be read as "ways to escape the covenantal curse and attain the blessing of life."[76] Our study shows that the primary focus of the blessing of Abraham in Gal 3:1–14 is redemptive and reconciliatory. Thus, the result of our study concurs with Sprinkle's conclusion on the soteriological emphasis of Hab 2:4 and Lev 18:5 in Gal 3:11–12. Although the concern of "where to live"—under the new age of Christ or under the law—is an issue in Galatians (e.g., Gal 4:8–10; 5:1), the motif is developed later in the letter and is not the primary focus in Gal 3:1–14. On the other hand, "where to live" may also be understood as subsidiary to the larger question of soteriology, as it is only by living "in Christ," not "under the law," that a person may be assured of ultimate salvation (Gal 5:1–4).

Second, since justification is identified as the blessing of Abraham in Gal 3:1–14, should justification then be understood in soteriological or covenantal categories? Justification has been understood traditionally in terms of a person's right standing before God. The issue in Galatians would then be perceived as Paul's opponents claiming that Torah observance is necessary for the individual's salvation.[77] In more recent years, scholars have begun to view justification in covenantal terms—how a person may be included within the covenant people of God.[78] Therefore, the issue in Galatians is seen as Paul's opponents insisting that Gentile Christians observe the Torah in order to be included in the covenant as God's people.[79]

We have seen that God initiated the Abrahamic promise in Gen 12:2–3 in order to reconcile humankind to himself, and he later formalized the promise by establishing it as a covenant with Abraham in Genesis 15, 17, and 22. The concept of Abraham's descendants as the people of God first arises in Gen 17:7–8, and it is reaffirmed in Exod 6:7 and Lev 26:12 under the Sinai covenant. We have also seen how the eschatological

---

76. Sprinkle, *Law and Life*, 133–42, 140.

77. E.g., Burton, *Galatians*, liv, lvii; Duncan, *Galatians*, xxxii–liv; Mußner, *Galater-brief*, 12–14, 24–26.

78. E.g., Wright insists that "Paul's doctrine of justification is not about 'getting in' . . . but about *the eschatological definition of the true community*." He continues to explain, "Of course, if someone who has not previously believed the gospel comes to do so, that event . . . forms a beginning, an entry point. But the language of 'justification' itself does not, for Paul, describe or denote that entry, but rather the definition of the community that has thereby come about" (Wright, "Justification and Eschatology," 123; emphasis in original).

79. E.g., Sanders, *Paul, the Law*, 111–13.

restoration of the covenantal relationship between Israel and God is not just a fulfillment of the Mosaic covenantal promises, but more so the Abrahamic promise, in which the inclusion of Gentiles as the people of God at the eschatological restoration is the fulfillment of the blessing for the nations. Therefore, the eschatological restoration of both Jewish and Gentile believers as members of God's people presupposes their redemption from sin and the covenantal curses.

Such a background is very likely the reason why Paul's language of justification in Gal 2:15—3:29 is intricately connected to the blessing of Abraham, redemption from the curse of the law, and membership in the people of God, the true offspring of Abraham. Certainly, the issue at stake was whether the Gentile believers need to observe the Torah in order to be included as the people of God. Westerholm has correctly affirmed that "recent scholarship has rightly underlined that it was in the context of *this* dispute, *not* a debate whether one is saved by human effort or by divine grace, that Paul formulated the doctrine of justification 'by faith, apart from the works of the law.'"[80]

Membership in the people of God, which directly involves the Abrahamic and Mosaic covenants, is the result of a person being justified by faith in Christ (Gal 3:7, 24–29). In this respect, justification may be understood in covenantal terms, but there is more. The Abrahamic and Mosaic covenants have their roots in the Abrahamic blessing of Gen 12:2–3, which is God's means of reconciling the alienated humankind to himself. Therefore, covenantal relationship with God is a part of God's soteriological plan. Hence, considering both the soteriological aspect of the blessing of Abraham in Genesis and the prophets, as well as how Paul appropriates the blessing of Abraham in Gal 3:6–14, justification has to be ultimately understood in broader soteriological terms, and not only in covenantal terms.[81] Justification involves God's act of reconciling the world to himself through the redemption of Christ, in whom sinners who believe in him

---

80. Westerholm, *Perspectives Old and New on Paul*, 441 (emphasis in original).

81. Interestingly, in his recent book, N. T. Wright also acknowledges that underlying his understanding of justification in covenant categories is the presupposition of "the problem of human sin, and the divine answer in terms of the rescue provided by the Messiah," because "the [Abrahamic] covenant always had in view *the liberation of the entire human race from the plight of Genesis* 3–11 . . . which means that God's single purpose through the Abrahamic covenant was to rescue human race from the present evil age" (Wright, *Justification*, 133; emphasis in original; see also 131–34). The difference between Wright and me is that he understands justification *as* "membership within God's family," but I see membership as a *result* of justification (see Wright, *Justification*, 116, 133).

may become the righteousness of God and be justified (cf. Rom 3:21–30; 2 Cor 5:18–21; Gal 3:6–14).[82]

Third, since the Spirit is the evidence and perpetuator of the blessing of Abraham, what then is the role of the Spirit in justification, both present and future? There has been lively discussion in recent years about the present and future aspects of justification in terms of their nature and interrelationship.[83] Most of the discussions about the role of the Spirit in justification are concerned with the role of the Spirit in relation to the present status of justification; few discuss the role of the Spirit in future justification.[84]

The nature of present and future justification and their relationship with the Spirit would demand a study in its own right. Nonetheless, the conclusion of our present study has important ramifications for the subject of justification and points towards the need for further research on the role of the Spirit in justification.

First, in the terms of systematic theology, our study confirms the substitutionary death of Christ as the formal cause of justification—Christ died on the cross in order that the blessing of Abraham (i.e., justification) may come to the nations (Gal 3:13–14a). Second, the reception of the Spirit is the evidence of present justification (Gal 3:2, 5, 14). Third, the Spirit perpetuates the blessing of Abraham by enabling obedience and producing righteous works in accord with the status of present justification, so as to guard the believer against the curse of the law. In other words, the work of the Spirit is the means by which present and future justification are ensured (cf. Gal 5:5–6). This third ramification on the role of the Spirit for future justification is by far the most important and significant contribution of this study. Such an understanding is in accord with the concept

---

82. For other critiques of understanding justification in covenantal categories, see, e.g., Westerholm, *Perspectives Old and New on Paul*, 440–45; Thielman, *Theology of the New Testament*, 272–74; Gathercole, "Justification," 219–41; Bird, "Justification," 109–30; Piper, *Future of Justification*.

83. See, e.g., Stuhlmacher, "Paul's View," 72; Cosgrove, "Justification in Paul," 653–55; Wright, *What Saint Paul Really Said*, 129–31; Seifrid, *Christ, Our Righteousness*, 82, 172; idem, "Paul, Luther, and Justification in Gal 2:15–21," 218–19; Rainbow, *Way of Salvation*, 155–74; Gaffin, "By Faith," 83–100. For those who argue against a future element in justification, see, e.g., Fung, *Galatians*, 232–35; VanLandingham, *Judgment and Justification*, 317–18; Baugh, "The New Perspective," 150–56.

84. See, e.g., Williams, "Justification and the Spirit," 91–100; Reginald H. Fuller, "Justification and the Holy Spirit," 499–505; Macchia, "Justification through New Creation," 202–17; Kärkkäinen, "Holy Spirit and Justification," 26–39; Anderson, "Holy Spirit and Justification," 292–305.

of the Spirit as the "guarantee" (ἀρραβών) of all God's promises, which would include future/final justification (2 Cor 1:22; 5:5; cf. Eph 1:14).[85] In 1 Cor 6:11, Paul also describes the Spirit as the means of justification.[86] This study helps us to understand specifically how believers are justified by the Spirit.

Scholars have constantly debated whether there is a transformative element in justification ever since the Reformation period.[87] Our study shows that Christ's substitutionary death on the cross is the formal cause of justification, while the Spirit functions as the evidence of the present status of justification. Therefore, the transforming work of the Spirit does not contribute to the initial and present status of justification.[88] Rather, the empowering work of the *Spirit of Christ* (cf. Rom 8:9–11; Gal 4:6) in the life of the believer in resisting sin *demonstrates* that the curse of the law has *indeed* been overcome by Christ's death on the cross, and in producing works of righteousness *demonstrates* that the believer has *indeed*

---

85. See also Cho, *Spirit and Kingdom*, 94–95, who notes that "Paul sees the Spirit received by faith as a crucial factor in guaranteeing the future righteousness/justification, not the works of Torah . . . By the Spirit, the Galatians are guaranteed their hope of the final realization of justification." However, as Cho's focus is to show that Paul's language of the Spirit is similar to the concept of the kingdom in the Synoptic Gospels, he has not developed further how the Spirit becomes the guarantee of future justification. For this reason, see below for a fuller discussion.

86. 1 Cor 6:11b: "but you have been cleansed, sanctified, and justified [δικαιόω] in the name of the Lord Jesus Christ and by the Spirit [ἐν τῷ πνεύματι] of our God." Thiselton takes the preposition ἐν to indicate instrument or agency (i.e., "by") (Thiselton, *First Corinthians*, 455). Fee contends that "regeneration, sanctification, and justification" are "the work of the Spirit in the believer's life" (Fee, *First Corinthians*, 247).

87. In contemporary discussion, those who argue that justification as solely declarative without transformation include: Moo, *Romans 1-8*, 65–70, 82–86; Schreiner, *Paul*, 203–9; those who include transformation are, e.g., Käsemann, "'The Righteousness of God,'" 168–82; Garlington, *Faith*, 155–61; Stuhlmacher, *Justification*, 62–67; Jüngel, *Justification*, 208–11. Nonetheless, scholars on both sides would agree that justification cannot be separated from sanctification. The difference is that the latter understands sanctification as included in justification, while the former sees the two as distinct but in conjunction with each other. In the former position, some understand justification as preceding sanctification in the order of salvation (e.g., Murray, *Redemption*, 97–105), while others understand justification to be distinct but concurrent with sanctification (e.g., Schreiner, *Paul*, 207–8). More recently, some view justification as a whole, rather than part of the order of salvation (e.g., Seifrid, *Christ, Our Righteousness*, 174–75; Gathercole, "Justification," 229–32).

88. My view on the evidential function of the Spirit for the present status of justification is thus congruous with the view that justification is forensic and declarative, but is not inclusive of transformation. It is also different from those who understand Christ's death and the believer's obedience as joint causes of justification.

been justified by faith in Christ. The Spirit in believers' lives is not just a passive "guarantee" (ἀρραβών; 2 Cor 1:22; 5:5; cf. Eph 1:14) of future justification. Rather, the active work of the Spirit in believers' lives bears the fruit that is necessary for final vindication and thereby functions as the proof necessary for final justification. By doing so, the Spirit is the means by which believers are vindicated at the final judgment that they have indeed been truly justified by faith in Christ.[89] In this manner, the believer's justification by faith in Christ begins with the Spirit as its evidence and consummates eschatologically by the Spirit as its vindication (cf. Gal 3:2-3; 5:5).[90]

My conclusion on the role of the Spirit as the evidence of present justification and the guarantor of future justification by enabling obedience and producing righteous works in accord with the status of present justification is also supported by a recent, but separate, work of Macchia.[91] Our conclusions are similar in that both of us recognize that the work of the Spirit is involved in the very substance of justification in its initiation and final vindication.[92]

However, our approach is different, and my work complement and rectify his in some ways. First, although Macchia mentions in passing that justification is the blessing of Abraham in Gal 3:8, he has yet to explain adequately the reason behind Paul's equation.[93] At the beginning of this chapter, I have shown clearly from the narrative framework and the the-

---

89. I am thankful to Beale, who pointed out to me the vindicating nature of future justification prior the publication of his work (see Beale, *New Testament Biblical Theology*, 497-526). Nonetheless, Beale has not associated the believers' final justification/vindication through good works with the work of the Spirit, with which I have further developed here. The divine work of ensuring final justification does not preclude human responsibility to obey and produce good works. As seen in our dicussion above, this is apparent in both the prophets and in Paul. Believers are commanded to "walk by the Spirit" (Gal 5:16, 25), and there are warnings against disobedience (Gal 5:21b; 6:7-9), because their actions will be judged at the final judgment (e.g., Rom 14:10-12; 1 Cor 3:13-15; 2 Cor 5:10). Therefore, since there is no righteousness apart from God, believers all the more have to depend on the empowerment of the Spirit by faith to produce righteous works (cf. Rom 8:12-13; Phil 2:12-13).

90. The dative πνεύματι ("through/by the Spirit") in both Gal 3:3 and 5:5 may be taken as "the manner in which" or "the instrument/means by which" (Bruce, *Galatians*, 150; Longenecker, *Galatians*, 103, 229; see also Wallace, *Greek Grammar*, 166n77).

91. See Macchia, *Justified in the Spirit*. Our work is independent of each other. Macchia published his work after I have completed mine, but while I was preparing my manuscript for publication.

92. Macchia, *Justified in the Spirit*, 206, 217, 294, 309-11.

93. Ibid., 196.

ology of the Pentateuch why the blessing of Abraham can be conceived as justification.[94] Second, like many other scholars, Macchia equates the blessing of Abraham with the promised Spirit.[95] However, as laid out in this study, I argue that the two are not equated and that the Spirit is the evidence and perpetuator of the blessing of Abraham. This delineation is important as it helps us understand specifically *how* the Spirit is involved in the process of justification and not just its association with justification.

The similar conclusion of our study, which is derived independently of each other, very likely confirms that both of us are on the right track in reclaiming the neglected role of the Holy Spirit in justification. Macchia's work complements mine in his commendable effort in tracing the historical theology of justification and "knitting [it] together" with the Spirit, as well as pointing out the different emphases of the Protestant and the Catholic theology of justification.[96] My work has its niche in tracing comprehensively the theological development of the blessing of Abraham and the promise of the Spirit in the OT that eventually leads to Paul's theology of justification.

## Conclusion

We began this study by questioning the common assumption that the blessing of Abraham is the promise of the Spirit in Gal 3:14 and the claims of a few scholars that the two motifs are unrelated in Gal 3:14. In chapter 2, based on the chiastic structure of Gal 3:6–14, the grammatical relationship between juxtaposed ἵνα clauses in Pauline usage, and the broader context of Galatians, I have shown that the blessing of Abraham is related to, but distinct from, the promise of the Spirit. Nevertheless, we noted at that point that a more precise relationship between the two motifs in Gal 3:14 can only be determined after further investigation of these two motifs in their original contexts and how they have been developed in other parts of the OT, the Second Temple literature, and in Paul.

From chapter 3, we saw that the blessing of Abraham is depicted in the narrative context of Genesis as God's plan to fulfill his original intention to bless humankind through Abraham (Gen 12:3; cf. Gen 1:28), so

---

94. See pp. 183–85 above.

95. Macchia, *Justified in the Spirit*, 265, where he states that "in receiving the blessing of Abraham, which is the indwelling Spirit, Gentiles change from participation in Israel's judgment to participation with Israel in restoration."

96. See esp. Macchia, *Justified in the Spirit*, 3–99, 293–300, 294.

that he may reconcile the alienated humankind to himself and reverse the curse of the fall. Therefore, the climax of the blessing of Abraham lies in the blessing for the nations. As the Abrahamic blessing for the nations remains largely unfulfilled in the Pentateuch, it continues to be developed in Genesis and other OT texts in two important ways. First, in Genesis, the means of blessing is extended from Abraham to his offspring, and this offspring very likely refers to a specific individual from the royal line of Judah who will reign over other nations (Gen 22:18; 26:4; 28:14; cf. Gen 17:6; 27:29; 35:11; 49:10). In chapter 4, we saw that this offspring was eventually identified with the ideal Israelite king who will reign over all the earth in Ps 72:17, and all the nations of the earth shall declare that they are blessed because of his righteous rule.

Second, the blessing for the nations is developed in Gen 17:5–6, where Abraham shall be "the father of many nations," and in Gen 35:11, where Jacob, who is renamed Israel, shall become "a nation and a company of nations." While it is unclear in Genesis how the nations will be associated with the patriarchs, we observed in chapter 4 that this motif is developed mainly in the restoration prophets. At the eschatological restoration of Israel, there will be people from other nations who will "join themselves to Yahweh" by keeping his covenant, and they shall also become the people of Yahweh (Isa 56:3–7; Zech 2:11 [MT 2:15]; cf, Isa 19:18–24). These nations shall turn from their wicked ways (Jer 3:17), worship Yahweh, and walk in his ways (e.g., Isa 2:2–3; 66:18–24; Jer 3:16; 4:2; Zech 8:20–23). Therefore, the promise that Israel shall become "a nation and a company of nations" (Gen 35:11) shall be fully realized at the eschatological restoration of Israel.

In chapter 4, we also examined the promise of the Spirit in the prophets and whether this promise is associated with the blessing of Abraham. As the Mosaic covenant was broken repeatedly in the history of Israel due to their persistent disobedience and failure to keep the covenantal stipulations, Israel forfeited the covenantal blessings of life and prosperity, and the prophets announced that the covenantal curses would be fully executed on Israel as Yahweh's judgment (e.g., Jer 11:1–17; Ezek 20:1–38; cf. Lev 26:1–39; Deut 28:1–68). Nonetheless, due to Yahweh's faithfulness in keeping the Abrahamic and Mosaic covenants (Lev 26:42; Deut 4:31), the prophets also proclaimed that Yahweh would restore his covenantal relationship with Israel after the judgment with a new and everlasting covenant (e.g., Jer 31:31–34; 32:36–44; Ezek 37:26). Yahweh's Spirit will be given as the means by which the covenantal blessings are restored to

## The Spirit's Relationship with the Blessing of Abraham in Galatians

Israel. The Spirit (1) restores life and prosperity to the people (Isa 32:15; 44:3; Ezek 37:14); (2) signifies the restoration of the covenantal relationship with Yahweh (Isa 44:1-5; Ezek 39:29); and (3) empowers the people to obey Yahweh (Ezek 36:27), so that the covenantal blessings may be perpetuated and the covenantal curses subverted permanently. Although the promise of the Spirit is made primarily to Israel as the people of Yahweh, I have argued that, considering the fact that the nations who have "joined themselves to Yahweh" are also called "the people of Yahweh" (Isa 56:3-7; Zech 2:11 [MT 2:15]), the promise of the Spirit may then also be extended and applied to these nations. I have also shown in chapter 4 that, at the eschatological restoration of Israel, not only are the Mosaic covenantal blessings fully restored to Israel, all the elements of the Abrahamic blessing—descendants, land, and blessing for the nations—are also fully realized. Therefore, the Spirit is associated not only with restoration of the Mosaic covenantal blessings, but also with the Abrahamic blessing.

On the other hand, in chapter 5, we observed that, in the Second Temple literature, the texts that mention the Abrahamic blessing for the nations and the promise of the Spirit do not associate the two motifs. The blessing of Abraham is often tied with obedience to the law, and the citation of the Abrahamic blessing for the nations appear to be incidental. Even if it is developed a little further, it is of secondary concern. The nature of the blessing is commonly understood to be material prosperity, although Philo includes spiritual and moral benefits as well. While the function of the Spirit in the Second Temple literature is similar to the OT, there is generally no expectation during that period that Gentile converts would receive the Spirit, except for the case of *Joseth and Aseneth*.

In contrast, we have seen in chapter 6 that, in accord with the Genesis narrative, Paul regards the blessing of Abraham as reconciliatory and redemptive, such that he refers to it as justification (Gal 3:6-14: cf. Gal 2:16). Also, Paul's understanding of Christ as the fulfillment of the Abrahamic blessing for the nations could very well be due to the tradition of identifying the specific offspring as the eschatological ideal Israelite king (Ps 72:17) and associating the rule of a Davidic king at the restoration of Israel (e.g., Isa 11:1-16; Ezek 37:24-27).

While Paul's pneumatology is similar to the OT and the Second Temple literature, he differs from the Second Temple literature in his understanding that the gift of the Spirit is received by faith in Christ Jesus, apart from observing the law and regardless of ethnicity (Gal 3:1-5, 14; 4:4-6). The scriptural basis of Paul's conviction most likely lies in his understanding that (1) obedience to the law is the result of the work of the Spirit and not the prerequisite of receiving the Spirit (cf. Ezek 36: 26–27); and (2) since Gentile converts are also called the people of Yahweh (cf. Isa 56:3–7; Zech 2:11 [MT 2:15]), they may also receive the gift of the Spirit that is promised to Israel as the people of God.

Although Paul does not cite the OT passages concerning the promise of the Spirit in Galatians, his arguments and his pneumatology in the letter are nonetheless deeply influenced by the prophets, as reflected in the following. (1) The Spirit is the source and sustenance of life for the believer (Gal 5:25; 6:8; cf. Ezek 37:14). (2) The reception of the Spirit is the evidence of the believers' present justification (Gal 3:1–5) and their status as the children of God (Gal 4:6). In other words, the Spirit signifies the believers' membership in God's people (cf. Isa 44:1–5; Ezek 39:29). (3) The work of the Spirit in believers' lives produces in them true obedience and righteousness in accord with the law (Gal 5:14, 22–25; cf. Ezek 36:26–27). The Spirit also enables them to overcome sin (Gal 5:16–21), so that the curse of the law, from which Christ has already redeemed the believers (Gal 3:10, 13), may be continually subverted (cf. Gal 5:18). It is through the Spirit by faith that the believers are ensured of their hope of righteousness—their future justification (Gal 5:5).

Therefore, based on our investigation of the blessing of Abraham and the promise of the Spirit in their original contexts and their development in the OT, the Second Temple literature, and in Paul, I conclude that the promise of the Spirit is not the content of the blessing of Abraham in Gal 3:14. Rather, the blessing of Abraham is identified with justification, and the Spirit functions as the evidence of receiving the blessing and the means of perpetuating the blessing.

This understanding of the relationship between the blessing of Abraham and the promise of the Spirit in Gal 3:14 bears significant hermeneutical and theological implications. First and most importantly, as these two motifs are closely related to Paul's argument on justification, the function of the Spirit in relation to the blessing of Abraham contributes to our understanding of the role of the Spirit in present and final justification. While Christ's substitutionary death on the cross is the formal basis of justification (Gal 3:13–14a), the Spirit's active work in the believer's life not only demonstrates the reality of the status of present justification by producing works of righteousness and overcoming the curse of the law by the empowerment to resist sin, it also serves as the guarantee of future justification by bearing the fruit necessary for final vindication.

## The Spirit's Relationship with the Blessing of Abraham in Galatians

Second, this interpretation helps us to see the integral connection between the so-called "doctrinal" (Galatians 1–4) and "ethical" (Galatians 5–6) sections of the letter. The former sets forth the principle of justification by faith with the reception of the Spirit as the evidence of justification. The latter elucidates how believers must rely on the Spirit of Christ by faith, because it is by the Spirit's work in the believer's life that the status of justification is maintained and guaranteed for final vindication.

Finally, in view of the influence of the prophets on Paul, we also need to consider the theology of the prophets on human responsibility and ability to keep the law in addition to the theology of Deuteronomy and the view of the law in early Judaism in order to understand Paul's argument in Gal 3:10–13. As the prophets hold individuals as accountable for their disobedience (e.g., Jer 17:10; 18:11–12; Ezek 18:1–32), emphasize their responsibility to obey "all the statutes of Yahweh" (Ezek 18:19, 21), and stress the human inability to keep the law adequately apart from divine intervention (e.g., Jer 13:23; 31:33–34; Ezek 11:19–20; 36:27), it is thus most likely that Paul's citation of Deut 27:26 in Gal 3:10 includes the implied premise of the impossibility to keep the law perfectly and has reference to individual obedience. By understanding the Spirit as the evidence of receiving the blessing of Abraham and the means by which the blessing is perpetuated, Paul is then asserting that without the divine initiation of reconciliation, redemption, and empowerment, humans are ultimately hopeless and impotent.

# Bibliography

## Primary Sources and Lexicons

Baillet, Maurice. *Qumrân Grotte 4 III (4Q482–4Q520)*. DJD 7. Oxford: Clarendon, 1982.

Bauer, Walter, et al. *A Greek-English Lexicon of the New Testament and Other Early Christian Literature*. 3rd ed. Chicago: University of Chicago Press, 2000.

Beentjes, Pancratius C. *The Book of Ben Sira in Hebrew: A Text Edition of All Extant Hebrew Manuscripts and a Synopsis of All Parallel Hebrew Ben Sira Texts*. VTSup 68. Leiden: Brill, 1997.

Botterweck, G. Johannes, et al., eds. *Theological Dictionary of the Old Testament*. Translated by John T. Willis et al. Rev. ed. 15 vols. Grand Rapids: Eerdmans, 1974–2006.

Brown, F., et al. *A Hebrew and English Lexicon of the Old Testament*. Oxford: Clarendon, 1907.

Burchard, Christoph, et al., eds. *Joseph und Aseneth: Kritisch herausgegeben*. Pseudepigrapha Veteris Testamenti Graece 5. Leiden: Brill, 2003.

Charlesworth, James H., ed. *The Old Testament Pseudepigrapha*. 2 vols. Garden City, NY: Doubleday, 1983.

———, et al., eds. *Rule of the Community and Related Documents*. Vol. 1, *The Dead Sea Scrolls: Hebrew, Aramaic, and Greek Texts with English Translations*, edited by J. H. Charlesworth. Princeton Theological Seminary Dead Sea Scrolls Project. Tübingen: Mohr Siebeck, 1994.

Clines, David J. A., ed. *The Dictionary of Classical Hebrew*. 8 vols. Sheffield: Sheffield Academic Press, 1993–2011.

García Martínez, Florentino, and Eibert J. C. Tigchelaar, eds. *The Dead Sea Scrolls Study Edition*. 2 vols. Leiden: Brill, 1997–1998.

Holm-Nielsen, Svend. *Hodayot: Psalms from Qumran*. Acta Theologica Danica 2. Aarhus: Universitetsforlaget, 1960.

Horgan, Maurya P. "Habakkuk Pesher." In *Pesharim, Other Commentaries, and Related Documents*, vol. 6B of *The Dead Sea Scrolls: Hebrew, Aramaic, and Greek Texts with English Translations*, edited by J. H. Charlesworth and F. M. Cross, 157–85. Tübingen: Mohr Siebeck, 2002.

Josephus, Flavius. *Josephus*. Translated by H. St. J. Thackeray et al. 10 vols. LCL. Cambridge, MA: Harvard University Press, 1926–1965.

Kittel, Gerhard, and Gerhard Friedrich, eds. *Theological Dictionary of the New Testament*. Translated by G. W. Bromiley. 10 vols. Grand Rapids: Eerdmans, 1964–1967.

*Bibliography*

Kohlenberger, John R., and James A. Swanson. *The Hebrew-English Concordance to the Old Testament: With the New International Version.* Grand Rapids: Zondervan, 1998.

Köhler, Ludwig, et al., eds. *The Hebrew and Aramaic Lexicon of the Old Testament.* 1st English ed. 5 vols. Leiden: Brill, 1994–2000.

Mansoor, Menahem, ed. *The Thanksgiving Hymns: Translated and Annotated with an Introduction.* STDJ 3. Leiden: Brill, 1961.

McCarthy, Carmel, ed. *Deuteronomy. BHQ* 5. Stuttgart: Deutsche Bibelgesellschaft, 2007.

Philo, of Alexandria. *Philo: With an English Translation.* Translated by Francis H. Colson and George Herbert Whitaker. 10 vols. and 2 supplementary vols. LCL. Cambridge, MA: Harvard University Press, 1929–1962.

———. *The Works of Philo: Complete and Unabridged.* Translated by Charles D. Yonge. Peabody, MA: Hendrickson, 1993.

Sparks, H. F. D., ed. *The Apocryphal Old Testament.* Oxford: Clarendon, 1984.

Sukenik, Eleazar L., ed. *The Dead Sea Scrolls of the Hebrew University.* Jerusalem: Magnes, 1955.

VanderKam, James C., ed. *The Book of Jubilees: A Critical Text.* CSCO 510. Leuven: Peeters, 1989a.

———, trans. *The Book of Jubilees.* CSCO 511. Leuven: Peeters, 1989b.

VanderKam, James C., and J. T. Milik. "Jubilees." In *Qumrân Cave 4. VIII: Parabiblical Texts, Part I,* 1–185. DJD 13. Oxford: Clarendon, 1994.

VanGemeren, Willem, ed. *New International Dictionary of Old Testament Theology and Exegesis.* 5 vols. Grand Rapids: Zondervan, 1997.

Vermes, Geza. *The Complete Dead Sea Scrolls in English.* Rev ed. London: Penguin, 2004.

Weeks, Stuart, et al., eds. *The Book of Tobit: Texts from the Principal Ancient and Medieval Traditions.* Fontes et subsidia ad Bibliam pertinentes 3. Berlin: de Gruyter, 2004.

Wise, Michael O., et al. *The Dead Sea Scrolls: A New Translation.* Rev. ed. San Francisco: HarperSanFrancisco, 2005.

Ziegler, Joseph. *Sapientia Iesu filii Sirach.* Septuaginta: Vetus Testamentum Graecum 12 Part 2. Göttingen: Vandenhoeck & Ruprecht, 1965.

## Secondary Literature

Achtemeier, Paul J. "Apropos the Faith of/in Christ: A Response to Hays and Dunn." In *Pauline Theology, Vol. 4: Looking Back, Pressing On,* edited by E. Elizabeth Johnson and David M. Hay, 82–92. Atlanta: Scholars, 1997.

Albl, Martin C. *"And Scripture Cannot Be Broken": The Form and Function of the Early Christian Testimonia Collections.* NovTSup 96. Leiden: Brill, 1999.

Alexander, Joseph A. *Commentary on the Prophecies of Isaiah.* Zondervan Commentary Series. Grand Rapids: Zondervan, 1970.

Alexander, T. D. "Abraham Re-Assessed Theologically: The Abraham Narrative and the New Testament Understanding of Justification by Faith." In *He Swore an Oath: Biblical Themes from Genesis 12–50,* edited by R. Hess et al., 7–28. Grand Rapids: Baker, 1994.

———. *From Paradise to the Promised Land: An Introduction to the Pentateuch*. 2nd ed. Grand Rapids: Baker, 2002.

———. "Further Observations on the Term 'Seed' in Genesis." *TynBul* 48 (1997) 363–67.

———. "Genealogies, Seed and the Compositional Unity of Genesis." *TynBul* 44 (1993) 255–70.

———. "Royal Expectations in Genesis to Kings." *TynBul* 49 (1998) 187–212.

Allen, Leslie C. *The Books of Joel, Obadiah, Jonah, and Micah*. NICOT. Grand Rapids: Eerdmans, 1976.

———. *Ezekiel 1–19*. WBC 28. Dallas: Word, 1994.

———. *Ezekiel 20–48*. WBC 29. Dallas: Word, 1990.

———. "Images of Israel: The People of God in the Prophets." In *Studies in Old Testament Theology*, edited by Robert L. Hubbard Jr. et al., 149–68. Dallas: Word, 1992.

———. *Jeremiah: A Commentary*. OTL. Louisville: Westminster John Knox, 2008.

———. "Structure, Tradition and Redaction in Ezekiel's Death Valley Vision." In *Among the Prophets: Language, Image, and Structure in the Prophetic Writings*, edited by Philip R. Davies and David J. A. Clines, 127–42. JSOTSup 144. Sheffield: JSOT, 1993.

Alter, Robert. *The Art of Biblical Poetry*. New York: Basic Books, 1985.

Amadi-Azuogu, Chinedu A. *Paul and the Law in the Arguments of Galatians: A Rhetorical and Exegetical Analysis of Galatians 2,14—6,2*. Bonner Biblische Beiträge 104. Weinheim: Beltz Athenäum, 1996.

Andersen, Francis I. *Habakkuk: A New Translation with Introduction and Commentary*. AB 25. New York: Doubleday, 2001.

Andersen, T. David. "Genealogical Prominence and the Structure of Genesis." In *Biblical Hebrew and Discourse Linguistics*, edited by Robert D. Bergen, 242–66. Dallas: Summer Institute of Linguistics, 1994.

Anderson, A. A. *The Book of Psalms*. 2 vols. NCBC. Greenwood, SC: Attic, 1972.

———. "Use of 'Ruah' in 1QS, 1QH and 1QM." *JSS* 7 (1962) 293–303.

Anderson, Jeffrey K. "The Holy Spirit and Justification: A Pneumatological and Trinitarian Approach to Forensic Justification." *EvRT* 32 (2008) 292–305.

Aquinas, Thomas. *Commentary on Saint Paul's Epistle to the Galatians*. Translated by F. R. Larcher. Aquinas Scripture Series 1. Albany, NY: Magi, 1966.

Arnold, Bill T. "Old Testament Eschatology and the Rise of Apocalypticism." In *The Oxford Handbook of Eschatology*, edited by Jerry L. Walls, 23–39. Oxford: Oxford University Press, 2008.

Attridge, Harold W. *The Interpretation of Biblical History in the Antiquitates Judaicae of Flavius Josephus*. Harvard Dissertations in Religion 7. Missoula, MT: Scholars, 1976.

Avemarie, Fredrich. "Paul and the Claim of the Law according to the Scripture: Leviticus 18:5 in Galatians 3:12 and Romans 10:5." In *The Beginnings of Christianity: A Collection of Articles*, edited by Jack Pastor and Menachem Mor, 125–48. Jerusalem: Yad Ben-Zvi, 2005.

Bachmann, Michael. "Keil oder Mikroskop? Zur jüngeren Diskussion um den Ausdruck '"Werke" des Gesetzes.'" In *Lutherische und neue Paulusperspektive: Beiträge zu einem Schlüsselproblem der gegenwärtigen exegetischen Diskussion*, edited by

## Bibliography

Michael Bachmann and Johannes Woyke, 69-134. WUNT 182. Tübingen: Mohr Siebeck, 2005.

———. *Sünder oder Übertreter: Studien zur Argumentation in Gal 2,15ff.* WUNT 59. Tübingen: Mohr Siebeck, 1992.

———. "Zur Argumentation von Galater 3.10-12." *NTS* 53 (2007) 524-44.

Balestier-Stengel, Guy. "Un aperçu sur les Jubilés: Le personnage d'Abram." *FoiVie* 89 (1990) 61-71.

Baltzer, Klaus. *Deutero-Isaiah: A Commentary on Isaiah 40-55.* Hermeneia. Minneapolis: Fortress, 2001.

Barclay, John M. G. *Obeying the Truth: A Study of Paul's Ethics in Galatians.* Studies of the New Testament and Its World. Edinburgh: T. & T. Clark, 1988.

Barrett, C. K. "Allegory of Abraham, Sarah, and Hagar in the Argument of Galatians." In *Rechtfertigung*, edited by Johannes Friedrich et al., 1-16. Tübingen: Mohr Siebeck, 1976.

———. *A Commentary on the Epistle to the Romans.* BNTC. London: Adam & Charles Black, 1957.

———. *A Critical and Exegetical Commentary on the Acts of the Apostles.* 2 vols. ICC 34. Edinburgh: T. & T. Clark, 1994-1998.

———. *The First Epistle to the Corinthians.* BNTC. Peabody, MA: Hendrickson, 1993.

———. *The Second Epistle to the Corinthians.* BNTC. Peabody, MA: Hendrickson, 1993.

Barrett, Michael P. V. "Pentecost and Other Blessings (Joel 2:21-28)." *BV* 29 (1995) 23-34.

Bauckham, Richard. *The Climax of Prophecy: Studies on the Book of Revelation.* Edinburgh: T. & T. Clark, 1993.

Baugh, S. M. "The New Perspective, Mediation, and Justification." In *Covenant, Justification, and Pastoral Ministry*, edited by R. Scott Clark, 137-63. Phillipsburg, NJ: P&R, 2007.

Baumbach, Günther. "Abraham unser Vater: Der Prozess der Vereinnahmung Abrahams durch das frühe Christentum." *Theologische Versuche* 16 (1986) 37-56.

Baumgarten, Joseph M. "Proselytes." In *EDSS* 2:700-1.

Beale, G. K. *A New Testament Biblical Theology: The Unfolding of the Old Testament in the New.* Grand Rapids: Baker Academic, 2011.

———. *The Temple and the Church's Mission: A Biblical Theology of the Temple.* NSBT 18. Downers Grove, IL: InterVarsity, 2004.

Beecher, Willis J. *The Prophets and the Promise.* Grand Rapids: Baker, 1963.

Bekken, P. J. "Abraham og Ånden. Paulus' anvendelse av Genesis 15:6 i Galaterbrevet 3:6 belyst ut fra jodisk materiale (Abraham and the Spirit: Paul's Application of Genesis 15:6 in Galatians 3:6 in Light of Jewish Material)." *TTKi* 71 (2000) 265-76.

Bellis, Alice Ogden. "Habakkuk 2:4b: Intertextuality and Hermeneutics." In *Jews, Christians, and the Theology of the Hebrew Scriptures*, edited by Alice O. Bellis and Joel S. Kaminsky, 369-85. SBLSymS 8. Atlanta: SBL, 2000.

Bennema, Cornelis. *The Power of Saving Wisdom: An Investigation of Spirit and Wisdom in Relation to the Soteriology of the Fourth Gospel.* WUNT/II 148. Tübingen: Mohr Siebeck, 2002.

Benton, Richard. "The Niphal and Hitpael of ברך in the Patriarchal Narratives." *KUSATU* 8/9 (2008) 1-17.

Berkley, Timothy W. *From a Broken Covenant to Circumcision of the Heart: Pauline Intertextual Exegesis in Romans 2:17-29*. SBLDS 175. Atlanta: SBL, 2000.

Berthelot, Katell. "La Notion de בן dans les Textes de Qumrân." *RevQ* 19 (1999) 171-216.

Berthoud, Pierre. "Le thème de Genèse 1 à 11." *RRef* 31 (1980) 250-64.

Best, Ernest. *A Critical and Exegetical Commentary on Ephesians*. ICC. Edinburgh: T. & T. Clark, 1998.

Bethune, Larry L. "Abraham, Father of Faith: The Interpretation of Genesis 15:6 from Genesis to Paul (Galatians, Romans)." PhD diss., Princeton Theological Seminary, 1987.

Betz, Hans D. *Galatians: A Commentary on Paul's Letter to the Churches in Galatia*. Hermeneia. Minneapolis: Fortress, 1979.

Biddle, Mark E. *Deuteronomy*. Smyth & Helwys Bible Commentary. Macon, GA: Smyth & Helwys, 2003.

Bird, Michael F. "Justification as Forensic Declaration and Covenant Membership: A Via Media between Reformed and Revisionist Readings of Paul." *TynBul* 57 (2006) 109-30.

Bird, Michael F., and Preston Sprinkle, eds. *The Faith of Jesus Christ: Exegetical, Biblical, and Theological Studies*. Peabody, MA: Hendrickson, 2009.

Blenkinsopp, Joseph. *Ezekiel*. Interpretation. Louisville: John Knox, 1990.

———. *Isaiah 1-39: A New Translation with Introduction and Commentary*. AB 19. New York: Doubleday, 2000.

———. *Isaiah 40-55: A New Translation with Introduction and Commentary*. AB 19A. New York: Doubleday, 2000.

———. *Isaiah 56-66: A New Translation with Introduction and Commentary*. AB 19B. New York: Doubleday, 2003.

Bligh, John. *Galatians: A Discussion of St. Paul's Epistle*. London: St. Paul, 1969.

———. *Galatians in Greek: A Structural Analysis of St. Paul's Epistle to the Galatians*. Detroit: University of Detroit Press, 1966.

Block, Daniel I. *The Book of Ezekiel: Chapters 1-24*. NICOT. Grand Rapids: Eerdmans, 1997.

———. *The Book of Ezekiel: Chapters 25-48*. NICOT. Grand Rapids: Eerdmans, 1997.

———. "Empowered by the Spirit of God: The Holy Spirit in the Historiographic Writings of the Old Testament." *SBJT* 1 (1997) 42-61.

———. "Gog and the Pouring out of the Spirit: Reflections on Ezekiel 39:21-29." *VT* 37 (1987) 257-70.

———. "The Prophet of the Spirit: The Use of *RWḤ* in the Book of Ezekiel." *JETS* 32 (1989) 27-49.

Bock, Darrell L. *Acts*. BECNT. Grand Rapids: Baker, 2007.

Bockmuehl, Marcus. "1QS and Salvation at Qumran." In *Justification and Variegated Nomism, Vol. 1: The Complexities of Second Temple Judaism*, edited by D. A. Carson et al., 381-414. Grand Rapids: Baker Academic, 2001.

Boers, Hendrikus. *The Justification of the Gentiles: Paul's Letters to the Galatians and Romans*. Peabody, MA: Hendrickson, 1994.

Bohak, Gideon. *Joseph and Aseneth and the Jewish Temple in Heliopolis*. SBL Early Judaism and Its Literature 10. Atlanta: Scholars, 1996.

Böhm, Martina. *Rezeption und Funktion der Vätererzählungen bei Philo von Alexandria: Zum Zusammenhang von Kontext, Hermeneutik und Exegese im frühen Judentum*. BZNW 128. Berlin: de Gruyter, 2005.

# Bibliography

Borgen, Peder. *Philo of Alexandria: An Exegete for His Time*. NovTSup 86. Leiden: Brill, 1997.

Braswell, Joseph P. "'The Blessing of Abraham' Versus 'the Curse of the Law': Another Look at Gal 3:10–13." *WTJ* 53 (1991) 73–91.

Brensinger, Terry L. "היה." In *NIDOTTE* 2:108–13.

Breuer, Joseph. *The Book of Jeremiah: Translation and Commentary*. Translated by Gertrude Hirschler. New York: Feldheim, 1988.

Briggs, Charles A., and Emilie G. Briggs. *A Critical and Exegetical Commentary on the Book of Psalms II*. ICC 15. Edinburgh: T. & T. Clark, 1907.

Bright, John. *Jeremiah: A New Translation with Introduction and Commentary*. AB 21. Garden City, NY: Doubleday, 1965.

Brondos, David. "The Cross and the Curse: Galatians 3.13 and Paul's Doctrine of Redemption." *JSNT* 81 (2001) 3–32.

Brown, Teresa R. "God and Men in Israel's History: God and Idol Worship in Praise of the Fathers (Sir 44–50)." In *Ben Sira's God*, edited by Renate Egger-Wenzel, 214–20. BZAW 321. Berlin: de Gruyter, 2002.

Bruce, F. F. *The Epistle to the Galatians: A Commentary on the Greek Text*. NIGTC. Grand Rapids: Eerdmans, 1982.

———. "The Spirit in the Letter to the Galatians." In *Essays on Apostolic Themes*, edited by Paul Elbert, 36–48. Peabody, MA: Hendrickson, 1985.

Brueggemann, Walter. *Genesis*. Interpretation. Atlanta: John Knox, 1982.

———. *Isaiah 40–66*. Westminster Bible Companion. Louisville: Westminster John Knox, 1998.

———. *Reverberations of Faith: A Theological Handbook of Old Testament Themes*. Louisville: Westminster John Knox, 2002.

———. *Theology of the Old Testament: Testimony, Dispute, Advocacy*. Minneapolis: Fortress, 1997.

Bryant, Robert A. *The Risen Crucified Christ in Galatians*. SBLDS 185. Atlanta: SBL, 2001.

Buber, Martin. "*Leitwort* Style in Pentateuch Narrative." In *Scripture and Translation*, edited by Martin Buber and Franz Rosenzweig, translated by L. Rosenwald and E. Fox, 114–28. Bloomington: Indiana University Press, 1994.

Burchard, Christoph. "Joseph and Aseneth." In *Outside the Old Testament*, edited by Marinus de Jonge, 92–110. CCWJCW 4. Cambridge: Cambridge University Press, 1985.

———. "Joseph and Aseneth: A New Translation and Introduction." In vol. 2 of *The Old Testament Pseudepigrapha*, edited by James H. Charlesworth, 177–247. Garden City, NY: Doubleday, 1985.

———. "Joseph und Aseneth: Eine jüdisch-hellenistische Erzählung von Liebe, Bekehrung und vereitelter Entführung." *TZ* 61 (2005) 65–77.

———. "Küssen in Joseph und Aseneth." *JSJ* 36 (2005) 316–23.

———. "The Text of Joseph and Aseneth Reconsidered." *JSP* 14 (2005) 83–96.

———. "Zum Text von Joseph und Aseneth." *JSJ* 1 (1970) 3–34.

Burke, Trevor J. *Adopted into God's Family: Exploring a Pauline Metaphor*. NSBT 22. Downers Grove, IL: InterVarsity, 2006.

Burkes, S. "Wisdom and Law: Choosing Life in Ben Sira and Baruch." *JSJ* 30 (1999) 253–76.

Burton, Ernest DeWitt. *A Critical and Exegetical Commentary on the Epistle to the Galatians*. ICC 33. Edinburgh: T. & T. Clark, 1921.

Byrne, Brendan. *Sons of God, Seed of Abraham: A Study of the Idea of the Sonship of God of All Christians in Paul against the Jewish Background*. AnBib 83. Rome: Biblical Institute, 1979.

Calvert-Koysis, Nancy. *Paul, Monotheism and the People of God: The Significance of Abraham Traditions for Early Judaism and Christianity*. JSNTSup 273. New York: T. & T. Clark, 2004.

Calvin, John. *The Epistles of Paul the Apostle to the Galatians, Ephesians, Philippians, and Colossians*. Translated by T. H. L. Parker. Edited by David W. Torrance and Thomas F. Torrance. Calvin's New Testament Commentaries 11. Grand Rapids: Eerdmans, 1965.

Caneday, Ardel. "'Redeemed from the Curse of the Law': The Use of Deut 21:22–23 in Gal 3:13." *TJ* 10 (1989) 185–209.

Carmignac, Jean, and P. Guilbert. *Les textes de Qumran: Traduits et annotés*. 2 vols. Autour de la Bible. Paris: Letouzey et Ané, 1961–1963.

Carroll, Robert P. *Jeremiah: A Commentary*. OTL. Philadelphia: Westminster, 1986.

Carroll Rodas, M. Daniel. "Blessing the Nations: Toward a Biblical Theology of Mission from Genesis." *BBR* 10 (2000) 17–34.

Carson, D. A., et al., eds. *Justification and Variegated Nomism, Vol. 1: The Complexities of Second Temple Judaism*. 2 vols. Grand Rapids: Baker Academic, 2001.

Cassuto, U. *A Commentary on the Book of Genesis: Part II—from Noah to Abraham Genesis VI 9–XI 32*. Translated by I. Abrahams. Jerusalem: Magnes, 1964.

Charles, R. H. "Jubilees." In *The Apocryphal Old Testament*, edited by H. F. D. Sparks, 1–140. Oxford: Clarendon, 1984.

Charlesworth, J. H. "Ladder of Jacob." In *ABD* 3:609.

Chazon, Ester G. "4QDibHam: Liturgy or Literature?" *RevQ* 15 (1992) 447–55.

———. "Is *Divrei Ha-Me'orot* a Sectarian Prayer?" In *The Dead Sea Scrolls: Forty Years of Research*, edited by Devorah Dimant and Uriel Rappaport, 3–17. STDJ 10. Leiden: Brill, 1992.

———. "Words of the Luminaries." In *EDSS* 2:989–90.

Chesnutt, Randall D. *From Death to Life: Conversion in Joseph and Aseneth*. JSPSup 16. Sheffield: Sheffield Academic, 1995.

———. "Perceptions of Oil in Early Judaism and the Meal Formula in Joseph and Aseneth." *JSP* 14 (2005) 113–32.

Childs, Brevard S. *The Church's Guide for Reading Paul: The Canonical Shaping of the Pauline Corpus*. Grand Rapids: Eerdmans, 2008.

———. *Introduction to the Old Testament as Scripture*. Philadelphia: Fortress, 1979.

———. *Isaiah*. OTL. Louisville: Westminster John Knox, 2001.

Cho, Youngmo. *Spirit and Kingdom in the Writings of Luke and Paul: An Attempt to Reconcile These Concepts*. Paternoster Biblical Monographs. Waynesboro, GA: Paternoster, 2005.

Christensen, Duane L. *Deuteronomy 21:10—34:12*. WBC 6B. Nashville: Thomas Nelson, 2002.

Christiansen, Ellen J. *The Covenant in Judaism and Paul: A Study of Ritual Boundaries as Identity Markers*. AGJU 27. Leiden: Brill, 1995.

Ciampa, Roy E. *The Presence and Function of Scripture in Galatians 1 and 2*. WUNT/II 102. Tübingen: Mohr Siebeck, 1998.

## Bibliography

———. "Scriptural Language and Ideas." In *As It Is Written: Studying Paul's Use of Scripture*, edited by Stanley E. Porter and Christopher D. Stanley, 41–57. SBLSymS 50. Atlanta: SBL, 2008.
Clines, David J. A. *The Theme of the Pentateuch*. 2nd ed. JSOTSup 10. Sheffield: JSOT, 1997.
Coggins, Richard J. *Sirach*. GAP. Sheffield: Sheffield Academic, 1998.
Cohen, Jeremy. *Be Fertile and Increase, Fill the Earth and Master It: The Ancient and Medieval Career of a Biblical Text*. Ithaca, NY: Cornell University Press, 1989.
Collins, C. John. "Galatians 3:16: What Kind of Exegete Was Paul?" *TynBul* 54 (2003) 75–86.
Collins, Jack. "A Syntactical Note (Genesis 3:15): Is the Woman's Seed Singular or Plural?" *TynBul* 48 (1997) 139–48.
Collins, John J. "Joseph and Aseneth: Jewish or Christian?" *JSP* 14 (2005) 97–112.
———. "The Literature in the Second Temple Period." In *The Oxford Handbook of Jewish Studies*, edited by Martin Goodman, 53–78. Oxford: Oxford University Press, 2002.
Conzelmann, Hans. *1 Corinthians: A Commentary on the First Epistle to the Corinthians*. Hermeneia. Philadelphia: Fortress, 1975.
Cook, D. "Joseph and Aseneth." In *The Apocryphal Old Testament*, edited by H. F. D. Sparks, 465–503. Oxford: Clarendon, 1984.
Cooke, G. A. *A Critical and Exegetical Commentary on the Book of Ezekiel*. ICC. Edinburgh: T. & T. Clark, 1937.
Cooper, Lamar E. *Ezekiel*. NAC 17. Nashville: Broadman & Holman, 1994.
Cosgrove, Charles H. *The Cross and the Spirit: A Study in the Argument and Theology of Galatians*. Macon, GA: Mercer University Press, 1988.
———. "Justification in Paul: A Linguistic and Theological Reflection." *JBL* 106 (1987) 653–70.
Craigie, Peter C. *The Book of Deuteronomy*. NICOT. Grand Rapids: Eerdmans, 1976.
Craigie, Peter C., Page H. Kelley, and Joel F. Drinkard. *Jeremiah 1–25*. WBC 26. Dallas: Word, 1991.
Cranfield, C. E. B. *A Critical and Exegetical Commentary on the Epistle to the Romans*. 6th ed. 2 vols. ICC 32. Edinburgh: T. & T. Clark, 1975–1979.
Cranford, Michael. "The Possibility of Perfect Obedience: Paul and an Implied Premise in Galatians 3:10 and 5:3." *NovT* 36 (1994) 242–58.
Crenshaw, James L. "The Book of Sirach." In *Introduction to Wisdom Literature; Proverbs–Sirach*, edited by Leander E. Keck, 601–867. NIB 5. Nashville: Abingdon, 1997.
———. *Joel: A New Translation with Introduction and Commentary*. AB 24C. New York: Doubleday, 1995.
Croatto, J. Severino. "The 'Nations' in the Salvific Oracles of Isaiah." *VT* 55 (2005) 143–61.
Dahood, Mitchell. *Psalms II, 51–100: A New Translation with Introduction and Commentary*. AB 17. Garden City, NY: Doubleday, 1968.
Dalton, William J. "The Meaning of 'We' in Galatians." *ABR* 38 (1990) 33–44.
Das, A. Andrew. *Paul and the Jews*. Library of Pauline Studies. Peabody, MA: Hendrickson, 2003.
———. *Paul, the Law, and the Covenant*. Peabody, MA: Hendrickson, 2001.
Davenport, Gene L. *The Eschatology of the Book of Jubilees*. StPB 20. Leiden: Brill, 1971.

Davies, Philip R. "'Old' and 'New' Israel in the Bible and the Qumran Scrolls: Identity and Difference." In *Defining Identities: We, You, and the Other in the Dead Sea Scrolls*, edited by Florentino García Martínez and Mladen Popović, 33–42. STDJ 70. Leiden: Brill, 2008.

Davila, James R. *Liturgical Works*. Eerdmans Commentaries on the Dead Sea Scrolls 6. Grand Rapids: Eerdmans, 2000.

Davis, Basil S. "The Meaning of προεγράφη in the Context of Galatians 3.1." *NTS* 45 (1999) 194–212.

Davis, Ellen F. *Swallowing the Scroll: Textuality and the Dynamics of Discourse in Ezekiel's Prophecy*. JSOTSup 78. Sheffield: Almond, 1989.

Deasley, Alex R. G. "The Holy Spirit in the Dead Sea Scrolls." *Wesleyan Theological Journal* 21 (1986) 45–73.

Delling, Gerhard. "Einwirkungen der Sprache der Septuaginta in 'Joseph und Aseneth.'" *JSJ* 9 (1978) 29–56.

Dempster, Stephen G. *Dominion and Dynasty: A Biblical Theology of the Hebrew Bible*. NSBT 15. Downers Grove, IL: InterVarsity, 2003.

Di Lella, Alexander A. "Ben Sira's Praise of the Ancestors of Old (Sir 44–49): The History of Israel as Parenetic Apologetics." In *History and Identity: How Israel's Later Authors Viewed Its History*, edited by Núria Calduch-Benages and Jan Liesen, 151–70. Berlin: de Gruyter, 2006.

Dillard, Raymond B. "Joel." In *Hosea, Joel, and Amos*, Vol. 1 of *The Minor Prophets: An Exegetical and Expository Commentary*, edited by Thomas E. McComiskey, 239–313. 3 vols. Grand Rapids: Baker, 1992.

Dodd, C. H. *According to the Scriptures: The Sub-Structure of New Testament Theology*. London: Nisbet, 1952.

Dohmen, Christoph. "Der Sinaibund als Neuer Bund nach Ex 19–34." In *Der neue Bund im alten*, edited by Erich Zenger, 51–84. Freiburg: Herder, 1993.

Donaldson, Terence L. "The 'Curse of the Law' and the Inclusion of the Gentiles: Galatians 3:13–14." *NTS* 32 (1986) 94–112.

———. *Paul and the Gentiles: Remapping the Apostle's Convictional World*. Minneapolis: Fortress, 1997.

Driver, S. R. *A Critical and Exegetical Commentary on Deuteronomy*. 3d ed. ICC 5. Edinburgh: T. & T. Clark, 1986.

Dumbrell, William J. "Abraham and the Abrahamic Covenant in Galatians 3:1–14." In *Gospel to the Nations*, edited by Peter Bolt and Mark Thompson, 19–31. Downers Grove, IL: InterVarsity, 2000.

———. *Covenant and Creation: A Theology of the Old Testament Covenants*. Nashville: Thomas Nelson, 1984.

Duncan, George S. *The Epistle of Paul to the Galatians*. Moffatt New Testament Commentary. London: Hodder & Stoughton, 1934.

Dunn, James D. G. "ΕΚ ΠΙΣΤΕΩΣ: A Key to the Meaning of ΠΙΣΤΙΣ ΧΡΙΣΤΟΥ." In *The Word Leaps the Gap: Essays on Scripture and Theology in Honor of Richard B. Hays*, edited by J. R. Wagner et al., 351–66. Grand Rapids: Eerdmans, 2008.

———. *The Epistle to the Galatians*. BNTC. Peabody, Mass.: Hendrickson, 1993.

———. *The New Perspective on Paul*. WUNT 185. Tübingen: Mohr Siebeck, 2005.

———. "Once More, ΠΙΣΤΙΣ ΧΡΙΣΤΟΥ." In *Pauline Theology, Vol. 4: Looking Back, Pressing On*, edited by E. Elizabeth Johnson and David M. Hay, 61–81. Atlanta: Scholars, 1997.

———. *Romans 1–8*. WBC 38a. Dallas: Word Books, 1988.

# Bibliography

Eastman, Susan G. "The Evil Eye and the Curse of the Law: Galatians 3.1 Revisited." *JSNT* 83 (2001) 69-87.

———. *Recovering Paul's Mother Tongue: Language and Theology in Galatians*. Grand Rapids: Eerdmans, 2007.

Ebeling, Gerhard. *The Truth of the Gospel*. Translated by David Green. Philadelphia: Fortress, 1983.

Eckstein, Hans-Joachim. *Verheißung und Gesetz: Eine exegetische Untersuchung zu Galater 2,15-4,7*. WUNT 86. Tübingen: Mohr Siebeck, 1996.

Edwards, Mark J., ed. *Galatians, Ephesians, Philippians*. Rev. ed. Ancient Christian Commentary on Scripture New Testament 8. Downers Grove, IL: InterVarsity, 2005.

Ego, Beate. "The Book of Tobit and the Diaspora." In *The Book of Tobit: Text, Tradition, Theology*, edited by Géza G. Xeravits and József Zsengellér, 41-54. JSJSup 98. Leiden: Brill, 2005.

Eichrodt, Walther. *Ezekiel: A Commentary*. Translated by Cosslett Quin. OTL. Philadelphia: Westminster, 1970.

Elliott, John H. "Paul, Galatians, and the Evil Eye." *CurTM* 17 (1990) 262-73.

Ellis, E. Earle. *Paul's Use of the Old Testament*. Edinburgh: Oliver & Boyd, 1957.

Endres, John C. *Biblical Interpretation in the Book of Jubilees*. Catholic Biblical Quarterly Monograph Series 18. Washington DC: Catholic Biblical Association, 1987.

Evans, Craig A. "Scripture-Based Stories in the Pseudepigrapha." In *Justification and Variegated Nomism, Vol. 1: The Complexities of Second Temple Judaism*, edited by D. A. Carson et al., 57-72. 2 vols. Grand Rapids: Baker Academic, 2001.

Evans, John F. "An Inner-Biblical Interpretation and Intertextual Reading of Ezekiel's Recognition Formulae with the Book of Exodus." ThD diss., University of Stellenbosch, 2006.

Falk, Daniel K. *Daily, Sabbath, and Festival Prayers in the Dead Sea Scrolls*. STDJ 27. Leiden: Brill, 1998.

———. "Psalms and Prayers." In *Justification and Variegated Nomism, Vol. 1: The Complexities of Second Temple Judaism*, edited by D. A. Carson et al., 7-56. 2 vols. Grand Rapids: Baker Academic, 2001.

Fee, Gordon D. *The First Epistle to the Corinthians*. NICNT. Grand Rapids: Eerdmans, 1987.

———. *God's Empowering Presence: The Holy Spirit in the Letters of Paul*. Peabody, MA: Hendrickson, 1994.

Feldman, Louis H. *Josephus's Interpretation of the Bible*. Hellenistic Culture and Society 27. Berkeley: University of California Press, 1998.

Finley, Thomas J. *Joel, Amos, Obadiah*. WEC. Chicago: Moody, 1990.

Fischer, Georg. *Jeremia 1-25: Übersetzt und ausgelegt*. HTKAT. Freiburg: Herder, 2005.

———. *Jeremia 26-52: Übersetzt und ausgelegt*. HTKAT. Freiburg: Herder, 2005.

Fitzmyer, Joseph A. *The Acts of the Apostles: A New Translation with Introduction and Commentary*. AB 31. New York: Doubleday, 1998.

———. "Habakkuk 2:3-4 and the New Testament." In *To Advance the Gospel: New Testament Studies*, edited by Joseph A. Fitzmyer, 236-46. New York: Crossroad, 1981.

———. *Tobit*. Commentaries on Early Jewish Literature. Berlin: de Gruyter, 2003.

Flury-Schölch, André. *Abrahams Segen und die Völker: Synchrone und diachrone Untersuchungen zu Gen 12,1-3 unter besonderer Berücksichtigung der inter-

*textuellen Beziehungen zu Gen 18;22;26;28; Sir 44: Jer 4 und Ps 72*. Forschung zur Bibel 115. Würzburg: Echter, 2007.
Frank, Yitzḥak. *Grammar for Gemara and Targum Onkelos: An Introduction to Aramaic.* Jerusalem: Ariel, United Israel Institutes, 2003.
Frettlöh, Magdalene L. *Theologie des Segens: Biblische und dogmatische Wahrnehmungen.* Gütersloh: Chr. Kaiser/Gütersloher, 1998.
Fuller, Daniel P. "Paul and the Works of the Law." *WTJ* 38 (1975) 28–42.
Fuller, Reginald H. "Justification and the Holy Spirit." *AThR* 83 (2001) 499–505.
Fung, Ronald Y. K. *The Epistle to the Galatians.* NICNT. Grand Rapids: Eerdmans, 1988.
Gaffin, Richard B. *"By Faith, Not by Sight": Paul and the Order of Salvation.* Waynesboro, GA: Paternoster, 2006.
Garland, David E. *1 Corinthians.* BECNT. Grand Rapids: Baker Academic, 2003.
Garlington, Don B. *An Exposition of Galatians: A Reading from the New Perspective.* 3rd ed. Eugene, OR: Wipf & Stock, 2007.
———. *Faith, Obedience, and Perseverance: Aspects of Paul's Letter to the Romans.* WUNT 79. Tübingen: Mohr Siebeck, 1994.
———. "Paul's 'Partisan ἐκ' and the Question of Justification in Galatians." *JBL* 127 (2008) 567–589.
———. "Role Reversal and Paul's Use of Scripture in Galatians 3.10–13." *JSNT* 65 (1997) 85–121.
Garscha, Jörg. *Studien zum Ezechielbuch: Eine redaktionskritische Untersuchung von 1–39.* Europäische Hochschulschriften 23. Bern: Lang, 1974.
Gaston, Lloyd. "Abraham and the Righteousness of God." *HBT* 2 (1980) 39–68.
Gathercole, Simon J. "The Doctrine of Justification in Paul and Beyond: Some Proposals." In *Justification in Perspective*, edited by Bruce L. McCormack, 219–41. Grand Rapids: Baker Academic, 2006.
———."Torah, Life, and Salvation: Leviticus 18:5 in Early Judaism and the New Testament." In *From Prophecy to Testament: The Function of the Old Testament in the New*, edited by Craig A. Evans, 126–45. Peabody, MA: Hendrickson, 2004.
Gignac, Alain. "Citation de Lévitique 18,5 en Romains 10,5 et Galates 3,12: Deux lectures différentes des rapports Christ-Torah?" *EgT* 25 (1994) 367–403.
Goldingay, John. *The Message of Isaiah 40–55: A Literary-Theological Commentary.* London: T. & T. Clark, 2005.
———. *Psalms.* 2 vols. Baker Commentary on the Old Testament Wisdom and Psalms. Grand Rapids: Baker, 2006–2007.
Goldingay, John, and David Payne. *A Critical and Exegetical Commentary on Isaiah 40–55.* 2 vols. ICC. London: T. & T. Clark, 2006.
Good, Edwin M. *Irony in the Old Testament.* Philadelphia: Westminster, 1965.
Gordis, Robert. "The Heptad as an Element of Biblical and Rabbinic Style." *JBL* 62 (1943) 17–26.
Goshen-Gottstein, Alon. "Ben Sira's Praise of the Fathers: A Canon-Conscious Reading." In *Ben Sira's God*, edited by Renate Egger-Wenzel, 235–67. BZAW 321. Berlin: de Gruyter, 2002.
Greenberg, Moshe. *Ezekiel 1–20: A New Translation with Introduction and Commentary.* AB 22. Garden City, NY: Doubleday, 1983.
———. *Ezekiel 21–37: A New Translation with Introduction and Commentary.* AB 22A. New York: Doubleday, 1997.

———. "Salvation of the Impenitent *Ad Majorem Dei Gloriam*: Ezek 36:16–32." In *Transformations of the Inner Self in Ancient Religions*, edited by Jan Assmann and Guy G. Stroumsa, 263–71. Studies in the History of Religions 83. Leiden: Brill, 1999.

———. "Three Conceptions of the Torah in Hebrew Scriptures." In *Die Hebräische Bibel und ihre zweifache Nachgeschichte: Festschrift für Rolf Rendtorff zum 65 Geburtstag*, edited by E. Blum et al., 365–78. Neukirchen-Vluyn: Neukirchener, 1990.

Groß, Heinrich. "Der Mensch als neues Geschöpf (Jer 31; Ez 36; Ps 51)." In *Weg zum Menschen: Zur philosophischen und theologischen Anthropologie*, edited by Rudolf Mosis and Lothar Ruppert, 98–109. Freiburg: Herder, 1989.

Groß, Walter. "Israel und die Völker: Die Krise des Yhwh-Volk-Konzepts im Jesajabuch." In *Der neue Bund im alten*, edited by Erich Zenger, 149–67. Freiburg: Herder, 1993.

Grüneberg, Keith N. *Abraham, Blessing, and the Nations: A Philological and Exegetical Study of Genesis 12:3 in Its Narrative Context*. BZAW 332. Berlin: de Gruyter, 2003.

———. *Blessing: Biblical Meaning and Pastoral Practice*. Grove Biblical Series. Cambridge: Grove, 2003.

Guthrie, Donald. *Galatians*. NCBC. Grand Rapids: Eerdmans, 1981.

Haak, Robert D. *Habakkuk*. VTSup 44. Leiden: Brill, 1992.

Hafemann, Scott J. "The Covenant Relationship." In *Central Themes in Biblical Theology: Mapping Unity in Diversity*, edited by Scott J. Hafemann and Paul R. House, 20–65. Grand Rapids: Baker Academic, 2007.

Hahn, Ferdinand. "Genesis 15:6 Im Neuen Testament." In *Probleme Biblischer Theologie*, edited by Hans W. Wolff, 90–107. Munich: Kaiser, 1971.

Hahn, Scott W. *Kinship by Covenant: A Canonical Approach to the Fulfillment of God's Saving Promises*. The Anchor Yale Bible Reference Library. New Haven, CT: Yale University Press, 2009.

Hals, Ronald M. *Ezekiel*. Forms of the Old Testament Literature 19. Grand Rapids: Eerdmans, 1989.

Hamerton-Kelly, Robert G. "Sacred Violence and the Curse of the Law (Galatians 3:13): The Death of Christ as a Sacrificial Travesty." *NTS* 36 (1990) 98–118.

Hamilton, James M., Jr. *God's Indwelling Presence: The Holy Spirit in the Old and New Testaments*. NAC Studies in Bible & Theology. Nashville: B&H Academic, 2006.

Hamilton, Victor P. *The Book of Genesis: Chapters 1–17*. NICOT. Grand Rapids: Eerdmans, 1990.

———. *The Book of Genesis: Chapters 18–50*. NICOT. Grand Rapids: Eerdmans, 1995.

Hanhart, Robert. *Sacharja*. Biblischer Kommentar. Altes Testament XIV/7. Neukirchen-Vluyn: Neukirchner, 1990.

Hanse, Hermann. "ΔΗΛΟΝ (Zu Gal 3,11)." *ZNW* 34 (1935) 299–303.

Hansen, G. Walter. *Abraham in Galatians: Epistolary and Rhetorical Contexts*. JSNTSup 29. Sheffield: JSOT, 1989.

———. "Paul's Three-Dimensional Application of Genesis 15:6 in Galatians." *TTJ* 1 (1989) 59–77.

Harmon, William. *A Handbook to Literature*. 9th ed. Upper Saddle River, NJ: Prentice Hall, 2003.

Harrington, Daniel J. "The Bible Rewritten." In *Early Judaism and Its Modern Interpreters*, edited by Robert A. Kraft and George W. E. Nickelsburg, 239–47. The Bible and Its Modern Interpreters 2. Atlanta: Scholars, 1986.

———. "Pseudo-Philo: A New Translation and Introduction." In vol. 2 of *The Old Testament Pseudepigrapha*, edited by James H. Charlesworth, 297-377. Garden City, NY: Doubleday, 1985.

Harrington, Hannah K. "Keeping Outsiders Out: Impurity at Qumran." In *Defining Identities: We, You, and the Other in the Dead Sea Scrolls*, edited by Florentino García Martínez and Mladen Popović, 187-203. STDJ 70. Leiden: Brill, 2008.

Harrisville, R. A. *The Figure of Abraham in the Epistles of St. Paul: In the Footsteps of Abraham*. San Francisco: Mellen Research University Press, 1992.

Hartley, John E. *Leviticus*. WBC 4. Dallas: Word, 1992.

Hays, Richard B. *Echoes of Scripture in the Letters of Paul*. New Haven, CT: Yale University Press, 1989.

———. *The Faith of Jesus Christ: An Investigation of the Narrative Substructure of Galatians 3:1—4:11*. 2nd ed. The Biblical Resource Series. Grand Rapids: Eerdmans, 2002.

———. "Galatians." In *2 Corinthians-Philemon*, edited by Leander E. Keck, 181-348. NIB 11. Nashville: Abingdon, 2000.

———. "ΠΙΣΤΙΣ and Pauline Christology: What Is at Stake?" In *Pauline Theology, Vol. 4: Looking Back, Pressing On*, edited by E. Elizabeth Johnson and David M. Hay, 35-60. 4 vols. SBLSymS 4. Atlanta: Scholars, 1997.

Heckel, Ulrich. *Der Segen im Neuen Testament*. WUNT 150. Tübingen: Mohr Siebeck, 2002.

Heim, Knut. "The Perfect King of Psalm 72." In *The Lord's Anointed: Interpretation of Old Testament Messianic Texts*, edited by Philip E. Satterthwaite et al., 223-48. Carlisle, UK: Paternoster, 1995.

Herrmann, J. "נחל and נחל in the OT." In *TDNT* 3:769-81.

Hess, Richard S. "The Genealogies of Genesis 1-11 and Comparative Literature." *Biblica* 70 (1989) 241-54.

Hieke, Thomas. *Die Genealogien der Genesis*. HBS 29. Freiburg: Herder, 2003.

Hildebrandt, Wilf. *An Old Testament Theology of the Spirit of God*. Peabody, MA: Hendrickson, 1995.

Hodge, Charles. *Commentary on the Epistle to the Romans*. New ed., 1886. Reprint, Grand Rapids: Eerdmans, 1955.

Hoehner, Harold W. *Ephesians: An Exegetical Commentary*. Grand Rapids: Baker Academic, 2002.

Hofius, Otfried. "'Werke des Gesetz': Untersuchungen zu der paulinischen Rede von den e1rga no&mou." In *Paulus und Johannes: Exegetische Studien zur paulinischen und johanneischen Theologie Und Literatur*, edited by Dieter Sänger and Ulrich Mell, 271-310. WUNT 198. Tübingen: Mohr Siebeck, 2006.

Holladay, William L. *Jeremiah 1: A Commentary on the Book of the Prophet Jeremiah, Chapters 1-25*. Hermeneia. Philadelphia: Fortress, 1986.

———. *Jeremiah 2: A Commentary on the Book of the Prophet Jeremiah, Chapters 26-52*. Hermeneia. Minneapolis: Fortress, 1989.

Hollander, Harm W. "The Testaments of the Twelve Patriarchs." In *Outside the Old Testament*, edited by Marinus de Jonge, 71-91. CCWJCW 4. Cambridge: Cambridge University Press, 1985.

Hollander, John. *The Figure of Echo: A Mode of Allusion in Milton and After*. Berkeley: University of California Press, 1981.

Hollenberg, D. E. "Nationalism and the Nations in Isaiah 40-55." *VT* 19 (1969) 23-36.

## Bibliography

Holtz, Traugott. "Christliche interpolationen in Joseph und Aseneth." *NTS* 14 (1968) 482–97.
Hong, In-Gyu. "Does Paul Misrepresent the Jewish Law? Law and Covenant in Gal 3:1–14." *NovT* 36 (1994) 164–82.
Hooker, Morna D. "'Beyond the Things Which Are Written': An Examination of 1 Cor 4:6." *NTS* 10 (1963) 127–32.
Hopkins, David C. "The First Stories of Genesis and the Rhythm of the Generations." In *The Echoes of Many Texts: Reflections on Jewish and Christian Traditions*, edited by Lou H. Silberman et al., 25–41. Brown Judaic Studies 313. Atlanta: Scholars, 1997.
House, Paul R. *Old Testament Theology*. Downers Grove, IL: InterVarsity, 1998.
Hubbard, David A. *Joel and Amos: An Introduction and Commentary*. Tyndale Old Testament Commentaries. Downers Grove, IL: InterVarsity, 1989.
Hübner, Hans. *Biblische Theologie des Neuen Testaments*. 3 vols. Göttingen: Vandenhoeck & Ruprecht, 1990.
Huey, F. B. *Jeremiah, Lamentations*. NAC 16. Nashville: Broadman, 1993.
Hughes, Julie. *Scriptural Allusions and Exegesis in the Hodayot*. STDJ 59. Leiden: Brill, 2006.
Humphrey, Edith M. *Joseph and Aseneth*. GAP. Sheffield: Sheffield Academic, 2000.
Hunn, Debbie. "ΠΙΣΤΙΣ ΧΡΙΣΤΟΥ in Galatians 2:16: Clarification from 3:1–6." *TynBul* 57 (2006) 23–33.
Hur, Ju. *A Dynamic Reading of the Holy Spirit in Luke-Acts*. JSNTSup 211. Sheffield: Sheffield Academic, 2001.
Inowlocki, S. *Des idoles mortes et muettes au Dieu vivant: Joseph, Aséneth et le fils de Pharaon dans un roman du Judaïsme hellénisé*. Monothéismes et Philosophie. Turnhout, Belg.: Brepols, 2002.
Jacobson, Howard. *A Commentary on Pseudo-Philo's Liber Antiquitatum Biblicarum: With Latin Text and English Translation*. 2 vols. AGJU 31. Leiden: Brill, 1996.
James, Montague R. *The Lost Apocrypha of the Old Testament: Their Titles and Fragments*. Translations of Early Documents. Series I: Palestinian Jewish Texts (Pre-Rabbinic) 14. London: Society for Promoting Christian Knowledge, 1920.
Janzen, J. Gerald. "Habakkuk 2:2–4 in the Light of Recent Philological Advances." *HTR* 73 (1980) 53–78.
———. *Genesis 12–50: Abraham and All the Families of the Earth*. International Theological Commentary. Grand Rapids: Eerdmans, 1993.
Jewett, Robert. *Romans: A Commentary*. Hermeneia. Minneapolis: Fortress, 2007.
Jobes, Karen H. "Jerusalem, Our Mother: Metalepsis and Intertextuality in Galatians 4:21–31." *WTJ* 55 (1993) 299–320.
Johnson, Bo. "Who Reckoned Righteousness to Whom?" *SEÅ* 51 (1986) 108–15.
Johnson, H. Wayne. "The Paradigm of Abraham in Galatians 3:6–9." *TJ* 8 (1987) 179–99.
Johnson, Marshall D. *The Purpose of the Biblical Genealogies: With Special Reference to the Setting of the Genealogies of Jesus*. SNTSMS 8. London: Cambridge University Press, 1965.
Johnston, George. "'Spirit' and 'Holy Spirit' in the Qumran Literature." In *New Testament Sidelights*, edited by Harvey K. McArthur, 27–42. Hartford, CT: Hartford Seminary Foundation, 1960.
Jonge, Marinus de. "The Testaments of the Twelve Patriarchs." In *The Apocryphal Old Testament*, edited by H. F. D. Sparks, 505–600. Oxford: Clarendon, 1984.

Joosten, Jan. *People and Land in the Holiness Code: An Exegetical Study of the Ideational Framework of the Law in Leviticus 17-26*. VTSup 67. Leiden: Brill, 1996.

Joüon, Paul. *A Grammar of Biblical Hebrew*. Translated by T. Muraoka. 2 vols. Subsidia Biblica 14. Roma: Editrice Pontificio Istituto Biblio, 1991.

Joyce, Paul M. *Divine Initiative and Human Response in Ezekiel*. JSOTSup 51. Sheffield: JSOT, 1989.

———. *Ezekiel: A Commentary*. LHBOTS 482. New York: T. & T. Clark, 2007.

Jüngel, Eberhard. *Justification: The Heart of the Christian Faith*. Translated by Jeffrey F. Cayzer. 3rd ed. Edinburgh: T. & T. Clark, 2001.

Kaiser, Otto. *Isaiah 1-12: A Commentary*. Translated by John Bowden. 2nd ed. OTL. Philadelphia: Westminster, 1983.

———. *Isaiah 13-39: A Commentary*. Translated by R. A. Wilson. OTL. Philadelphia: Westminster, 1974.

Kaiser, Walter C., Jr. "The Promise of God and the Outpouring of the Holy Spirit." In *Living and Active Word of God*, edited by Morris Inch and Ronald Youngblood, 109-22. Winona Lake, IN: Eisenbrauns, 1983.

———. *The Promise-Plan of God: A Biblical Theology of the Old and New Testaments*. Grand Rapids: Zondervan, 2008.

———. "Psalm 72: An Historical and Messianic Current Example of Antiochene Hermeneutical *Theoria*." *JETS* 52 (2009) 257-70.

Kärkkäinen, Veli-Matti. "The Holy Spirit and Justification: The Ecumenical Significance of Luther's Doctrine of Salvation." *Pneuma* 24 (2002) 26-39.

Käsemann, Ernst. *Commentary on Romans*. Translated by Geoffrey W. Bromiley. Grand Rapids: Eerdmans, 1980.

———. "'The Righteousness of God' in Paul." In *New Testament Questions of Today*, translated by W. J. Montague, 168-82. Philadelphia: Fortress, 1969.

Kee, H. C. "The Testaments of the Twelve Patriarchs: A New Translation and Introduction." In vol. 1 of *The Old Testament Pseudepigrapha*, edited by James H. Charlesworth, 775-828. 2 vols. Garden City, NY: Doubleday, 1983.

Keown, Gerald L., et al. *Jeremiah 26-52*. WBC 27. Waco, TX: Word, 1995.

Knibb, Michael A. *The Qumran Community*. CCWJCW 2. Cambridge: Cambridge University Press, 1987.

———. "Rule of the Community." In *EDSS* 2:793-96.

Knight, George W. *The Pastoral Epistles: A Commentary on the Greek Text*. NIGTC. Grand Rapids: Eerdmans, 1992.

Koch, Dietrich-Alex. *Die Schrift als Zeuge des Evangeliums: Untersuchungen zur Verwendung und zum Verständnis der Schrift bei Paulus*. Beiträge zur historischen Theologie 69. Tübingen: Mohr Siebeck, 1986.

———. "Der Text von Hab 2:4b in der Septuaginta und im Neuen Testament." *ZNW* 76 (1985) 68-85.

Kohn, Risa L. "'With a Mighty Hand and an Outstretched Arm': The Prophet and the Torah in Ezekiel 20." In *Ezekiel's Hierarchical World*, edited by Stephen L. Cook and Corrine L. Patton, 159-68. SBLSymS 31. Atlanta: SBL, 2004.

Konkel, A. H. "נכר." In *NIDOTTE* 3:108-9.

Kraemer, Ross S. *When Aseneth Met Joseph: A Late Antique Tale of the Biblical Patriarch and His Egyptian Wife, Reconsidered*. New York: Oxford University Press, 1998.

Kraus, Hans-Joachim. *Psalms 60-150*. Translated by Hilton C. Oswald. CC. Minneapolis: Fortress, 1993.

# Bibliography

Kruger, Hennie A. J. "Subscripts to Creation: A Few Exegetical Comments on the Literary Device of Repetition in Gen 1–11." In *Studies in the Book of Genesis: Literature, Redaction and History*, edited by André Wénin, 429–45. BETL 155. Sterling, VA: Uitgeverij Peeters, 2001.

Kruse, Colin G. "Paul, the Law and the Spirit." In *Paul and His Theology*, edited by Stanley E. Porter, 109–30. PAST 3. Leiden: Brill, 2006.

Kuck, David W. *Judgment and Community Conflict: Paul's Use of Apocalyptic Judgment Language in 1 Corinthians 3:5—4:5*. NovTSup 66. Leiden: Brill, 1992.

Kugel, James L. "The Ladder of Jacob." *HTR* 88 (1995) 209–27.

———. *The Ladder of Jacob: Ancient Interpretations of the Biblical Story of Jacob and His Children*. Princeton, NJ: Princeton University Press, 2006.

Kugler, Robert A. *The Testaments of the Twelve Patriarchs*. GAP. Sheffield: Sheffield Academic, 2001.

Kuhn, Heinz-Wolfgang. *Enderwartung und gegenwärtiges Heil: Untersuchungen zu den Gemeindeliedern von Qumran*. Studien zur Umwelt des Neuen Testaments 4. Göttingen: Vandenhoeck & Ruprecht, 1966.

Kutsch, Ernst. "Ich will meinen Geist ausgiessen auf deine Kinder." In *Wort, das Weiterwirkt: Aufsätze zur praktischen Theologie in memoriam Kurt Frör*, edited by Kurt Frör et al., 122–33. Munich: Kaiser, 1981.

Kuula, Kari. *The Law, the Covenant and God's Plan*. 2 vols. Publications of the Finnish Exegetical Society 72. Göttingen: Vandenhoeck & Ruprecht, 1999.

Kvalvaag, Robert W. "The Spirit in Human Beings in Some Qumran Non-Biblical Texts." In *Qumran between the Old and New Testaments*, edited by Frederick H. Cryer and Thomas L. Thompson, 159–80. JSOTSup 290. Sheffield: Sheffield Academic, 1998.

Kwon, Yon-Gyong. *Eschatology in Galatians: Rethinking Paul's Response to the Crisis in Galatia*. WUNT/II 183. Tübingen: Mohr Siebeck, 2004.

Lagrange, Marie-Joseph. *Saint Paul: Épître aux Galates*. 2nd ed. Études Bibliques. Paris: J. Gabalda, 1950.

Lambert, David. "Did Israel Believe That Redemption Awaited Its Repentance? The Case of Jubilees 1." *CBQ* 68 (2006) 631–50.

Lambrecht, Jan. "Abraham and His Offspring: A Comparison of Galatians 5,1 with 3,13." *Biblica* 80 (1999) 525–36.

Lapsley, Jacqueline E. *Can These Bones Live? The Problem of the Moral Self in the Book of Ezekiel*. BZAW 301. Berlin: de Gruyter, 2000.

Leaney, A. R. C. *The Rule of Qumran and Its Meaning*. New Testament Library. Philadelphia: Westminster, 1966.

Lee, Chee-Chiew. "ברך in Genesis 35:11 and the Abrahamic Promise of Blessings for the Nations." *JETS* 52 (2009) 467–82.

———. "Once Again: The Niphal and Hithpael of ברך in the Abrahamic Blessing for the Nations." *JSOT* 36 (2012) 279–96.

Lemke, Werner E. "Circumcision of the Heart: The Journey of a Biblical Metaphor." In *A God So Near*, edited by Brent A. Strawn and Nancy R. Bowen, 299–319. Winona Lake, IN: Eisenbrauns, 2003.

Lemmer, H. R. "Mnemonic Reference to the Spirit as a Persuasive Tool." *Neot* 26 (1992) 359–88.

Léonas, Alexis. "A Note on Acts 3,25–26: The Meaning of Peter's Genesis Quotation." *ETL* 76 (2000) 149–61.

# Bibliography

Leuenberger, Martin. *Segen und Segenstheologien im alten Israel: Untersuchungen zu ihren religions- und theologiegeschichtlichen Konstellationen und Transformationen.* Abhandlungen zur Theologie des Alten Und Neuen Testaments 90. Zürich: Theologischer Verlag Zürich, 2008.

Levin, Yigal. "Understanding Biblical Genealogies." *CurBS* 9 (2001) 11–46.

Levine, Amy-Jill. "Tobit: Teaching Jews How to Live in the Diaspora." *BRev* 8 (1992) 42–51, 64.

Levine, Baruch A. *Leviticus: The Traditional Hebrew Text with the New JPS Translation.* JPSTC. Philadelphia: JPS, 1989.

Lietzmann, Hans. *An die Galater.* Handbuch zum Neuen Testament 10. Tübingen: Mohr Siebeck, 1932.

Lightfoot, Joseph B. *St. Paul's Epistle to the Galatians: A Revised Text with Introductions, Notes and Dissertations.* 7th ed. London: Macmillan, 1881.

Lindsay, Dennis R. "Works of Law, Hearing of Faith and Πίστις Χριστοῦ in Galatians 2:16—3:5." *SCJ* 3 (2000) 79–88.

Lohfink, Norbert. "Covenant and Torah in the Pilgrimage of the Nations (the Book of Isaiah and Psalm 25)." In *The God of Israel and the Nations: Studies in Isaiah and the Psalms*, edited by Norbert Lohfink and Erich Zenger, translated by Everett R. Kalin, 33–84. Collegeville, MN: Liturgical, 2000.

Longenecker, Bruce W. *The Triumph of Abraham's God: The Transformation of Identity in Galatians.* Nashville: Abingdon, 1998.

———. "'Until Christ Is Formed in You': Suprahuman Forces and Moral Character in Galatians." *CBQ* 61 (1999) 92–108.

Longenecker, Richard N. *Galatians.* WBC 41. Dallas: Word, 1990.

Longman, Tremper. *How to Read Genesis.* Downers Grove, IL: InterVarsity, 2005.

Lührmann, Dieter. *Galatians.* Translated by O. C. Dean. CC. Minneapolis: Augsburg, 1992.

Lundbom, Jack R. *Jeremiah 1–20: A New Translation with Introduction and Commentary.* AB 21A. New York: Doubleday, 1999.

———. *Jeremiah 21–36: A New Translation with Introduction and Commentary.* AB 21B. New York: Doubleday, 2004.

———. *Jeremiah 37–52: A New Translation with Introduction and Commentary.* AB 21C. Garden City, NY: Doubleday, 2004.

Lunt, H. G. "Ladder of Jacob: A New Translation and Introduction." In vol. 2 of *The Old Testament Pseudepigrapha*, edited by James H. Charlesworth, 401–11. Garden City, NY: Doubleday, 1985.

Luther, Martin. *Lectures on Galatians.* Translated by Richard Jungkuntz. Luther's Works 26–27. St. Louis: Concordia, 1963–1964.

Macchia, Frank D. "Justification through New Creation: The Holy Spirit and the Doctrine by Which the Church Stands or Falls." *ThTo* 58 (2001) 202–17.

———. *Justified in The Spirit: Creation, Redemption, and the Triune God.* Pentecostal Manisfestos. Grand Rapids: Eerdmans, 2010.

Mack, Burton L. *Wisdom and the Hebrew Epic: Ben Sira's Hymn in Praise of the Fathers.* Chicago Studies in the History of Judaism. Chicago: University of Chicago Press, 1985.

Mann, Thomas W. "'All the Families of the Earth': The Theological Unity of Genesis." *Int* 45 (1991) 341–53.

## Bibliography

Marböck, J. "Die 'Geschichte Israels' als 'Bundesgeschichte' nach dem Sirachbuch." In *Der neue Bund im alten*, edited by Erich Zenger, 177–97. Freiburg: Herder, 1993.

Marshall, I. Howard. "Acts." In *Commentary on the New Testament Use of the Old Testament*, edited by G. K. Beale and D. A. Carson, 513–606. Grand Rapids: Baker, 2007.

———. *New Testament Theology: Many Witnesses, One Gospel*. Downers Grove, IL: InterVarsity, 2004.

Martens, Elmer. "Ezekiel's Contribution to a Biblical Theology of Mission." *Direction* 28 (1999) 75–87.

Martin, Troy. "Apostasy to Paganism: The Rhetorical Stasis of the Galatian Controversy." *JBL* 114 (1995) 437–61.

Martyn, J. Louis. *Galatians: A New Translation with Introduction and Commentary*. AB 33a. New York: Doubleday, 1997.

———. "Paul's Understanding of the Textual Contradiction between Habakkuk 2:4 and Leviticus 18:5." In *The Quest for Context and Meaning: Studies in Biblical Intertextuality in Honor of James A. Sanders*, edited by Craig A. Evans and Shemaryahu Talmon, 465–73. BibIntS 28. Leiden: Brill, 1997.

Matera, Frank J. *Galatians*. Sacra pagina. Collegeville, MN: Liturgical, 1992.

Mathews, Kenneth A. *Genesis 1–11:26*. NAC 1A. Nashville: Broadman & Holman, 2005.

———. *Genesis 11:27—50:26*. NAC 1B. Nashville: Broadman & Holman, 2005.

Matties, Gordon H. *Ezekiel 18 and the Rhetoric of Moral Discourse*. SBLDS 126. Atlanta: Scholars, 1990.

Mays, James L. *Micah: A Commentary*. OTL. Philadelphia: Westminster, 1976.

McComiskey, Thomas E. *The Covenants of Promise: A Theology of the Old Testament Covenants*. Grand Rapids: Baker, 1985.

———. "Zechariah." In *Zephaniah, Haggai, Zechariah, and Malachi*, vol. 3 of *The Minor Prophets: An Exegetical and Expository Commentary*, edited by Thomas E. McComiskey, 1003–1244. 3 vols. Grand Rapids: Baker, 1998.

McConville, J. G. *Deuteronomy*. Apollos Old Testament Commentary 5. Leicester: Apollos, 2002.

McGrath, Alister E. "Justification." In *DPL* 517–23.

McKane, William. *A Critical and Exegetical Commentary on Jeremiah*. 2 vols. ICC. Edinburgh: T. & T. Clark, 1986–1996.

McKenzie, John L. *Second Isaiah: Introduction, Translation, and Notes*. AB 20. Garden City, NY: Doubleday, 1968.

Melugin, Roy F. "Israel and the Nations in Isaiah 40–55." In *Problems in Biblical Theology*, edited by H. T. C. Sun and K. L. Eades, 246–64. Grand Rapids: Eerdmans, 1997.

Merrill, Eugene H. *Haggai, Zechariah, Malachi: An Exegetical Commentary*. Chicago: Moody, 1994.

———. "חלל." In *NIDOTTE* 1:1032–35.

Merwe, C. H. J. van der, et al. *A Biblical Hebrew Reference Grammar*. Biblical Languages: Hebrew 3. Sheffield: Sheffield Academic, 1999.

Metso, Sarianna. *The Serekh Texts*. Library of Second Temple Studies 62. London: T. & T. Clark, 2007.

———. *The Textual Development of the Qumran Community Rule*. STDJ 21. Leiden: Brill, 1997.

Meyers, Carol L., and Eric M. Meyers. *Haggai, Zechariah 1–8: A New Translation with Introduction and Commentary*. AB 25B. Garden City, NY: Doubleday, 1987.

———. *Zechariah 9–14: A New Translation with Introduction and Commentary*. AB 25C. New York: Doubleday, 1993.
Milgrom, Jacob. *Leviticus 17–22: A New Translation with Introduction and Commentary*. AB 3A. New York: Doubleday, 2000.
———. "Leviticus 26 and Ezekiel." In *The Quest for Context and Meaning: Studies in Biblical Intertextuality in Honor of James A. Sanders*, edited by Craig A. Evans and Shemaryahu Talmon, 59–62. BibIntS 28. Leiden: Brill, 1997.
Miller, Patrick D. "Syntax and Theology in Genesis 12:3a." *VT* 34 (1984) 472–76.
Mitchell, Christopher W. *The Meaning of BRK: 'To Bless' in the Old Testament*. SBLDS 95. Atlanta: Scholars, 1987.
Mitchell, H. G., et al. *A Critical and Exegetical Commentary on Haggai, Zechariah, Malachi and Jonah*. ICC 25. Edinburgh: T. & T. Clark, 1912.
Moberly, R. W. L. *The Bible, Theology, and Faith: A Study of Abraham and Jesus* Cambridge: Cambridge University Press, 2000.
———. "אמן." In *NIDOTTE* 1:427–33.
———. "Righteousness of Abraham (Gen 15:6)." In *Studies in the Pentateuch*, edited by J. A. Emeron, 103–30. Leiden: Brill, 1990.
Montague, George T. *The Holy Spirit: Growth of a Biblical Tradition*. 1976. Reprint, Peabody, MA: Hendrickson, 1994.
Moo, Douglas J. *The Epistle to the Romans*. NICNT. Grand Rapids: Eerdmans, 1996.
———. "The Law of Christ as the Fulfillment of the Law of Moses: A Modified Lutheran View." In *Five Views on Law and Gospel*, edited by Stanley N. Gundry, 319–76. Grand Rapids: Zondervan, 1996.
———. "'Law,' 'Works of the Law,' and Legalism in Paul." *WTJ* 45 (1983) 73–100.
———. *Romans 1–8*. WEC. Chicago: Moody, 1991.
Moore, Carey A. *Tobit: A New Translation with Introduction and Commentary*. AB 40A. New York: Doubleday, 1996.
Morales, Rodrigo J. *The Spirit and the Restoration of Israel: New Exodus and New Creation Motifs in Galatians*. WUNT/II 282. Tübingen: Mohr Siebeck, 2005.
———. "The Words of the Luminaries, the Curse of the Law, and the Outpouring of the Spirit in Gal 3,10–14." *ZNW* 100 (2009) 269–77.
Morland, Kjell A. "Expansion and Conflict: The Rhetoric of Hebrew Bible Citations in Galatians 3." In *Recruitment, Conquest, and Conflict: Strategies in Judaism, Early Christianity, and the Greco-Roman World*, edited by Peder Borgen et al., 251–71. ESEC 6. Atlanta: Scholars, 1998.
———. *The Rhetoric of Curse in Galatians: Paul Confronts Another Gospel*. ESEC 5. Atlanta: Scholars, 1995.
Morris, Leon. *The Epistle to the Romans*. Pillar New Testament Commentary. Grand Rapids: Eerdmans, 1988.
Motyer, J. Alec. *The Message of Exodus: The Days of Our Pilgrimage*. The Bible Speaks Today. Downers Grove, IL: InterVarsity, 2005.
Moule, C. F. D. *An Idiom Book of New Testament Greek*. 2nd ed. Cambridge: Cambridge University Press, 1959.
Mounce, William D. *Pastoral Epistles*. WBC 46. Nashville: Thomas Nelson, 2000.
Moyise, Steve. *Evoking Scripture: Seeing the Old Testament in the New*. London: T. & T. Clark, 2008.

# Bibliography

———. "Quotations." In *As It Is Written: Studying Paul's Use of Scripture*, edited by Stanley E. Porter and Christopher D. Stanley, 15–28. SBLSymS 50. Atlanta: SBL, 2008.

Müller, Mogens. "Die Abraham-Gestalt im Jubiläenbuch: Versuch einer Interpretation." *SJOT* 10 (1996) 238–57.

Murphy, Frederick J. *Pseudo-Philo: Rewriting the Bible*. New York: Oxford University Press, 1993.

Murray, John. *The Epistle to the Romans*. NICNT. Grand Rapids: Eerdmans, 1959.

———. *Redemption, Accomplished and Applied*. Grand Rapids: Eerdmans, 1955.

Mußner, Franz. *Der Galaterbrief*. 2nd ed, HTKNT 9. Freiburg: Herder, 1974.

Nelson, Richard D. *Deuteronomy: A Commentary*. OTL. Louisville: Westminster John Knox, 2002.

Neyrey, Jerome H. "Bewitched in Galatia: Paul and Cultural Anthropology." *CBQ* 50 (1988) 72–100.

Nickelsburg, George W. E. "The Bible Rewritten and Expanded." In *Jewish Writings of the Second Temple Period*, edited by Michael E. Stone, 89–156. Literature of the Jewish People in the Period of the Second Temple and the Talmud 2. Philadelphia: Fortress, 1984.

Niehaus, Jeffrey. "An Argument Against Theologically Constructed Covenants." *JETS* 50 (2007) 259–73.

———. "Covenant: An Idea in the Mind of God." *JETS* 52 (2009) 225–46.

Noth, Martin. *A History of Pentateuchal Traditions*. Translated by Bernhard W. Anderson. Englewood Cliffs, NJ: Prentice-Hall, 1972.

Nötscher, Friedrich. "Heiligkeit in den Qumranschriften." *RevQ* 2 (1960) 315–44.

Nowell, Irene. "The Narrative Context of Blessing in the Old Testament." In *Blessing and Power*, edited by Mary Collins and David Power, 3–12. Concilium. Edinburgh: T. & T. Clark, 1985.

———. "Tobit." In *1 & 2 Kings–Judith*, edited by Leander E. Keck, 973–1071. NIB 3. Nashville: Abingdon, 1999.

Nwachukwu, Mary S. C. *Creation-Covenant Scheme and Justification by Faith: A Canonical Study of the God-Human Drama in the Pentateuch and the Letter to the Romans*. Tesi Gregoriana: Serie Teologia 89. Rome: Editrice Pontificia Universita Gregoriana, 2002.

Obeng, E. A. "Abba, Father: The Prayer of the Sons of God." *ExpTim* 99 (1988) 363–66.

O'Brien, Peter T. "Justification in Paul and Some Crucial Issues of the Last Two Decades." In *Right with God: Justification in the Bible and the World*, edited by D. A. Carson, 69–95. Grand Rapids: Baker, 1992.

Oeming, Manfred. "Der Glaube Abrahams: Zur Rezeptionsgeschichte von Gen 15,6 in der Zeit des zweiten Tempels." *ZAW* 110 (1998) 16–33.

———. "Ist Genesis 15:6 ein Beleg für die Anrechnung des Glaubens zur Gerechtigkeit?" *ZAW* 95 (1983) 182–97.

Orlov, Andrei A. *From Apocalypticism to Merkabah Mysticism: Studies in the Slavonic Pseudepigrapha*. JSJSup 114. Leiden: Brill, 2007.

Oswalt, John N. *The Book of Isaiah: Chapters 1–39*. NICOT. Grand Rapids: Eerdmans, 1986.

———. *The Book of Isaiah: Chapters 40–66*. NICOT. Grand Rapids: Eerdmans, 1998.

———. "The Nations in Isaiah: Friend or Foe; Servant or Partner." *BBR* 16 (2006) 41–51.

# Bibliography

Otzen, Benedikt. *Tobit and Judith*. GAP. London: Sheffield Academic, 2002.

Pedersen, Johannes. *Israel, Its Life and Culture: I-II*. London: Oxford University Press, 1926.

Pelser, G. M. M. "The Opposition Faith and Works as Persuasive Device in Galatians." *Neot* 26 (1992) 389-405.

Penn, Michael. "Identity Transformation and Authorial Identification in Joseph and Aseneth." *JSP* 13 (2002) 171-83.

Pennington, A. "The Ladder of Jacob." In *The Apocryphal Old Testament*, edited by H. F. D. Sparks, 453-64. Oxford: Clarendon, 1984.

Petersen, David L. *Haggai and Zechariah 1-8: A Commentary*. OTL. Philadelphia: Westminster, 1984.

———. *Zechariah 9-14 and Malachi: A Commentary*. OTL. Louisville: Westminster John Knox, 1995.

Philip, Finny. *The Origins of Pauline Pneumatology: The Eschatological Bestowal of the Spirit Upon Gentiles in Judaism and in the Early Development of Paul's Theology*. WUNT/II 194. Tübingen: Mohr Siebeck, 2005.

Philonenko, Marc. *Joseph et Aséneth: Introduction, texte critique, traduction et notes*. StPB 13. Leiden: Brill, 1968.

Piper, John. *The Future of Justification: A Response to N. T. Wright*. Wheaton, IL: Crossway, 2007.

Pohlmann, Karl-Friedrich. *Das Buch des Propheten Hesekiel (Ezechiel)*. 2 vols. Das Alte Testament Deutsch 22. Göttingen: Vandenhoeck & Ruprecht, 1996.

Porter, Stanley E. "Allusions and Echoes." In *As It Is Written: Studying Paul's Use of Scripture*, edited by Stanley E. Porter and Christopher D. Stanley, 29-40. SBLSymS 50. Atlanta: SBL, 2008.

———. "Further Comments on the Use of the Old Testament in the New Testament." In *The Intertextuality of the Epistles: Explorations of Theory and Practice*, edited by Thomas L. Brodie et al., 98-110. New Testament Monographs 16. Sheffield: Sheffield Phoenix, 2006.

———, ed. *Paul and His Opponents*. PAST 2. Leiden: Brill, 2005.

———. "The Use of the Old Testament in the New Testament: A Brief Comment on Method and Terminology." In *Early Christian Interpretation of the Scriptures of Israel: Investigations and Proposals*, edited by Craig A. Evans and James A. Sanders, 79-96. JSNTSup 148. Sheffield: Sheffield Academic, 1997.

Potter, Harry D. "The New Covenant in Jeremiah 31:31-34." *VT* 33 (1983) 347-57.

Preuss, Horst Dietrich. *Old Testament Theology*. Translated by Leo G. Perdue. 2 vols. OTL. Louisville: Westminster John Knox, 1995.

Prinsloo, Willem S. *The Theology of the Book of Joel*. BZAW 163. Berlin: de Gruyter, 1985.

Puech, Émile. "Hodayot." In *EDSS* 1:365-69.

———. "Quelques aspects de la restauration du Rouleau des Hymnes (1QH)." *JJS* 39 (1988) 38-55.

Pyne, Robert A. "The 'Seed,' the Spirit, and the Blessing of Abraham." *BSac* 152 (1995) 211-22.

Rabinovits, Chaim Dov. *Commentary to the Book of Yehezkel*. Translated by Zvi Faier. Da'ath Sofrim: Torah, Prophets, Sacred Writings. New York: Vagshal, 2001.

Rad, Gerhard von. *Genesis: A Commentary*. Translated by John H. Marks. Rev. ed. OTL. Philadelphia: Westminster, 1972.

# Bibliography

———. *Old Testament Theology*. Translated by D. M. G. Stalker. 2 vols. Edinburgh: Oliver and Boyd, 1962–65.

———. *The Problem of the Hexateuch and Other Essays*. Translated by E. W. Trueman Dicken. Edinburgh: Oliver & Boyd, 1966.

Rainbow, Paul A. *The Way of Salvation: The Role of Christian Obedience in Justification*. Waynesboro, GA: Paternoster, 2005.

Rapp, Hans A. *Jakob in Bet-el: Gen 35,1–15 und die jüdische Literatur des 3. und 2. Jahrhunderts*. HBS 29. Freiburg: Herder, 2001.

Rashi. *Pentateuch with Targum Onkelos, Haphtaroth and Rashi's Commentary: Genesis and Exodus*. Translated by M. Rosenbaum and A. M. Silbermann. Jerusalem: The Silbermann Family, 1972.

Reiterer, Friedrich. "Der Pentateuch in der spätbiblischen Weisheit Ben Siras." In *A Critical Study of the Pentateuch: An Encounter between Europe and Africa*, edited by Eckart Otto and J. H. Le Roux, 160–83. Munich: Lit, 2005.

Renaud, Bernard. "L'alliance éternelle d'Éz 16,59–63 et l'alliance nouvelle de Jér 31,31–34." In *Ezekiel and His Book*, edited by J. Lust, 335–49. BETL 74. Leuven: Uitgeverij Peeters, 1986.

Rendtorff, Rolf. "Ez 20 und 36,16ff im Rahmen der Komposition des Buches Ezechiel." In *Ezekiel and His Book*, edited by J. Lust, 260–65. BETL 74. Leuven: Uitgeverij Peeters, 1986.

Renz, Thomas. *The Rhetorical Function of the Book of Ezekiel*. VTSup 76. Leiden: Brill, 1999.

Reventlow, Henning G. "Die Völker als Jahwes Zeugen bei Ezechiel." *ZAW* 71 (1959) 33–43.

Ridderbos, Herman N. *The Epistle of Paul to the Churches of Galatia*. Translated by Henry Zylstra. NICNT. Grand Rapids: Eerdmans, 1953.

Roberts, J. J. M. *Nahum, Habakkuk, and Zephaniah: A Commentary*. OTL. Louisville: Westminster John Knox, 1991.

Robertson, Archibald, and Alfred Plummer. *A Critical and Exegetical Commentary on the First Epistle of St. Paul to the Corinthians*. 2nd ed. ICC 31. Edinburgh: T. & T. Clark, 1914.

Robertson, O. Palmer. *The Books of Nahum, Habakkuk, and Zephaniah*. NICOT. Grand Rapids: Eerdmans, 1990.

Robson, James. *Word and Spirit in Ezekiel*. LHBOTS 447. New York: T. & T. Clark, 2006.

Ross, Allen P. *Creation and Blessing: A Guide to the Study and Exposition of the Book of Genesis*. Grand Rapids: Baker, 1988.

Routledge, Robin. "Is There a Narrative Substructure Underlying the Book of Isaiah?" *TynBul* 55 (2004) 183–204.

Rowland, Christopher. "The Eschatology of the New Testament Church." In *The Oxford Handbook of Eschatology*, edited by Jerry L. Walls, 56–72. Oxford: Oxford University Press, 2008.

Rudman, Dominic. "Zechariah 8:20–22 & Isaiah 2:2–4 Parallel Micah 4:2–3: A Study in Intertextuality." *BN* 107/108 (2001) 50–54.

Ruprecht, Eberhard. "Vorgegebene Tradition und theologische Gestaltung in Genesis 12:1–3." *VT* 29 (1979) 171–88.

Sailhamer, John H. "Creation, Genesis 1–11, and the Canon." *BBR* 10 (2000) 89–106.

———. *The Pentateuch as Narrative: A Biblical-Theological Commentary*. Library of Biblical Interpretation. Grand Rapids: Zondervan, 1992.

Sanders, E. P. *Paul and Palestinian Judaism: A Comparison of Patterns of Religion.* London: SCM, 1977.

———. *Paul, the Law, and the Jewish People.* Philadelphia: Fortress, 1983.

Sanders, James A. "Habakkuk in Qumran, Paul and the Old Testament." In *Paul and the Scriptures of Israel,* edited by Craig A. Evans and James A. Sanders, 98–117. JSNTSup 83. Sheffield: Sheffield Academic, 1993.

Sänger, Dieter. "Erwägungen zur historischen Einordnung und zur Datierung von 'Joseph und Aseneth.'" *ZNW* 76 (1985) 86–106.

Sarna, Nahum M. *Genesis: The Traditional Hebrew Text with New JPS Translation.* JPSTC. Philadelphia: JPS, 1989.

Scharbert, Josef. "בָּרַךְ." In *TDOT* 2:279–308.

Schenker, Adrian. "Unwiderrufliche Umkehr und neuer Bund: Vergleich zwischen der Wiederherstellung Israels in Dt 4,25–31; 30,1–14 und dem neuen Bund in Jer 31,31–34." *FZPhTh* 27 (1980) 93–106.

Schiffman, Lawrence H. "Non-Jews in the Dead Sea Scrolls." In *The Quest for Context and Meaning: Studies in Biblical Intertextuality in Honor of James A. Sanders,* edited by Craig A. Evans and Shemaryahu Talmon, 153–71. BibIntS 28. Leiden: Brill, 1997.

Schneider, Gerhard. *Die Apostelgeschichte.* 2 vols. HTKNT 5. Freiburg: Herder, 1980–1982.

Schodde, George H. "The Book of Jubilees Translated from the Ethiopic." *BSac* 43 (1886) 455–86, 727–45.

Schoeps, Hans J. *Paul: The Theology of the Apostle in the Light of Jewish Religious History.* Translated by Harold Knight. Philadelphia: Westminster, 1961.

Scholer, David M. "An Introduction to Philo Judaeus of Alexandria." In *The Works of Philo: Complete and Unabridged,* translated by Charles D. Yonge, xi–xviii. Peabody, MA: Hendrickson, 1993.

Schreiner, Josef. *Jeremia 1—25,14.* NEBKAT 3. Würzburg: Echter, 1981.

———. *Jeremia 25,15—52,34.* NEBKAT 9. Würzburg: Echter, 1984.

———. "Patriarchen im Lob der Väter (zu Sir 44)." In *Textarbeit: Studien zu Texten und ihrer Rezeption aus dem Alten Testament und der Umwelt Israels,* edited by Klaus Kiesow and Thomas Meurer, 425–41. Alter Orient und Altes Testament 294. Münster: Ugarit, 2003.

Schreiner, Thomas R. "Is Perfect Obedience to the Law Possible? A Re-Examination of Galatians 3:10." *JETS* 27 (1984) 151–60.

———. *New Testament Theology: Magnifying God in Christ.* Grand Rapids: Baker Academic, 2008.

———. "Paul and Perfect Obedience to the Law: An Evaluation of the View of E. P. Sanders." *WTJ* 47 (1985) 245–78.

———. *Paul, Apostle of God's Glory in Christ: A Pauline Theology.* Downers Grove, IL: InterVarsity, 2001.

———. *Romans.* BECNT 6. Grand Rapids: Baker, 1998.

———. "'Works of Law' in Paul." *NovT* 33 (1991) 217–44.

Schultz, Richard L. *The Search for Quotation: Verbal Parallels in the Prophets.* JSOTSup 180. Sheffield: Sheffield Academic, 1999.

Schüngel-Straumann, Helen. *Tobit: Übersetzt und ausgelegt.* HTKAT. Freiburg: Herder, 2000.

# Bibliography

Scott, James M. *Adoption as Sons of God: An Exegetical Investigation into the Background of ΥΙΟΘΕΣΙΑ in the Pauline Corpus*. WUNT/II 48. Tübingen: Mohr Siebeck, 1992.

———. "'For as Many as Are of Works of the Law Are under a Curse' (Galatians 3:10)." In *Paul and the Scriptures of Israel*, edited by Craig A. Evans and James A. Sanders, 187–221. JSNTSup 83. Sheffield: Sheffield Academic, 1993.

———. *Paul and the Nations: The Old Testament and Jewish Background of Paul's Mission to the Nations with Special Reference to the Destination of Galatians*. WUNT 84. Tübingen: Mohr Siebeck, 1995.

Segal, Michael. *The Book of Jubilees: Rewritten Bible, Redaction, Ideology and Theology*. JSJSup 117. Leiden: Brill, 2007.

Seifrid, Mark A. *Christ, Our Righteousness: Paul's Theology of Justification*. NSBT 9. Downers Grove, IL: InterVarsity, 2000.

———. "Paul, Luther, and Justification in Gal 2:15–21." *WTJ* 65 (2003) 215–30.

Sekki, Arthur E. *The Meaning of Ruah at Qumran*. SBLDS 110. Atlanta: Scholars, 1989.

Siker, Jeffrey S. *Disinheriting the Jews: Abraham in Early Christian Controversy*. Louisville: Westminster John Knox, 1991.

Silva, Moisés. "Abraham, Faith, and Works: Paul's Use of Scripture in Galatians 3:6–14." *WTJ* 63 (2001) 251–67.

———. "Faith Versus Works of the Law in Galatians." In *Justification and Variegated Nomism, Vol. 2: The Paradoxes of Paul*, edited by D. A. Carson et al., 217–48. Grand Rapids: Baker Academic, 2004.

———. "Galatians." In *Commentary on the New Testament Use of the Old Testament*, edited by G. K. Beale and D. A. Carson, 785–812. Grand Rapids: Baker, 2007.

———. *Interpreting Galatians: Explorations in Exegetical Method*. 2nd ed. Grand Rapids: Baker, 2001.

Ska, Jean L. "L'éloge des pères dans le Siracide (Sir 44–50) et le canon de l'Ancien Testament." In *Treasures of Wisdom: Studies in Ben Sira and the Book of Wisdom*, edited by N. Calduch-Benages and J. Vermeylen, 181–93. BETL 143. Leuven: Leuven University Press, 1999.

Skehan, Patrick W., and Alexander A. Di Lella. *The Wisdom of Ben Sira*. AB 39. New York: Doubleday, 1987.

Skinner, John. *A Critical and Exegetical Commentary on Genesis*. 2nd ed. ICC 1. Edinburgh: T. & T. Clark, 1930.

Smith, Barry D. "'Spirit of Holiness' as Eschatological Principle of Obedience." In *Christian Beginnings and the Dead Sea Scrolls*, edited by John J. Collins and Craig A. Evans, 75–99. Acadia Studies in Bible and Theology. Grand Rapids: Baker Academic, 2006.

Smith, D. Moody. "The Pauline Literature." In *It Is Written: Scripture Citing Scripture*, edited by D. A. Carson and H. G. M. Williamson, 265–91. Cambridge: Cambridge University Press, 1988.

Smith, Gary V. "Structure and Purpose in Genesis 1–11." *JETS* 20 (1977) 307–19.

Smith, Ralph L. *Micah–Malachi*. WBC 32. Waco, TX: Word, 1984.

Smith, Robert S. *Justification and Eschatology: A Dialogue with "the New Perspective on Paul."* Reformed Theological Review Supplement Series 1. Doncaster, Aus.: Reformed Theological Review, 2001.

Speiser, E. A. *Genesis: A New Translation with Introduction and Commentary*. AB 1. New York: Doubleday, 1969.

# Bibliography

Sprinkle, Preston M. "Law and Life: Leviticus 18.5 in the Literary Framework of Ezekiel." *JSOT* 31 (2007) 275-93.

———. *Law and Life: The Interpretation of Leviticus 18:5 in Early Judaism and in Paul.* WUNT/II 241. Tübingen: Mohr Siebeck, 2008.

Standhartinger, Angela. *Das Frauenbild im Judentum der hellenistischen Zeit: Ein Beitrag anhand von "Joseph und Aseneth."* AGJU 26. Leiden: Brill, 1995.

Stanley, Christopher D. *Arguing With Scripture: The Rhetoric of Quotations in the Letters of Paul.* London: T. & T. Clark, 2004.

———. *Paul and the Language of Scripture: Citation Technique in the Pauline Epistles and Contemporary Literature.* SNTSMS 74. Cambridge: Cambridge University Press, 1992.

———. "'Under a Curse': A Fresh Reading of Galatians 3:10-14." *NTS* 36 (1990): 481-511.

Stanton, Graham N. "The Law of Moses and the Law of Christ: Galatians 3:1—6:2." In *Paul and the Mosaic Law*, edited by James D. G. Dunn, 99-116. Grand Rapids: Eerdmans, 2001.

Starcky, Jean. "Les quatre étapes du messianisme à Qumran." *RB* 70 (1963) 481-505.

Strong, John. "Ezekiel's Use of the Recognition Formula in His Oracles against the Nations." *PRSt* 22 (1995) 115-33.

Stuart, Douglas K. *Hosea–Jonah.* WBC 31. Waco, TX: Word, 1987.

Stuhlmacher, Peter. "The Apostle Paul's View of Righteousness." In *Reconciliation, Law, and Righteousness: Essays in Biblical Theology*, translated by Everett R. Kalin, 68-93. Philadelphia: Fortress, 1986.

———. *Revisiting Paul's Doctrine of Justification: A Challenge to the New Perspective.* Downers Grove, IL: InterVarsity, 2001.

Stuhlmueller, Carroll. *Creative Redemption in Deutero-Isaiah.* AnBib 43. Rome: Biblical Institute, 1970.

Tate, Marvin E. *Psalms 51-100.* WBC 20. Dallas: Word, 1990.

Tengström, S. "רוח." In *TDOT* 13:365-96.

Thielman, Frank. *Theology of the New Testament: A Canonical and Synthetic Approach.* Grand Rapids: Zondervan, 2005.

Thiselton, Anthony C. *The First Epistle to the Corinthians: A Commentary on the Greek Text.* NIGTC. Grand Rapids: Eerdmans, 2000.

Thompson, J. A. *The Book of Jeremiah.* NICOT. Grand Rapids: Eerdmans, 1980.

Thompson, Michael B. *Clothed with Christ: The Example and Teaching of Jesus in Romans 12.1—15.13.* JSNTSup 59. Sheffield: JSOT, 1991.

Tidiman, Brian. *Le livre d'Ézéchiel.* 2 vols. CEB 4. Vaux-sur-Seine, Fr.: Edifac, 1985-1987.

———. *Le livre de Zacharie.* CEB 18. Vaux-sur-Seine, Fr.: Edifac, 1996.

Treier, Daniel J. "The Fulfillment of Joel 2:28-32: A Multiple-Lens Approach." *JETS* 40 (1997) 13-26.

Tschuggnall, Peter. "'Das Wort ist kein Ding': Eine theologische Einübung in den literaturwissenschaftlichen Begriff der Intertextualität." *ZKT* 116 (1994) 160-78.

Ulrichs, Karl F. *Christusglaube: Studien zum Syntagma pistis Christou und zum paulinischen Verständnis von Glaube und Rechtfertigung.* WUNT/II 227. Tübingen: Mohr Siebeck, 2007.

Van Pelt, M. V., et al. "רוח." In *NIDOTTE* 3:1073-78.

## Bibliography

VanderKam, James C. "The Book of Jubilees." In *Outside the Old Testament*, edited by Marinus de Jonge, 111–44. CCWJCW 4. Cambridge: Cambridge University Press, 1985.

———. *The Book of Jubilees*. GAP. Sheffield: Sheffield Academic, 2001.

———. "The Origins and Purposes of Jubilees." In *Studies in the Book of Jubilees*, edited by M. Albani et al., 3–24. Texte und Studien zum antiken Judentum 65. Tübingen: Mohr Siebeck, 1997.

VanGemeren, Willem A. "The Spirit of Restoration." *WTJ* 50 (1988) 81–102.

VanLandingham, Chris. *Judgment and Justification in Early Judaism and the Apostle Paul*. Peabody, MA: Hendrickson, 2006.

Vieweger, Dieter. "Die Arbeit des jeremianischen Schülerkreises am Jeremiabuch und deren Rezeption in der literarischen Überlieferung der Prophet Ezechiels." *BZ* 32 (1988) 15–34.

Vos, Johannes Sijko. *Traditionsgeschichtliche Untersuchungen zur paulinischen Pneumatologie*. Van Gorcum's Theologische Bibliotheek 47. Assen, Neth.: Van Gorcum, 1973.

Wakefield, Andrew H. *Where to Live: The Hermeneutical Significance of Paul's Citations from Scripture in Galatians 3:1–14*. SBL Academia Biblica 14. Atlanta: SBL, 2003.

Wallace, Daniel B. *Greek Grammar Beyond the Basics: An Exegetical Syntax of the New Testament*. Grand Rapids: Zondervan, 1996.

Waltke, Bruce K. *Genesis*. Grand Rapids: Zondervan, 2001.

———. "Micah." In *Obadiah, Jonah, Micah, Nahum, and Habakkuk*, vol. 2 of *The Minor Prophets: An Exegetical and Expository Commentary*, edited by Thomas E. McComiskey, 591–764. Grand Rapids: Baker, 1993.

Waltke, Bruce K., and M. O'Connor. *An Introduction to Biblical Hebrew Syntax*. Winona Lake, IN: Eisenbrauns, 1990.

Waltke, Bruce K., and Charles Yu. *An Old Testament Theology: An Exegetical, Canonical and Thematic Approach*. Grand Rapids: Zondervan, 2007.

Walton, John H. *Genesis*. The NIV Application Commentary. Grand Rapids: Zondervan, 2001.

Wan, Sze-kar. "Abraham and the Promise of Spirit: Points of Convergence between Philo and Paul." In *Things Revealed: Studies in Early Jewish and Christian Literature in Honor of Michael E. Stone*, edited by Ester G. Chazon et al., 209–24. JSJSup 89. Leiden: Brill, 2004.

Watson, Francis. *Paul and the Hermeneutics of Faith*. London: T. & T. Clark, 2004.

Watts, John D. W. *Isaiah 1–33*. WBC 24. Waco, TX: Word, 1985.

———. *Isaiah 34–66*. WBC 25. Waco, TX: Word, 1987.

Watts, Rikki E. "Echoes from the Past: Israel's Ancient Traditions and the Destiny of the Nations in Isaiah 40–55." *JSOT* 28 (2004) 481–508.

Weinfeld, Moshe. "Jeremiah and the Spiritual Metamorphosis of Israel." *ZAW* 88 (1976) 17–56.

Weiser, Artur. *The Psalms: A Commentary*. OTL. Philadelphia: Westminster, 1962.

Wenham, Gordon J. *Exploring the Old Testament, Vol. 1: A Guide to the Pentateuch*. 4 vols. Downers Grove, IL: InterVarsity, 2003.

———. *Genesis 1–15*. WBC 1. Waco, TX: Word, 1987.

———. *Genesis 16–50*. WBC 2. Waco, TX: Word, 1994.

Wenk, Matthias. *Community-Forming Power: The Socio-Ethical Role of the Spirit in Luke-Acts*. Journal of Pentecostal Theology Supplement Series 19. Sheffield: Sheffield Academic, 2000. Reprint, London: T. & T. Clark, 2004.

Westerholm, Stephen. *Perspectives Old and New on Paul: The "Lutheran" Paul and His Critics*. Grand Rapids: Eerdmans, 2004.

Westermann, Claus. "Arten der Erzählung in der Genesis." In *Forschung am Alten Testament*, 9-91. Munich: Kaiser, 1964.

———. *Blessing in the Bible and the Life of the Church*. Translated by Keith Crim. Overtures to Biblical Theology. Philadelphia: Fortress, 1978.

———. *Genesis 1-11*. Translated by John J. Scullion. CC. Minneapolis: Augsburg, 1984.

———. *Genesis 12-36*. Translated by John J. Scullion. CC. Minneapolis: Augsburg, 1985.

———. *Genesis 37-50*. Translated by John J. Scullion. CC. Minneapolis: Augsburg, 1986.

———. *Isaiah 40-66: A Commentary*. Translated by D. M. G. Stalker. OTL. Philadelphia: Westminster, 1969.

Whybray, R. N. "Ben Sira and History." In *Treasures of Wisdom: Studies in Ben Sira and the Book of Wisdom*, edited by N. Calduch-Benages and J. Vermeylen, 137-45. BETL 143. Leuven: Leuven University Press, 1999.

Wilcox, Max. "Upon the Tree: Deut 21:22-23 in the New Testament." *JBL* 96 (1977) 85-99.

Wildberger, Hans. *Isaiah 1-12: A Commentary*. Translated by Thomas H. Trapp. CC. Minneapolis: Fortress, 1991.

———. *Isaiah 13-27: A Commentary*. Translated by Thomas H. Trapp. CC. Minneapolis: Fortress, 1997.

———. *Isaiah 28-39: A Commentary*. Translated by Thomas H. Trapp. CC. Minneapolis: Fortress, 2002.

Williams, Sam K. *Galatians*. Abingdon New Testament Commentaries. Nashville: Abingdon, 1997.

———. "The Hearing of Faith: ΑΚΟΗ ΠΙΣΤΕΩΣ in Galatians 3." *NTS* 35 (1989) 82-93.

———. "Justification and the Spirit in Galatians." *JSNT* 29 (1987) 91-100.

———. "Promise in Galatians: A Reading of Paul's Reading of Scripture." *JBL* 107 (1988) 709-20.

Williamson, Paul R. *Abraham, Israel and the Nations: The Patriarchal Promise and Its Covenantal Development in Genesis*. JSOTSup 315. Sheffield: Sheffield Academic, 2000.

———. *Sealed with an Oath: Covenant in God's Unfolding Purpose*. NSBT 23. Downers Grove, IL: InterVarsity, 2007.

Williamson, Ronald. *Jews in the Hellenistic World: Philo*. CCWJCW 1 Part II. Cambridge: Cambridge University Press, 1985.

Willis, John T. "Exclusivistic and Inclusivistic Aspects of the Concept of 'The People of God' in the Book of Isaiah." *ResQ* 40 (1998) 3-12.

Willitts, Joel. "Context Matters: Paul's Use of Leviticus 18:5 in Galatians 3:12." *TynBul* 54 (2003) 105-22.

Wilson, Todd A. *The Curse of the Law and the Crisis in Galatia: Reassessing the Purpose of Galatians*. WUNT/II 225. Tübingen: Mohr Siebeck, 2007.

## Bibliography

Winkle, D. W. van. "The Relationship of the Nations to Yahweh and to Israel in Isaiah 40–55." *VT* 35 (1985) 446–58.
Winston, David. *The Wisdom of Solomon: A New Translation with Introduction and Commentary.* AB 43. Garden City, NY: Doubleday, 1979.
Wintermute, O. S. "Jubilees: A New Translation and Introduction." In vol. 2 of *The Old Testament Pseudepigrapha*, edited by James H. Charlesworth, 35–142. Garden City, NY: Doubleday, 1985.
Wisdom, Jeffrey R. *Blessing for the Nations and the Curse of the Law: Paul's Citation of Genesis and Deuteronomy in Gal 3.8–10.* WUNT/II 133. Tübingen: Mohr Siebeck, 2001.
Wolff, Hans W. *Anthropology of the Old Testament.* Translated by Margaret Kohl. London: SCM, 1974.
———. "Das Kerygma des Jahwisten." *EvT* 24 (1964) 73–97.
———. *Joel and Amos: A Commentary on the Books of the Prophets Joel and Amos.* Translated by Waldemar Janzen et al. Hermeneia. Philadelphia: Fortress, 1977.
Wong, Ka Leung. *The Idea of Retribution in the Book of Ezekiel.* VTSup 87. Leiden: Brill, 2001.
Wright, Christopher J. H. "אָב." In *NIDOTTE* 1:219–23.
———. "נחל." In *NIDOTTE* 3:77–81.
———. *The Mission of God: Unlocking the Bible's Grand Narrative.* Downers Grove, IL: InterVarsity, 2006.
Wright, N. T. *The Climax of the Covenant: Christ and the Law in Pauline Theology.* Minneapolis: Fortress, 1992.
———. *Justification: God's Plan and Paul's Vision.* Downers Grove, IL: InterVarsity, 2009.
———. *Paul: In Fresh Perspective.* Minneapolis: Fortress, 2005.
———. *What Saint Paul Really Said: Was Paul of Tarsus the Real Founder of Christianity?* Grand Rapids: Eerdmans, 1997.
Young, Edward J. *The Book of Isaiah: The English Text, with Introduction, Exposition, and Notes.* 3 vols. NICOT. Grand Rapids: Eerdmans, 1965–1972.
Young, Norman H. "Who's Cursed—and Why? (Galatians 3:10–14)." *JBL* 117 (1998) 79–92.
Zerwick, Maximilian. *Biblical Greek: Illustrated by Examples.* Scripta Pontificii Instituti Biblici 114. Rome: Editrice Pontificio Istituto Biblico, 1963.
Zimmerli, Walther. *Ezekiel 1.* Translated by Ronald E. Clements. Hermeneia. Philadelphia: Fortress, 1979.
———. *Ezekiel 2.* Translated by James D. Martin. Hermeneia. Philadelphia: Fortress, 1983.
———. "Knowledge of God According to the Book of Ezekiel." In *I Am Yahweh*, edited by Walter Brueggemann, translated by Douglas W. Stott, 29–98. Atlanta: John Knox, 1982.

www.ingramcontent.com/pod-product-compliance
Lightning Source LLC
Chambersburg PA
CBHW050850230426
43667CB00012B/2226